THE COMPLETE IDIOT'S GUIDE® TO

Direct Marketing

COLLECTION MANAGEMENT

6/18/12	9- 1	2/2/19

by Robert W.

ALPHA
A Pearson Education Co

To the Karps: Ken, Terri, Maddy, and Emily

Copyright © 2002 by Robert W. Bly

International Standard Book Number: 0-02-864210-4
Library of Congress Catalog Card Number: 2001092309

04   03   02   8   7   6   5   4   3   2   1

Interpretation of the printing code: The rightmost number of the first series of numbers is the year of the book's printing; the rightmost number of the second series of numbers is the number of the book's printing. For example, a printing code of 02-1 shows that the first printing occurred in 2002.

Printed in the United States of America

Publisher
Marie Butler-Knight

Product Manager
Phil Kitchel

Managing Editor
Jennifer Chisholm

Acquisitions Editor
Mike Sanders

Development Editor
Nancy D. Warner

Production Editor
Katherin Bidwell

Copy Editor
Susan Aufheimer

Illustrator
Brian Moyer

Cover Designers
Mike Freeland
Kevin Spear

Book Designers
Scott Cook and Amy Adams of DesignLab

Indexer
Lisa Wilson

Layout/Proofreading
Svetlana Dominquez
Mary Hunt
Kimberly Tucker
Mark Walchle

Contents at a Glance

Part 1: Getting Started in Direct Marketing   **1**

  1 Direct Marketing 101   3
Understanding direct marketing and the direct marketer's mindset.

  2 Planning Your Direct Marketing Campaign   19
How to determine your market, your list, and your offer.

  3 Make Your Buyers an Offer They Can't Refuse   31
Testing offers that increase response.

  4 Mailing Lists   47
Finding, selecting, and testing the right lists.

  5 Writing Copy That Sells   61
The secrets of writing powerful direct response copy—revealed.

  6 Producing and Printing Your Direct Marketing Campaign   75
Get your mailing, ad, catalog, or postcard designed, printed, and mailed.

Part 2: Direct Response Formats and Media   **85**

  7 The Direct Mail Package   87
The anatomy of a successful direct mail package, what components you need, and how they work together.

  8 Direct Mail: Longer Formats   101
Magalogs, minilogs, bookalogs, and other alternatives to the traditional direct mail package.

  9 Direct Mail: Short Formats   115
Self-mailers, postcards, snap packs, and other short-form direct mailers.

  10 Catalogs   129
Selling mail order merchandise via a printed catalog.

  11 Profits from Postcard Decks   145
Designing and writing cards and running them in the most profitable decks.

  12 Alternative Media   157
A guide to using free-standing inserts, package inserts, and other alternative media.

  13 Direct Response Advertising   169
Using classified, small display, and full-page ads for lead generation and mail-order sales.

Part 3: Electronic Direct Marketing   **185**

14   Direct Response TV and Radio   187
Doing direct marketing over cable and broadcast media.

15   Telemarketing   199
Selling over the telephone.

16   The Internet: Direct Marketing for the Digital Age   209
Online marketing with banner ads, e-mail, Web sites,
and e-zines.

Part 4: Direct Marketing Applications   **223**

17   Direct Marketing to Consumers   225
Selling consumer merchandise through mail order.

18   Business-to-Business Direct Marketing   233
Reaching business executives, professionals, entrepreneurs,
and other business prospects via direct response marketing.

19   Selling Services   251
Using direct marketing to sell services instead of products.

20   Selling "Information Products"   263
Direct marketing of newsletters, magazines, books, soft-
ware, seminars, and other "information products."

21   Lead Generation   277
Generating qualified inquiries with direct marketing.

22   Nonprofit Marketing   287
Fundraising, political, and other nonprofit direct
marketing.

Part 5: Measuring and Monitoring Your Results   **301**

23   Testing Your Way to Direct Marketing Success   303
Determining what works for you in direct marketing
via statistically valid scientific testing.

24   Tracking and Analyzing Response   315
Measuring and analyzing responses.

25   Database Marketing   323
How to build a customer and prospect database and
conduct a database-marketing campaign.

Appendixes

A   Glossary   335

B   Resources   339

    Index   347

Contents

Part 1: Getting Started in Direct Marketing   1

1   Direct Marketing 101   3

Understanding the Direct Marketing Jargon 4
The Evolution of Direct Marketing 7
How Direct Marketing Differs from Other Advertising 9
   Creativity..9
   Branding 10
   Entrepreneurship 10
   Selling 10
   Design 11
   Copy 11
   Campaign Consistency..12
The Direct Marketing Mindset 12
The Direct Marketing Customer 15
Arrows in the Direct Marketer's Quiver 16

2   Planning Your Direct Marketing Campaign   19

What Are You Selling? 20
What Products Sell Best via Direct Marketing?.................20
   Not Available in Stores 21
   Story Rich 21
   Priced for Direct Response Markup 21
   An Element of Fun, Mystery, or the Unusual.............21
   Refillable or Requires Updating...............................22
   Different from Competing Products...........................22
Planning Your Front and Back Ends 22
Determining Your Marketing Objectives 23
Taking Aim at Your Target Market..............................24
   Business Prospects 26
Choosing Campaign Specifics 26
Determining Your Key Sales Appeal or Theme 26
Identifying Supporting Facts and Sales Arguments 27
Planning Your Offer..28
Don't Forget Project Planning and Management 29

3   Make Your Buyers an Offer They Can't Refuse   31

What Is an Offer—And Why It's Important 32
One Step or Two Step?...33

The Four Types of Offers 34
   Hard Offers *34*
   Soft Offers *34*
   Negative Offers *34*
   Deferred Offers *36*
Selecting Response Options 36
   By Phone *36*
   By Fax *37*
   By Mail *37*
   By E-Mail *37*
   Through the Web *38*
Choosing Payment Options 38
   With a Check..*38*
   With a Money Order *38*
   With Cash..*38*
   With a Credit Card *39*
   C.O.D...*39*
   Bill-Me...*39*
   Purchase Order (P.O.) *40*
How to Make Your Offer Stronger...............................41
Getting the Buyer to Act Now, Buy More,
  and Pay Up Front...42
   Quick-Response Bonus *42*
   Deadline or Expiration Date................................*42*
Satisfaction Guaranteed or Your Money Back..................43
Must Direct Marketers Charge Sales Tax? 43
Taking Credit Card Orders...44

4 Mailing Lists   **47**

A List of Available Lists 47
Where Can You Rent Good Mailing Lists? 49
   List Owners *50*
   List Managers *50*
   List Brokers *50*
Evaluating Mailing Lists and List Recommendations........51
Questions to Ask About Your Lists 54
Placing Your List Order 56
Getting Rid of Duplicate Names 57
Earn Extra Income by Marketing Your Mailing
  List to Others 57
   Getting More Brokers to Recommend Your List *58*

5 Writing Copy That Sells   **61**

Long Copy Versus Short Copy: Which Works Best?.........62
Determining Copy Content, Tone, and Style 63

Creating a Winning Copy Platform 64
The Motivating Sequence 65
Step 1: Get Attention 65
Step 2: Identify a Problem, Need, or Want 65
Step 3: Position Your Product as the Solution 66
Step 4: Prove Your Case 66
Step 5: Ask for the Order 67
Writing a Powerful Headline 67
Features and Benefits 68
Selling to Experts 68
Enthusiasts 68
Engineers and Scientists 69
Equipment 69
Practicality 70
More Tips for Writing Better Body Copy 70
Be as Concise as Possible 70
Speak the Reader's Language 71
Negative Selling Can Work 72
Don't Reveal Your Hand Too Early 72

**6 Producing and Printing Your Direct
   Marketing Campaign   75**

Calculating the Cost per Thousand 75
Graphic Design Guidelines 77
Photography and Illustration Considerations 78
Printing Preparation 79
Letter Shop...82
Postal Regulations 84

Part 2: Direct Response Formats and Media   85

7 The Direct Mail Package   87

The Outer Envelope..88
The Big Tease 88
Blind Mailings 89
The Sales Letter 91
Personalized Versus Nonpersonalized 91
Using a Johnson Box 92
Using a Salutation 93
Determining the Length 93
Signing the Letter 94
Body Copy 94
Talk About the Reader's Needs 94
Start Off with a Strong "Lead" 95

State the Offer Up Front 95
Get Personal...96
Narrow the Focus 97
Know How Much to Tell..97
Use Graphics to Highlight Key Points 98
The Brochure 98
The Lift Note 98
The Buck Slip or Premium Sheet.....................................99
Order Forms That Close the Deal 99
Business Reply Envelopes (BREs).....................................99

8 Direct Mail: Longer Formats   101

Why and When to Use Long-Copy Formats 101
Long-Copy Direct Mail Formats 102
Magalogs 102
Tabloids...104
Faux Reports 104
Issuelog 104
Minilogs...105
Bookalogs..105
Organizing Your Long-Form Mailing 106
Designing Long-Form Mailings.......................................107
Copywriting Techniques That Work in Long Formats 108
Understanding the Buyer's "Core Complex" 108
Creating a Customer Profile 109
Keep the "Information Density" Level High 111
The Four U's 112

9 Direct Mail: Short Formats   115

Working with Self-Mailers 115
Choosing Your Format..116
Postcards 116
Double Postcards 117
Posterboard 118
Folded Self-Mailers 118
Snap Packs..118
Dimensional Mailers 119
Urgent Mailers 119
Cost Considerations 119
Putting Self-Mailers to Work 119
Mailings to Customers 119
Continuity 120
Short Message 120
Low-Response Offers 120

The Elusive Target *120*
Mail Order *121*
Large Volume *122*
The Secret of Self-Mailing Success 122
Writing an Attention-Grabbing Outer-Panel Headline....124
Boosting Response Rates to Your Self-Mailers 125

10 Catalogs   129

Writing Powerful Catalog Copy 129
Merchandising Your Catalog 131
Catalog Marketing Techniques That Work 132
Catalog Selling Starts on the Cover 134
Ideas to Boost Your Catalog Sales 135
Checklist for Effective Catalog Copy 137
Determining Your Proper Copy "Tone" 139
Calculating Your Catalog Real Estate 140

11 Profits from Postcard Decks   145

What Is a Postcard Deck? 146
Advertising in Postcard Decks 146
Selecting the Right Postcard Decks *147*
Reviewing Postcard Market Segments *147*
Determining Card Deck Advertising Costs........................*148*
Measuring Card Deck Results *149*
Don't Most People Just Throw Postcard Decks Away? 149
Writing Your Postcard's Headline 150
Mention a Free Offer *150*
Provide a Benefit Headline *151*
Ask a Question..*151*
Use a Command Headline *151*
Use a News Headline *152*
Use Mail-Order Headlines..*152*
Writing the Body Copy 152
Illustrating Your Postcard 154

12 Alternative Media   157

Why Alternative Media? 157
Alternative Media Options 158
Bind-In and Blow-In Programs *158*
Free-Standing Inserts *159*
Package Inserts..*159*
Co-Op Mailings *160*
Statement Stuffers *160*
Take-Ones *161*

Ride-Alongs *161*
Sampling Program *161*
Getting Started in Package Inserts................162
Producing and Shipping Package Inserts 163
Size and Format.. *164*
Choosing an Insert Format *164*
Key Coding for Response Tracking *164*
Fulfillment *165*
Shipping the Inserts *165*
Big Advertising with Billboards.....................165
Transit Advertising: Ads on the Move............167
Integrating Alternative Media into Your
Marketing Mix 167

13 Direct Response Advertising   169

Big Versus Small Ads 169
Media Buying for Direct Response Advertising 170
Getting Your Space Ads to Sell More Product.................172
Advertise the Right Product for the Right Audience *172*
Using an Attention-Getting Headline *173*
Getting to the Point *174*
Using a Reader-Friendly Layout *175*
Giving the "Why They Should Buy"—And Proving It *175*
Avoiding Generalities *176*
Start with the Prospect, Not the Product *177*
Promise the Reader a Reward for Reading the Copy...........*178*
Using a Friendly, Conversational Style *178*
Don't Forget a Strong Call to Action *179*
Making Money with Classified and Small
Display Ads 179
Writing an Effective Classified Ad *180*
Phrasing the Offer *180*
Reducing Word Count (Advertising Costs)......181
Placing Your Classified Ads 181
Testing Your Ad 182
Advertising in the Yellow Pages and Business
Directories 183

Part 3: Electronic Direct Marketing   185

14 Direct Response TV and Radio   187

Infomercial: The Commercial That Sells Like a Show 188
Common Infomercial Blunders to Avoid *188*
Key Elements of Infomercial Production *189*
Getting Your Infomercial on the Air *190*

xi

Shorter Formats 192
Other DRTV Options: HSN and QVC 194
Direct—Response Radio...194
 Reaching Listeners Through Radio *194*
 Buying Radio Time.....................................*195*
 Writing Effective Radio Commercials *196*

15   Telemarketing   199

Why Telemarketing Works 199
Creating a Winning Telemarketing Script....................201
 The Benefit-Statement Script...........................*202*
 The Prospect Need-Qualification Script *203*
Becoming a Telemarketing Master 205
 Shift Your Delivery to Accommodate Prospect Mood *205*
 Improving Your Telemarketing Technique *206*
Telemarketing and Direct Mail: A Powerful
 One-Two Punch 206
Telemarketing's Dynamic Duo: Feedback and
 Flexibility 207

16   The Internet: Direct Marketing for the Digital Age   209

Integrating E-Commerce into Your Direct
 Marketing Program 210
Building a Web Site 211
 Need-to-Know Information *211*
 Want-to-Know Information *212*
Designing Your Home Page 213
Taking Product Orders on Your Site 214
Links and Affiliate Programs 215
Banner Advertising 216
Internet Direct Mail...216
E-Zines and E-Zine Classified Ads 219
Advertising in Other Marketer's E-Zines 220

Part 4:   Direct Marketing Applications   223

17   Direct Marketing to Consumers   225

Getting Started in Consumer Mail-Order
 Merchandise..225
 Meeting Your Mail-Order Customers *226*
 Using Low-Cost Marketing Methods to Minimize
  Your Risk *226*

Expanding Your Marketing with the Profits You Make 226
Consumer Direct Mail Percentage Returns 227
What's in a Direct Mail Company Name? 228
"Romancing" the Buyer 229
Overcoming Buyer Resistance with Endorsed
Mailings 232

18 Business-to-Business Direct Marketing   233

Getting Down to Business-to-Business 234
The Business Buyer Wants to Buy 234
The Business Buyer Is Sophisticated 234
The Business Buyer Will Read a Lot of Copy 234
A Multi-Step Buying Process 235
Multiple Buying Influences 235
Business Products Are More Complex 236
Selling Business Opportunity Offers 236
Reaching the SoHo Market 237
Industrial Marketing 238
Be Technically Accurate 238
Check the Numbers 239
Be Concise 239
Simplify 240
Talk to the Users to Determine Their Needs 240
*Understand How the Promotion Fits into the
Buying Process* 241
Know How Much to Tell 241
Don't Forget the Features 242
*Include Case Histories to Demonstrate Proven
Performance* 242
Selling Tech Products to Non-Tech Executives 243
Using Premiums 244
Getting a Response 244
Writing High-Tech Product Copy 245
Selling to Middle Managers 246
Selling to Corporate Executives 248

19 Selling Services   251

Service Selling Is Different 251
Working the Phone Lines 252
Referral Marketing 252
Testimonials 253
Direct Mail: The Powerhouse of Service Marketing 255
The Prospect Letter 256
The Reply Card 256

Advertising Your Services...257
  Where Should You Advertise?...............................*258*
  Writing Your Ad...*259*

20 Selling "Information Products"   **263**

Understanding Information Marketing and
  the Information Buyer..264
  Look for Niche Areas..*264*
  Research Your Market...*264*
  Cultivate the Information-Hungry Core Buyer................*264*
  People Pay for Tightly Focused Information...................*265*
  *Transform Editorial Matter into Powerful
    Promotional Copy*..*265*
  Determined Responses...*266*
Selling Information in the Information Age...................267
  Narrow the Focus..*267*
  Seize a Subject..*267*
  Plan the Back End Before You Start Marketing...............*268*
  Test Your Concept with Classified Ads........................*268*
  The Importance of the Bounce-Back Catalog..................*268*
  Create Low-, Medium-, and High-Priced Products............*269*
  Let Your Buyers Tell You What Products to Create...........*269*
  Be the Quality Source..*269*
Building the Buyer's Trust in You.............................270
Types of Information Products You Can Sell................271
  Magazine Subscriptions...*271*
  Newsletters..*271*
  Directories...*272*
  Books..*272*
  Booklets and Special Reports..................................*272*
  Audio Cassettes...*273*
  Video Tapes..*273*
  CD-ROMs..*274*
  Software..*274*
  Seminars..*274*
Online Products...275

21 Lead Generation   **277**

Sales Leads Support the Sales Force.............................277
  Increasing Sales Force Efficiency.............................*278*
  Reaching the Buying Committee...............................*279*
Direct Mail Formats That Work Best for Lead
  Generation...280
  Direct Mail Letter..*280*

Self-Mailers 281
Postcards 281
Successful Lead-Generating Copy Features 282
Solo Versus Series Mailing 283
Market Size and Handling Capacity 283
Evaluating Your Response 284
Other Lead-Generating Methods...............................285

22   Nonprofit Marketing   287

What Motivates People to Donate?............................287
You Asked Them To 288
They Can Afford It..288
They're Proven Donors 289
They Support Organizations Like Yours......................289
They Want to Make a Difference 290
They Want to See Immediate Results 290
They Want to Be Recognized for Their Good Works 290
They Want the Premium You Are Offering 290
They Want to Be Heard 291
Your Cause Is Endorsed by a Celebrity 291
You Help Them Fight Back 292
They Want to Be Part of Your Inner Circle 292
You Give Them a Forum for Their Opinions 292
You Give Them Access to Inside Information 293
What Makes Fundraising Different? 293
You Have No Commercial Product 293
You Offer No Solutions for Individual Prospects 294
You Have a Single Cause—Not a Full "Product Line" 294
You Target Multiple Audiences 294
Your Approach Is Somewhat Restricted 295
Writing Powerful Fundraising Copy 295
Begin with a Worthy Cause 295
Lead with Emotions 296
Follow with Facts..296
Use Plenty of "You" References 296
Explain the Urgency 296
Offer a Gift as a Token of Appreciation 297
Appeal to Their Need for Prestige 297
Give Options for Giving 297
Get More from Your P.S. 297
Ask for the Next Donation 297
Marketing a Political Candidates 298
Past Performance 298
Future Promise 299

Credibility *299*
Ideology *299*

Part 5: Measuring and Monitoring Your Results   301

23 Testing Your Way to Direct Marketing Success   303

Why Not Learn While You Test?....................................304
Tracking Results with Key Codes..................................304
Using Employees to Help Track Response.....................305
Statistically Valid Responses 306
How Many Test Pieces Must You Mail?.........................307
Rolling Out After a Successful Test 309
What Should You Test? 310
Ten Essential Rules of Tested Direct Marketing 311
When the Verdict Goes Against You..............................312

24 Tracking and Analyzing Response   315

Counting Returns 315
Response Metrics 316
Lifetime Customer Value...318
Response Boosters 319

25 Database Marketing   323

What Is Database Marketing? 324
Database Marketing Is Measurable 324
Gain Competitive Advantage and Control......................325
Building Profitable Private Prospecting Databases 325
Demographic Overlays 328
Modeling Your Marketing Database 329
Uni-Variate Analysis *330*
Bi-Variate Analysis *330*
Factor Analysis *331*
Cluster Analysis..*331*
Discriminant Analysis *332*
CHAID Analysis *332*
Choosing the Right Methodology.................................333

Appendixes   **301**

  A **Glossary**   **335**

  B **Resources**   **339**

     Index   **347**

Foreword

Every day is full of negotiations. Bargains are struck—often without words—thousands of times a day as we go about our business.

You give me a $7.95 … I'll give you a steak sandwich.

You pass to the left … I'll pass to the right.

You take out the trash … I'll cook dinner.

So customary and habitual are these transactions that we scarcely notice them. Yet, each one involves subtle or elaborate acts of persuasion.

A customer must be persuaded that your product is better, cheaper, more convenient, more durable, or more stylish than a competitor's. A jury must be convinced that the defendant is guilty or innocent. Even personal relationships require an element of salesmanship. It may be called courtship, seduction, or just a pick-up line … but it is a form of marketing—selling oneself to the opposite sex.

There are private acts of marketing—such as when an auto dealer sells a car or when a teenager convinces his parents to let him use it.

And there is mass marketing, when investors are lured into overpriced stocks by an enthusiastic analyst's report … or voters, stirred up with the passion of self-righteous envy by a clever demagogue, elect the scoundrel. Everywhere you look, in almost every transaction, someone is being persuaded of something.

"It's a beautiful day, isn't it," says one person.

"Yes," comes the reply, "it's lovely." Yet, without the leading question, a different judgment might have been provoked. "It's a little chilly," he might have been thinking.

All through our lives, we suggest, urge, plead, argue, tease, demand, and bully to get others to do what we want. For without cooperation from others, few things are possible. Commerce and trade would cease. All forms of organization—except for the most brutal slavery—would dissolve. Even the species itself would likely perish—for if men and women could not get together, few children would be born … and fewer still would survive.

Though this process is central to so much of human life, it is rarely examined or reduced to practical advice. Plato and Erasmus described the elements of successful rhetoric. Lawyers study the reaction of juries and learn how to persuade them. Hitler would practice giving speeches in front of a mirror—refining his gestures and body language to produce just the effect he was looking for.

But persuasion has been most often studied and most highly developed at a commercial level. More sales means more profits. And selling necessarily involves the techniques of salesmanship. Those techniques make the difference between profits and losses, success and failure, for countless businesses and individual salesmen. Thus, they are a subject of keen interest.

Billions of dollars are spent on advertising campaigns—involving thousands of hours of careful research, focus groups, and brainstorming sessions. In the end, it is not always clear whether the effort increased sales or depressed them. But in one area of sales, direct marketing, the results speak for themselves. Direct marketers are accustomed to judging sales efforts in numbers and dollars—R.O.I., dollars per name, percent response, and pay up rates. The numbers tell us what logic and theory cannot—what persuasive techniques actually work.

In this book, Bob Bly surveys the vast world of direct marketing to tell us what works—simply and directly. You will find out everything from how to use a bounce-back offer to how to select the proper mailing list for your sales campaign.

Bly's book is a good place to begin a direct marking campaign. It is also a good place to end one. It would be a good idea to run through a checklist of what actually works in order to avoid costly mistakes—and then to subject your unsuccessful campaigns to a 'post-mortem' review. Often, marketing campaigns fail for the simplest and most basic reasons.

You will find little theory in Bly's book and much helpful, practical information. You may use it to raise money for your favorite charity, elect a Senator, sell a condominium, or meet your future spouse. It's up to you.

—Bill Bonner

Bill Bonner is President and CEO of Agora Publishing and author of "The DailyReckoning.com".

Introduction

You don't have to be a direct marketing "addict" to successfully use direct marketing methods to increase your sales and profits. But you probably do have to be one to write a book about it—and fortunately, I am.

Like many of my fellow direct marketers, I find that direct marketing has a certain appeal—call it a "romance," if you will—that other marketing lacks. When I see a Calvin Klein ad featuring an anorexic teen model and the words "Ah, the smell of it," I want to barf. My idea of fun is to get, read, and open a *Time Life Books* mailing with pages of fascinating copy and color pictures on World War II or Ancient Egypt.

As a kid, I was the kind of customer that direct marketers hate: I accepted every free offer and, because I was a child with no money, canceled immediately and kept whatever was sent to me. I had more single copies of *Psychology Today* and *Intellectual Digest* than any 11-year-old needed, plus three leather-bound editions of *Moby Dick*, which I never actually read all the way through.

Direct marketing is the most measurable, and arguably the most effective, type of marketing in the world. You write an ad or mailer, send it out, then sit back and count the reply cards, orders, and checks that come pouring in—when all goes well, that is. Unlike general advertisers, who have to content themselves with such nebulous measurements as brand awareness and corporate image, we direct marketers can tell, down to the penny, which ad pulled best, or which mailing won the test.

The Complete Idiot's Guide to Direct Marketing is written to give you the information, tools, resources, and strategies you need to make direct marketing work for your business. You will learn how to use direct mail, space ads, radio and TV, the Internet, and other direct-response media to generate leads or sales—or both. You will see how direct marketing can help you acquire new customers as well as sell more goods and services to existing customers.

While the experience of others can point the way, and the techniques and tips in this book can help you avoid costly mistakes, do not be mislead into thinking there is one magic formula—and if you had it, you would never mail an unsuccessful direct mail piece again. If there truly was such a formula and I had it, Bill Gates would be my houseboy. No direct marketing practitioner, including me, has a "silver bullet" that can make all your direct marketing problems go away or get you a 100 percent response rate.

I tell clients that hiring an experienced direct marketing agency, consultant, or copywriter is no guarantee of success. All you are really buying is the expectation that the promotion will be more successful, because of the expert's experience—nothing more. I also tell clients that no direct marketing expert knows in advance, or can predict with any certainty, which headline, offer, or promotion will be the winner and which will bomb. At best, experts can come up with test-worthy ideas based on their experience—but that is all.

And so it is with *The Complete Idiot's Guide to Direct Marketing.* After reading the book, you will have a pretty good idea of how to use direct marketing to build your business, and you will have the tools to do it yourself or evaluate the campaigns others create for you. But direct marketing is a discipline that takes a lifetime to master. That's both the challenge and the fun. You will never achieve the ultimate result, because you can always do better—but in attempting to do even better, you will never be bored.

Fun—the fun of learning, of testing, of trying new things, of seeing tangible results from your efforts, and of making a profit—is just ahead of you. There is a long and pleasurable road awaiting you, with big rewards along the way. Now, what was once a country back road is now a superhighway, with the bumps smoothed out and some of the curves removed.

Questions and comments on *The Complete Idiot's Guide to Direct Marketing* may be sent to:

Bob Bly
Direct Response Copywriter
22 E. Quackenbush Avenue
Dumont, NJ 07628
Phone 201-385-1220
Fax 201-385-1138
E-mail rwbly@bly.com
Web site www.bly.com

How This Book Is Organized

Just as a direct mail package is organized into different components, each with its own function, this book is organized into five parts, each with its own objective.

Part 1, "Getting Started in Direct Marketing," introduces you to the world of direct marketing, showing you how to plan, create, and execute successful direct marketing programs and campaigns.

Part 2, "Direct Response Formats and Media," guides you in how to use the various formats and media available in the direct marketer's arsenal.

Part 3, "Electronic Direct Marketing," reveals the successes direct marketers are having on the Internet, in telemarketing, in radio and TV, and other electronic media.

Part 4, "Direct Marketing Applications," shows you the most popular product categories in direct marketing, what works in promotion, and how to adapt those tactics to your own efforts, even if you are in an entirely different industry.

Part 5, "Measuring and Monitoring Your Results," tells you how to conduct tests, collect and analyze responses, and interpret results so you know, to the penny, how profitable or unprofitable every promotion is—and use this knowledge to cut your losses and expand your winners.

Extras

One of the power copywriting principles discussed in Chapter 5, "Writing Copy That Sells," is: If you want to make sure people read something on a page, put it in a box. Well, in this book, I've used boxes throughout the chapters to highlight advice or ideas I think are extra important and I don't want you to miss.

Insider's Buzzwords

Like other industries, direct marketing has its own special jargon. In Insider's Buzzwords, I define key terms you are likely to encounter in reading direct marketing publications, attending seminars, or speaking with vendors. This way you'll feel more confident and knowledgeable.

Warning!

Here, I alert you to common mistakes that can hurt your response or even prevent your promotion from working altogether. I have seen a 10,000-piece mailing generate zero replies just because it contained a single one of these deadly errors—an error you can easily avoid.

Success Story

The best way to become adept at direct marketing is to study what works and what doesn't, and learn from those successes and failures. Throughout the book I will highlight winning direct marketing campaigns and point out the techniques they used that you can adapt to your own efforts.

Surprising Secrets

There are a number of direct marketing principles that defy common sense but are true nevertheless. For instance, did you know that in fundraising, the person who just made a donation is the one most likely to donate again? You'll find surprising secrets like this one in these boxes.

Marketing Tip

This box highlights very powerful response-boosting or cost-cutting techniques I want to make sure you read and at least consider applying to your own marketing campaigns.

Acknowledgments

Because almost everything is grist for the direct response copywriter's mill, the list of people I ought to thank is nearly infinite. However, given the limitations of space and memory, I acknowledge a select group who have had the most influence over my career (my apologies if you are not on this list and should be—I goofed):

Richard Armstrong	Brian Kurtz
Peter Beteul	Dr. Jeffrey Lant
William Bonner	Dr. Andrew Linick
John Finn	Chris Marett
John Forde	Michael Masterson
Celine Goget	Ed McClean
Dennison Hatch	Milt Pierce
Buddy Hayden	Steve Roberts
Don Hauptman	Sig Rosenblum
Richard Stanton Jones	David Yale
Bob Jurik	

Thanks to my agent, Bob DiForio, for creating the opportunity to write a direct marketing book for *The Idiot's Guide* series, and to Mike Sanders, my editor at *The Idiot's Guide* series, for making the book stronger, tighter, and more reader friendly. Special thanks to Fern Dickey for reading the entire manuscript and making many helpful suggestions, almost all of which I actually used.

Thanks to my wife, Amy, and children, Alex and Stephen, for enduring the neglect that the preparation of this book necessitated.

Finally, I'd like to acknowledge authors and publications who graciously allowed me to reprint their ideas in various sections of this book:

Chapter 1. Richard Armstrong's letter was printed under the title "Don't Cry for Me Madison Avenue" in *Advertising Age* magazine.

Chapter 5. The section on long copy versus short copy is adapted from a privately published article written by Paul Tracy and is used with permission.

Chapter 7. Some of the advice on order forms is from copywriter David Yale.

Chapter 10. The discussion on hurdle rates is reprinted from *Target Marketing* with permission of the author, Stephen Lett.

Chapter 12. Some of this material is adapted from the article "Alternative Media" and is reprinted from *Target Marketing* with permission of the author, Stephen Lett. Other material is from Leon Henry, reprinted with his permission.

Chapter 13. Some of the information on Yellow Pages advertising is reprinted with permission of its author, Richard Armstrong.

Chapter 14. Some of the information on infomercials is adapted from material written by Dan Kennedy and is reprinted with permission.

Chapter 18. The Success Story about the pigeon mailing is reprinted with permission of Shell Alpert.

Chapter 20. The beginning of this chapter is reprinted with permission from Don Hauptman's privately published article "Marketing Information."

Chapter 21. The opening section on how direct mail generates leads to support the sales force is adapted from an article by Rene Gnam.

Trademarks

All terms mentioned in this book that are known to be or are suspected of being trademarks or service marks have been appropriately capitalized. Alpha Books and Pearson Education cannot attest to the accuracy of this information. Use of a term in this book should not be regarded as affecting the validity of any trademark or service mark.

Part 1

Getting Started in Direct Marketing

If you are new to direct marketing, this part will bring you up to speed quickly, showing you what direct marketing is about and what you need to know to get started. If you are an old pro, this part will give you a welcome refresher and perhaps give you some fresh ideas you can test to bolster your response rates.

First, you will be introduced to direct marketing, both as a method of selling as well as a way of thinking. Then, the steps necessary for planning a successful direct marketing campaign will be outlined.

In addition, I discuss the all-important offer and the enormous boost the "right offer" can give your response rates as well as how to find, select, and test mailing lists. Writing direct response copy that sells is covered along with tips on getting your campaigns produced, printed, and mailed.

Chapter 1

Direct Marketing 101

> ### In This Chapter
>
> ➤ What is direct marketing?
>
> ➤ The evolution of direct marketing
>
> ➤ Direct marketing versus general advertising
>
> ➤ Understanding the direct marketing mindset
>
> ➤ Knowing the direct marketing customer
>
> ➤ Direct marketing media and formats

Every day we're bombarded by advertising messages. But notice that the advertisements you see seem to be of two types. The first category seems to concentrate on being memorable. For example: James Brolin as the pitchman for Meineke Mufflers, the talking M&M's, and State Farm's "Like a Good Neighbor" campaign.

The second category of advertisements focuses on getting you to place an order or at least make a direct inquiry for more information about the product being advertised. These include those four-page letters asking you to subscribe to various magazines; infomercials that ask you to call an 800 number to order an ab machine or Taebo exercise video; a Publishers Clearinghouse sweepstakes mailing; or a Victoria's Secret or Sharper Image catalog.

Those types of advertisements—those that ask for the order now instead of later—are examples of direct marketing. You've heard the term direct marketing before. And you've seen countless examples. This book is written to help you use direct marketing to make your business more successful and profitable.

If you manage or own a traditional business, you'll learn how to apply proven direct marketing techniques to generate more leads, more customers, more orders, more sales. Instead of having to ring doorbells, pound the pavement, or schmooze at networking luncheons, you'll have more people lined up to hire you or buy from you than you could ever hope to handle. So you'll be able to charge the prices you want, and be highly selective about who you do business with—and who you don't.

If you manage or own a direct marketing business … or are thinking of starting one … *The Complete Idiot's Guide to Direct Marketing* will provide you with tips, techniques, and ideas you can immediately apply to start or jump-start your direct response business. You'll learn from the successes (and failures) of other direct marketers, and apply these lessons to boost your own response rates and avoid costly mistakes.

Understanding the Direct Marketing Jargon

Direct marketing is any type of marketing that seeks some sort of reply from the reader, typically by phone, mail, e-mail, or fax. Direct marketing print materials usually have response coupons (see the following figure) or reply cards you can use to request more information or order the product. Direct marketing TV and radio commercials typically use toll-free 800 numbers (and nowadays, 900 numbers as well). Many encourage prospects to respond via e-mail or visit a Web site.

There are a lot of terms associated with direct marketing, and many of them are listed here to give you a basis for many of the topics that will be covered in this book:

➤ **Direct response** and direct marketing mean the same thing. Direct response seeks an immediate action on the part of the reader. This could be to call a toll-free number, visit a showroom, try a product, mail a reply card, go to a home page, or see a demonstration.

➤ **Database marketing** is a form of direct marketing in which you repeatedly communicate with prospects whose names and other information are contained in a database you own or rent.

Marketing Tip

The best prospects for direct marketing promotions are those who are proven mail order buyers. Look for lists of prospects who have bought a product similar to yours, at a similar price. Conversely, if you mail to lists of people who have not been identified as mail order customers, your response rates will most likely be low. See Chapter 4, "Mailing List," for more information on how to exploit this fact to your advantage.

Write, Stay Home, and Make $100,000 a Year

by Bob Bly

Dear Writer:

The writing life is a great life. I love staying home, avoiding the rat race, and getting paid good money to sit at my beloved Kaypro computer, thinking, reading, and writing for my clients.

Now I want to show you how to stay at home writing while earning $500 a day—or $50,000 to $75,000 to $100,000 a year or more as a freelance commercial writer handling assignments for local and national clients. What will you write? Ads, sales letters, brochures, direct mail packages, speeches, annual reports, press releases, audio-visual scripts, and dozens of other lucrative assignments.

How much will you earn? $500 per day...$1,000 or more per assignment... $1,000 to $2,000 a week...$100,000 and more per year. All working from the comfort of home.

Now the secrets of how to earn a six-figure income as a freelance writer are revealed in my two-volume, 300+ page writer's manual. I call it *Secrets of a Freelance Writer.* My readers call it the best information they have ever seen on how to double, triple, even quadruple your freelance writing income.

The Secrets Revealed

Here's just a sampling of the writer's secrets my manual reveals:

* The best clients for freelance writers—where to find them, how to reach them (see Chapter 2)
* How to get paid big money from local businesses for your ideas and advice (Chapter 11)
* How to earn thousands of dollars "ghostwriting" articles and speeches for busy executives (Chapter 7)
* How to write a sales letter that brings you 5 to 10 new prospects to call on for every 100 letters you mail (Chapter 3)
* How to write small classified ads that can bring in thousands of dollars in immediate new business for you (Chapter 3)
* How to get clients to hire you by mail (Chapter 3)
* How to earn $125 to $200 per hour as a Communications Consultant (Chapter 11)

* Secrets of the country's highest paid copywriters—and how you can get the same fees they do (Chapter 6)
* Plus detailed pricing guidelines on what to charge for press releases, booklets, audiovisual scripts, speeches, direct mail ...and dozens of other assignments (Chapter 2)

My material tells you everything you need to succeed. Nothing is left out. For the first time, all the secrets of the high-paid commercial writers are revealed in full detail.

Here's What My Readers Say:

"With Bob's practical ideas and clear business advice, I have been able to land jobs I would never have thought of before and establish myself as a highly successful full-time professional freelance writer."
—Joe Vitale, Houston, TX

"Reading *Secrets of a Freelance Writer,* particularly the tips on contracts, saved me at least $10,000 in six months."
—Catherine Gonick, Jersey City, NJ

"I made $30,000 in my first nine months working part-time 17 hours per week. And I love it! Thanks, Bob. I'm not sure I ever would have put the pieces together on my own."
—Kathie Friedley, Takoma Park, MD

"I have found *Secrets of a Freelance Writer* extremely helpful, wonderfully practical, and clearly inspiring—invaluable for any serious writer. I am a very avid reader of this type of material and nowhere have I found a book so loaded with practical, step-by-step instructions."
—James C. Magruder, Racine, WI

"I'm reading—and enjoying—*Secrets of a Freelance Writer.* Thanks for writing such a practical and information-packed book."
—Doug Toft, Minneapolis, MN

"I've just completed the three busiest, most financially rewarding months of my writing career, and part of the credit goes to you for sharing your 'secrets.' I've had little time for (low-paying) pieces o'cake, but no complaints."
—Irwin Chusid, Montclair, NJ

"I just finished your fascinating *Secrets of a Freelance Writer.* What an education! Thanks for the inspiration."
—Jim Travisiano, Barboursville, VA

"I wanted to say a brief word of thanks for your help in getting me started in the right direction in a freelance career. I've been writing ad copy for a national advertising company for seventeen years, dreaming of having my own business. Now that dream is a reality."
—William W. Bennett, Lancaster, CA

Try *Secrets* Risk-Free for 90 Days

To order *Secrets of a Freelance Writer,* just fill in the coupon and mail with your check for $19.95 plus $2.50 shipping and handling. I'll rush a copy to you immediately. If you are not 100% delighted with my material, simply return it within 90 days and I will refund your money in full—no questions asked.

The writing life is a great life—especially if you are getting paid handsomely to sit home and do it. Why not enjoy the good life now instead of later? Send for my instructions and get started today. There is no risk or obligation of any kind. And your satisfaction is guaranteed.

Sincerely,
Bob Bly
174 Holland Avenue
New Milford, NJ 07646
(201) 599-2277

YES, I'd like to make $100,000 a year or more as a freelance writer. Please send me the two-volume set *Secrets of a Freelance Writer.* I understand that if I am not 100% delighted with this material, I may return it within 90 days for a full refund—no questions asked. On that basis, here is my check for $22.45 ($19.95 + $2.50 shipping and handling).

Name _____

Address _____

City _____

State _____ Zip _____

NJ residents add 6% sales tax ($1.20). Canada residents add $2 (U.S.dollars).

❑ I have enclosed an extra $2 for special rush first-class delivery.

Mail To: Bob Bly, Dept. WDD
174 Holland Avenue
New Milford, NJ 07646

Because direct marketing must do the whole selling job, the copy is usually longer than it is in general advertising. (Source: John Doe marketing company)

➤ **Advertising** refers to promotional messages that are paid for by a sponsor (the advertiser) and carried in print or broadcast media. These include newspaper ads, magazine ads, trade journal ads, Yellow Pages ads, directory ads, radio commercials, TV commercials, and billboards.

➤ **Business-to-business marketing** is designed to sell products or services to business, industry, or professionals rather than consumers. Ads that appear in trade journals are a prime example of business-to-business marketing. So are industrial catalogs. People often think of business-to-business advertising as technical advertising, but not all business-to-business products are technical. A catalog selling paper clips, envelopes, and other office supplies to business offices is business-to-business, but hardly technical.

➤ **Consumer marketing** is designed to sell products or services to individual consumers, families, and households. Examples include most of the TV commercials, radio commercials, and newspaper ads you see, hear, and read every day. Victoria's Secret catalogs are definitely consumer marketing, as are all the sneaker commercials featuring basketball stars.

Joe Lane, a specialist in business-to-business marketing, defines consumer advertising as "simple thoughts for simple folks." But that's an overstatement. While it's true that most consumer advertising deals with simple products—soap, detergent, beer, hamburgers—not all of it does. Brochures written to describe cars, VCRs, and stereo systems, for example, often get quite technical in their discussion of features and functions.

➤ **Direct mail** is unsolicited advertising or promotional material (that is, material the recipient has not requested) sent to an individual or company through the mail. A four-page sales letter asking you to subscribe to *Time* or *Newsweek* is an example of direct mail. So is that big package Publishers' Clearinghouse sends you every now and then.

➤ **High-tech advertising** promotes software, computer hardware, electronics, and other technology products. Most of it is aimed at business buyers; some of it is designed to appeal to consumers. So high-tech marketing is not necessarily business-to-business marketing, although most high-tech advertising is probably business-to-business.

➤ **General advertising**, also known as **image advertising**, doesn't seek an immediate response, but instead aims at building an image or creating an awareness of a product, brand, or company over an extended period of time.

Examples include TV commercials for consumer products such as fast foods (McDonald's, Wendy's, Burger King), soft drinks (Coke, Pepsi), and packaged goods such as shampoos, soaps, dishwashing liquids, and household cleaners. The institutional or corporate advertising that appears in *Forbes* and *Fortune* is another example of the genre. While targeted at business, it exists to promote a corporate image, not generate orders for a specific product.

➤ **Industrial marketing** refers to marketing used to advertise and promote products and services aimed primarily at engineers and other buyers working in traditional U.S. "smokestack" industries, such as chemical processing, pulp and paper, construction, mining, food processing, oil and gas, water and wastewater treatment, and so forth. All industrial advertising is business-to-business advertising, but there's a lot of business-to-business advertising that isn't industrial (for example, firms promoting accounting, legal, and other professional services are business-to-business, but not industrial). In 1983, the leading trade magazine in the field of business-to-business marketing changed its name from *Industrial Marketing* to *Business Marketing*. Some people use the two terms interchangeably, but this is inaccurate.

➤ **Junk mail** is a popular term for direct mail and is often used in a derogatory sense. Many professionals who work in direct marketing consider the term a put-down of their industry and take great offense whenever the words "junk mail" are used. In fact, whenever a major media story on the direct mail industry refers to direct mail as "junk mail," numerous direct marketers protest by writing letters to the editors to both the offending newspaper and the direct mail trade magazines. Everyone else knows and uses this familiar term all the time. I suspect the average citizen doesn't have much of an idea of what direct marketing or direct response is—nor do they care.

➤ **Mail order** is the selling of products through the mail. In mail-order selling, the buyer typically purchases the product directly from an ad, mailing, or catalog without visiting a store or seeing a salesperson. The product is then shipped by mail or UPS; again, with no middleman involved. Some marketers consider "mail order" a dated term and prefer to call it direct marketing.

➤ **Marketing** refers to the activities required to get a customer to give you money in exchange for your product or service. Although many people (including me) commit the language sin of using the terms advertising and marketing interchangeably, they are not the same. Marketing consists of four key components: the product, the price, distribution, and promotion. Advertising is part of promotion. (Other parts of promotion include trade shows, direct mail, catalogs, sales brochures, the Internet, and publicity.)

Surprising Secrets

In 1999, direct marketers spent $176.5 billion on advertising and generated $1.53 trillion in sales. Direct response sales are projected to grow by 8.8 percent annually through 2004 versus 5.3 percent annual sales growth for the U.S. economy as a whole.

The Evolution of Direct Marketing

No one can say for sure when direct marketing was first introduced. Possibly the first direct marketer in the United States was Ben Franklin, who published a book catalog asking for mail orders. He reassured buyers with this printed guarantee: "Those persons who live remote, by sending their orders to said B. Franklin, may depend on the same justice as if present" (*Catalog Success*, January 2001, p. 25.). Today the money-back guarantee is a staple of all successful direct marketing (see the following figure).

A cornerstone of successful direct marketing is a strong money-back guarantee. (Source: Phillips Publishing)

> **It doesn't get any safer than this**
> # Our 100% Risk-Free Guarantee
>
> As you can see from this Investor Bulletin, we do everything in our power to make it possible for you to get 50% or more a year, investing in best-in-class Internet stocks that meet our rigorous selection criteria. And we believe our service is "one-of-a-kind" and offers extraordinary value.
>
> Still, you may have the tiniest hesitation, and that's why our guarantee can make your decision totally risk-free. If you change your mind within the first 60 days, just let us know. You'll promptly receive a 100% refund of every penny. What's more, if at any time after those first 60 days you don't feel like continuing, just let us know and we'll refund the unused portion of your service immediately. And of course, all the materials you've received will be yours to keep.
>
> We want to make it simple and easy for you to enjoy very high returns from The Internet Age, and this guarantee is our way of making it clear that you don't have to take on any additional risk just to enjoy additional profits.
>
> Mark Burkhardt   Bryan Perry

Another pioneer in direct marketing was Dick Sears. A railroad station agent, Sears came into possession of a shipment of gold watches that he thought other station agents might want to buy. In 1886, he sent a letter describing the watches and, to his surprise, sold out the lot. From this he went on to build mail-order giant Sears, Roebuck. His first ads for Sears had the then-revolutionary offer in the headline, "send no money now"—a line still used in direct marketing copy today.

Lester Wunderman, co-founder of the direct marketing ad agency Wunderman Cato Johnson, is credited with having invented the term "direct marketing" in a speech he gave on October 1, 1961 to the Hundred Million Club in New York, an organization of leaders in the direct mail business.

In the 1990s, Jeff Bezos pioneered direct marketing on the World Wide Web by launching Internet bookseller Amazon.com. The Internet has already had an enormous effect on the direct marketing industry (Forrester Research estimates that sales to consumers over the Internet will reach $187.9 billion by 2004). But so far, the real success stories seem to be traditional brick-and-mortar companies adding the Internet to their arsenal of marketing tactics, rather than pure dot.coms that rely on Internet sales as their sole source of revenue.

Warning!

The best advice I ever heard on direct marketing creativity is from freelance copywriter Peter Betuel, who says, "Don't get trapped by personal preferences." What's important is not what appeals to you. The issue is whether what you write and design appeals to your potential customer. "I hate it" is not a meaningful critique of a direct marketing promotion. Instead, ask yourself, "Will my customers buy it?" Or, to quote an old advertising saying: It isn't creative unless it sells.

How Direct Marketing Differs from Other Advertising

There are a number of differences that distinguish direct marketing from the general or "image" advertising as practiced by Madison Avenue advertising agencies. These differences will be discussed in the following sections.

The most important of these is the particular mindset of the direct marketer, which I believe is focused more on profit and less on "creativity" than is general advertising.

Creativity

The most common—and damning—criticism you will ever get from a general advertiser is, "This isn't very creative." A true direct marketer doesn't care whether your promotion is a marvel of creativity or a near carbon copy of something else, as long as it works. Again, the focus is on results, not aesthetics.

Branding

In their book *How to Write a Successful Marketing Plan* (NTC), Roman Hiebing and Scott Cooper define branding as "a process of establishing and managing the images, perceptions, and associations that the consumer applies to your product." General advertisers are obsessed with branding; entire books have been written about branding on the Internet. But direct marketers care about getting orders, not building brands—and the two often conflict.

"Build your business, not your brand," advises Howard Sewell in an article in *DM News* (February 14, 2001). "With all due respect to its many proponents, branding is a luxury you cannot afford. For all the dot.coms that spent millions creating a brand (a certain sock puppet comes to mind), there are hundreds more using cost-effective marketing strategies to generate new business from people who have never heard of them. Branding may be a worthy goal for Coke or Nike, but with your budget, forget it."

Entrepreneurship

Although direct marketing is increasingly being used by mainstream marketers, it has its roots in entrepreneurial enterprises, often selling odd or unusual products advertised as being "not available in stores." A good example is the kitchen gadgets sold in infomercials by Ron Popeil of Ronco. Some of the early mail-order firms sold "patent medicines," elixirs, and other cures for a variety of ailments. Medicine is still a popular category today, especially nutritional supplements.

One of the legendary entrepreneurs of direct marketing is Joe Karbo, a failed TV producer. He made a fortune running an ad with the classic headline, "The Lazy Man's Way to Riches." The ad sells a $10 book telling how to become rich running mail order ads! The ad also contained another classic line whose wisdom still rings true today, "Most people are too busy making a living to make any money."

Selling

Direct marketers view their mission as selling, not entertainment or image building. When creative directors at general ad agencies look at a copywriter's portfolio, the copywriter knows the job interview is going well if the creative director smiles, chuckles, or nods in admiration. The creative director at a direct marketing agency is

10

likely to ask the copywriter, "Which of these are controls?"—meaning, are the promotions profitable enough that the client is running them again and again? The focus is on results, not aesthetics.

Design

General advertisers strive for clean, even gorgeous graphics. Direct marketers don't. In fact, there's some evidence that, for certain products and audiences, "ugly" direct marketing pieces *outpull* "clean" ones! One direct marketer I know deliberately made a typo on page one of his sales letters; he said readers noticed the typo, helping the letter gain their attention. I am not saying you should deliberately design your direct marketing pieces to be shlocky, but there is evidence that fine art does not enhance direct marketing results and may, in fact, depress them.

Direct response graphic designer par excellence Ted Kikoler says the primary function of design is to make the copy readable. This contrasts sharply with the approach of some general advertising art directors who view copy as a mere "design element" (and not their favorite one at that). These attitudes explain in part why Ted's mailings are so successful and why so many general ad campaigns fail to produce tangible results.

Copy

While the age-old debate of long versus short copy is an issue we'll take up at length in Chapter 5, "Writing Copy That Sells," many direct marketers today still live by the old credo, "In direct response, copy is king."

Direct marketing is a selling medium, and for most offers, words sell more effectively than pictures. Therefore direct marketing remains a copy-intensive, copy-dominated medium. General advertising, on the other hand, increasingly has fewer and fewer words, relying instead on images.

Insider's Buzzwords

Pull refers to the amount of response a direct marketing promotion generates. To say one ad "outpulled" another means it generated more sales.

Insider's Buzzwords

In his book *Advertising Terminology* (Needham & Grohmann), Victor Grohmann defines a **campaign** as "a series of coordinated advertisements using a definite theme or appeal planned to accomplish a specific task." Famous examples include the Pillsbury Doughboy for Pillsbury, and the Marlboro Man for Marlboro cigarettes.

Campaign Consistency

General advertisers place a great premium on *ad campaigns*—a series of advertisements maintaining graphic consistency from one ad to the next. Direct marketers, by comparison, place a premium on creating a test mailing or ad that can beat the "control"—their current best-performing mailing or ad. To beat the control, the test by definition has to be different; if it is similar, it will merely generate similar results. Thus, graphic consistency is not a goal of the direct marketer. In fact, it's a weakness.

This fact is demonstrated in renewal mailings for subscriptions. Often, to reduce mailing costs, every effort in a renewal series (which can run to eight letters or more) uses the same size and color outer envelope. Experience shows that when you vary the size or color of the outer envelope in one effort in the series, the response for that effort increases considerably.

One possible reason is that if every mailing looks the same, the prospect thinks he or she has gotten the piece before and throws it away without opening it on that assumption. But whatever the reason, graphic consistency—which increases memorability in general advertising—can reduce response in direct marketing.

The Direct Marketing Mindset

As mentioned earlier, the major difference between direct marketers and general advertisers is their mindset—the way they think. Since a number of well-known direct marketers have written about the direct marketing mindset eloquently and at length, I will quote from them directly here to make my point.

The first is from a letter to the editor written by my friend, copywriter Richard Armstrong. It was first published in *Advertising Age* magazine many years ago. I reprint it in its entirety:

Ever since Madison Avenue finished its feeding frenzy on the direct-marketing industry, there's been a lot of talk in the trade press recently about "a new era of creativity in direct response." With an influx of creative talent from Madison Avenue, so the argument goes, direct marketers will at last learn something about building an image for their clients.

It has been suggested that old-fashioned direct marketers like myself are the advertising equivalent of hit-and-run drivers. In our reckless pursuit of profits, we neglect the long-term consequences of our actions. We would, for example, gladly print our direct mail on toilet paper if we thought it would cut the cost per thousand.

All this is about to change, however, now that Madison Avenue has taken over the direct-marketing agencies. At last, we junk mailers are going to discover the secrets of Madison Avenue creativity. Specifically, we're going to learn—fanfare and timpani roll—how to create an image.

Well, speaking on behalf of my fellow direct marketers: Thanks, but no thanks. Or, to put it more bluntly, if the people responsible for Mr. Whipple have something to say about image to the people responsible for L.L.Bean … well, we're listening.

Meanwhile, maybe there's a thing or two you can learn from us. In fact, there are five ways direct marketers build an image that general advertisers would be wise to remember:

1. *Direct marketers offer iron-clad guarantees.*

Nothing builds a company's image in the customer's mind better than a good guarantee and a commitment to honor it, yet general advertisers rarely use this age-old technique. The value of a guarantee was forcefully brought home to me on a recent trip to Maine.

Nearly every native I met had a story to tell me about L.L. Bean, and most of these tales revolved around Bean's legendary guarantee. I heard about kayaks returned after 10 years and cheerfully replaced, refunds made for scuffed hiking boots and moth-eaten sweaters, all after years of use.

Surely some of these accounts were exaggerated, but does it matter? A company whose customers are willing to stretch the truth to convince others certainly doesn't have an image problem.

2. *Direct marketers go beyond building an image to building a relationship.*

Does your grandmother have an image? Does your wife or husband? I guess they do. But you actually have more than just an image of these people; you have a relationship with them. Thanks to general advertising, I have an image of IBM. But thanks to direct marketing, I have a relationship with Lillian Vernon.

Nothing carnal, mind you. But my relationship with Lillian is based on an intimate communication which has been maintained over a period of years. I've received letters from her. I've spoken with her assistants on the phone. I've had my problems resolved, my questions answered, and ——in return for being such a good friend—I've received gifts and discounts. As far as I'm concerned, Lillian Vernon's image couldn't be better.

3. *Direct marketers seldom change their image; they merely enhance it.*

Pepsi-cola has had about five images in my lifetime. Coca-cola has had three images in the last month. The "Kiplinger Letter," by contrast—a financial newsletter sold primarily by direct mail—has not only kept the same image for the past 35 years, they've actually been mailing the same promotion.

Direct marketers take an additive approach to their image to let it grow and sink deep roots in the consumer's mind. General advertisers, on the other hand, take an overhaul approach: When the product's image shows signs of fading, wipe it out and create a new one. Thus the $25 million that a client spends on one campaign will be rendered worthless by the $30 million he spends on the next. In the long run, which approach works best?

4. *Direct marketers personalize their companies.*

To their credit, general advertisers have caught on to this technique in recent years. But as thrilled as Madison Avenue was with the success of Frank Perdue and Lee Iacocca as spokesmen for their own companies, we direct marketers reacted with a yawn. We've been doing this for years!

What better way to create an image for your company than to incarnate it in the form of a real human being? From the home-grown pears of Harry & David to the elegant attire of J. Peterman, customers trust the product because they trust the man behind it.

5. *Direct marketers create a good image for themselves by maintaining a good image of their customers.*

When a company has a good image of me, I have a good image of it. When a company treats me like a fool, my image of it goes down. It's as simple as that.

Direct mail has gotten a bad rap recently and, unfortunately, much of the criticism has come from the hybrid agencies that were spawned by Madison Avenue's takeover of direct-marketing companies. I'm thinking especially of a recent advertisement by Scali, McCabe, Sloves Direct that attacked "junk mail" for being ugly, insulting, and demeaning to its readers.

I don't agree. I do confess that much of the direct mail I receive contains gimmicky involvement devices—"Yes/No" stickers and the like—but I don't find these particularly insulting. Nowhere near as insulting as "Ring around the collar," for example.

If anything, I find my direct mail treats me as much more of an intellectual than I really am. In recent weeks, I've received mail from The Nation, The New Republic, *and* National Review *which sought to engage my mind on a variety of political, social, and economic issues to which I previously had given scarcely a moment's thought. This is heady stuff for a guy who gets a kick out of* Baywatch.

Granted, these are upscale products. But even my most downscale direct mail makes certain flattering assumptions about me which Madison Avenue's television commercials rarely do: 1) that I can read; 2) that I can think; 3) that I am capable of making a decision; and 4) that I'm an individual who acts on free will, not a couch potato who mindlessly accepts whatever electrons are beamed at him from the nearest Sony.

So, like most Americans, I read or skim almost all of my direct mail. And like most Americans, I consider Madison Avenue's "creative" television commercials to be excellent opportunities for going to the bathroom. The next is by legendary Madison Avenue adman David Ogilvy, from his book Ogilvy on Advertising *(Vintage Books, 1989):*

For all their research, most advertisers never know for sure whether their advertisements sell. Too many other factors cloud the equation. But direct-response advertisers, who solicit orders by mail or telephone, know to a dollar how much each advertisement sells. So watch the kind of advertising they do. You will notice important differences between their techniques and the techniques of general advertisers. For example:

General advertisers use 30 second commercials. But the direct response fraternity have learned that it is more profitable to use two minute commercials. Who, do you suppose, is more likely to be right?

General advertisers broadcast their commercials in expensive prime time, when the audience is at its peak. But direct response advertisers have learned that they make more sales late at night. Who, do you suppose, is more likely to be right?

In their magazine advertisements, general advertisers use short copy, but the direct response people invariably use long copy. Who, do you suppose, is more likely to he right it?

I am convinced that if all advertisers were to follow the example of their direct response brethren, they would get more sales per dollar. Every copywriter should start his career by spending two years in direct response. One glance at any campaign tells me whether its author has ever had that experience.

And in a letter to the editor published in *DM News* (February 12, 2001, p. 56), Anne Carman, director of direct marketing for Children's Hospital Foundation, talks about the direct marketer's passion for results:

> *I live by our numbers, care passionately about our database, love the creativity of coming up with ideas and test strategies, and love the thrill of watching returns coming in to meet or beat projections, or even to prove an idea wrong. It's a great game, the stakes are very high, but we have the best mission in the world so the motivation never dies.*

Success Story

Bob Kalian, a New York entrepreneur, realized that "free" was one of the most powerful words in direct marketing, so he decided to build an entire business around it. He self-published a directory of free information and free offers (remember, this was before the glut of free information on the Internet). Then he ran an ad for it with the headline, "Thousands of Free Gifts." The body copy of his small display ad contained the word free more than 32 times. Eventually Bob sold over half a million copies of his free things book and retired, a self-made mail-order millionaire.

The Direct Marketing Customer

Direct marketing buyers come in all ages, sizes, and colors. In Chapter 2, "Planning Your Direct Marketing Campaign," and Chapter 4, we will go into how to select the right prospects for your direct marketing campaign in detail.

Surprising Secrets

Believe it or not, the prospect most likely to respond to your offer is the one who just responded to your last promotion. Fundraisers, for example, know that they will get the most donations by mailing to a list of donors who have just given! Common sense might cause you to reason, "Recent donors just gave money so they'll be tapped out." While that seems logical, test results consistently prove the opposite: The most recent buyers are the most responsive. This is why mailing lists often offer a "hotline" selection which allows you to rent only the names of customers who have bought recently—usually within the last 6, 12, or 24 months.

Not everyone responds to direct marketing offers. About half of Americans do, and half don't. Overwhelmingly, a key factor in direct-marketing success is to target only those prospects who are proven responders to direct marketing.

In print advertising, for example, ads run in publications that have other mail-order ads usually pull much better than the same ads running in publications that do not carry other mail-order advertising. As the late direct response copywriter Paul Bringe said, "Fish where the fish are biting."

The same principle applies in direct mail. Mailings that attempt to sell products directly to the recipient typically do better when mailed to response lists—that is, lists of people who have previously responded to and bought products from direct mail solicitations.

Arrows in the Direct Marketer's Quiver

Many people think that direct mail and direct marketing are the same thing, but as we've noted, the terms are not synonymous. Direct mail is an important weapon in the direct marketer's arsenal, but by no means the only one. Here's the complement of tools you, as a direct marketer, have at your disposal:

➤ **Space Ads.** Print advertisements reach, at a low CPM (cost per thousand), the entire subscriber base of a newspaper or magazine. Therefore, it is extremely cost-effective when marketing to large markets. For instance, if you want to sell software to chemical engineers, run an ad in *Chemical Engineering* magazine. See Chapter 13, "Direct Response Advertising," for details.

➤ **Direct mail.** Direct mail is unsolicited promotional material sent to prospects via the post office. Direct mail works when you want to cost-effectively target a select group of prospects, such as plant managers. Direct mail is covered in detail in Chapters 7 through 9.

➤ **Catalogs.** A catalog is a bound booklet or brochure offering a number of different products, usually of the same category (for example, lingerie, jewelry), for the same usage (for example, home office equipment, gardening tools and products), or for the same audience (for example, gamblers, investors). The catalog is one of the only direct-marketing mediums, aside from Web sites, through which multiple products can be offered effectively in a single promotion. You'll find more information on catalogs in Chapter 10, "Catalogs."

➤ **Postcard decks.** Because of their space constraints, postcards are typically best for promoting free offers for lead generation, such as a free catalog or free demo disk. They can also be used to sell simple products that do not require a lot of explanation, like business cards and mailing labels. See Chapter 11, "Profits from Postcard Decks."

➤ **TV and radio.** TV and to a lesser degree radio are proven direct marketing media. TV is especially attractive for products that benefit from a visual demonstration, such as exercise machines or engine additives. TV and radio ads are covered in Chapter 14, "Direct Response TV and Radio."

➤ **Telemarketing.** Although most people, when asked, say they "hate" telemarketing, businesses wouldn't make telemarketing calls unless it was profitable. When you hit the right person with the right proposition at the right time, telemarketing can generate sales. And the hit rate doesn't have to be high for the telemarketing campaign to be profitable. Read Chapter 15, "Telemarketing" for a more complete discussion on telemarketing.

➤ **Internet.** The Internet is the "hot" new medium in direct marketing. Options for Internet marketing include Web sites, banner ads, and e-mail marketing. Internet marketing is discussed in Chapter 16, "the Internet: Direct Marketing for the Digital Age."

➤ **Alternative media.** The term "alternative media" refers to any marketing vehicle not in the categories just listed. An example is the free-standing inserts for Orek vacuum cleaners or Harriet Carter you find in your Sunday newspaper. For details see Chapter 12, "alternative Media."

The Least You Need to Know

➤ The best direct response prospects are those who have previously responded to direct response offers.

➤ Successful direct marketing promotions ask for the order (or at least for an inquiry for more product details) and give the prospect a reason to respond now instead of later.

➤ In direct marketing, response is the name of the game. Do not let image building, brand awareness, or other secondary communications objective interfere with the primary objective of getting the prospect to respond.

➤ Direct marketers do limited market tests in small quantities to see whether an offer or promotion is profitable before rolling out to a larger-scale campaign. If the test fails, they redesign it or drop it and move on to something else.

Chapter 2

Planning Your Direct Marketing Campaign

> ## In This Chapter
>
> ➤ Selecting the product or service to promote
>
> ➤ Establishing objectives and selecting the market
>
> ➤ Choosing the medium, format, tone, and style
>
> ➤ Determining your unique selling proposition
>
> ➤ Identifying supporting features and benefits
>
> ➤ Creating your offer and scheduling your campaign

You wouldn't spend $100,000 on a new advertising campaign without carefully setting goals and objectives. Yet, many advertisers will dash off a quick sales letter and mail it to thousands of customers without a second thought.

Planning is the professional approach. Your plan need not be elaborate or complex, but by analyzing your audience, selecting your message, and establishing sales goals, you increase your direct marketing campaign's chances for success.

This chapter will show you how to plan a direct marketing project of any scope and size from a simple postcard to a nationwide media blitz reaching thousands—or even hundreds of thousands—of prospects.

What Are You Selling?

The first question you should always ask when planning a direct marketing campaign is, "What am I selling?" Finding the answer is not always as simple as you might think.

Do you feature one product or a product line? Do you sell the deluxe version, the midline model, or the low-cost basic model? Selling the deluxe brings in more money per order, but the higher price might hurt response. Do you sell the product with supplies and accessories as a package, or do you sell the basic product now, then up-sell the buyer on supplies and accessories after the initial purchase?

Let's say you are selling a complete line of equipment used in chemical plants. You have many different products that perform a variety of functions, but each is purchased by the same customer. Do you highlight individual products, one per mailing? Or should each mailing sell your full product line? Maybe your products are pretty similar to the competition's. In that case, would you be better off stressing service, price, fast delivery, or the reliability and reputation of your firm, rather than trying to convince the customer that the products themselves are superior? What, exactly, are you selling?

Surprising Secrets

Although you might expect that offering your customers lots of choices will pull more orders, the opposite is usually true: Offering too many response options can actually depress response. The simpler your offer is, and the easier it is to understand, the better the response. Don't clutter your product offering with too many options, models, colors, and choices. The fewer the choices, the better. If you are going to offer multiple products, or different ordering options, keep everything clear and simple.

What Products Sell Best via Direct Marketing?

Although theoretically almost anything can be sold via direct response (with the possible exceptions of ice and ice cream), some products are better suited for direct marketing than others.

The following sections can help you evaluate the potential of a product to be sold via direct marketing. You don't need all of these factors to be successful, but you do need at least some of them.

Not Available in Stores

The easier the product is to get in stores, the more difficult it will be to sell via mail-order. If the direct response product is available only by mail, and not in stores, "not available in stores" is a magnetic lure to many mail-order buyers. However, many products are sold both retail and via mail order. For these products, the convenience of buying mail order is what attracts buyers.

Story Rich

If the product is story rich, it means there is a lot you can say about the product. The story can include how it originated, how it was made, and, of course, the many benefits it offers users.

Products sold through full-page ads and solo direct mail packages are usually story-rich, so the copywriter can weave a story that captivates and compels the reader to order. Catalog products can be more like commodity items, and can be sold by showing a picture of the product, along with the price and a brief description.

Priced for Direct Response Markup

A $6 product is difficult to sell via mail order. The price is too low to profitably sell it directly from a space ad or direct mail package. You can sell the $6 product only if it's one of many items in a *bounce-back* or other catalog.

Direct response products ideally sell for at least $10. If you are going to promote the product via direct mail, it should sell for at least $25 or more, and preferably $50 or more. The selling price should be at least five times the cost of goods or higher. If you are selling low-priced units, consider a bundle or minimum order of $30 or more. Another way to raise the average unit of sale is to offer a "free gift with purchase." For example, www.gazelle.com, an online hosiery site, offered a free gift with orders of $40 or more.

Insider's Buzzwords

The term **bounce-back** refers to an insert, order form, or catalog of related products inserted into the box in which your main product is shipped. It is called a "bounce-back" because, when the customer wants to order one of your other products, he sends the order card in the insert to you—so part of the insert is "bouncing back" to you.

An Element of Fun, Mystery, or the Unusual

Direct response buyers tend to like gimmicks, gadgets, and unusual, hard-to-find products. A good example is Ron Popeil's pocket fisherman, a fishing rod you can fold up and carry in your pocket.

Marketing Tip

Ice cream is not an ideal mail-order product because it is difficult and expensive to ship to the consumer without melting. Delicate, fragile, and oversize items are also difficult to ship. The ideal mail-order product is compact enough to be shipped economically, and rugged enough so it won't break or spoil in transit.

Rarities and collectibles sell well via direct marketing. Exclusivity and the promise of inside information also appeal to mail-order buyers. An example is the *Boardroom Reports* promotion that begins, "What the airlines don't tell you …." One of my favorites was a full-page newspaper ad selling a lump of coal from the Titanic as a collectible.

Refillable or Requires Updating

The next section covers the importance of having additional products, known as back-end products, to sell your direct response customers after they buy your initial offering. A refillable product, or one that requires updating, has its own back-end built into it.

A good example is Day-Timer. When you buy a Day-Timer, the company gains a customer who will in all likelihood come back each year to buy refill pages for the new year. Another good refillable mail-order product is vitamins. When you use up the vitamins, you have to order more to keep up with the regimen.

Different from Competing Products

Try to identify or create in your product one unique selling point that differentiates it from all other products in its class, in at least one aspect. Your copy will come across stronger if it focuses on a unique aspect of your product that the consumer can't get when buying competing products.

Hamilton Knife, for example, sells a machine tool oil that makes tools last up to five times longer because of the superior lubrication. The lubrication is superior because the oil is literally magnetic, so it clings to the cutting edge better. In magnetic materials, the atoms are polarized, or aligned in one direction. Hamilton's ad headline, "Unique 'polarized oil' makes machine tools last five times longer," capitalizes on the unique difference of polarized oil versus regular oil. This is their unique selling proposition, which is explained at great length in their inquiry fulfillment materials.

Planning Your Front and Back Ends

To succeed in direct marketing, you cannot have just one product (exceptions are rare). The reason is that the majority of direct response businesses make most of their profits on the *back end*—selling related products to people who have purchased the *front end*, or primary product.

The greatest expense in direct marketing is acquiring a new customer. It costs approximately five times as much to acquire a new customer than it does to sell additional products (the back-end product line) to existing customers. Therefore, if you do not have a back end—additional products to sell people who have bought your main product from you—you are leaving money on the table.

Insider's Buzzwords

The **front-end** product is the product you sell the customer from your ad or mailing. **Back-end** products are other products you sell to this customer once she has purchased the front-end product.

Which product should be your front end and which should be your back end? A good front-end product has broad appeal to the majority of your target market. For instance, if you are selling advice on how to get a career in the travel and tourism industry, your front-end product could be a special report, "100 Best Careers in Travel and Tourism," since it covers all the career opportunities and therefore has the broadest appeal.

A good back-end product complements the front-end product. For instance, Dan Poynter of Para Publishing (1-800-PARA-PUB) sells as his front-end *The Self-Publishing Manual,* a book on how to self-publish your own book. Many forms are involved in publishing a book (such as copyright forms and ISBN registration), so a natural back-end product for Dan, which he sells from his catalog, is a collection of all the necessary forms.

Back-end products should relate to the front-end product; that is, they ideally address the same consumer need, fear, concern, or problem. If you sell vitamins, for example, a book on blood pressure is a good back-end product; a book on investing in mutual funds, unrelated to health, is not.

Back-end products are usually smaller than the main product, less expensive to produce, and priced lower. But this is not always the case. A percentage of customers who buy your product will buy a related product at a much higher price, and up-selling your list on more expensive offers can often be profitable.

Determining Your Marketing Objectives

When asked to state their marketing objective, many people simply answer, "to increase profits and sales," or "to get leads for new business." But how many leads? Of what quality? How much profit? How many sales?

The first step in planning a mailing is to set concrete, measurable goals—and the more specific the better. Why is this important? Because if you don't have a goal set with specific results that you want to get from the mailing, then how do you know whether the mailing has achieved its objective? Only by setting a specific sales objective can you determine whether the mailing is successful.

Many people say, "A 2-percent response is good." But good for *whom?* For a mailer asking people to pay $495 to attend a seminar, a 2-percent response is excellent—and highly profitable. But if you're going for leads, not sales, and you offer a free gift (such as a book, coffee mug, or calendar), with no strings attached, to everyone who requests your brochure, it's easy to get 2 percent, and 20 percent or more is possible!

Comparing a sales-generating mailing with a lead-generating mailing, or a free gift offer with a straight offer, is like comparing apples and oranges. You have to set objectives that make sense in terms of your audience, your product, your offer, and your sales methods. One manufacturer may want leads for salespeople to pursue; another sells its product direct through a catalog. The type of response you want, and how *much* response you want, is an individual decision that you must make.

A better way to set objectives than tracking percentage response is to look at break-even. A goal of "100-percent break-even" means the revenue generated by the promotion equals its cost. A goal of 200 percent break-even means that for every $1 you spend in marketing, you get $2 in sales. Chapter 25, "Database Marketing," gives details on how to calculate your break-even point.

Marketing Tip

Many direct marketers are happy to get 130 percent to 150 percent of break-even, because they know their profits will be made in the back end. Some are even satisfied if they break-even or even operate at a small loss on the front end to acquire a mail-order customer. If you get 200 percent to 300 percent of break-even on promotion selling your front-end product to new customers, you are doing very well indeed.

Taking Aim at Your Target Market

To whom are you selling? Who is your audience? Who is the prospective buyer? Who will receive, read, and hopefully respond to your letter? The beauty of direct marketing is that you can use it to reach *only* those people who are potential buyers for your product or service. This is sometimes called "target marketing."

Think about your customers. Are they male or female? Young or old? Rich or poor? New wave or grassroots? Corporate or entrepreneurial? City slickers or country folk? Married or single? What do they do for a living? Where do they live? What are their hobbies and interests? If you can accurately describe your typical customer, chances are there's a list of them available.

In some cases, you may be selling one product to many different types of customers, each with different interests and concerns. In such a situation, you can use a standard brochure to describe the product in general, then tailor your cover letter to your different markets. For example, a broker selling investments might stress low risk in a letter to retired couples, but highlight tax-free in a letter to doctors, lawyers, and other high-income professionals.

In business-to-business marketing, you often have to reach multiple buying influences within each client company. Let's say you're selling sales training seminars to medium-size firms. Mail aimed at sales managers would talk about the fantastic competitive edge their salespeople will have—and all the extra sales they will generate—after taking your program. A letter sent to the human resources or training manager might stress your firm's reputation, testimonials from satisfied training managers who have hired you to give programs, and the great training materials you provide with each course.

A key component of successful direct marketing strategy is generating a profile of your target market or "ideal customer," then selecting mailing lists or other media outlets that most closely fit this profile.

The following selection factors, available on many mailing lists, should be kept in mind as you develop your Ideal Prospect Profile:

➤ **Geographic.** Most lists can be segmented by location: state, SCF (sectional center facility, which is the first three digits of your zip code), zip code, county, and metropolitan area. All zip codes included under a given SCF share the same first three digits.) If you are planning a mailing designed to get business people to attend a conference in New York City, you might mail only to executives located within a 100-mile radius of midtown Manhattan.

➤ **Demographic.** Some lists provide quantitative characteristics of a given population: age, sex, income level, wealth, race, and other vital statistics of a personal nature. A great many mailing lists, for instance, allow selection by sex (male or female).

➤ **Psychographic.** This segmentation refers to the psychological make-up of your target audience and is more difficult to identify. A mailer sponsoring a seminar on "How to Become a Published Author," for example, might mail seminar invitations to members of the AARP (American Association for Retired Persons) on the assumption that many retirees are looking for something to occupy their time and might consider writing for publication. The premise is unproven, however, and a test mailing to this list might fail to generate sufficient response. A better choice might be the *Writer's Digest* subscription list, because people have indicated their interest in writing by buying a magazine on the subject.

Surprising Secrets

Experience proves that buyers who buy often and spend more are better prospects than those who buy infrequently and spend less. Also, contrary to what might seem logical, those persons most likely to respond to a new mail order offer are those who have recently responded to a previous mail-order offer! This is why "hotlines"—the segment of a list comprised of the most recent buyers—are priced higher than the rest of the list.

➤ **RFM** (recency, frequency, monetary). Three important selection criteria for mail-order buyers are frequency (how often they buy through the mail), recency (the date of their last purchase), and amount (how much they spent). Many list descriptions provide a dollar amount for "average order," representing the average amount spent by people on the list.

Business Prospects

Selections on business lists include job function, title, plant size, industry (often specified by SIC code, which is short for Standard Industrial Classification), number of employees, annual sales, and types of products purchased.

Choosing Campaign Specifics

Chapter 1, "Direct Marketing 101," outlines the major communications vehicles available to direct marketers and their application: direct mail, ads, telemarketing, the Internet, and alternate media. Your choice will depend on budget, audience, product, and offer, as well as available media. For example, if there is no magazine reaching your target audience, you may have to do direct mail instead. If you choose direct mail, think about what type of mailing piece you want to send out. Will it be big or small? Flat or bulky? Expensive or low-budget? Will it be a full-blown direct mail package with letter, color brochure, inserts, order forms, and reply cards, or just a simple postcard?

Whether you use mail, online marketing, or print ads, will the copy be hard-sell, or will you go for a low-key, professional approach? Will it be splashy and bright, or quiet and dignified?

Many different media formats are available. Selecting the right one is based largely on subjective judgment, knowledge of the audience, the type of offer, and your budget.

Determining Your Key Sales Appeal or Theme

Next, decide which sales appeal to stress in your copy. Your product may have many features that appeal to buyers. And, depending on whether you're after leads or sales, you may decide to mention all of them or just some of them. But successful advertising copy in direct mail or any other format is copy that focuses on *one* key sales appeal.

First, you pick the key sales appeal. This is the benefit that is most important to your customer. If your customers are primarily concerned with cost, the sales appeal would be, "saves money." If they are more concerned with performance, your key benefit might be "performance guaranteed" or "highest reliability." Then, you write a mailing piece based on this theme. Sure, you'll talk about other features and benefits. But these will be presented so that they support and reinforce the main message.

Why does successful advertising copy highlight one key benefit rather than many? If you stress every point, no point stands out, and the reader doesn't remember your sales pitch. If you highlight one key point, and drive it home over and over, you get your message across, and it sticks in the reader's mind.

How do you know which product benefit is most important to your customer? Experience tells you. For example, you could run two ads, or test two mailings. One says "easy to install," while the theme of the other is "maintenance-free." By seeing which draws the best response, you know whether the customer is more concerned with easy installation or minimal maintenance. If they both pull the same response (unlikely but possible), continue to test them on other mailing lists. You may find that different sales themes work best with different lists.

Another way to find out what customers want is through some type of market research. This can be as informal as speaking to a few customers at a trade show, or as elaborate as a formal survey or focus group. While this type of research can suggest sales appeals to test, it cannot answer definitely which will be the winner. Only a live test can do that. Your own experience, or that of your sales force, can provide guidance to help you decide which theme to use.

Once you've selected a theme or key sales appeal, you can test it, and see if you were right. If one theme doesn't work so well, you can easily switch to another. That's a major advantage of direct mail, it's easy to test and inexpensive to change.

Identifying Supporting Facts and Sales Arguments

Make a list of all the other sales arguments you might include in your copy. Remember to talk about benefits, not just features. A feature is a descriptive fact about a product or service, such as size, weight, material, form, or function. A benefit is what the user of the product gains as a result of the feature.

For example, a feature of my wristwatch is that it is luminescent: The hands and numbers glow in the dark. The benefit is that I can easily read the time, even at night or in a dark room.

How do you uncover benefits? Easy.

Divide a sheet of paper into two columns—features on the left and benefits on the right. Look at your product, or study the sales literature written about it. In the left column, list every fact (feature) about your product. Now, in the right-hand column, try to think of how the customer can benefit from each feature. In other words, how does the feature save the buyer time or money, make the buyer's job easier, or satisfy the buyer's needs in some other way?

As an example of how to create a features/benefits list, here's one for a common object—a number 2 pencil:

Features	Benefits
Pencil is a wooden cylinder that surrounds a graphite core	Can be resharpened as often as you like to ensure clean, crisp writing
One end is capped by a rubber eraser	Convenient eraser lets you correct writing errors cleanly and quickly
Eraser attached with a metal band	Tight-fitting band holds eraser snugly in place—won't fall off
Pencil is $7^{1}/_{2}$ inches long and	Lasts a long time
$^{1}/_{4}$ inch in diameter	Slender shape makes it easy to hold, with a comfortable grip
Number 2 hardness	Writes smoothly yet crisply
Yellow exterior	Bright, attractive; stands out in a pen holder or desk drawer
Sold by the dozen	Convenient 12-pack saves trips to the stationery store
Also available by the gross at a discount	Accommodates the needs of schools and business offices; saves money
Made in the U.S.A.	A quality product; supports our economy

This example may seem trivial because of the simplicity of the product. But creating a features/benefits list is immensely helpful in preparing to write copy about unfamiliar or more complex products and services.

Planning Your Offer

Now that you know your main sales theme and your supporting sales arguments, you have to determine the offer you want to make. The offer is simply what you send to people who respond to the mailing, combined with what they have to do to get it.

Successful direct marketing usually has a free offer, a discount offer, or offers something free along with your paid order. One of the main reasons people respond to mailings is to save money. Another is to get something free.

Also, people are afraid of being hooked by unethical mail-order schemes or high-pressure salesmen, so your offer should have no strings attached. Stress that your offer is free, that there is no obligation to buy, that you have a money-back guarantee. Shoppers don't want to commit themselves to a purchase. Buyers want to be assured that they won't be ripped off. Your offer should address these needs.

The action you want your prospect to take is part of the offer. Use phrases like "Send no money now," "Try it FREE for 15 days," "Mail the no-obligation Trial Request Form today," "Call us toll-free," or "Complete and mail the enclosed reply card." These phrases move the reader to action.

Many different offers are possible. Should you offer a 30-day trial, a free pamphlet, a pocket calculator, a one-year guarantee, or 20 percent off the price? Choose an offer you feel your prospects would best respond to. Then test it. See which offer works best.

The offer is important and can have a tremendous effect on your response. When in doubt about which offer is best, test one against the other and measure the results. Chapter 3, "Make Your Buyers an Offer They Can't Refuse," provides additional guidance on how to formulate and improve direct response offers.

Don't Forget Project Planning and Management

Budget and objectives determine the scope of a campaign. For example, if you want to generate 100 orders, and you anticipate a one percent response rate to your mail piece, you must mail 10,000 pieces. At $500 per thousand pieces mailed, your cost is $5,000. If you have only $2,500 total to spend, you can mail half the quantity or try a less expensive format or medium, such as a postcard or e-mail blast.

Timing is critical to some campaigns, less important to others. Some offers can be mailed year-round with continued strong response. Others are seasonal. For example, for catalog marketers selling gift items, the Christmas season is the most important, and they mail heavily in September, October, and November.

The other concern is whether you need a single mailing or a series of mailings. If your market is large, and your budget limited, you can probably mail one piece for many months or even many years before exhausting all the names available.

On the other hand, if you have a small market, you need a variety of different promotions. If you mail just one piece over and over again, it will soon experience a decline in response rate and wear out.

How many pieces should be in your mailing series, and at what intervals should they be mailed? A typical schedule for large direct marketing companies is to mail to their house list of customers monthly or every other month, and to their database of prospects three or four times a year.

Let's say you decide to do six mailings during the year. You can spread them out, one every other month, to keep your name in front of the prospect throughout the year. Another approach is to do a "blitz" mailing where you hit them with the six mailings in a short period of time, say one a week

Marketing Tip

Although timing varies by product category, the best month for mail-order sales is January, especially for self-help and self-improvement offers (perhaps it has something to do with New Year's Eve resolutions). Mailing in January can give you a 20-percent lift in response. By comparison, mailing in July can depress your response 20 percent.

for six weeks. The first method ensures that the prospect knows about you all year long, while the second method probably makes more of an impression.

Successful direct marketing is as much art as science, more trial and error than anything else. You come up with an idea, test it in the mail, and refine your work based on the results. The advantage is that you *can* measure results, an advantage not available with many other types of marketing.

The Least You Need to Know

➤ Your markup on a product sold via direct response should be at least 5:1.

➤ It is very difficult to profitably sell a product or take an order via direct response for less than $50; but there are numerous exceptions.

➤ Before you start marketing a product via direct response, make sure you have a related line of additional products to sell those customers once they buy.

➤ The only way to know what headline or sales appeal will work best is to test. In direct marketing, test results are the only opinion that matters.

➤ Spend time planning and testing a variety of offers. The offer (e.g., adding a premium) can make a huge difference in response rates—often much larger than you would expect.

Chapter 3

Make Your Buyers an Offer They Can't Refuse

In This Chapter

➤ One-step versus two-step offers

➤ The four types of offers

➤ Response and payment options

➤ Premium and discounts

➤ Act-now incentives

➤ Creating effective guarantees

"YOU MAY HAVE ALREADY WON $10 million."

"The GREATEST SPORTS BLOOPERS VIDEO—yours FREE with your paid subscription to Sports Illustrated."

"Affix the token to the reply card for your FREE sample issue."

"Buy one—get one free."

"FREE tote bag when you become a member."

Direct marketers rely heavily on finding and phrasing the proper offer to wake up bored consumers, get them to take notice, and persuade them to respond to the marketers' ads and mailings.

The offer is of utmost importance to the success of any direct marketing piece or campaign. The strategic planning, selection, and testing of offers can make or break a campaign, regardless of how well-designed or well-written the piece is.

As a rule, the more valuable and risk-free the offer seems to the reader, the better your response.

The presentation of the offer—the copy used to describe it, the graphics, the emphasis it receives—is also of critical importance. The more you emphasize and stress the offer in copy and graphics, the higher your response rate. The clearer and more understandable your offer, the better your response. The lack of a clear, distinct offer can significantly depress response.

What Is an Offer—And Why It's Important

I define the "offer" as follows: *What your prospects get when they respond to your ad or mailing, combined with what they have to do to get it.*

Note that the offer has two components:

1. What the prospect gets
2. What the prospect has to do to get it

Consider the following example of an offer: "For a free brochure on the Widget 2000, complete and mail the enclosed reply card today." What the prospect gets is a brochure describing your product. What they have to do to get it is fill in and mail a reply card.

There is one simple reason why offers are so important: They can have an enormous effect on the responses your marketing campaign generates.

It is not uncommon for a successful offer test to increase response rates 10 to 30 percent or more over the existing control (the "control" is the top-performing mailing piece the marketer had been using until the test beat it). In some cases, I have seen offer "A" outpull offer "B" for the same product by 10:1. A simple change in offer can transform a marginal campaign into a major winner.

One of the most successful offers in recent years is AOL's direct mail campaign. They send you an AOL CD-ROM and offer 10, 30, even 50 hours or more of free service.

How do I know this offer is successful for them? The same way you know whether any direct marketing campaign is successful: It is repeated again and again. If the mailing were not profitable, AOL would not continue to mail it. And I have probably received it over a dozen times.

Success Story

A software company was selling an accounting program consisting of five modules (accounts receivable, accounts payable, general ledger, payroll, and inventory at $29 each) for $145, with limited success, via direct mail. Their ad agency changed the mailing to advertising "Accounting software modules (accounts payable, accounts receivable, payroll, inventory)—only $1 each." Inside, you discovered you would get these modules at this price if you purchased the general ledger module for $141. Although the asking price was still $145 for both offers, the "accounting modules for $1" offer outpulled the "five modules for $145" offer by 10:1, making the mailing immensely profitable.

One Step or Two Step?

Depending on what you are selling, you can use either a one-step offer or a two-step offer.

In one-step direct marketing, also known as "mail order," you sell your product directly off the printed page. The prospect gets your direct mail package or sees your ad, reads it, and orders the product. There is no salesperson involved, no showroom or store to visit. The entire transaction takes place without customization, according to the precise ordering instructions spelled out on the order form. Example: You get a gift catalog in the mail, flip through it, and see an item you want. You call the toll-free number, give the operator the item number and your credit card, and the item pictured in the catalog is delivered right to your door.

One-step direct marketing is used primarily for products with low to moderate cost; and for products that do not require a high degree of customization or customer education.

In two-step direct marketing, also known as "lead generation," the prospect who responds to your promotion is not placing an order; rather, he or she is asking for more information about the product or service being advertised. The marketer sends the requested brochure or other materials requested. In some cases, the prospect can receive this material, read it to get his or her questions answered, and then place an order using an enclosed order form. In other cases, the prospect may be visited or telephoned by a sales representative who answers any questions and closes the sale.

Two-step direct marketing is used for medium to high-priced products, especially those that do not have a fixed price, but must be quoted based on the customer's requirements. It is also used for products requiring a high degree of customization or explanation.

The Four Types of Offers

You will hear direct marketers talk about "hard" versus "soft" offers. What do they mean?

Hard Offers

In mail-order selling, a hard offer usually requires the prospect to pay for the product in advance. The seller ships the product only after payment is received via check, money order, or credit card. Use of a hard offer eliminates credit and collection problems, because there is no billing; everyone pays up front.

Soft Offers

By comparison, the soft offer in mail-order selling is the classic "bill me" offer. Here, the prospect can order and receive the product with no money up front. The seller sends a bill and is paid later.

Negative Offers

In addition to hard and soft offers, there are two other basic categories of business-to-business offers: negative and deferred.

Rather than define them, I will give you the exact wording of these offers as you would use them in a reply card or an order form.

The negative offer reads as follows:

[ ] Not interested right now because:

_____

(Please give reason—thank you.)

Typically, reference to the negative offer is made in the P.S. or elsewhere in the body of the letter, using the following language:

P.S. Even if you are not interested in [name of product or service], please complete and return the enclosed reply card. Thank you.

The negative offer provides a response option for people who are prospects (that is, they have a need or problem your product addresses), but for some reason or another, do not want to buy from you or get more information on your product.

Normally, a person not interested in your offer will not respond to your mailing. By using a negative offer option, you will get response from a small portion of these people.

The negative offer should be used when you are testing a mailing on a new product, service, or offer you haven't promoted before using direct mail. The reason you use the negative offer is that without it, if you get a low or no response to your mailing, you don't know whether it's the mailing piece that's ineffective, or whether the product, service, or offer isn't right for the market.

With the negative offer option, people will *tell you* why they are not interested in your offer. Perhaps the price is too high. Or your technology is not compatible with the systems they are already using. Or they don't like your type of product, or don't use it.

This information not only helps you readjust your marketing plans; it also reveals why prospects didn't buy —something that's good to know if you're the person who wrote or designed it.

A second benefit of the negative option is that it can increase slightly your overall response rate. You might object and say, "But all the people who check the negative option box have told us they are not prospects."

But quite the opposite is true: If someone took the time to tell you why your offer isn't right for them, they *are* a prime prospect. They're telling you they have some sort of need, but your product *as described in the mailing* didn't seem quite right ... and that they want you to get back to them with a product, service, or offer that is right for them.

Actually, your product or service may be ideal for them, but your ad or mail copy may not have communicated this effectively, or else they misunderstood or didn't read carefully enough.

That's okay. By completing the negative offer option box, your prospects have set themselves up in perfect position for follow-up and closing by a skilled salesperson.

If you have ever been a salesperson, then you know the most difficult prospect to sell is the one you can't reach—the one who never responds to your letters or returns your phone calls, or the one who says he or she is not interested, but won't say why.

A prospect who fills in the blank space on your reply card where it says "please give reason why you are not interested" has framed a specific objection which can be overcome with the proper selling argument.

Deferred Offers

A deferred offer is a variation on the negative offer. Here's how it's phrased:

[ ] Not interested right now.
   Try us again in

_____

   (month/year)

The deferred offer encourages a response from prospects who do not have an immediate need but may have a future requirement for your product or service.

The deferred offer option box says to the prospect, "If you have no immediate requirement but may have a future need, you can use this box to let us know that you have a future need, without getting calls from salespeople now."

When do you use the negative—as opposed to the deferred—offer option? Use the negative offer option when testing a new offer or when you think many prospects might not respond for specific reasons. Use the deferred offer when you think a significant number of prospects are more likely to need your services in the future, rather than immediately.

Selecting Response Options

We have talked about the need to keep offers simple and not offer the reader too many options. The reason is that the more options you offer (blue versus red versus purple; standard versus premium versus premium with optional amplifier), the more difficult it is for the prospect to make a decision. The prospect then puts the card aside to think it over. He or she then forgets about it or loses enthusiasm, and the card is never returned.

The one area in which you should offer plenty of options, however, is response options. Different customers like to order in different ways. George likes to sit with his catalog, study it carefully, fill out the order form, and mail it with a personal check. Sally is an impulse buyer; when she sees something she wants, she picks up the phone, calls, and pays with a credit card. David is a computer geek and only wants to order online at your Web site.

People like to communicate with you when they want, in the way they want. As a rule of thumb, the easier you make it for your prospect to respond, the more responses you will receive. The following sections outline the response options you should consider offering your buyers.

By Phone

Experience shows offering a toll-free phone number can often (though not always) increase orders. I wouldn't omit ordering by phone as an option unless you have determined, through careful testing (see Chapter 23, "Testing Your Way to Direct Marketing Success"), that it does not pay for you.

By Fax

Since the advent of the fax machine, direct marketers—especially those marketing to businesses—have increasingly designed reply forms so they can be faxed easily. Add your fax number to order forms in your catalog.

By Mail

Business reply mail is still the most popular response method for direct marketing. Business reply cards work well for lead-generation and bill-me offers. For hard offers, where you are asking for either a check or credit card information, you need to supply a business reply envelope.

While the prevailing wisdom is to use business reply mail, some direct marketers who sell low-priced goods want to avoid the cost. They provide a return envelope, but it is not postage paid. Instead, there is a small box in the upper right that says, "Place stamp here," requiring the buyer to provide the postage.

Some novices—and occasionally, a few fundraisers—place live return postage on every reply envelope. I advise against this practice, as it is costly: If you get a 2 percent response, you are throwing away return postage for 98 out of every 100 pieces mailed.

By E-Mail

A recent phenomenon is giving customers an e-mail address to which they can respond. The problem is that e-mail does not provide a secure mechanism for paying with a credit card, and it requires you to write out the details of your order. Right now, e-mail response is mainly used for direct marketers seeking inquiries.

Warning!

A reply card printed on card stock is difficult to fax. If you want fax replies, consider an $8^{1}/_{2} \times 11$ inch fax–back sheet. Print your fax–back on white or light colored stock; dark paper often is not readable when faxed. When in doubt, print a sample first and test it in the fax before printing the full run.

Marketing Tip

Novices are intimidated by business reply mail, but you can get a business reply permit for a nominal fee from your local post office. Your graphic designer (see Chapter 6, "Producing and Printing Your Direct Marketing Campaign") can use your permit number in designing business reply cards and envelopes for you; or you can do it yourself following the instruction booklet your post master gives you when you get your permit.

Through the Web

If you send the prospect to your home page, he or she may get lost meandering around the site and never reach your order page. When you offer a Web site address as a response mechanism, whether offline or online, it should direct the prospect to the page on your Web site specifically designed as an order form for the offer.

If you do not have such a page on the site, consider omitting the Web as a response mechanism. Experience shows that sending buyers to a home page as an option in a paper direct mail campaign can actually depress orders.

Choosing Payment Options

As with response options, payment options help boost response: The more ways you allow customers to pay, the better. Here are the commonly used payment options for mail order selling.

With a Check

Be sure to tell the customer how to make out the check ("payable to American Widget Company"). Clever direct marketers have used payment with check as a marketing ploy with success. For instance, Joe Karbo, in his mail order ads for "The Lazy Man's Way to Riches," told customers he would hold their check for 30 days uncashed while they tried his product. This created a perception of trustworthiness that made his no-risk trial offer stand out.

With a Money Order

Believe it or not, many poorer people do not have checking accounts, but still want to order your products. Accept money orders and say that you do in your copy.

With Cash

I don't recommend encouraging people to stick cash in an envelope—too many potential problems. I have done it in the past and found that people will pay cash for inexpensive offers in the $1 to $5 range at most.

I heard a story about a direct marketer who ran small ads saying "FREE condom—$1 shipping and handling," and received thousands of dollar bills in the mail. His objective was not to sell condoms for a dollar a pop, but to build a list of mail-order buyers interested in sex offers.

With a Credit Card

Accepting credit cards increases your response rates and eliminates the pay-up problems you can have with bill-me orders. Another advantage of taking credit cards is that doing so allows you to take till-forbid and installment orders.

In an installment order, the purchase price is billed to the buyer's credit card in multiple installments instead of all at once. The benefit is buyer perception of a lower price. After all, which sounds more affordable to you—"$58" or "three easy payments of $19"?

In a till-forbid order, a monthly, quarterly, or other ongoing fee (such as for a service subscription or insurance premium) is charged to the credit card until the customer says to stop.

Some products—such as sets of collectibles or home study courses—are naturals for installment payments. If a home study course costs $19 per lesson, and there are 12 lessons, you can ship lessons and bill the student monthly until the course is completed.

Even if you don't offer installment payments, you can still state your price this way. For instance, instead of $24.95 a year, say, "$1.95 a month, billed annually."

In a till-forbid order, you continue to ship product or supply service—and bill the buyer for it on some agreed-upon schedule—until the buyer cancels. Subscriptions to online services like America Online are sold this way. You are billed for the service monthly unless you tell AOL otherwise.

Marketing Tip

Should you use supermarket pricing—for example, $19.95 instead of $20? Probably yes, since the supermarket price sounds less expensive. Sales resistance increases at certain price barriers in direct marketing, such as $50 and $100. Stating the price as $49.95 creates the perception that you are below the $50 barrier.

C.O.D.

Cash on delivery (C.O.D.) means the mail carrier collects the payment from you when he or she delivers your merchandise. With so many people working during the day, the chances of someone being home to receive the package and make the C.O.D. payment are slim, and so offering this option has fallen out of favor. Very few direct marketers still sell C.O.D.

Bill-Me

Bill-me is the classic soft offer in mail order selling. The customer orders the product without sending payment. If the customer likes it and wants to keep it, he or she pays your invoice. If the customer doesn't like it, he or she returns the product and owes you nothing.

Selling with bill-me offers is standard practice in certain direct response product categories, such as magazine subscription selling. The magazine publisher sends a mailing offering a "free trial issue" for which you "send no money now." If not 100-percent satisfied, you may cancel within 30 days, keeping the issue at no cost and with no further obligation of any kind.

The following example shows a bill-me offer. If you are not satisfied, you may cancel your subscription, tear up the invoice you receive, and owe nothing.

A classic soft offer in magazine subscription selling a free issue offer.

(Source: Stocks and Commodities Magazine)

The advantage of bill-me offers is higher up-front response; the disadvantage is that many bill-me buyers are not committed to purchasing and either cancel or just don't bother to pay their bill. Therefore the real measure of a bill-me offer is not how many people respond up front, but how many actually buy.

Purchase Order (P.O.)

For bill-me offers aimed at organizations, some marketers ask the buyer to provide a purchase order number; a few even ask for an actual purchase order. Marketers who do this feel it gets a more serious buyer than someone who just checks the bill-me box without writing a P.O. One newsletter publisher who specializes in newsletters aimed at the higher education market told me that when the buyer gives a P.O. number, the buyer almost always pays the invoice as long as he or she is satisfied with the product.

How to Make Your Offer Stronger

There are a number of proven techniques for making your offer more attractive and improving the response it generates:

➤ **Premiums.** A premium is a free bonus gift the customer gets for placing an order—or sometimes just for making an inquiry. A premium can be information (a special report or booklet), more of the product (buy 100 now and get 20 more free), a complimentary product (buy a water purifier and get three filter refills free), or an unrelated gift item (a free pocket calculator, cordless phone, radio, digital camera).

➤ **Discounts.** Direct response buyers like to get a discount, and copy often states that the products cost less because they are sold via direct marketing ("Buy at our factory-direct prices and save!" "eliminates the middleman"). Build the discount into your pricing. For instance, if you want to get $249 for your software program, set the retail price at $349. Then you can advertise "act now and save $100!"

➤ **Loss leaders.** A loss leader means you sell your front end at a deep discount and plan to make it up on the back end. Loss leaders work well for continuity mailings, in which you are ordering a series of videos, books, or other items. For example: Easton Press sells a continuity series of leather-bound classic books for $45 each. They offer the first book in the series, *Moby Dick,* as a loss leader for $5.95. They do not make money selling *Moby Dick* at $5.95, but the offer draws people into the series; a percentage go on to buy more books at full price.

➤ **Sweepstakes.** Recently in the news for alleged deceptive practices, sweepstakes have long been established as proven sales boosters. Sweepstakes have been known to boost response rates by 50 percent or more. But like everything else in direct marketing, you have to test. A sweepstakes may or may not be right for your offer and your audience.

➤ **Extra support and service.** Some marketers offer extra support and service as an incentive. IBM, for instance, ran a promotion for its servers where the buyer would get free installation and "turn on" (making sure the server was installed and working properly in the network) if they bought before a certain date.

Warning!

Sweepstakes are strictly regulated and must follow both federal and state guidelines. Consult your attorney or a direct marketing attorney. One protective measure you should take is to print on your sweepstakes promotion the phrase, "Void where prohibited by law."

Getting the Buyer to Act Now, Buy More, and Pay Up Front

You can offer one premium or multiple premiums, discounts, or other incentives. Some marketers use multiple incentives to motivate specific purchasing behavior. These include …

Quick-Response Bonus

The quick-response bonus is usually an extra premium given to encourage a buyer to respond to the mailing as quickly as possible. Sometimes the mailing specifies an expiration date before which the buyer must respond in order to earn the bonus.

Deadline or Expiration Date

The simplest and strongest time-limited offer has a specific expiration date ("This offer expires December 31, 2002"). If you do not want to print an expiration date (some marketers avoid printing expirations on mailings because it dates the promotion), you can set a limited period for responses ("You must reply within the next 15 days to take advantage of this special offer").

These are the typical bonuses offered to encourage speedy payment:

➤ **Cash with order bonus.** Many marketers, especially those who sell to businesses, are afraid they will lose orders if they do not offer a bill-me option. And it's probably true, since many businesses need an invoice to pay for products and services purchased. The accounting department won't pay from an order form. The prospect could charge his or her credit card, put the item on an expense account, and get reimbursed, but perhaps the prospect does not want to. The marketer is afraid to insist on cash with the order, but would certainly prefer it. The solution is to offer both payment with order and bill-me options, but to give a bonus to buyers who pay up front.

Marketing Tip

In situations where you don't want to print an expiration date or specific time period on your promotion, you can say, "But hurry. This offer is for a limited time only. And once it expires, it may never be repeated again."

➤ **Up-sell bonus.** This is an extra gift given if you buy more product with your initial order. For example: Buy one bottle of vitamins and get 10 percent off. Buy two and get 15 percent off. Buy three and get 20 percent off plus a free pill case for taking vitamins when you travel.

Satisfaction Guaranteed or Your Money Back

Almost all direct marketers offer, in some form, money-back guarantees of satisfaction. The reason: It works. You are asking your customer to take a leap of faith—to buy a product the buyer has never seen, from someone he or she doesn't know. The money-back guarantee takes the risk off the customer's shoulders and onto yours. You can then tell the prospective customer, "You know you must be satisfied, because if you are not, just return the product and we will refund your money in full. That way, there's no risk!"

What are the elements that make a guarantee strong and effective? See the following:

➤ **Length.** The longer the guarantee, the better. I recommend 30-, 60-, or 90-day guarantees. Anything shorter causes the buyer to become suspicious and feel rushed when the package arrives for its trial period.

➤ **Conditions.** The more unconditional the guarantee, the better. Make your guarantee "no strings attached." Trust the buyer and give him or her the benefit of the doubt. Accept return products and give refunds even if the buyer is slightly late in requesting the refund or has soiled or ruined the product.

➤ **Emphasis.** Do not hide your guarantee, bury it on page eight, or print it in four-point type. Print the guarantee in the same type size as the body copy or bigger. Put the headline "Your Money-Back Guarantee of Satisfaction" in large, boldface type. Surround the guarantee with a certificate-style border to make it stand out. Feature it prominently on your order form.

Warning!

Don't put caveats in your guarantee language, such as "money back if returned in *undamaged* condition." How do you know the customer is to blame for the damage? Maybe the shipping company or post office dropped it.

Must Direct Marketers Charge Sales Tax?

According to the *San Jose Mercury News*, 46 states and 7,000 local jurisdictions in the United States charge sales taxes, often on different items and at varying rates. Rates typically range from 5 to $8^1/_4$ percent.

Traditionally, mail-order operators in the United States collect sales tax only on orders placed by customers whose mailing addresses are in their state. Says mail-order attorney Kalvin Kahn in his book, *Mail Order Laws*, "You need not collect and pay the sales tax of the state of your purchaser unless you have a 'physical presence'—an office, warehouse, or salespersons—in that state."

According to the Direct Marketing Association, the 1992 Supreme Court decision in *Quill Corporation* v. *North Dakota Department of Revenue* ruled in favor of direct marketers. It affirmed that, without congressional authorization, state governments can't force out-of-state mail-order companies to collect the sales taxes imposed by the state on in-state merchants.

Marketing Tip

Canadian direct marketers collect Goods and Services Tax (G.S.T.) on all orders from customers within Canada. The G.S.T. is currently 7 percent. Canadian direct marketers do not charge sales tax on orders placed from customers in the United States. U.S. direct marketers do not charge G.S.T. or any other sales tax on orders placed from customers in Canada.

Prior to *Quill* v. *North Dakota,* there had been many proposals at both the federal and state levels to force mail-order firms to collect sales tax from all customers. The recent Supreme Court ruling, which upholds the 1967 ruling of *National Bellas Hess,* makes it illegal for states to ask you or try to force you to collect sales tax if you don't have a physical location in that state.

This law has been challenged several times in recent years. While it is still in place, one of the greatest threats to small mail-order operators is that the courts may someday require you to collect sales tax in every state.

This would make your order forms unbelievably complex and would be an administrative and accounting nightmare. Order forms would have to be redesigned, and computer software modified to account for the different sales tax rates in the various states. Software and tax-rate tables would have to be updated annually since sales tax rates do change periodically.

Taking Credit Card Orders

As discussed earlier, you can seriously increase your orders by accepting credit cards as payment. It's easy and convenient for the customer, and that makes it more likely for them to order.

Mediamark Research reports that the average age of credit card holders in the United States is 45.6 years. Of 220 million Americans, 144 million have Visa, 93 million have MasterCard, 41 million have Discover, and 25 million have American Express. Experience shows that having a merchant account can increase your sales volume 30 to 200 percent.

The only problem is that it's hard for some businesses, particularly small direct response businesses, to gain the ability to accept credit cards. Banks are very reluctant to authorize credit card acceptance, mainly because they have been burned too many times by fraudulent businesses.

So, many businesses go on, accepting only checks or money orders for payment, and miss out on the added sales they would get through credit cards. There is a way, though, for businesses that can't get bank authorization to accept credit cards.

The major credit cards in this country are Visa, MasterCard, Discover, and American Express. If your business caters to certain market segments, you may want to consider other types of credit cards. For example, if many of your customers are Japanese, you probably want to accept orders from JCB (Japan Credit Bureau) cardholders. For European customers, consider Diner's Club. You might also want to think about Carte Blanche cards.

To get established as a Visa and MasterCard merchant, start with your own bank. If you have a good relationship with them, they are your best bet. Another option you may want to add is American Express. They are easy to deal with, and seem to have no bias against the Internet businesses.

Marketing Tip

If you have a long-term, good relationship with your bank, that can give you some powerful leverage. Be willing to use that leverage to get what you want. After all, banks are in business for the same reason as the rest of us—to serve their customers and to make a profit.

The typical American Express cardholder has an affluent lifestyle, high household income, and is an impulsive buyer. Many businesses give their employees American Express credit cards for travel and other business expenses. So if you are selling products or services to business people, by all means call American Express for a merchant account application.

When you fill out your merchant account applications, whether it be for your bank, American Express, or whoever—be truthful, but give them as high an average per-order dollar figure as you can. They like to see average orders of $20 or more.

Higher average orders and higher sales volumes can reduce the percentage of each sale you will pay to the credit card issuer. This fee can vary anywhere from 1.5 percent to 5 percent, depending on your average size order, sales volume, and other factors. But even if you have to pay 5 percent, it's well worth it.

Another way to get a merchant account is to work with an Independent Sales Organization (ISO), which acts as a middleman between small businesses and banks. They will charge an additional fee for each transaction, so you will be paying a bit more than the standard percentage charged for credit-card transactions. There will also be an application fee. Here are the typical charges to expect, as of this writing:

➤ *Application fees.* Usually, these range from $95 to $400 and may or may not be refundable.

➤ *Point of sale terminal purchase or lease.* The terminal you use to process the charge and check for fraudulent numbers is usually available from a bank for around

45

$300. You will only be able to get this price, though, if a bank authorizes you. If working through an ISO, prices will range from $400 to even as high as $1,500. You can usually lease the terminal, though, at an average of $45 per month. The best thing to do, though, is to find an ISO that will provide computer software that can be used in place of a terminal. This will usually cost only around $150.

➤ *Service fees.* Banks charge between 2 and 5 percent for processing a credit card purchase. ISO's charge higher, usually 3 to 7 percent. They also usually charge a per transaction fee of 20 to 25 cents, and a monthly statement fee of $5 to $10.

Why all these fees? ISO's only want to work with legitimate businesses and ones that will stay with them for a long period of time, if a business can afford these fees, they are considered less of a risk.

Shop around. Get as much information as you can about each ISO you are considering, and read it thoroughly. Look for hidden charges and unreasonable requirements.

All of these services will require you to fill out an application. Be totally truthful with everything on the application and don't let the representative talk you into putting anything else down.

The reason is, if the banks affiliated with the ISO you use were to find out that any information on your application is false, you would probably be immediately cancelled and your business name and address would go on a "black list." This would prevent you from being able to accept credit cards for an indefinite period of time. Don't let this happen to you.

Most of the ISO's out there are legitimate, but there are a few that may put down spurious information, rather than lose the fees they'd receive. Be sure to look everything over twice. If you do, you'll probably find an ISO that will work with you to expand your business through the acceptance of credit cards. See the appendix for a list of companies that can grant you merchant status for accepting various credit cards.

The Least You Need to Know

➤ Offers are important. The right offer can increase response rates 10 percent to 30 percent or more—sometimes 1,000 percent!

➤ Putting a deadline or time limit in your mailing or ad almost always increases response rates.

➤ Premiums and discounts are extremely effective in closing the sale and getting the order.

➤ Not offering a money-back guarantee is a mistake and will depress your response rate.

Chapter 4

Mailing Lists

In This Chapter

➤ Determining the profile of your target market

➤ Dealing more effectively with list vendors and brokers

➤ Identifying the right mailing list

➤ Marketing your mailing lists to others

Direct mail success is dependent on the selection of your mailing lists—names and addresses of people to whom advertisers will send a direct mail solicitation. But the mailing list isn't just the way you reach your market—it *is* the market! If you cannot identify and rent appropriate lists, your chances of success are poor.

Except for your offer (the product and its price), mailing list selection is the most important factor in determining direct mail response. Outstanding copy and design, for example, might pull double the response of a poorly conceived mailing piece, but a good list can out pull a weak list by a ratio of 10:1 (a difference, for example, of a 1 percent response or a 10 percent response).

Approximately 30,000 different lists are available for rental, representing a combined database of some one billion names. There are few persons in the United States whose names are not on at least one of those mailing lists.

A List of Available Lists

The basic categories of available mailing lists include the following:

➤ **House lists.** An in-house list usually contains your customers, people who have bought from you; and your prospects, people who have inquired but not bought.

House lists are best because they frequently pull double or more the response of even the best-performing rented lists.

➤ **Compiled lists.** These are lists of people or businesses compiled from published sources, such as industry directories and the Yellow Pages. Compiled lists frequently provide the best means of reaching large groups of specific audiences. For example, you can rent compiled lists of all attorneys in New York City or all radiologists in the United States. For mail-order offers, however, compiled lists generally do not pull as well as response lists.

➤ **Response lists.** A response list is a list of proven mail-order buyers. Mail-order offers usually get the best return through mailings to response lists of buyers who have purchased through the mail a product similar to yours and in the same price range. For example, a $10 book on small business success is likely to sell best to test lists of people who have bought similar books in the $8 to $15 price range.

➤ **Attendee/membership/seminar lists.** These lists contain individuals who have attended a specific trade show or industry event, belong to an industry association or professional group, or paid for seminar participation. Since relatively costly trade show attendance, memberships, and seminars are usually sold through direct mail, excellent results are possible from such lists.

➤ **Subscription lists.** Subscriber lists are some of the best and largest lists on the market. Two types of subscription lists exist: controlled circulation and paid circulation. With controlled circulation, the readers receive the magazine free, provided they can prove to the publisher that they fall into a certain professional category (for example, to receive a free computer magazine, the reader must work in the data processing department at a firm of a certain minimum size). Proof is accomplished by completing a subscription request form or qualification card. With paid circulation, the reader pays for a subscription and is not required to provide additional data other than name and address.

➤ **Donor lists.** Used primarily by fundraisers, these lists contain the names of people who have contributed money to charities and nonprofit organizations.

➤ **Credit card holder lists.** These names are useful because the prospects can respond to your offer using a credit card. Also, credit card holders are somewhat "upscale" (demonstrated by the fact that they earn enough money to qualify for a credit card).

➤ **Opt-in lists.** These are lists of people who have given their permission for marketers to send them promotional e-mail messages.

➤ **Merged database lists.** This type of list simplifies selection because merging lists eliminates duplicate names and offers the remaining names as a single, master unduplicated list. One example of a merged database list is the International

Thomson Retail Press (ITRP), a master list of 175,737 executives in wholesale, manufacturing, retail, and service industries derived from highly selective, qualified, trade publication subscriber lists. Such databases allow list users to reach a large portion of a specific market without having to track down obscure, hard-to-find, or poorly managed lists.

Mailing lists are usually rented for one-time usage. If you want to do a second mailing, you must rent the list again. The next section will tell you how to do this.

Marketing Tip

Controlled circulation and paid circulation both have their pros and cons. Controlled circulation lists offer the advantage of greater selectability. Because the subscribers have given a lot of information about themselves, you can select portions of the list according to certain characteristics, which might include job title, job function, size of company, or even the types of products purchased. For mail-order promotions, paid subscriber lists may be the better choice, because those on the list have purchased a product (the magazine) through the mail.

Where Can You Rent Good Mailing Lists?

The names and addresses of people who respond to your original mailing, however, become your property and can be added to your own in-house list.

Mailing lists are generally available from three sources:

1. A list owner
2. A list manager
3. A list broker

A fourth source, of course, is to compile your own lists from appropriate sources, for example, membership directories, warranty cards, or visitors to your retail outlets.

List Owners

Many marketers and private organizations rent their own in-house mailing lists to other businesses. If you wanted to rent a list of people who attended, say, the Chemical Exposition, you could call the show sponsor and see if the list is available.

List Managers

Because the administrative details of list rentals are time consuming, many list owners hire outside firms called list managers, to manage and market their lists for them. If a list management firm handles a list, you would rent it from that firm, rather than the owner. Also, list managers aggressively promote their lists (to generate commissions from rentals), and list management firms place many of the ads in direct marketing publications featuring lists.

List Brokers

A list broker is a third-party agent that acts as liaison between the list owner or manager and the mailing list user. Unlike list managers who work primarily for the list owner, list brokers work primarily for you, the list user. Also, while managers have a vested interest in promoting their own lists, brokers can be more objective in their recommendations.

The best way to find a good list broker is through referral. Call colleagues, associates, and others who rent mailing lists and ask for recommendations. You can also find brokers in the Yellow Pages under "Mailing Lists" and ads in such direct mail publications as *Direct Marketing, Target Marketing,* and *DM News.*

Marketing Tip

Since all brokers have access to the same lists, they differ by the service, advice, expertise, and recommendations they offer clients. It is estimated that ap-proximately 80 percent of all list rentals are made through brokers.

The broker's key function is to provide timely and in-formed recommendations about which lists you should test and why. A detailed report on each recom-mended list should be provided. Be suspicious of bro-kers who regard your request for more information as an affront or a waste of their time.

In addition to providing list recommendations and in-formation, your broker should handle the administra-tive aspects of list rental and delivery, follow up on all administrative details, and make sure your lists are de-livered by deadline. Brokers do not charge list users for their services, but are paid a commission from the list owner or manager; hence, there is no extra fee for renting through a broker instead of going directly to the list owner.

Evaluating Mailing Lists and List Recommendations

Although the mailing list supplier can make recommendations, only you can be responsible for making the final decision concerning which lists to test. You can make a better choice by taking the time to study the broker's list recommendations.

Information about a list is traditionally provided in a format known as a "data card" (see the following figure). This document (sometimes an $8\frac{1}{2}$-by-11-inch sheet of paper or a computer printout) contains basic information on the list.

For each list, you should look for the following elements:

➤ **List size.** These range in size from less than 2,000 names to one million names or more. The traditional approach to direct mail is to test a small portion of the list, then mail to a larger portion if the test is successful. For this reason, some mailers avoid small lists because the opportunity to expand after a successful test is limited by the total number of names available. On the other hand, to the mailer seeking unusual or hard to find prospects, such small specialized lists may be the only means of reaching certain markets.

➤ **Cost per thousand.** Prices typically range from $55 to $95 per thousand names, with specialized lists going for $100 to $150 per thousand and more. Be wary of firms offering so-called "bargain lists" selling for $5, $10, or even $25 per thousand, because often these are absolutely worthless.

➤ **List description.** Each data card contains a paragraph or two about the background of the list: its source, history, a profile of the type of buyers it represents, and a description of the product they bought, the publication they subscribe to, or the seminar they attended. Read the description to get a feel for the market represented by the list.

➤ **Average size of order.** Given as a dollar amount, this represents the average size of the mail-order purchase made by the buyers on the list. Average size of order is a good indication of whether people on this list might be willing to pay your price.

Marketing Tip

When you rent lists of similar prospects (for example, gardening enthusiasts, fishermen), there is likely to be duplication of names between lists. When ordering, ask your broker whether they can get you a net-net arrangement. In a net-net arrangement, you pay for each name only once, even if the name appears on two or more of the lists you are using.

A data card for the Oracle Magazine subscriber list.

(Source: Edith Roman Associates)

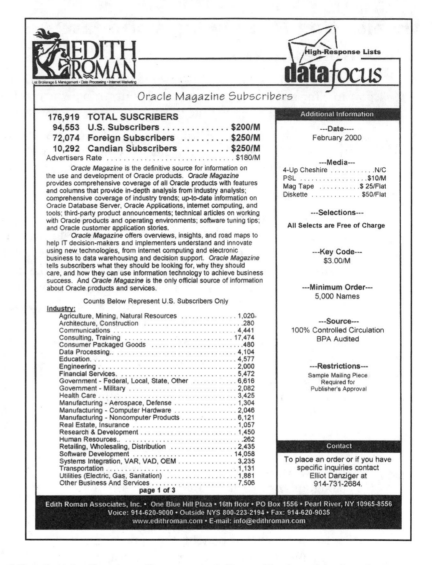

> ➤ **Percentage of list that is direct mail-generated.** You will often see the phrase, "95 percent direct mail generated" or "100 percent direct mail generated." This indicates the percentage of names on the list obtained through response to direct mail. Higher percentages are better because direct mail-generated prospects and customers are more likely to respond to direct mail than people who became prospects or customers through other avenues. (Surveys indicate that as many as one third of Americans do not respond to direct mail solicitations.)

> ➤ **Hotline.** This is a segment of the list that represents "hot" customers who have recently made a mail-order purchase usually within the last 6 to 12 months (the more recent, the better). Hotlines typically rent for $5 more per thousand than the rest of the list.

➤ **Active versus inactive, and buyer versus prospect.** Customer lists almost always pull better than prospect lists. If you're thinking of testing a list of newsletter subscribers, for example, rent the list of current (active) subscribers, rather than the list of former (inactive) subscribers whose subscriptions have expired.

➤ **List-usage report.** Try to get the list supplier to tell you how well the list pulled for other people who rented it, especially those with offers similar to yours. This information probably won't appear on the data card, but it may be contained in a separate list-usage report available from the broker. List-usage reports usually show rental activity by tests (initial mailings) and continuations (rental of additional names following a successful test). If a high percentage of the mailers who tested are also listed under continuations, they are getting test results profitable enough to warrant continued use of the list—a good sign that the list works.

➤ **Selections.** The data card indicates the selection criteria by which the list can be segmented. In general, the more selections, the better, because selectability allows you to mail only to those people who are closest to your target profile.

➤ **Frequency of updating.** Question the list's "cleanliness"—that is, are the names current and is the list frequently updated? Many list suppliers guarantee their lists to be clean and will refund postage costs on pieces returned (called pixies) in excess of some certain small percentage. Because approximately one fifth of the population moves every year, compiled and prospect lists get dated quickly. As a rule, a list should be updated (meaning that names no longer current are removed) at least once a year.

Marketing Tip

When renting a list from a mail-order catalog company, obtain the names of people who have actually bought from the catalog, not those who merely requested a free catalog but did not buy.

Warning!

If you don't see it on the data card, ask the list broker when the list was last updated. Also ask when the next update is scheduled. "A list that was updated recently *and* updates frequently will pull better than a file that updates less often," writes Barbara Gill in *Newsletter Industry Monitor* (March 2001, p. 8).

The list is the most important variable in your direct-mail campaign, and lists must always be tested. Even two lists that appear similar may yield widely varying results. One company sold software to a particular niche market covered by two trade magazines with similar content and aimed at the same audience. Yet in testing, the subscriber list of magazine A outpulled the subscriber list of magazine B 3:1. No one involved expected this result or could explain it—which is why you *must* test everything in direct marketing!

Questions to Ask About Your Lists

Data cards are the standard format for communicating list information to potential users, but they don't tell the whole story. Here are seven critical questions you should ask before renting any list—questions that aren't always answered on the data card.

How are the names generated—direct mail, catalog, Internet, or telemarketing?

Telemarketing-generated mail-order customers can become conditioned not to respond to direct mail. Why fill out a lengthy order form when someone will take the information from you in a quick conversation over the phone? Experience shows that telemarketing-generated lists often respond at a much lower rate to direct mail than direct mail-generated lists.

If you rent subscriber lists, be aware that many high-tech publishers are turning to the Internet instead of telemarketing or direct mail to acquire and re-qualify subscribers. And many high-tech catalogers are now generating as many orders on their Web sites as they are with their paper catalogs. Whether Internet-generated subscribers, inquirers, and buyers will continue to be mail responsive remains to be seen. But look for more of these names, especially on high-tech subscriber and customer lists.

What's this buyer really interested in?

The two-paragraph description on the data card doesn't really get you inside the mind of the buyer. You need to go deeper. If it's a catalog list, for instance, get a copy of the catalog and look through the merchandise.

Considering a test of an Internet list? Visit and spend time on the Web site from which the names were generated. And for subscriber lists, study the *media kit* and flip through several issues of the magazine.

What mailers have tested and then continued on the file?

Ask for a list of tests and continuations. What percentage of tests result in a continuation? Are there any mailers that are similar in product and price range to your own? This is a good indication that your own offer has a chance to be profitable with this list.

Insider's Buzzwords

A **media kit** is a folder sent to a magazine's potential advertiser, giving them information on how and whether they should run an ad in that publication. The media kit typically includes a rate card (giving ad rates), a sample issue, an editorial calendar (listing special issues or articles and when they are scheduled to run), and a description of the magazine's audience, content, and purpose.

How clean is the list?

Many data cards give you the date the file was last updated. What's most important is the percentage of the file has been updated within the past 3, 6, 9, and 12 months—often referred to as the "hotline" names. Why is this so important? Remember the RFM (recency, frequency, monetary) formula from Chapter 2, "Planning Your Direct Marketing Campaign": The more recently a customer has bought, the more likely they are to buy again. So don't just assume that the entire file has been updated. Ask.

Is the list owner excluding its best customers from its rental file?

Some do. And if they do, then by how much does that change the average unit of sale for those that are left?

If it's a mail order list, are there any deferred-credit buyers on the file?

These are people who have ordered on a bill-me basis and have not yet paid. Many turn out to be no-pays, so deferred-credit buyers can reduce the average unit of sale—and your response.

Are there any selections that the list owner holds out for its special mailers, but does not offer on the card?

For example, a cataloger may offer you selections by type of merchandise purchased or dollar amount that are not on the data card. Also, many publishers are collecting information on the subscriber's "preferred address"—whether they prefer to receive mail at home or work.

Many business-to-business mailers have gotten a lift in results by mailing to business prospects at home versus office addresses, probably because the prospect is overwhelmed at work, but has more time when at home.

Success Story

A Florida-based car rental company tested the idea of marketing car rentals by mail and selling them by the week. Its market was consumers. What lists would you test if you were that company? Recommendations included Disney World visitors, airline passengers, and families with young children. The winning list? Florida condo owners. Reason: The condo owners frequently visited Florida to use their condos, didn't bring their cars, and needed a rental car for a week at a time—an ideal fit for the rental firm's offer.

Finding and testing mailing lists is like Sherlock Holmes solving a mystery. Like Holmes, you need evidence to support your intuition. The more information you have, the less clueless and more successful you'll be.

Placing Your List Order

Most brokers and managers require a minimum order of 5,000 names per list (not per order). By ordering all lists through a single broker, you may be able to get volume discounts ranging from 10 to 60 percent.

Traditionally, brokers are paid only for the actual number of names rented. However, there is a movement in the list industry to create a new payment structure in which brokers are compensated for the consulting service they provide, not just for the net number of names rented.

Do not be surprised if some brokers actually request an up-front retainer for making recommendations. In most cases, this fee will be credited toward list rental, so that the consultation costs you nothing if you buy from the broker who gave you the advice.

Almost all mailing list owners reserve the right to review your mailing piece before accepting your list order. Be sure to send two sample mailing pieces to your list supplier so this can be taken care of promptly. Although most mailings are approved, list owners occasionally deny use (especially if your offer is competitive to theirs or if they think it will offend their customers in some way).

When ordering, you must specify the medium on which you wish to receive the names. The most common format is mailing labels, either pressure-sensitive (peel and stick) or Cheshire. Cheshire is the format preferred by letter shops that use automated equipment to cut the paper into single labels and affix these labels to envelopes. (Be sure to check with your letter shop to see what kind of labels it wants before you place your list order.)

If you are hiring a letter shop or computer service firm to produce a personalized letter (one imprinted with the recipient's name and address), order your list on magnetic tape or floppy disk, depending on whether a mainframe or micro-based system is used. For telephone follow up, you can order an extra copy of the list on telemarketing cards or printed on sheets of computer paper; some lists are also accessible as online databases.

Be aware of special services that brokers offer. These include key coding of mailing labels (essential for determining response when testing several mailing pieces or lists), title addressing, telephone numbers, and duplicate sets of labels.

Getting Rid of Duplicate Names

If you rent five mailing lists, they may have duplicate names, especially if they target the same market segment. How can you avoid sending two, three, four, or more of the same mailing piece to the same prospect?

In a merge/purge operation, a computer service bureau runs your lists through a computer (usually a mainframe), eliminating duplicates. A list free of duplicates reduces costs by eliminating mailing to the same person.

Of course, there is a fee for merge/purge service. As a rule of thumb, merge/purge pays for itself only when you are mailing a total of 30,000 names or more. Most list brokers can provide merge/purge in-house or outsource it to a service bureau.

Success Story

A manufacturer of factory safety equipment had brisk catalog sales, except to Fortune 1000 companies, where response rates were lower than those from small and mid-size firms. He thought perhaps the mail rooms were identifying the catalogs as promotional mail and throwing them away, so they never reached the buyer. His list house used a computer to split the lists into two piles: Fortune 1000 prospects and others. The catalogs for the Fortune 1000 prospects were then mailed in a plain white envelope; the others went out the usual way, with no envelope. Sales to the Fortune 1000 prospects picked up dramatically.

Earn Extra Income by Marketing Your Mailing List to Others

As you build your direct response business, you grow one of your most valuable assets: your customer list, also known as the "house file." Not only can you generate a large volume of additional sales by offering these customers additional products (see Chapter 25, "Database Marketing"), but you can also rent their names—at a handsome profit—to other direct marketers.

Say you charge $150 per thousand to rent your names. That comes to 15 cents a name. If you have 100,000 names, every time you rent the full list you make $15,000. Do that 10 times a year, and you gross $150,000 just from renting your house file to others.

Getting More Brokers to Recommend Your List

A list broker has a potential universe of 30,000 lists to select from and recommend to a client—including yours. Here are eight offers you can make to get more list brokers to recommend more of your lists for more tests, more often:

1. **Free test.** If you strongly believe your list will do well with a particular mailing, offer to do a 5,000-name test for free. The potential revenue of the roll-out far exceeds the modest cost of giving away a few thousand names for a test. Such an offer catches the broker's attention and shows you are interested in helping users get results, rather than making a quick buck with numerous, small, one-shot tests.

2. **Guarantee.** If you don't want to offer a free test, offer a guarantee of performance. For example, if the list isn't profitable for a proven direct mail piece, there's no charge ... or, the mailer can test another 5,000 names from one of your other list properties. This strategy works when selling to brokers who shy away from free tests because it costs them a 5,000-name commission.

3. **Net-net deal.** Help brokers reduce their clients' list rental costs. In a net-net arrangement, your list is merged/purged with other lists the mailer is testing. The mailer pays only for unduplicated names from your list. Depending on the level of duplication, this can make it anywhere from 10 to 50 percent cheaper to use your list.

4. **Discounted run charges.** Run charges (a small service charge for computer time needed to duplicate the list on disk, tape, or paper) for lists are typically $5 to $10 per thousand names. A broker who is on the border about using your list may be swayed if you offer to cut or even eliminate run charges for a test. The lower the cost per thousand, the better the chance of reaching or beating break-even on the test.

5. **Exclusives.** To build closer relationships with key brokers, offer them an exclusive. Special selects are an attractive offer. A broker whose client sells Windows NT applications might be interested in your list of corporate data center managers. By offering the broker a selection of companies that have NT installed (something that is not listed on the data card for this file) you increase the odds that the list will pay off for the broker. Another exclusive you can offer is a "first." When a list is updated, or new hotline names become available, call your favorite broker and give him or her first crack at these fresh names.

Marketing Tip

There are perhaps millions of companies that use mailing lists, but—according to Standard Rate and Data Service (SRDS)—there are only 754 list brokerage companies. Yet 80 percent of list orders are placed by brokers, not mailers.

6. **Variable pricing.** A software company promoting a $250 program can afford a higher cost per thousand than can a publisher selling a $19 book. Perhaps it's time list owners started offering tiered pricing based on the break-even economics of the particular mailing. This is a radical idea for mailing lists, but advertising space reps have already adopted this pricing model. Many publications, for example, have one rate for corporate advertisers, and lower rates for retail and mail-order advertisers. Why not price your list based at least partially on the mailer's ability to make a test pay off? In fact, the list industry has taken a small step in this direction for years, offering reduced rates for fund-raising mailings. Adding tiers to pricing can help price list rentals more realistically, so a broader range of mailers have a chance to mail the list at a profit.

7. **Better product.** Use the merge/purge processing service National Change of Address (NCOA) to keep your list clean. Add more "selects" (criteria by which you can segment your list) with "demographic overlays" (explained in the section with the same name in Chapter 25). The better the quality and selectivity of the list, the more likely brokers are to recommend it to their mailers. Some list owners and managers offer to model their file against the mailer's customers, allowing the mailer to select prospects with similar characteristics (again, see Chapter 25). This can multiply response rates many times over on tests and continuations. If you don't know how to do this modeling in-house, there are many database consulting firms ready to assist you.

8. **Superior knowledge.** The more brokers know about the market a given mailing list reaches, the better able they are to make an intelligent decision about whether to recommend the list for a test. List owners and managers often boast about how many well-known direct marketers have tested their lists, but brokers are much more interested in continuations. What percentage of those who tested the list rolled out? Seventy percent or better is impressive.

Another big selling point is whether someone with a product and offer similar to the broker's client's tested the list, and rolled out. That means the odds are good the list will work for the client's mail campaign, too.

As a rule, the more data on the data card, the better. Write a clear, descriptive profile of the names on the list and the type of buyers they are. Include such useful things as size of average order, availability of hotline names, whether the prospects are buyers or inquirers, when the list was last updated,

Warning!

Incidentally, don't bother trying to sway brokers with fancy brochures and elaborate mailers. Brokers primarily just want to see a data card. It's the information—not the format—that makes or breaks a list promotion.

and how the names were generated—direct mail, retail, catalog, credit card, sweepstakes, telemarketing, or Internet.

But don't send brokers stacks of data cards that haven't been well targeted to the broker's clientele. If the brokers have to go through the pile to find the relevant lists, they're doing your work—and they'll resent it.

Other things that rarely work are gifts, giveaways, and other special promotions. There's a conflict in a broker accepting a gift, such as a vacation or laptop computer, for recommending a particular list. It looks especially bad if the list doesn't work.

The biggest mistake a list owner or manager can make is not carefully analyzing the marketing challenges of direct marketers before approaching their list brokers with list suggestions. The quickest way to lose credibility is to recommend your lists when they are clearly inappropriate for the mail campaign. Don't recommend the Omaha Steaks customer file for a fundraising mailing for Vegetarians Against Animal Slaughter.

Do that even one time, and you may never get the broker's ear again. And with direct marketing being a relatively small and close-knit community, that's a mistake you cannot afford to make.

The Least You Need to Know

➤ Rent lists from list brokers, rather than list owners directly. List brokers will recommend alternative lists to test, while list owners are interested only in marketing their own lists.

➤ Have your broker send you data cards on the lists he or she recommends and study them carefully. Ask the broker which lists performed best for offers similar to yours.

➤ Do not make assumptions about which list will be the best for you; test several.

➤ Compiled lists are good for reaching everyone in a particular market niche. Response lists generate higher response rates for mail-order offers.

➤ You can earn additional revenue (10 cents per name or more) every time you rent your list to other marketers.

Chapter 5

Writing Copy That Sells

In This Chapter

➤ Does long copy sell better than short copy

➤ Finding the right tone and style

➤ Determining your sales theme

➤ The motivating sequence

➤ How to write a powerful headline

➤ More tips for writing copy that sells

Direct marketers are frequently criticized by nondirect marketers for using long copy. "Why do you use all that copy?" "It's too cluttered." "Nobody reads any more—just use bullets." "You need more pictures—too many words." "Who's going to read all that text?"

The simple reason why direct marketing is a copy-driven medium is that it attempts to do the entire selling job—and to do that, you need a lot of words.

Think about it. Retail ads just have to bring you into the store; the sales display and the sales clerks can do the rest. Yellow Pages ads just have to get you to pick up the phone and call; a sales rep explains the service, gives you the pricing, and closes the deal. Consumer ads for packaged goods don't even try to make a sale; they just communicate a product feature ("tastes great") or promote an image (for example, Calvin Klein makes you sexy).

The poor direct mail package or direct response space ad has to do all of those things—and more. It gets your attention. Says what the product is. Explains its features and benefits, and shows what it looks like. The copy has to answer all questions and overcome objections, since there is no salesperson to do that. It even has to take your credit card information and explain the terms and conditions.

Long Copy Versus Short Copy: Which Works Best?

Sales letters come in many lengths, ranging from 1 page to 16 and sometimes more. Conventional direct marketing wisdom holds that long copy most often will outperform short copy. The maxim is, "The more you tell, the more you sell."

Some copywriters who maintain that much of what we think we know about direct mail is dubious have challenged such a notion. They question whether what held true in the past applies to copywriting today—after all, times change.

Anecdotal evidence that people are less willing to spend time reading mail than in the past includes complaints from companies that their customers inadvertently toss out as solicitations some bills they receive. Several reasons are given as to why people may be less willing to spend time reading mail now than in the past.

Marketing Tip

A useful technique for short copy is including a brief letter making major points along with an enclosure, such as a fact sheet, flyer, brochure, or other enclosure. "I like the idea of enclosures," says copywriter Paul Tracy. "When I receive a solicitation with an enclosure and am unable to immediately make up my mind as to purchasing, I like to save the enclosure until I finally decide. The letter can be thrown away and the enclosure saved. There is then no need to put everything back in the envelope where it might not be noticed. I like the notion of including the necessary contact information on the enclosure. A well-organized enclosure that contains all the relevant points is easier to review than a letter."

One reason is that people are busier. In families where both spouses are employed or in single-head-of-household families, people do not want to spend much time reading mail. Another reason is that people receive more mail than they used to. When people find their mailboxes full of solicitations, they start looking for things to toss out. Furthermore, television may have played a role in shortening people's attention spans. Often, people discard mail they cannot quickly understand.

There are situations in which short copy is appropriate. Letters sent to generate leads are such a case. When trying to generate leads, the prospect's interest needs to be sparked. A more sustained sales effort can be made at the closing. In other situations, well-known products do not require copy that is as long as unfamiliar brands. The well-known products do not need long copy to build their credibility; they already have credibility. For example: The success of double postcards used to sell subscriptions to publications the reader is already familiar with, such as *Business Week*.

Products or services that are uninteresting to the audience (for example, banking services) generally should have short copy. Prospects are unlikely to read long copy about something they find boring. Copy directed at busy people (for example, businesspeople, doctors, other professionals) should be short for the most part. Harried people want to understand quickly what the offer is; they do not have time to wade through pages and pages of copy.

Of course, many situations call for long copy. Copy directed at people who enjoy reading are such cases. For example, long copy aimed at soliciting magazine subscriptions and book club memberships is appropriate. High-involvement items, such as health items and investment newsletters call for long copy. People interested in such things want a lot of information; the information is important to them.

Similarly, special-interest products pertaining to things about which the prospect would like to learn more call for long copy. Such products might deal with, for example, home car repair or golfing techniques.

Fundraising from a sympathetic audience calls for long copy. A letter for a good cause can go on with one compelling anecdote after another and not get boring. The more information provided to the audience the greater the chance of winning their hearts and getting a contribution. A fundraising letter from an organization named the Parents Television Council, of which the late Steve Allen was honorary chairman, calls for help in getting Howard Stern off television. The letter goes on for pages with remarks in questionable taste made by Stern; it never gets boring.

There is no simple rule for copy length that applies to all situations. Copy should be as long as it needs to be to get across the points the copywriter has to make, without losing the reader's interest. The proper copy length is a matter of judgment and contingent on the specifics of what is being sold and to whom.

Determining Copy Content, Tone, and Style

The biggest factor determining the content of your copy—what you say—is not your product, although that's important. It's your customer and what he or she wants and needs to know about the product to make a purchase decision.

Marketing Tip

"Start with the prospect, not the product," advises copywriter Don Hauptman, the author of the classic mail order ad "Speak Spanish Like a Diplomat!" Think about the prospect—his or her hopes, dreams, fears, desires. Focus your copy on a core need, belief, or concern to tap deep into existing attitudes, beliefs, and desires, and you will elicit a more powerful response—one that will cause the prospect to open his or her pocketbook and write you a check.

Appeal to the basic human desires: to make money, save money, save time, have better relationships, better health, feel better, be happy. Here, for example, is an appeal to greed (the desire to make money) from a highly successful direct mail package selling a financial newsletter: "A Rare Opportunity to Turn $5,000 Into $3.52 Million." And another for a health product: "Have a 'Washboard Stomach' in 60 Days or Less!" Or this one from a successful diet promotion: "Eat Yourself Thin."

Notice that the product name is not mentioned. The focus is on the reader, his or her problems, and the benefits the reader wants—not on the brand or the manufacturer. This is a major difference between direct response versus general advertising.

Creating a Winning Copy Platform

A "copy platform" is a document that serves as a preliminary blueprint for the copy about to be written. The reason to create a copy platform is to allow everyone who has a say in the copy to review the writer's theme and intent before the copy is committed to paper or disk. That way, changes can be made early, eliminating wasted time and effort.

Here is a concise one-paragraph copy platform for a direct mail package to sell subscriptions to a financial newsletter covering the Vanguard family of mutual funds:

> *The "Big Idea" of this package is that, if you join us, you can double your Vanguard profits or better. That is, with our service, you can increase your returns from Vanguard funds 50 to 100 percent versus what you were making before you subscribed. We are the only service that can make this promise.*

Even if you are a solo operator with no one to answer to, you may still want to write a copy platform before you proceed with a draft and show it to a few people whose opinions you trust.

The Motivating Sequence

The copy in virtually all direct marketing promotions follows a well-established formula for persuasive writing known as "The Motivating Sequence." The steps are as follows:

1. Get attention.
2. Identify the problem or need.
3. Position your product as the solution or answer.
4. Prove your product is the best solution or answer.
5. Ask for the order.

Step 1: Get Attention

Your prospect is bombarded by things demanding his or her attention, from TV commercials and the day's mail and e-mail, to project deadlines and kids crying for attention. Therefore, your headline or teaser has to work super hard just to get your prospect's attention for a few seconds.

One way to gain attention is to make a big promise or deliver important news. For example: "The IRS Owes You $10,470. Here's How to Get Your Money in as Little as 90 Days."

Another way is to make an appeal to self-interest. For example: "To Every Reader Who'd Like to Have More Money."

A third technique is to ask a question to which the reader would want to know the answer. For example: "What do Japanese managers have that American managers sometimes lack?" and "Has the IRS Gone Mad?"

Basically, get their attention!

Step 2: Identify a Problem, Need, or Want

Once you grab the prospect's attention, you have to lure him or her into the body copy or you quickly lose a potential client. Attention spans today are short. To make a bridge between your attention getter and the proposition you are making to the prospect, dramatize early in your copy (immediately after the headline or teaser) the problem your product solves or the need it fills. For example (for an investment newsletter) …

> *If you have invested in the Internet, the odds are high that you've put your money in the wrong stocks.*

Why is this step necessary? Doesn't the prospect already know about the need? Maybe yes, maybe no. But regardless, chances are the prospect isn't thinking about that subject at the moment your ad appears or is plucked from the mailbox. By clearly stating the problem or need, you orient your prospect and place that individual in a receptive mood for what is to come.

Step 3: Position Your Product as the Solution

Once you identify the problem or need, quickly transition to your product as the solution or answer. This transition should be done in just a couple of sentences. Here is a neat example from a fundraising letter:

> *Some day, you may need the American Red Cross.*

> *But right now, the Red Cross needs you.*

And from a sales letter offering consulting and training services …

> *Harland Company, the second-largest check printer in North America, had a problem: Customers wanted faster turnaround than the four to five days they offered.*

> *In my proven training seminar, "Achieving Performance Excellence," I helped Harland executives identify waste in their processes which, if eliminated, could cut cycle time substantially.*

> *The result? Now 97 percent of Harland's jobs are completed in less than two days. And operating costs have been reduced $600,000 a year.*

> *Printing companies nationwide—including Harland Company, West Texas Printing, Victor Cornelius, Ennis Tag and Label, and Intelmail—say that my "Achieving Performance Excellence" training programs are helping them attain and keep a competitive edge.*

Step 4: Prove Your Case

Remember, the reader is skeptical. Just because you say your cream can clear up acne doesn't mean the reader believes you. You have to prove your case.

A variety of techniques for proving your case are fortunately at your disposal. These include …

➤ A list of satisfied customers.

➤ Testimonials from satisfied customers.

➤ Case histories or product success stories.

➤ A description of features, advantages, and benefits.

➤ Media reviews or third-party endorsements.

➤ Certifications, licensing, lab tests, and benchmark performance results.

➤ The number of units sold.

➤ Years in business.

➤ Superior methodology, principle of design or operation, or other feature differentiating you from the competition and making you better.

Step 5: Ask for the Order

The last step is to ask for the order by presenting the offer and asking the reader to accept it. (Chapter 3, "Make Your Buyers an Offer They Can't Refuse," goes into more detail about how to formulate and present attractive offers.)

Direct marketing absolutely depends on a clear, well-stated offer. It is never vague about what to do next, nor does it hesitate to ask for direct action on the part of the reader (for example, "Order now and save 15 percent").

Writing a Powerful Headline

Copywriter par excellence Michael Masterson, along with many other experts, says that the headline is the most important part of your copy. You should spend more time coming up with a strong headline than on any other part of your promotion.

The strongest headline in direct marketing is not one that builds a brand image or awareness, but speaks directly to the reader's self-interest. For example: The Institute of Children's Literature has had great success with an ad selling a home correspondence course in how to write children's books and stories. The ad's headline, "We're looking for people to write children's books," does not contain a benefit. Nor does it promise a reward. Instead, it selects a specific audience—people who want to write and publish children's books.

These people want to be authors. Their dream is to publish a book. So there's no need to sell them on the benefits of writing. Instead, the ad breaks the rule by grabbing the attention of a select, highly motivated audience and then building their interest in the course.

Features and Benefits

In Chapter 2, "Planning Your Direct Marketing Campaign," you learned how to compile a list of the features and benefits of your product. Now that you are writing your copy, how much of this should you include? Benefits only? Which ones? Benefits and features? Which?

Perhaps the oldest—and most widely embraced—rule for writing direct response copy is, "Stress benefits, not features." But even this sacred commandment doesn't always hold true.

Specifically, there are five selling situations in which features should be given equal (if not top) billing over benefits and promise-oriented copy. Read the following sections to find out more.

Selling to Experts

As new homeowners, most people know beans about insulation. So they most likely need to be sold on the benefits: How much will the insulation reduce my winter fuel bills? What's the benefit of insulating my attic floor versus the roof? Why is an R value of 11 better than 9? Will the house actually become warmer and less drafty?

But could you imagine repeating this discussion in a mailing aimed at insulation contractors and installers? Of course not, because these contractors are experts in insulation. They already know what insulation can do and why it is important. So copy should stress the features of insulation—R values, price, volume discounts, types of materials available, installation techniques.

These insulation experts are interested in only one thing: Do you have the products they need to help them do their job correctly and at a good profit? A discussion of features and pricing will give these knowledgeable pros the information they need to make a decision.

Marketing Tip

When writing to enthusiasts, *think* like an enthusiast. Don't assume that the hobbyist shares your lack of interest in the nuts-and-bolts aspects of whatever it is you are selling.

Enthusiasts

An ad for Porsche reads, "The 944 has a new 2.5-liter, 4-cylinder, aluminum-silicon alloy Porsche engine—designed at Weissach, and built at Zuffenhausen. It achieves maximum torque of 137.2 ft.-lbs. as early as 3,000 rpm, and produces 143 hp at 5,500 rpm. The 944 also has the Porsche transaxle design, Porsche aerodynamics, and Porsche handling."

Now, I'm the type who couldn't care less about cars or which one I drive ... but then again, I'm probably not the kind of buyer Porsche is after. But if the Porsche ad was aimed at automobile enthusiasts, then perhaps its features-oriented approach was just right for tickling their fancy.

Remember, enthusiasts and hobbyists have a love for their obsession that is quite alien to the rest of us, but very real to them.

Engineers and Scientists

Vivian Sudhalter, director of marketing for Macmillan Software, is responsible for selling expensive software to scientists who use computers to analyze complex laboratory data. I asked Vivian what works for her in direct mail—and what doesn't.

"Despite what tradition tells you, the engineering and scientific market does not respond to promise- or benefit-oriented copy," she says. "They respond to features. Your copy must tell them exactly what they are getting and what your product can do. Scientists and engineers are put off by copy that sounds like advertising jargon. They resent it if you talk down to them. When writing copy, don't try to be clever, just give information about the product."

Sudhalter's lead-generating self-mailer for Macmillan's Asyst and Asystant software follows this model. The copy has a scientist-to-scientist tone and talks about such arcane matters as Hermitian matrices, spectral slicing, and QR factorization.

Yet, it is successful, having generated a 4 percent response with Macmillan's in-house prospect list. Vivian tells me that she has conducted many tests of feature-oriented versus benefit-oriented mailings, and the feature-oriented mailings win every time.

Equipment

Copy that sells equipment and systems must not only stress the benefits, but it also must describe how the product works and what it can do. And it must list complete specifications—so the buyer can make an intelligent decision.

If someone buys a newsletter, that person subscribes because of how he or she will benefit from the information it contains. Features, such as whether it is 8 or 12 pages long, or whether the editor reads 287 publications instead of 240, are secondary. Either the information is useful to that person, or it isn't.

But the situation is different with tangible items. For example, if someone is looking through a catalog that sells computer furniture through the mail, the catalog better provide some specific information. For instance the catalog should give desk dimensions so the buyer can decide if the printer will fit on the printer shelf—or even if the desk will fit through the front door.

Benefits may generate initial interest in a product, but with many customers, you make or lose the sale based on whether you mention a particular feature. Copy that doesn't highlight *all* the key features can cost you sales.

Practicality

Is your product sold on glitz and glamour, hopes and dreams? Or is it bought for more practical reasons? Products with practical appeal must be supported by feature-oriented copy that gives your prospect the assurance that he or she is buying a good solution to a problem.

For example, the dozens of "How to Get Rich Quick" books sold through mail-order ads are appealing to the buyer's dreams, rather than to hard reality. (How many of the people who buy such books actually become rich?)

And so the copy—quite appropriately—concentrates 100 percent on the promise of riches beyond the dreams of avarice, without revealing the actual *features* of the plan ... which would only be a disappointment.

On the other hand, if the same person needed a new gas furnace for the home, he or she would look at your product with much more attention to detail. Here, copy would have to concentrate on explaining technical features, and on building confidence in the performance of the product and the reliability of the manufacturer. Features would likely have equal billing with benefits in your brochure or mail package.

More Tips for Writing Better Body Copy

Here are some principles to guide you in writing the copy for your ad, mailer, or other direct response campaign elements.

Be as Concise as Possible ...

... but say what needs to be said. This is a favorite rule among not only copywriters, but all writers (except experimental novelists and counterculture journalists). "Omit needless words!" writing instructors exclaim, urging us to cut copy to the bone.

But I can think of at least three situations in which conciseness is not a virtue, and extra words can make the writing better.

The first situation is when you need to explain something that may be clear to some readers, but not to others.

Let's say you're writing a computer catalog and you want to describe the machine's internal memory. The most concise description would read, 640 MB of RAM. Do most people today know what RAM is? You might, but does your mother? So, to make it clear to everyone, add words like: 640 MB of internal memory. But is 640 MB a number people can visualize? Does it mean anything to them? If not, you may need to add even more words to make the benefit clear: "Features 128K of internal memory—enough to run the most sophisticated multimedia applications and business software and store as much information as 10 sets of encyclopedias!"

The second reason to use extra words is to add emphasis—to ensure that the reader understands you.

For example, mail-order copywriters are fond of emphasizing the "free gift" you'll receive when you join a record club or subscribe to a magazine. Any grammarian can tell you that "free gift" is a redundancy—a gift by definition is free, so the adjective "free" is superfluous. But the copywriter's job is to sell, not to write compositions for an English class. And as a copywriter, you realize that the consumer's natural reaction is to think that the gift comes with strings attached. So you add the word "free" to emphasize that there are no strings attached—that the gift is indeed just that: a gift.

The third situation in which more words work better than less is in highly personal copy—copy that speaks to the reader's needs as an individual.

An engineer is probably dispassionate when it comes to pump selection, but shopping for a life insurance policy is an emotional purchase as well as a rational one. The most concise approach to writing an ad for life insurance would be to list the monthly payments, amount of insurance, and criteria for acceptance, but the successful ad will talk about the emotional issues—caring for one's family, planning for the future—on a person-to-person level. That takes extra words, but the words are well spent.

Speak the Reader's Language

Every business-writing text warns us to avoid jargon and write in plain, simple terms. But jargon, if properly applied can make copy more effective. The most common exception to the "avoid jargon" rule is in copy aimed at special audiences—farmers, chemists, fishermen, architects, warehouse managers, snow boarders, and so on.

Jargon can strengthen your link to these specialists because it shows them that you are "in the know," that you understand their business and empathize with their problems. If you don't speak their language, or if your copy defines terms that they already know, the readers suspect that you lack expertise in their business.

Simple words are the easiest to understand. And, because copy is written to communicate, short words are best—usually. An exception to the rule is when you want to use a big word to make your subject seem more important or impressive. For example, let's say you're selling expensive, top-quality reproductions of antique pistols. The simplest description of the product is "guns." But

Surprising Secrets

Jargon sometimes can make a product seem more impressive or more valuable. Listerine, we are told, is the only mouthwash that kills "halitosis." Sounds impressive, until you realize that halitosis is a word concocted by the Listerine people to sell more mouthwash.

"firearms," though a bigger word, sounds more distinctive. And that's why it works better: The reader might pay $295 for a firearm, but not for a mere "gun."

Or take a luxury item like a Mont Blanc pen. There's something unsettling about paying $100 or more for a pen; a pen is something you get for 99 cents at a drug store. But paying $100 or more for a "writing instrument" is somehow more acceptable.

Giving a product a more impressive title can convey an image of added value. Recently, I received a brochure promoting a "selling system." The system turned out to be an in-plant seminar. But somehow the term "selling system" sounds more impressive than calling it a "course," "seminar," or "training session."

Negative Selling Can Work

I have run into clients who will always change a negative statement into a positive one or eliminate it altogether. "Too negative" they write in the margin after crossing out the offending copy.

The logic behind this rule of avoiding negatives is perhaps that people have imperfect memories. If your headline reads, "New cherry fizz contains no salt," they're likely to remember it as, Cherry fizz contains salt."

But some situations call for a negative. A radio commercial for a New York furniture store begins with this harsh warning: "Don't buy furniture today!" That makes you stop and listen, because it's unusual to hear an advertiser tell you not to buy. The commercial goes on to say that you can save hundreds of dollars if you hold off until the big furniture sale this coming Saturday.

In Advertising 101 in college, the professor told us not to mention the competition in advertising because it gives them free exposure. Goodrich commercials used to say, "We're Goodrich, not Goodyear"; everybody remembered Goodyear and forgot Goodrich.

This rule makes sense when there's no clear leader, no number-one brand. Everybody's competing against everybody else, so you can win customers by selling the advantages of your product over all the others.

But in markets where there's clearly a leader in the field, you've got to convince people to switch from the comfortable favorite to you, the up-and-comer. And often, the reason is that you're similar to the leader, but you do one thing better. To get that message across, you can't avoid talking about—and comparing yourself with—number one.

Don't Reveal Your Hand Too Early

If you study successful direct mail packages, you will find that many do not reveal the nature of what they are selling—or even that you are reading a sales pitch—until you have read a few paragraphs or even a few pages.

In an ad, for instance, you might spend a paragraph describing the reader's problem before you get to the product and how it solves the problem. Reason: The reader may not be aware of the problem the product solves, or may not think of it too often.

Here's the lead paragraph of an ad for an industrial product. The lead "warms up" before getting to the point:

> *Sugar entrained (trapped) in evaporators and pans means sugar lost in condenser discharge streams. And if it isn't bad enough that wasting sugar costs you money, the sugar you dispose of in your refinery or factory wastewater decomposes. This results in biological oxygen demand, a depletion of oxygen in the water that's a major source of pollution.*

A waste of space? No, because many of the people running sugar refineries don't realize that entrainment (trapping a particular substance during a process of evaporation) is this serious. The copy has to point to the problem and highlight its adverse effects before the ad can begin to sell the solution.

On the other hand, an ad stressing a product's energy efficiency should begin with a talk about energy savings. Copy that explains the negative consequences of wasting energy would be wasting words, because buyers already know how precious and costly energy is.

The Least You Need to Know

➤ The first step in writing successful copy is to get the reader's attention.

➤ The quickest way to engage the reader in your message is through appeal to self-interest, promise of a big benefit, or the revelation of important news or information.

➤ Back up your claims with proof—the more, the better. Consumers are skeptical; you have to work hard to get them to believe you.

➤ Write in a friendly, conversational language. Sound like one friend talking to another and speak the prospect's language; if that means using technical jargon, then by all means use it.

Chapter 6

Producing and Printing Your Direct Marketing Campaign

In This Chapter

➤ Calculating cost per thousand

➤ Working with the graphic design

➤ Using photography and illustrations

➤ Printing and the letter shop

➤ Understanding postal regulations

Various direct marketing promotions require design and print production; of these, direct mail is the most complex. Therefore we'll focus in this chapter on direct mail, but keep in mind that most of these graphic design and production tips can apply to brochures, catalogs, and other promotions as well.

Calculating the Cost per Thousand

Direct mail seeks to generate maximum sales at minimum cost. (That's basically the goal of all marketing, only direct marketers know it, while many general marketers seem not to.) There are two ways to maximize your direct marketing profits:

➤ Increase your response

➤ Decrease your cost per thousand

Most marketers are naturally more enthusiastic about the first method, maximizing response. This is the fun part. It's where the creativity comes in. But don't neglect the second method, decreasing cost.

Say you are selling a $30 product. By using a cheaper paper stock, you reduce the cost per thousand by $30. That's equivalent to getting an extra order, putting just as much money in your pocket.

Cost per thousand can be calculated using this simple formula:

$L_1 + L_2 + P_1 + P_2 = CPM$ (cost per thousand pieces mailed)

L_1 = Mailing list rental per thousand

L_2 = Letter shop assembly of the mail piece per thousand

P_1 = Postage per thousand

P_2 = Production (printing) per thousand

All four variables are recurring costs. You incur expense for mailing list rental, letter shop charges, postage, and printing every time the package is mailed.

By comparison, copywriting and graphic design are one-time charges. You incur the cost in the creation of the package, but once the package is proven successful, you can mail it again and again without further compensation to the writer or designer (the exception being copywriters and designers who charge royalties, mailing fees, or other performance bonuses for winning packages).

These one-time expenses are not figured into the cost-per-thousand calculation when determining the profitability of a mailing. The nonrecurring costs are usually not significant in large-scale consumer mailings where, spread out over hundreds of thousands or millions of packages mailed, they come to just a few pennies per package.

Surprising Secrets

The cost per thousand can actually be cheaper for the same mailing piece when mailed in large quantities versus small quantities. The reason is that larger runs enjoy economies of scale in printing and production that smaller runs do not. For instance, an offset printer may charge $70 to print 500 fliers, but only $10 more ($80) to print 1,000. Therefore, the cost per sheet is 8 cents apiece for the 1,000 print run but almost twice as much—14 cents—for the shorter run.

On business-to-business mailers aimed at narrow niche markets, especially when an elaborate dimensional mailer is used, the creative costs can be a significant cost factor. For instance, if you pay $10,000 to an agency to design and write a mailer aimed at automobile manufacturers and your list has only 100 names, the creative costs alone come to $100 per package mailed.

Graphic Design Guidelines

In general advertising, some marketers have criticized art directors as viewing their designs as works of art, rather than tools to sell products. I have had more than one art director refer to the copy I gave him as a "design element"—and when I saw the layout, realized that the copy was the design element the art director seemed to enjoy working with least.

In direct marketing design, the objective is not to create an aesthetically pleasing and award-winning work; it is to get people to read the copy—because it's primarily the copy that sells, not the layout or the pictures.

Good direct marketing design attracts the eye to the page and makes the copy easy to read. Direct marketing designers are usually adept at selecting readable typography to fit the layout. You rarely see them use techniques that obscure the copy or interfere with readability, such as setting copy against a tint or using reverse type (light print on a darker background) on body copy.

Ted Kikoler, one of the leading direct mail designers in North America, offers these guidelines for typing and laying out your sales letters:

➤ Always use old-fashioned typewriter type, such as Courier or Prestige, never desktop publishing fonts like Helvetica or Times Roman.

➤ Use a serif typeface (type with little finishing strokes on top and bottom, like the book you're reading right now). The best is Prestige or Courier. The larger version, Pica (10 characters per inch), is easier to read than the smaller one, Elite (12 characters per inch).

➤ Indent all paragraphs five spaces.

➤ Use wide margins. Long line lengths with narrow margins fill too much of the page, making it look like there's more to read than there actually is. A good line length is 6.5 inches, which is 65 characters Pica or 80 characters Elite.

➤ Add one line of space between all paragraphs.

➤ Make the right-hand margin ragged right. Never justify it.

➤ Try to avoid paragraphs longer than six lines. If you have a longer paragraph, break it into two or more paragraphs.

➤ Indent entire paragraphs you want to highlight by 10 characters on each side.

➤ Always have the bottom of the first page end mid-sentence. This is an effective page turner and gets the reader over to page two. Also, add "over, please" to the bottom right.

➤ Use a desktop publishing font (for example, Times Roman bold) in the headline of the letter for emphasis. You can also set the headline off from the body of the letter by putting it in a ruled box or a Johnson box (a box around the heading), putting white space around it, or using a second color.

➤ The main body copy should be black, but an accent color can be used for subheadings.

➤ Make the signature legible.

➤ Shorten the first name of the writer to sound friendlier and to close the gap between reader and writer. Bill sounds better than William, Kathy sounds better than Katherine.

➤ When using a personalized letter, try to avoid using subheadings, especially all capital letters and centered above the paragraph. Keep the logo on the front page. Use a blue signature.

➤ Underscore words that should be emphasized. A good technique is to read the copy aloud and listen to the words you emphasize. These are the ones to underscore.

➤ Indent the entire body copy of the P.S. by five characters so the letters "P.S." stand out. If it's all flush left, it gets lost.

Of course, your direct mail package may have other inserts in addition to a letter, such as a circular or brochure. These are often printed in color and illustrated with photos or drawings.

Photography and Illustration Considerations

Direct marketers have a cost problem associated with photos and artwork other marketers don't: cost per thousand. In the beginning of the chapter, we talked about the importance of keeping cost per thousand low. Therefore, you do not want photos and artwork to add to your cost per thousand.

Unfortunately, many stock photo and art houses base their licensing fees for visual images on usage. If you are producing an annual report, usually this isn't a problem. After all, you're going to print this year's annual report only once and never again.

But a successful direct mail package can be mailed for years in quantities in the millions. Buying visuals based on number of pieces mailed is therefore uneconomical for most direct marketing.

The visual images for most (not all) direct marketing are pretty straightforward—product shots, diagrams, photos of satisfied customers. More and more marketers are getting serviceable images using digital cameras.

Printing Preparation

When preparing your direct mail package for the printer, make sure that the Bar Code Clear Zone is clear. That's the bottom right corner of the envelope.

A bar code is a series of lines that can be read by an optical scanner for mail processing. The bar code zone is $4^3/_4$ inches by $^5/_8$ inches. You can have solid colors there, but the color and the density is important. One mailer changed a solid blue front to one that graduated from 100 percent at the top of the envelope to 20 percent at the bottom. That was approved by the post office. Other color variations may also be acceptable. Always check with the post office and have them sign off on your design.

Marketing Tip

If you lack the time, skill, or inclination to take your own photos, you can hire photographers and illustrators to create images for you. Negotiate to buy all rights for a reasonable one-time fee.

The bar code must show through the window no matter where it slides within the envelope. You can make this happen in several ways. Use a bigger address piece (typically the order form). This might be expensive if it throws off the press fit. If that's the case, try using a smaller envelope—for example, a #9 instead of a #10. Make sure the background color behind the address is not too dark. Again, check with the post office.

The printed permit information in the *indicia* must be correct and up to date. If you are mailing first-class and doing any presorts, the indicia must say "presort." You can get your mailing permit from your local post office. If you are using a letter shop to handle the mailing, you may be able to use their permit number.

Insider's Buzzwords

The **indicia** is a preprinted postal permit that serves as postage in lieu of a stamp or meter.

If you are using a covered window, you can't bleed into it with most printing processes. If you will be using stamps, be sure to have the envelope manufactured with the proper glue line. When overseas, check to see if the envelope needs to say "Printed Matter." This is simply a postal requirement. There is no significance, except that if you don't follow their requirements, your piece may not be mailable.

If you're using a textured stock like a Laid Finish, decide how you want the pattern to be positioned. A diagonal-seam envelope with straight-laid lines will waste a lot of paper. Try a booklet style or accept a random pattern to save money.

Dick Goldsmith of the Horah Group gives these 19 tips for cutting your printing costs:

1. **Plan in advance.** Nothing can be more costly than last-minute changes. Make a dummy of your package so you can make sure that it all works. For instance: Make sure everything fits into the outer envelope; the order form fits into the *BRE;* the outer envelope window is big enough to ensure that you get the pre-barcoding discount; and you've gotten a reply mail permit from the post office.

2. **Allow enough time** so as not to incur rush charges.

3. **Bid out all jobs.** Don't let a printer become complacent about pricing. Take advantage of times when printers are hungry for work.

4. **Ask your printers which sizes work best for them.** Ask them to suggest alternatives that would save you money yet not really affect the design of your piece.

5. **Prepare your disks correctly.** Send them to your printer with all necessary files. Disks must be accompanied by a hard copy of what you believe is on them. They should also be accompanied by all original artwork. Transmittal instructions must include the names and versions of programs used to prepare them.

6. **Proofread your artwork.** Don't make changes to your proofs. After film is made and you see proofs, changes mean that new film has to be prepared. This is expensive.

7. **Reduce paper weight.** You pay for paper by the pound. If you use fewer pounds you save money on paper and possibly postage as well. Use the lightest weight paper that does the job for you.

8. **Use a lower grade of paper.** Familiarize yourself with different paper stocks. Ask your printer or paper supplier for samples. Maybe your catalog will sell just as much merchandise printed on newsprint as it would on expensive coated and heavy stock.

9. **Don't bleed if you don't have to.** Bleeds (having the ink on the page run to the edge of the paper) require extra paper and extra cutting. Do you really need them?

Insider's Buzzwords

The **BRE** is a business reply envelope. The customer uses the BRE to mail her completed order form and payment information to the seller, who has prepaid the return postage. See Chapter 7, "The Direct Mail Package," for details.

10. **Make lot changes simple for the printer.** If you are testing prices or other copy, don't put the changes in type that reverses out of four colors (for example, white type printed over a color photo). Don't use colored type made out of multiple colors. Use black or 1 PMS (black with a second color) with nothing behind it or as a surprint (printing over an already printed area).

11. **Use standing dies.** When designing envelopes, use dies that already exist. (A die is a hardened steel engraving stamp used to print an inked image.) If your printer or envelope converter doesn't have exactly the one you're looking for, ask the printer what is close to what you want. The printer probably has something that will work just fine and you'll save a lot of money.

12. **Don't date material.** Don't print the date that the offer will expire unless it's absolutely essential. If the mail goes out late, you don't want to have to reprint. If you have leftover material, you might be able to use it next time.

13. **Combine pieces that print on the same or similar paper onto one press form,** such as a letter and flyer. You can also tint one-half of a sheet so that it looks like it's on another color paper.

14. **Try to combine pieces on one press form if you have multiple lots.** If you are printing an 8½ by 11 letter on a press that can print four letters on one sheet, combine the test lots (e.g., four versions of a letter) to reduce printing plate changes. If you are testing three prices with 10,000 pieces each and you are running an additional 70,000 pieces of your control, print the three test pieces and 10,000 of the control on one press form. Then, change the necessary plates (hopefully only one) and run the additional 60,000 control pieces "four up" (four letters on one sheet).

15. **Print near your letter shop to help reduce freight costs,** or ask your printer to include delivery of the printed pieces to your letter shop in his quotation.

16. **Project future needs.** If you know that you will mail 300,000 pieces in the next six months and they're not all mailing at once, you can still preprint some components such as business reply envelopes.

17. **Print continuous forms to work most efficiently with laser printers.** In laser printing, you pay by the inch.

18. **Check your bills carefully.** The price may not be one you've agreed upon with the salesperson. There might be charges for extras that were to be included, there might be charges for extras that were not your problem, but the billing department didn't know that.

19. **Design your art so that you can use it more than once.** Perhaps your brochure art can also be used for a space ad or on the Web. Art from a "take one" display can be used on a lift letter. This becomes rather simple these days if you are using a computer to help you design your pieces. Take full advantage of these capabilities.

Since profitability in direct marketing depends on the ratio of response to costs, lowering your printing costs by $100 adds as much to your bottom line as generating another $100 in orders.

Letter Shop

When computer personalization was introduced decades ago, the extra cost per thousand was tremendous, especially for small quantities. And so, even though these letters pulled better, the extra response didn't always justify the increased cost.

But with modern technology drastically reducing the cost of personalization, personalized direct mail now commonly proves more responsive, more profitable, *and* more cost-effective than form letters—even in small test quantities! For example, an ink-jet system can generate custom mailings for a little more than the cost of mailing labels—and at far less cost than tractor-fed laser printers.

Many mailing programs can benefit from using personalization. One proven application is in mailings to customers. People who have dealt with you in the past expect you to address them personally. Personalized letters gain their attention and can result in higher response and more orders. Personalization "is worth its weight in gold, particularly if you have an established relationship with the recipient," reports *Marketing News*.

Marketing Tip

Cost of personalizing mailings depends on several factors, including the package format and the quantity to be mailed. As a rule of thumb, ink-jet is the most cost-effective method of personalization available for a cost-per-thousand equivalent to labels. Impact and laser personalization are more expensive, but can also pay off in many applications.

In addition, an article in *Mail Order Digest* observes: "Most business-to-business mailings lend themselves to personalization, as do consumer packages for insurance, financial services, fund raising, subscriptions, and any kind of sweepstakes or check mailings."

Other areas where personalization has been effective at increasing response include time-limited offers and specials, membership, billing and collection, renewals, dealer and distributor mailings, and database marketing.

Equipment on the market today is designed to make the cost of personalization affordable for business-to-business marketers and other mailers who mail smaller quantities. And letters are not the only element of the mailing that can be personalized.

You can personalize your outer envelopes, self-mailers, flyers, reply cards, order forms—virtually any element in the package. For instance, you can add an OCR (optical character recognition) code to reply elements that enables incoming coupons to be scanned for automated tabulation of direct mail results.

Here are 10 tips for maximizing response to personalized mailings:

1. Always include a letter in a personalized package. A sales letter conveys a much more personal feel than a brochure or self-mailer.

2. Print the recipient's name and address on the letter above the salutation, and use his or her name in the salutation (for example, "Dear Mr. Smith").

3. Put a specific date on the letter, as you would when writing a personal letter to a friend (for example, "January 16, 2002," not "January 2002").

4. Indent the first line of each paragraph five spaces.

5. Avoid handwritten margin notes, arrows, starbursts, and other such devices. Effective in nonpersonalized mailings, they defeat the "me-to-you" mood personalization helps create.

6. Use short paragraphs.

7. Set the body of the letter in a typewriter typeface such as Courier or Prestige.

8. *Selectively* use any available data on your prospect list to extend personalization beyond the mere insertion of a name. For example, if you are trying to reactivate old accounts, remind prospects of the last time they bought from you, inserting the specific date into the body of the letter, if available. However, be careful not to overdo variables.

9. Do not overuse the prospect's name. Constantly referring to the prospect by name in the letter ("... and so, Mr. Jones ...") gives a phony ring to your copy. You wouldn't talk to the prospect in person this way or insert his or her name six times in a short, personal note, would you? Don't do it in direct mail, either.

10. On reply cards, ask recipients to indicate whether they are Mr., Mrs., Miss, or Ms. Add this information to your database so you can correctly identify sex in subsequent mailings.

One common mistake you should avoid is changing the copy after the piece has been designed without checking with the mailing house first. This can result in disaster, because inserting or deleting text can affect the placement and alignment of the personalized elements.

Another common mistake is not checking a sample letter by inserting it into its envelope to make sure the personalization is properly aligned and shows through the window.

A third common mistake is not planning for imperfect or incomplete data on the mailing list. For instance, how will you handle consumer lists where some names don't have titles (Mr./Mrs./Ms./Miss) available? (Solution: Put the full name in the salutation, for example, "Dear Terry Jones").

Postal Regulations

Mail can be sent first class or third-class bulk rate. In mail-order selling, third class is usually used because of the lower cost per thousand. Nationwide, average delivery time for a third-class bulk-rate mailing takes about $2^1/_2$ weeks.

The cost of third-class mail varies depending on how the mail is sorted. Your local post office can issue a bulk rate permit and provide a manual explaining the different sorting options and mailing rates. As of this writing, the cost for a third class bulk rate up to $6^1/_8$ inches by 11 inches and 3.3 ounces is approximately 25 cents per piece.

The cost savings can be considerable for offers that are mailed in large quantities (say over 100,000 pieces or more). And for lower-priced consumer products with low profit margin, the lower cost per thousand helps you reach break-even sooner. You have to mail at least 200 pieces to qualify for the bulk rate.

When mailing to corporations or executives, business-to-business direct marketers sometimes prefer first-class to third-class mail. First-class mail usually gets delivered just two or three days after it's mailed.

One advantage of first-class mail is that it is more likely to reach its destination. Nondelivery rate for third-class mail is around 10 percent, which means 100 out of every 1,000 third-class packages aren't delivered to their destinations.

The drawback to first-class mail is the expense, especially as the weight of the mailing package increases. As of this writing, first-class mail costs 34 cents up to one ounce, and 55 cents up to two ounces.

The Least You Need to Know

➤ Direct mail seeks to generate maximum profits at minimum cost. Do whatever you can to reduce your cost per thousand without diminishing response.

➤ Be a production cheapskate. If there's a less expensive envelope or grade of paper available, use it. The recipient won't care.

➤ Avoid proprietary (nonstandard) sizes and formats. They cost extra and limit your choice of vendors for the job.

➤ With personalized mailing, inspect them periodically to make sure the right letter is going in the right envelope. If you are one off, the envelope for Shirley James will contain Sam Jones's letter, and your mailing will be a disaster.

Part 2
Direct Response Formats and Media

The media and format you select for your direct response campaign can significantly improve response rates. This part presents the available media and format choices in depth, and gives you guidelines on selecting which one is right for your product.

You will learn how to put together a direct mail package, and utilize the individual elements including the outer envelope, sales letter, brochure, buck slip, lift letter, and reply form.

Then, we will move on to the alternative direct mail formats appropriate for long-copy mailings: magalogs, minilogs (digests), and bookalogs. In addition, we look at how to effectively use short-copy formats including self-mailers, postcards, double postcards, and snap packs. Tips on catalog marketing, marketing postcard decks, free-standing inserts, and package inserts are next. Finally, how to use classified and display ads to generate leads and orders are covered.

Chapter 7

The Direct Mail Package

In This Chapter

➤ Direct mail: still working after all these years

➤ Outer envelopes: to tease or not to tease?

➤ The sales letter sells and the brochure tells

➤ Lift notes and buck slips

➤ Designing effective order forms

Despite the growth of fax, e-mail, and Web sites, mail is still a vital part of business communication. According to a survey by the United States Post Office, 75 percent of business executives read mail as soon as it is received, and 65 percent feel strongly that letters are important when conducting official business.

A Gallup Study indicates that direct mail is the most common communications medium, used by 77 percent of U.S. companies. In the survey, marketing managers rated direct mail as the best communications tool for generating sales, educating business decision makers on complex issues, selling products directly to businesses, and notifying business prospects about new products and services. Sixty-five percent of the companies using direct mail have increased direct mail budgets in the past five years by an average of 25 percent.

There are many different direct formats we will explore in this part of the book. This chapter focuses on the most popular and, in many instances, the most effective format: the standard direct mail package consisting of an outer envelope, sales letter, brochure, other inserts (lift notes, buck slips), and reply element.

The Outer Envelope

It's impossible to mail a sales letter without an outer envelope. Or is it? You can always print your sales message on a sheet of paper, fold it, and mail it without an outer envelope. We call this a self-mailer, and discuss it in Chapters 8, "Direct Mail: Longer Formats," and 9, "Direct Mail: Short Formats." But if you are sending a multicomponent mailing—letter, brochure, reply form—an outer envelope is the way to go.

The first issue to decide is whether to mail first class or third class as discussed in detail in Chapter 6, "Producing and Printing Your Direct Marketing Campaign." The next issue is what size envelope to use. Common choices include #10 (standard business-size envelope), 6 by 9 inches, and jumbo (9 by 12 inches).

Color and paper stock are also choices that have to be made. A plain white envelope is a good choice for mailing to businesses and professionals, but a bright color can stand out and gain attention. Kraft (an official-looking brown color) can help make a mailing look important. Some letter shops offer outer envelopes that look like Fedex packages, Express Mail, or Western Union telegrams to convey an urgent feel.

The next issue is whether to use a teaser. Should you put promotional copy on the outer envelope or should you leave it plain?

Marketing Tip

For mailing to business prospects and professionals, the #10 envelope (standard business-size) is a popular choice, but one way to stand out is to be different from everyone else. If all your competitors are using #10 mailings, consider testing a 6-by-9-inch direct mail package. Some tests have shown jumbos to outpull these smaller formats, but not always enough to justify the extra cost of the larger format.

The Big Tease

A "teaser" is copy (which can also include graphics) placed on the outer envelope of the mailing. The major advantage of using teasers is that they can, in some instances, increase response rates. The major disadvantage is that sometimes they can lower response rates. After all, the teaser tips off the reader instantly that he or she is holding a piece of advertising mail, and therefore the reader can throw it away without risk of losing something important or personal.

Contrary to popular opinion, the purpose of an outer envelope teaser is not just to get people to open the envelope. A plain, unmarked envelope will always get opened, so why would you need a teaser? The true purpose of the teaser is to create an expectation for what is inside the envelope, making the reader more receptive to the message and offer. The most effective teasers promise a big reward or benefit for reading the mailing inside the envelope, arouse curiosity, or state a powerful offer up front.

A letter aimed at helping computer resellers increase their sales by offering their customers financing comes in an envelope with the teaser:

> *"Now close more and bigger sales, more often."*

A successful mailing for a financial newsletter arouses curiosity with this headline:

> *"Inside: The One Internet Stock You Must Own Now. (Hint: It's Not the One You Think.)"*

Another successful mailing, for a book club for chemical engineers, puts the offer right on the outer envelope:

> *"Why are we giving away this special 50th anniversary edition of Perry's Handbook (a $129 retail value) practically for free?"*

You never know which teaser will work best until you test.

Blind Mailings

If your instinct or experience tells you your audience is likely to throw away promotional mail, you may want to test a "blind" envelope (see the following example). A blind envelope is an outer envelope designed to make your package appear to be normal business or personal correspondence, rather than direct mail.

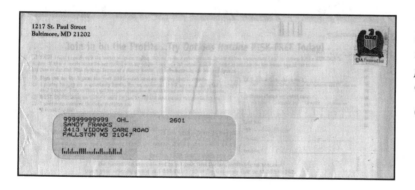

The blind "official" envelope looks like personal mail. You can't tell it's promotional until you open it and look inside.

(Source: Agora Publishing)

Here is a list of things to think about with your blind mailing:

➤ Use a #10 envelope or Monarch envelope—the sizes used for personal correspondence. (A 6-by-9–inch envelope, for example, is immediately perceived as direct mail.) With a computer, type the recipient's name and address directly on the outer envelope. This can be done by a letter shop or in-house. (Many printers and office supply catalogs now offer envelopes on continuous sheets that can be fed into your personal computer's printer.)

➤ Use a good quality stock for envelopes. Better paper creates a better impression and makes your piece look classy and important.

Warning!

If you are using a letter shop to computer-personalize your envelopes, ask to see a sample first. Many of the inkjet and some of the laser systems produce an undesirable computer-generated appearance. (This is especially true of desktop publishing systems.) Your envelopes should look as if they were typed on a typewriter.

Marketing Tip

What if you can't afford first-class postage or computer-typed envelopes? When mailing third class, use a meter instead of an indicia. An indicia seems to scream, "This is advertising mail!" but the meter doesn't make it as obvious (you have to turn the envelope sideways to read the tiny print that says "BLK RT," which means bulk rate).

➤ Consider mailing first class instead of third-class bulk rate. The cost difference is approximately $100 per thousand pieces mailed. This is insignificant for the typical business-to-business marketer who mails only a few thousand pieces. Once you get into quantities of tens of thousands, the added cost starts to become more of a factor.

➤ When mailing first class, have your letter shop affix a "live" stamp to the envelope rather use than use a meter or indicia. The additional cost for affixing the stamp is minimal and the results will be worth it: A letter sent in a #10 business envelope that looks personally typed and is mailed first class with a 34-cent stamp is almost always opened.

➤ Affix Cheshire labels directly to a reply card or form so the label shows through a clear window on the outer envelope.

➤ Instead of a fancy paper stock, have your envelopes printed on plain 24-lb. white weave. Reason: The white labels will match the envelopes in color and texture, making the label almost invisible and creating the illusion, at first glance, that the recipient's name and address was typed directly onto the envelope.

You will see many mailings in which a person's name appears hand-typed below the company logo and a return address in the upper left corner of the outer envelope. Doing this can increase response, probably because it helps maintain the illusion that the letter is personal correspondence.

Why not take this approach to the next logical step? Don't use a company letterhead at all. Instead, take a blank white #10 envelope, and type *your name only* (or someone else's name) and a return address in the upper-left corner. No logo. No company name. Use New Courier typeface, which looks like it came from a typewriter. When printed, each envelope will look as if the sender personally typed his or her name and return address on the outer envelope, and it is virtually impossible to tell that the envelope was printed. I have tested this in small quantities (unscientifically, I admit) with good preliminary results.

A variation of the blind envelope is the "official" envelope, which is designed to look like it's an official notice, such as those you might receive from the government or the IRS (see the following figure). Be careful: If you are too deceptive and scare the reader, the technique may backfire by angering the recipient.

"Official" envelopes border on deception, looking like they came from some recognized authority like an industry association or government agency.

(Source: Southwest Research.)

The Sales Letter

There's an old saying in direct marketing, "the letter sells, the brochure tells." The sales pitch is made in the letter; the brochure, as we'll discuss in a few minutes, plays only a supporting role—communicating information that can't easily be incorporated into the letter.

The advantage of a letter versus a brochure is that letters are a more personal medium. Unlike a catalog or annual report, a letter is signed by an individual, and therefore can be written "I" to "you." A friendly, personal, conversational style is the key to successful direct mail letter writing. Make it sound like one friend talking to another, enthusiastically sharing news about a great new product you have discovered, and you've hit the right tone.

The key components of the sales letter are covered in the sections that follow.

Personalized Versus Nonpersonalized

"Should I personalize?" You probably ask yourself that question every time you plan a mailing. And, if you're like most marketers, the question makes you hesitate—because you're never quite certain of the answer.

Is personalized direct mail effective? Yes. Experience proves and the experts agree that a personalized direct mail letter or package will almost always outpull the same letter

Marketing Tip

When computer personalization was introduced decades ago, the extra cost per thousand was tremendous, especially for small quantities. And so, even though these letters pulled better, the extra response didn't always justify the increased cost. But with modern technology drastically reducing the cost of personalization, personalized direct mail can at times prove more responsive *and* more profitable than form letters. It's a proposition worth testing.

or package when not personalized. But, it's not enough for personalized mailings merely to pull better than nonpersonalized mailings. As Bob Stone, author of *Successful Direct Marketing Methods* (NTC Business Books, 1996) observes, "They have to outpull by enough *to pay for the extra cost of personalization.*"

For mailings aimed at a mass audience, nonpersonalized direct mail seems to work well. When mailing to existing customers, personalization often pays off. Personalization also makes sense with exclusive offers, such as membership solicitations, and when mailing to high-level executives or wealthy individuals.

Using a Johnson Box

A Johnson box is a box above the salutation containing some lead-in headline or copy. Such above-the-salutation copy can also be used without placing it in a box.

On a personalized letter, I often omit the Johnson box and start with the salutation, since the very fact it's personalized is enough to get the reader reading. When I am using a form letter, I almost always use a Johnson box to gain the reader's attention.

Marketing Tip

When doing a major mailing to an association membership list, consider joining that association. For instance, if you are mailing to the National Association for Printing Leadership (NAPL) and you join, your letter can then carry the salutation "Dear Fellow NAPL Member." People are more likely to read something that identifies them as a member of the group, thinking it might be official association business. And the use of "Fellow" immediately establishes a relationship between you and reader.

Using a Salutation

When the letter is not personalized, you need a form salutation. "Dear Friend" is serviceable, but I recommend something more specific. If you are mailing to marketing directors, the obvious choice is "Dear Marketing Director."

But sometimes you can't pinpoint your audience that precisely. Say you are selling to people in marketing, but not all are managers. Some are entrepreneurs and company presidents; others may work at ad agencies or be market researchers. In that case try "Dear Marketing Professional." It covers everyone in the audience, and the term "professional" is flattering to the reader.

Determining the Length

The letter length depends on your audience, the subject matter, and your sales objective (leads versus orders). Here are some rules of thumb to guide you:

➤ **Does the type of letter matter?** Lead-generating letters are usually one or two pages. Letters selling mail-order products are usually two to four pages.

➤ **How busy is the audience?** Everyone is busy today, but some more than others. You can send a four-page letter to a retiree and he or she will read it, but a busy doctor may not.

➤ **Is the prospect a reader?** Letters for magazine subscriptions and book clubs are longer because the marketer knows that audience reads. Letters for CD and video clubs are usually shorter because these folks are not known readers.

The simpler the product and offer, the shorter the letter can be. A Florida company offering property tax assessment services found that a postcard worked best, because the proposition was so simple: "Hire us to review your property taxes, and if we get you a refund, give us half as a fee; if we don't, our services are free."

The best advice concerning length comes from Abraham Lincoln who, when asked how long a man's legs should be, answered "long enough to reach the ground." Your letter should be long enough to convince the reader to take the desired action—no more, no less.

Marketing Tip

I recommend using subheadings in any letter of two pages or more. Reason: Breaking up writing into short sections makes the copy easier to read. Subheadings also permit quick scanning.

Signing the Letter

Who should sign your letter? For many products and offers, it's not a critical issue. In other cases, it's more important. Here are some quick guidelines:

➤ When writing to niche markets, have the letter signed by someone who is like the audience. For instance, if you are selling programming tools to computer programmers, have your letter signed by your company's head programmer, not the marketing vice president.

➤ Have the letter come from the person who created or supports the product, not the person who sells it. For example, if you are selling software, have the Chief Programmer sign the letter, not the VP of Marketing.

➤ Use a celebrity or well-known name. People notice letters that come from Jimmy Carter or Bill Gates. (Of course you can only do this with their permission.)

➤ Print the signature in blue by using blue as the second color in a two-color printing job (see Chapter 6). The second color can also be used sparingly to highlight selected words or phrases.

But what about the heart of the sales letter—the copy itself?

Body Copy

Here are a few tips and suggestions you can use to make your sales letter more believable, engaging, and persuasive.

Talk About the Reader's Needs

Too many mailings are manufacturer oriented. They talk about the sellers' pet interests, rather than the reader's problems and needs. But the reader is more concerned with what's on his or her mind than what is on yours.

Here's the opening of a letter mailed to creative directors, ad managers, and editors:

> *"International Stock Photography Ltd. is a quality stock house serving the advertising, corporate, and editorial markets. Our files contain some of the finest images available ..."*

This lead is advertiser oriented. It boasts about the advertiser's firm, but fails to tell the reader why he or she should care or how the service can solve the reader's business problems. Compare this with the following letter from a company selling beach property:

"If you love the city … but long for cool ocean breezes and quiet moonlit beaches, then you should know that your dreams can come true with your own oceanfront vacation home."

This letter succeeds because it addresses a need—the reader's need to get away from the city on vacation. It is also effective because it promises a reward ("your dreams can come true"), paints a picture of the reward ("cool ocean breezes and quiet moonlit beaches"), and gets right to the point (you can own an oceanfront home).

Start Off with a Strong "Lead"

Experienced direct mail marketers know that the average reader scans a letter for just five seconds before deciding whether to read it or throw it away. If your opening doesn't hook the reader within five seconds, you've lost the prospect. Therefore, it pays to put your strongest sales argument right up front. Don't "warm up" with chitchat or secondary sales arguments. Don't hold back the most important point for the "big finish." If you do, most readers will never get to it.

For example, if your new heating system cuts fuel costs 50 percent, don't start off with:

"Good morning. I'd like to spend a few minutes chatting with you about an important subject. It's a vital piece of equipment that's keeping your toes toasty even while we speak … but one that's costing you much more money than it should."

Instead, get right to the point:

"Now you can cut your fuel bills by 30 percent, 40 percent, even 50 percent or more. The enclosed Technical Bulletin tells you how it's done …"

State the Offer Up Front

Many lead-generating sales letters focus on getting the reader to send for free literature. The reader is told …

"To receive a free copy of our new product bulletin, just complete and mail the enclosed business reply card."

This offer is usually made in the letter's last paragraph. You can increase response by stating the offer in the opening of the letter, as well as at the end. Many people will only glance at the lead paragraph of a direct mail letter and then throw the letter away. You can get some of these people to respond by putting the offer up front, as in this sales letter offering life insurance policies for children:

"There's no gift more meaningful ... for the children you love, than the one discussed in a new free pamphlet. It is yours with my compliments if you'll just mail the enclosed card."

The offer is repeated twice more—once in the fourth paragraph and again in the last paragraph.

Get Personal

A letter, unlike an ad or TV commercial, is a personal communication. And that's how it should sound—like one person talking to another. A formal, stiff, "corporate" tone is inappropriate for direct mail. Pompous writing alienates the reader; friendly, conversational writing wins the reader over. You can't fool the reader into thinking direct mail is personal mail. But, if you write warmly, sincerely, and naturally, the reader will react as if you had sent a personally written letter ... even though the reader knows you haven't.

Personal pronouns help make writing sound like natural conversation, as do contradictions and an occasional colloquial or slang expression. Here's a sample of appropriate copy style for direct mail. This is from a letter selling mail-order booklets on telephone technique:

"I wish you could meet Helen ... She's the woman who writes 'Your Telephone Personality,' our special training program to improve the way people handle their telephone. She's so warm, perceptive, and pleasant, you couldn't help but be favorably impressed."

Surprising Secrets

Take microcomputers, for example, which are used by several kinds of businesses. Freelance writers are interested primarily in word-processing capability and reasonable cost. A small business might be more concerned with service and customized software. A large corporation would want to know if the microcomputer is compatible with current equipment and if multiple micros can be linked in a network. A single mailing that attempted to cover all these points would have far less impact than separate mailings tailored to the three distinct audiences.

This mailing comes alive, because it deals with a flesh-and-blood person and not just sales talk, statistics, and product specifications.

Narrow the Focus

The most powerful reason for turning to direct mail is that it lets you target your message to select groups of special-interest readers. Yet a surprising number of industrial marketers fail to exploit this opportunity.

Aim your mailing at a narrow audience and highlight the solutions your product offers to the reader's specific problems. The same product may offer different benefits to different groups of users.

Know How Much to Tell

A client asked me to prepare a mailing to generate inquiries about a new evaporator. The people on his mailing list were engineers who were already familiar with evaporators. So the mailings, which consisted of a short letter and a reply card, focused on the specific advantage of my client's evaporator over all others.

A month later, this same client wanted to do a mailing on a new type of inspection and maintenance service for waste treatment equipment. Since such a service was unique and had never been offered before by any manufacturer, the reader needed to be educated from scratch.

The mailing consisted of a letter and reply card, plus an additional element—a pamphlet explaining how the program worked. More complete information was needed because the reader was unfamiliar with what was being offered.

Surprising Secrets

Direct mail writers use a P.S. because it stands out from the rest of the letter and therefore gets read. The P.S. can be used to either restate an important point (such as the offer or guarantee) or highlight an additional point not covered in the letter. In an article in *Target Marketing* magazine (February 2001, p. 75), Pat Friesen says that the "P.S." is one of the most widely read elements of a sales letter, and that 30 percent or more of all people read the P.S. first.

Use Graphics to Highlight Key Points

If you want to make sure the recipient reads a particular sentence, highlight it in yellow. If you want to make sure the reader reads a particular paragraph, put a box around it. Or put a handwritten note "Important" in the margin with an arrow pointing to the paragraph. Use graphics to emphasize parts of the letter you don't want readers to miss.

Marketing Tip

You may get additional orders from people who do not respond to your mailing immediately, but save the brochure for future reference. To encourage the recipient to hold onto your brochure, add some valuable information to it. A mailing for a casino, for instance, had the rules of black jack printed on the back panel of the brochure.

The Brochure

Do you need a brochure? Not always. And there are several reasons not to have one. A brochure adds expense, and it makes the piece look more promotional. A letter by itself has a more personal look and feel.

The advantage of a brochure is that it's illustrated: You can show pictures of your product—the various makes and models, applications, and satisfied customers enjoying its use. Some offers naturally lend themselves to color product photos. These include fashion, jewelry, travel, and real estate. Could you imagine a Victoria's Secret catalog without pictures of young female models in bras?

Brochures are also good vehicles for including information too detailed to be smoothly integrated into the letter copy, such as technical specifications. Brochures can also present other visuals, such as graphs and charts.

The Lift Note

The lift note is a second, smaller letter, usually printed on Monarch-size paper, enclosed along with the main letter. The original lift note had a headline printed on the outer flap that read ...

> *"Frankly, I'm puzzled why you have chosen not to accept our offer."*

Today the flap copy of most lift notes are written along those lines:

> *"Read this note only if you have decided NOT to order."*

The lift note is a last-minute pitch getting the reluctant customer to change his or her mind.

The Buck Slip or Premium Sheet

A buck slip is a small insert placed in the envelope along with the letter and other elements. It is often used to highlight the premium, although it can also be used to restate the guarantee or for other purposes. In a #10 mailing, a buck slip typically measures 4 by 9 inches. If you have multiple premiums that won't fit on a buck slip, you can use an 8½-by-11–inch piece of paper. This is called a premium sheet.

Order Forms That Close the Deal

While no sales rep worth his or her salt would neglect closing tools, order forms often don't get the attention they need from marketers, copywriters, and designers.

Here are several tips for boosting the closing power of your direct mail order forms:

➤ **Restate the guarantee on your order form.** Direct mail buyers can't see, feel, or handle the goods, so they're bound to be a little bit uneasy. A strong guarantee helps set them at ease, and a signature under the guarantee lets them know that a real person stands behind it.

➤ **Make the form easy to follow and fill in.** Guide prospects to the important parts of the form. You can do this by boxing important elements and highlighting them with a 10 percent to 15 percent tint of the form's spot (second) color. Don't make the tint darker than 15 percent, or the type in the boxes will be hard to read. Use color tints, a "handwritten" "X," or pointing fingers to point prospects to information they must fill in.

➤ **Give designers the room they need to create powerful closing tools.** Order forms don't have to be small. Larger order forms such as 5½ by 8½ inches and 8½ by 11 inches are becoming popular, especially since they are easier to fax than are small forms.

Marketing Tip

When using order forms bigger than 4 by 9 inches make sure that the forms will fold to fit the reply envelope, and indicate folding points in the margins.

Business Reply Envelopes (BREs)

A BRE is a business reply envelope—typically a #9 envelope, which is slightly smaller than the regular #10 business size envelope. The BRE is optional with lead generation and soft offers, but strongly recommended when you are generating orders. People will not send mail orders with payment (credit card information, check, or money order) unless you supply a BRE.

The BRE can be plain or have some copy on the envelope. This copy is intended to create the perception that the order being placed is important or urgent. Typical BRE teasers include: "Priority Order enclosed," "Urgent," and "Immediate processing requested."

The Least You Need to Know

➤ The most critical parts of the direct mail package are the outer envelope teaser and the beginning (headline and first paragraph) of the sales letter.

➤ The letter is more important than the brochure: "The letter sells, the brochure tells."

➤ Lift notes, buck slips, and new envelope teasers can often lift response 10 to 20 percent or more.

➤ Stress the benefits of your product and how the reader will come out ahead by buying it.

➤ Lead with your strongest benefit or sales point. Do not wait until the end to spring it on the reader; she may never get that far.

Chapter 8

Direct Mail: Longer Formats

In This Chapter

➤ Special formats for long-copy mailings

➤ Advantages of using magalogs, digests, and faux reports

➤ Organizing and designing long-copy direct mail

➤ Writing long copy that compels and sells

Although the classic direct mail package described in Chapter 7, "The Direct Mail Package," is the most widely mailed format, there are other direct mail formats that can sometimes work as well or even beat it.

In this chapter, we look at the various formats for long-copy mailings. These include magalogs, tabloids, faux reports, minilogs, and bookalogs. In the next chapter we go in the other direction and look at short-form mailings that work.

Why and When to Use Long-Copy Formats

First, let's define long copy. The long-form formats described in this chapter basically give you an alternate layout for any direct mail piece which, if done as a standard sales letter, would run eight pages or longer. A two- or even four-page letter simply doesn't have enough copy to fill a magalog or digest.

Why would you use these alternative formats? One reason is your direct mail package has tired, so your response needs to be lifted. Sometimes simply changing the format can lift response. If you have a successful direct mail package and response is dropping off, you might consider such a format test.

Another reason is to match the format with the amount of information you need to convey. One of the limitations of a sales letter is that it's a fairly linear format: You start at "Dear Friend" and read through to "Sincerely yours." Therefore sales letters are a natural for copy that makes one central argument. But say you have many features and sales arguments you want to highlight. In an alternative format, such as a *magalog*, you can have numerous sidebars in which to highlight different sales arguments—features, testimonials, benefits, supporting facts.

Alternative formats are also better suited for visual presentation than are sales letters, which are traditionally text without photos or drawings. Magalogs, for instance, have the size and space to allow clear, dramatic reproduction of full-color photos and complex diagrams.

Long formats are popular with information marketers, especially newsletter publishers and seminar providers. They are also used frequently to sell nutritional supplements and sometimes consumer gadgets and appliances, such as mixers and blenders.

Insider's Buzzwords

A **magalog** is a direct mail piece designed to look like a magazine. Pages are approximately the same size as a magazine.

Long-Copy Direct Mail Formats

Let's take a look at the more popular long-copy direct mail formats that have been developed. Note that all of these forms, except the bookalog, are self-mailers—they don't require an envelope.

Magalogs

A magalog is a direct mail piece disguised to look like a magazine (see the following figure). The name "magalog" comes from "magazine catalog." (I've always thought it should be "magamail" for "magazine direct mail.")

A magalog is typically 7 by 10 inches, or 8½ by 11 inches, and printed in four colors. Minimum length is eight pages, average length is 16 to 24 pages, and a few are even longer. When estimating length, figure approximately 400 to 500 words of copy per printed magalog page.

The front cover usually has an attention-getting headline, some subheads or bullet points that hint at what's inside, and one or more photos. It may also have a "fake" masthead that helps further the illusion of it being a magazine instead of a promo-tion (for example, "Special Consumer's Issue"). The inside front cover is often a table of contents or an introductory cover letter.

A magalog is a direct mailer disguised to look like a magazine.

(Source: Phillips Publishing)

Magalogs can be written as a series of independent "spreads" (two facing pages) or as a long article with sidebars. If you write it as a long article with sidebars, the article, with a headline, begins on page three, opposite the inside front cover.

In the spread approach, each spread covers a different topic and has its own head-line. A magalog selling subscriptions to *Men's Health* magazine uses this approach.

One spread is about flat abs; a second about sex and relationships; a third about nutrition and diet.

The mailing label goes on the bottom of the back cover. The rest of the back cover can have teasers or other promotional copy and photos designed to get the recipient to open the magalog and start reading.

The order form usually appears on the inside back cover. This way, when the recipient tears off, completes, and mails the order form, the mailing label is on the opposite side, and the mailer can read the key code and know what mailing and list the order is from. If there are premiums, these are usually discussed on the page opposite the inside back cover.

Surprising Secrets

The goal of the magalog is not to "fool" the reader into thinking they are looking at a magazine, but to create an editorial-style (as opposed to selling-style) publication that engages the reader *as if it were* a magazine and not a direct mail promotion.

Tabloids

A tabloid is similar to a magalog except it is oversized—approximately the size of the *New York Times* or *The National Enquirer*. Otherwise, the guidelines given for creating a magalog all apply.

Tabloids have two advantages over magalogs: the larger size stands out and gets attention, and there is more room for visual presentation. The disadvantage of tabloids is higher printing cost and therefore higher cost per thousand in the mail.

Faux Reports

A faux report (fake report) is a magalog-size self-mailer printed in two colors instead of four. The design is plainer than that of a magalog, more like a business report than a consumer magazine.

Faux reports are a better choice than magalogs when you want the mailer to convey the look and feel of serious, important information. Using a faux report instead of a magalog eliminates the need to have color photos, so it is recommended when good color photos are not available or the offer does not need to be illustrated.

Issuelog

An issuelog is very close in appearance and style to a faux report. The difference is that while the faux report looks like a special report, an issuelog looks like an issue of a newsletter.

Issuelogs so far have been used mainly to sell newsletter subscriptions. The design and copy have the look, feel, and style of a newsletter issue, so the recipient almost thinks he or she is reading a sample issue.

Minilogs

Also known as a "digest" or "reportalog," a minilog is a half-size magalog. It is made by printing on 8$^1/_2$-by-11 sheets, folding them to 5$^1/_2$-by-8$^1/_2$ pages, and saddle stitching (binding the pages by stapling them through the spine) to form a booklet. Although minilogs can be designed and printed either in two or four colors, most are two-color publications.

Because of its smaller page size, the minilog is not as well suited as the magalog for visual presentation and sidebars, although both can be used. Therefore, the minilog is the format of choice when you want to have the look and feel of a magalog, but don't need elaborate illustrations or a lot of sidebars (and have a more linear presentation).

Bookalogs

Bookalogs are direct mail packages published in the format of thin (usually 60 to 80 pages) paperback books. The book is usually mailed in an envelope with a short (one- to two-page) cover letter, business reply envelope, and order form, although an order form is also printed in the back of the book.

The big advantage of a bookalog is that, looking like a book, it has a higher perceived value than ordinary direct mail: People think they are getting a free book, and "free book inside" is often used on the outer envelope. Because people see a book, they read it as editorial and not promotional copy, believing it to be more credible and objective than a sales letter.

The disadvantages of a bookalog are twofold. First, cost. They are expensive to produce and mail. Second, the small page size and traditional book format are not well suited to sidebars and visual presentation. Therefore bookalogs, like sales letters, work best with linear copy: You expect the reader to start on page one and read through to "The End" (although they may not, which is why you break the book into short chapters).

Marketing Tip

In reality, you are not locked into any of the formats described here. Your choice of format is limited only by your own creativity and today's printing technology. The bookalog and magalog are fairly recent inventions. Perhaps the next format innovation will be yours (mine, the sandwichlog—a direct mail package printed on a ham and cheese hero—never really caught on).

Organizing Your Long-Form Mailing

A special challenge of writing long-form copy, especially in nonletter formats, is organization. Because personal letters are short, you're probably comfortable having to write a one- or two-page sales letter. But how do you organize and arrange thousands of words in a magalog or minilog?

Here are some organizing principles that you can use to organize your entire document, as well as individual spreads and sidebars:

➤ **Order by location.** A magalog selling a telescope and a book on astronomy has a sidebar on the planets of the solar system. To organize the sidebar, it starts with Mercury (the planet nearest the sun) and ends with Pluto (the planet farthest out).

➤ **Order by increasing difficulty.** Computer manuals often start with the easiest material and, as the user masters basic principles, move on to more complex operations. A minilog selling an options trading course starts with simple trading, then gets into advanced techniques later on.

➤ **Alphabetical order.** This is a logical way to arrange a minilog selling nutritional supplements and vitamins (A, B-3, B-12, C, D, E, and so on).

➤ **Chronological order.** Here you present the facts in the order in which they happened. This technique is often used in sidebars of magalogs selling financial newsletters. The newsletter editor's major successes and predictions (for example, "I told subscribers to sell all their stocks three weeks before the October 1987 crash") are laid out in chronological order.

➤ **Problem/solution.** Another format appropriate to case histories and many types of reports, the problem/solution organizational scheme begins with "Here's what the problem was" and ends with "Here's how we solved it." Many products (diets, for example) fit well within this organizational scheme.

➤ **Inverted pyramid.** This is the newspaper style of news reporting where the lead paragraph summarizes the story and the following paragraphs present the facts in order of decreasing importance.

➤ **Deductive order.** You can start with a generalization, and then support it with particulars. Scientists use this format in research papers that begin with the findings and then state the supporting evidence. It's a great way to persuade a prospect to see your point of view.

➤ **Inductive order.** Another approach is to begin with specific instances, and then lead the reader to the idea or general principles the instances suggest. This is another excellent way to get the reader to buy into your reasoning and arguments.

➤ **List.** The simplest and perhaps most effective organizational scheme is often to organize your mailing (or at least part of it) as a list. A recent digest promoting a financial newsletter offered readers "The 7 best places to invest your money today." Another promotion from the same publisher for a different newsletter advertised, "The 5 tech stocks you must own now."

However you organize your long-copy mailing, make sure the key selling points pop out. This can be done with strong headlines and subheads.

Designing Long-Form Mailings

Many of the choices you face when designing long-format mailings are dictated by the format you select. A bookalog, for example, must look like a paperback book. That means small page sizes and mostly black text on a white background. A magalog, by comparison, looks like a color magazine, with sidebars and lots of photos.

Some other design tips are as follows:

➤ **Make the headlines big and bold.** Large headlines capture the reader's eye.

➤ **Use large, bold subheads.** These help guide the reader through the body copy. This is especially important in long formats, where the reader can get lost in all that copy.

➤ **Use sidebars.** Putting important or supporting information in sidebars—especially information that doesn't fit well into the main article—helps get it read. Sidebars can be printed on light tints or surrounded by borders to make them stand out.

➤ **Make the artwork big.** A single, large photo gains more attention than several smaller ones. Also, a page with one large, color photo is less expensive to print than a page with multiple photos, because there are fewer color separations to be made.

➤ **Use captions on your photos.** Captions get high readership.

➤ **Find a consistent graphic style and stick with it.** Give the publication a uniform graphic look. Stick with one or two typefaces, and vary size and font. Don't mix and match half a dozen typefaces or page layouts; it confuses the reader and looks amateurish.

➤ **Design with the reader in mind.** If you are promoting a laser eye surgery center in Spanish Harlem, print your magalog in English and Spanish. If you are marketing to senior citizens, make the type large—at least 10 point.

The main purpose of the design, of course, is to make the copy easy to read. But what should the copy in a magalog or digest say?

Copywriting Techniques That Work in Long Formats

By the very fact that you have chosen a long-copy format, you are making several assumptions. First, you are assuming that your reader is someone who will read long copy. We make this assumption, for example, when selling information products, such as newsletters and books (see Chapter 20, "Selling 'Information Products'").

We also assume a reader who will read long copy when mailing to people with special interests—for example, selling nutritional supplements to lists of people who have proven a concern about their health by buying other supplements or books on alternative medicine.

Finally, we are assuming that our product is "story rich"—meaning there is a lot we can say about it that the reader would care about. But how do we know, exactly, what the reader cares about, and what points we should include in our copy?

Understanding the Buyer's "Core Complex"

"Core complex" refers to the buyer's basic values—beliefs, attitudes, feelings, desires. Are they liberal or conservative? Religious or patriotic or both? Do they embrace technology or resist change of any kind?

Warning!

The reason you can't rely on market research is that people will say one thing, then do the opposite. For instance, say Joe is in a focus group for a new luxury car costing $90,000. Sally, the person next to Joe, when asked if she might buy it, says "yes." Now Joe is asked—would he buy the car? Joe can't really afford it and would never spend that much on a car anyway. But Joe answers, "Yes, I might buy one." Why? Because he doesn't want Sally to think he's a loser. The direct marketer's credo as far as market research seems to be: The only consumer votes worth tallying are the ones consumers make with their dollars. Orders are the only response that is really meaningful.

There is a belief—false, in my opinion—among packaged goods and other general advertisers that, through market research, you can determine precisely what people will buy and what advertising will motivate them to do so. Although opinions vary among individuals, direct marketers as a group are somewhat skeptical—or at least cautious— about putting too much faith in market research.

It actually makes sense for general advertisers to rely on market research more than direct marketers do. General advertising does not produce direct sales. Therefore, the effectiveness of general advertising is difficult to measure. Since general advertisers cannot accurately evaluate the sales performance of one ad versus another, they rely on nondirect measurements, such as surveys and studies.

Unable to test sales propositions, general advertisers plan massive campaigns, based on a single theme or message, to build brand awareness. Naturally they want to feel they are choosing the right message and creative approach. They use market research to confirm that their messages are the right ones and that their ads and commercials "pre-test" well with audiences before airing.

Sometimes, traditional market research results in a blockbuster campaign, but often not through statistical analysis as the advertiser had hoped. For example, a copywriter was reading through the transcript of a focus group (an interview session conducted with a small group of consumers) to get inspiration for promoting a cooking oil. What caught his attention was a line in the transcript where one consumer said, "After cooking the chicken, I poured the oil from the pan back into the cup, and it was all there except for one teaspoon." This demonstration was turned into a successful TV commercial.

But direct marketers don't take this "all or nothing" approach. We find an idea, test it on a small scale. If it works, we roll out cautiously. If it flops, we keep testing until we find an approach that makes money. But how do we determine which ideas are test worthy and should be tried even in small trials? Direct marketers find that getting to core buyer motivations is more qualitative and intuitive.

One approach is to talk with a lot of people to get a feel for the "pulse" of the market. What are potential buyers of your product most worried about in their lives that your product can help them solve? What are their fears, hopes, dreams, and desires? What do they like and dislike about other products in your category?

Often, the answer may surprise you. Copywriter Joe Sacco had to create advertising for a new needle for diabetics. What is the sales appeal? It's hard to know if you are not a diabetic, and Joe wasn't. To his surprise, patients said they wanted needles that are "sharp"—and he built a successful campaign around this. If you have ever used a needle, you know why sharp is better: It penetrates the skin easier and therefore with minimum pain.

Creating a Customer Profile

Part of any copy platform should be a profile of the buyer's core complex. Since market research cannot give us a scientific formula for correctly creating a winning promotion, we need to determine, using our nonqualitative methods, our best guess as to the core concerns of our potential customer.

Ask the following questions: Who are these people? What do they believe? What is their attitude toward our product? What outcomes do they desire? What is their feeling concerning health care, the stock market, or whatever proposition we are selling to them? Then write down a customer profile as part of the copy platform you create (as described in Chapter 5, "Writing Copy That Sells") as an outline for your mailing.

For instance, in Chapter 5, I showed a portion of the copy platform I wrote before creating a mailing for a mutual fund newsletter aimed at Vanguard fund investors (refer to the section "Creating a Winning Copy Platform"). Since we couldn't rent Vanguard's customer list, we had to mail to more general lists of known investors, which means we didn't even know whether they held Vanguard funds or not.

The mailing was set to "drop" (be mailed) during the bearish market of early 2001 when a lot of investors had been badly burned. In the copy platform, I wrote the following customer profile to help us determine the tone and approach we would take in our mailing:

➤ **Primary audience:** Vanguard mutual fund investors.

➤ **Secondary audience:** Other mutual fund and stock market newsletter subscribers.

➤ **What they believe:** Vanguard is a solid family of funds—a good investment. If you own Vanguard, you will do well.

➤ **What they know, but may not admit out loud:** Some Vanguard funds do much, much better than others, but they don't know which will do best over the next 6 to 12 months—and Vanguard isn't really helping them pick the best ones.

➤ **What they fear:** The Vanguard funds they own right now are not the ones that are going to outperform the rest in the next 12 months, and some of the ones that traditionally have been strong (for example, index funds) won't continue to perform well in a bearish market. They are not going to make as much profit as they did in the past and may not recover what they lost in the recent market correction.

➤ **What they want:** Someone to optimize their Vanguard portfolio—weed out the bad funds and move money into the ones that will be the top performers over the next 12 months.

Every direct mail package is based on a set of assumptions—about the product, the market, and the prospect. Articulating these assumptions in writing is very helpful to the copywriter, especially in long-copy formats where it's easy to meander and wander off track.

With a written copy platform, you can always check to make sure the information you include to flesh out your magalog is there to advance the key selling proposition, not just to fill space.

Keep the "Information Density" Level High

Especially when you are writing your first long-copy mailings, there is a tendency for the copywriter to run out of steam and start coasting. But long copy works and holds the reader's attention only when every paragraph—indeed every sentence—has something interesting, important, and valuable to say.

Every sentence in your mailing must help communicate one of what copywriters call the "four P's"—promise, picture, prove, and push:

Promise—Describe the primary benefit. How the readers will come out ahead by buying the product (for example, overcome fatigue).

Picture—Help the readers visualize the benefit (for example, a picture of a happy customer playing tennis because your vitamin supplement gave them more energy).

Prove—Prove you can deliver the benefit.

Push—Ask for the order.

Nothing kills the selling power of a long-copy format mailing faster than superficial copy. Copy that talks in vague generalities, rather than in specifics. Copy that rambles without authority on a subject, rather than shows customers that you understand their problems, their desires, and their needs.

Surprising Secrets

Don Hauptman, author of the famous mail-order ad "Speak Spanish Like a Diplomat!" says that when he writes a direct mail package, more than 50 percent of the work involved is in the reading, research, and preparation. Less than half his time is spent writing, rewriting, editing, and revising. Recently, a client hired me to write an ad on a software package. After reading the background material and typing it into my PC, I had 19 single-spaced pages of notes.

What causes superficial copy? The fault lays with lazy copywriters who don't bother to do their homework (or copywriters who don't know any better). To write strong copy—specific, factual copy—you must dig for facts. You must study the product, the prospect, and the marketing problem. There is no way around this. Without facts, you cannot write good copy. But with the facts at their fingertips, even mediocre copywriters can do a decent job.

How much research is enough? I often collect at least twice as much information as I need—preferably three times as much. Then I have the luxury of selecting only the best facts, instead of trying desperately to find enough information to fill up the page.

The Four U's

Another challenge of long-copy formats is keeping the quality level of the copy high throughout the entire piece. In short copy used by general advertisers, there may only be a couple of paragraphs or sentences, so each one is refined and polished to perfection. But in a 10,000-word magalog, how can you be sure each subheading, bullet, and line is as strong as it should be? Copywriter Michael Masterson advises checking every key line against what he calls the "four U's" to make it as powerful as possible:

➤ **Ultra-specific:** Specifics sell and get noticed (for example, "How 197,259 investors became millionaires this year").

➤ **Urgent:** Give the reader a reason to act now instead of later (for example, "Pending changes in tax laws may soon eliminate this loophole. Act now to get your $7,500 deduction before it vanishes into thin air").

➤ **Useful:** What's in it for the reader? Is there a benefit? (For example, "Lower your cholesterol and blood pressure eating grilled sausage!")

➤ **Unique:** Offer something the competition does not, stress a feature they don't (for example, "High fat diet actually reverses arthritis").

After writing your first draft, check every line of copy—every bullet, every subhead—against this "four U's" checklist. Edit and rewrite those that don't meet the criteria to make them as strong as possible.

The Least You Need to Know

➤ Format selection can make a big difference in response rates. It is often worth testing the same basic copy in two different formats (for example, #10 direct mail package versus magalog).

➤ Long formats are well suited for "story-rich" products where the more you tell, the more you sell.

➤ Long formats are not advised for commodity products and products bought on impulse, where short copy seems to work better.

➤ Before you write, decide how you will organize your material. Making an outline is very helpful.

113

Chapter 9

Direct Mail: Short Formats

> **In This Chapter**
>
> ➤ Do self–mailers work?
>
> ➤ Using postcards, double postcards, and folded self–mailers
>
> ➤ Knowing when to use snap packs and dimensional mailers
>
> ➤ Understanding the economies of scale
>
> ➤ Making small format mailings more effective

Self-mailers, the most popular short-copy format, have traditionally gotten a bad rap from direct marketing consultants, copywriters, and agencies. "Self-mailers don't work," these professionals tell us. "They generate low response. People don't read them. They are thrown away because they look like brochures or advertising matter. A letter and reply card will nearly always outpull a self-mailer."

But many clients feel differently. "Self-mailers are easy to produce and wonderfully inexpensive. And we do get good results with them in many situations," one client recently told me. Are self-mailers the sure road to direct mail disaster … or a powerful secret weapon? This chapter discusses the facts.

Working with Self-Mailers

It's true that a standard package consisting of a letter, brochure, and reply element will often outpull a self-mailer. One company, a tool manufacturer, decided they would use a double postcard (a simple self-mailer consisting of a four-panel postcard) to offer their mail-order catalog to consumers. The price of the catalog was one dollar.

At the insistence of their ad agency, they tested this double postcard against a package consisting of a letter and reply card. Both had the same graphics and copy. The only difference was the format. The results? The letter and reply card generated three times as many orders for the catalog as the double postcard. Demonstrating once again that letters usually do pull better than self-mailers.

But not always. Self-mailers work well in many situations. They are especially effective for products with which the prospect is already familiar, and therefore doesn't have to be educated about or sold on. This is why double postcards are so effective in subscription marketing for well-known publications, such as *Business Week*. The prospect already knows the product and whether he or she wants it. The only real question is whether the offer is attractive enough—and the double postcard has enough space to communicate the offer.

Surprising Secrets

Self-mailers, with their lower cost per thousand, are the format of choice when selling offers with low profit margins or response rates.

Choosing Your Format

When producing a short-copy mailing, there are a number of proven formats you can choose from:

➤ Postcards

➤ Double postcards

➤ Posterboards

➤ Folded self-mailers

➤ Snap packs

➤ Dimensional mailers

➤ Urgent mailers

Each will be discussed in the following sections.

Postcards

Postcards (see the following figure) can be a variety of sizes. But to qualify for the lowest first-class rate, a postcard must be designed for automated mailing at the post office—meaning they can be processed by machine instead of by hand. The size range for automated postcard mailings is from 3 by 5 inches to a maximum of 4 by 6 inches as of this writing.

FREE Trial Reservation Card

PLACE

FREE

STICKER

HERE

☑ **YES!** Please enter in my name a FREE four-week trial subscription to BARRON'S. If I like BARRON'S, I'll receive 13 additional weeks (17 weeks in all) for only $39. That's the regular price of a 13-week subscription, so my first four weeks will cost me nothing.

No Cost. No Obligation. If I decide BARRON'S is not for me, I'll return your subscription invoice marked "cancel" and owe nothing at all. In either case, the first four weeks are mine to keep with your compliments.

Send No Money Now.
We'll bill you later.

**SATURDAY
DELIVERY
AVAILABLE**

The cost of your subscription may be tax-deductible.
Offer good in continental U.S. for a limited time only. For
New Subscribers Only.

```
B104000842655          17BNBB
Mr. Bob Bly
22 E Quackenbush Ave Ste 3
Dumont NJ 07628-3093
```

E-mail address_____
☐ I prefer not to be contacted via e-mail about other products and services from BARRON'S.

▼ Detach here and mail today ▼   DPC-18

A postcard is a "quick and dirty" format—one of the cheapest available.

(Source: Barron's)

"For a quick marketing message, postcards pack a lot of punch," says copywriter Shira Linden. "There are no worries about whether the envelope will get opened."

Self-promotion consultant Ilise Benen says postcards can be ideal for lead generation or as a reminder to prospects of your existence and your offer. They can also be used to convey a quick message about a special offer or sale, or to spark action by prospects who have already received your material, but haven't taken the next step.

Postcards do not contain a reply element, so they work best when they encourage the recipient to call a toll-free number or go to a Web site. Be sure to put the phone number or Web site address in large, bold type.

Marketing Tip

The postcard itself can serve as its own reply element. Just print a line that says, "To accept this offer, put this postcard in an envelope and mail it to us at the following address." There's no need for the prospect to fill in anything because the prospect's mailing address is already on the postcard's mailing label.

Double Postcards

A double postcard, as the name implies, is a self-mailer consisting of two attached postcards. There is a perforation separating the two cards.

One card has the address label on the front and some promotional copy on the back. The second card is a business reply card. You tear it off and return it to accept the offer. Often double postcards

117

are laser printed or applied with an ink jet so the reply card already has the prospect's name and address on it.

Double postcards are used primarily in magazine subscription marketing, where their low cost per thousand sometimes makes them more profitable than standard #10 direct mail packages. The format is underused elsewhere, so there's an opportunity for you to break through the clutter and apply this low-cost format to your own marketing.

Posterboard

A posterboard is a stiff, 8$\frac{1}{2}$-by-11–inch sheet mailed flat. A double postcard is affixed to the sheet under a glassine (transparent plastic) panel. The panel is transparent so the recipient's address, imprinted on the double postcard, shows through.

The sheet has ample room for copy and visuals, and for maximum effect, is usually printed in four colors.

Folded Self-Mailers

Self-mailers come in all sizes and shapes. Some of the more common ones include:

➤ 11-by-17–inch sheet folded once to form four panels

➤ 11-by-25–inch sheet folded twice to form six panels

➤ 11-by-25–inch sheet folded twice to form six panels, with one third of the sheet cut in half to form a short fold-over panel

➤ 8$\frac{1}{2}$-by-11–inch sheet folded twice to form six panels

➤ 8$\frac{1}{2}$-by-14–inch sheet folded three times to form eight panels

Of these, the 8$\frac{1}{2}$-by-11-inch sheet folded twice (called a "tri-fold") is perhaps the most popular, because it's so simple. You fold a letter-size piece of paper twice. The recipient's address goes on the outer panel.

When you open it, the top two thirds have the promotional message. The bottom third is a business reply card the prospect can tear off and return to the advertiser.

Snap Packs

A snap pack is a self-mailer consisting of multiple "plies" or sheets. The plies are accessed by tearing off perforated tabs at either end of the piece. The plies are usually single sheets printed on lightweight stock, but you can use other elements as plies—for example, a business reply envelope can be one of the plies.

Dimensional Mailers

Dimensional mailers include pop-up mailings and other structural pieces that have three dimensions. Because of the high cost per thousand, they are usually used only for high-end, lead-generating offers.

Urgent Mailers

Several letter shops and envelope manufacturers offer what they call "urgent" mailing formats. These are short letters mailed in outer envelopes designed to resemble Federal Express, Express Mail, Western Union, or other express or overnight delivery services.

Cost Considerations

The main reason why people use self-mailers is that self-mailers are much cheaper to produce and mail than are standard direct mail packages. With a self-mailer, you have only one piece of paper to print. A standard direct mail package has at least five: outer envelope, letter, brochure, order card, and reply envelope. Plus, all these elements must be coordinated, folded, and stuffed. And they are often computer-personalized. All of which costs money.

Depending on size and format, the self-mailer can be produced for a small fraction of the cost of a full-scale package. Creative costs are also lower. Copywriters and art directors charge much less to produce self-mailers than they charge for a full package.

As a result, even though the direct mail package might generate a greater amount of total leads, the self-mailer might give you a lower cost per lead, because it is so inexpensive to produce and to mail. In a case where the direct mail package pulls only a little better than a self-mailer, but costs a lot more to produce, the self-mailer may be the more economical choice.

Putting Self-Mailers to Work

When should you consider using or testing a self-mailer? There are several situations, each of which will be covered in the following sections.

Mailings to Customers

Bob Milroy, an executive vice president with Alexander Marketing Services, a Michigan-based ad agency, recommends self-mailers for mailing to your in-house list of customers and prospects. "Your customers and prospects—people who already know you—are more likely to read whatever you send them than people who don't know you, such as names on outside rented lists," says Milroy. "Even though a self-mailer is obviously promotional material, your customers will probably read it, because it's from you. You don't have to overcome obstacles to readership."

If you mail regularly to customers and prospects, try switching to self-mailers on half your list and see how it works. Remember, there is less need to grab attention and persuade the reader to open the envelope as there is when mailing cold to prospects. You might create a standard letterhead and call your monthly mailings "sales bulletins" or "bargain-of-the-month announcements" or use some other title that indicates value.

Surprising Secrets

Some companies produce monthly self-mailers that resemble newsletters. Because they look like information, these quasi–newsletters get higher readership than regular direct mail packages.

Continuity

Jim Alexander, president of Alexander Marketing, has another suggestion. "Self-mailers are good for continuity in a series of mailings," Jim observes. In a series of mailings, for example, you might alternate between letters and self-mailers. In a self-promotional mailing series for his agency, Jim mailed a series of letter and nonletter packages over 18 months. Total response was 30 percent.

Short Message

Jim also recommends self-mailers for communicating a short, pithy message to readers. Perhaps you just want to announce a change of address, a price change, a special sale, or some other event that doesn't require a lot of explanation or embellishment. You can do it on the back of a postcard for much less than it costs to send a letter package.

Low-Response Offers

If your type of offer typically pulls a small response, using an expensive mailing package may not allow you to break even. Self-mailers can be an economical alternative. This is why they are so popular for seminar promotion. The typical seminar mailing pulls only $1/4$ to $1/2$ of one percent. But it can be profitable if promoted with a low-cost self-mailer.

The Elusive Target

In certain marketing situations, we are sometimes not sure who exactly is the right person to sell our product to. In such a case, a self-mailer may do better than a standard package for the simple reason that self-mailers get passed along from person to person until they end up on the right person's desk. Envelope packages, on the other hand, are usually thrown away by the recipient if he or she is not interested in the offer.

Some direct marketers actually encourage pass-along by printing specific instructions under the address label. A self-mailer for an IBM seminar on project planning and control contains these instructions:

> *ATTENTION MAIL ROOM PERSONNEL (OR ADDRESSEE):*
>
> *This announcement about important seminars should go to the person who works with the DP department, such as: manager of operations, manager of production, vice president of planning, administrative vice president, vice president of finance, etc. DP managers should also receive this announcement.*

For many offers, such as seminars, it's difficult to know who in an organization is the right prospect. The pass-along notice can help get your mailing into the right hands.

Mail Order

Double postcards and other inexpensive self-mailers are being used by publishers and mail-order companies to sell products directly through the mail. Because a double postcard is so much simpler to produce than the usual, lengthy, mail-order package, you can mail to many more potential buyers at a much lower cost. Even if overall response rate per thousand pieces mailed is lower, the self-mailer may actually generate more orders for the same amount of money spent.

However, self-mailers don't give you the opportunity to do as thorough a selling job as you can in a complete mail-order package. With a self-mailer, you have only one piece of paper to work with. A standard mailing package gives you a larger, more flexible forum for selling. For this reason, self-mailers aren't effective when used for complex offers or products that require a lot of explanation and selling.

If you are going to try to sell directly from a self-mailer, make sure the following conditions exist:

➤ The use and nature of the product are already familiar to the reader.

➤ The mechanism for ordering the product is greatly simplified.

➤ The price is low enough that the purchase of the product could be considered an "impulse" buy.

➤ The bargain is readily apparent.

For example, I recently received a small self-mailer offering me a discount price and free gift for subscribing to *Business Week*. Since I am already familiar with *Business Week*, I don't need to be sold on the magazine. Telling me the price, offering a gift, and giving me a reply element might be enough to get me to write a check.

On the other hand, if someone sent me the same simple self-mailer offering an accounting software package for my computer, I would not order based on price and a free gift. I would need to know a lot more about the product—how it works, what it can do for me—before placing an order. A traditional mailing package could provide that information better than a self-mailer could.

Large Volume

If you have an extremely large mailing list, and no way of separating the most likely prospects from so-so prospects, you may simply not be able to afford to send a full-blown mail package to the list. A self-mailer is the only economical way of reaching everyone on the list with news about your offer. On the other hand, if you can segment the list, and pick out your prime prospects, you might consider mailing a full-scale package to the better portion of the list. Then, use a self-mailer to cover the remainder.

Xerox did this with a mailing selling its Conference Copier, a *$3,295* piece of office equipment. (The Conference Copier is a blackboard that at the touch of a button produces a hard copy of whatever is written on the board.)

The cream of the list, consisting of 500 key corporate decision-makers, received a series of costly three-dimensional mailings announcing the product. The theme of the mailing was how communications in meetings have evolved from primitive writing tools to modern office technology (such as the Conference Copier). Mailings contained such elaborate objects as a miniature Rosetta stone and a quill pen and parchment.

The second group consisted of 15,000 intermediate-level prospects. They received a simpler mailing, which invited them to attend a demonstration of the product at a local hotel.

Then, to cover the rest of the list, Xerox sent out *200,000* four-color self-mailers offering a free 15-day trial of the product. The self-mailer has generated many sales.

"We have learned that it is possible to sell high-priced equipment directly by mail and phone," says Dick Martin, manager of advertising and sales promotion for Xerox Direct Marketing. "And we do."

The Secret of Self-Mailing Success

Why can the self-mailer work so well for large lists, especially when you cannot segment "hot" prospects from the rest of the list? Think about the people you are reaching, and you realize that people on the list fall into one of three categories:

Category 1: People who are not interested in your product and would not buy it for any reason.

This group also includes people who do not respond to direct mail for any offer. You are not going to get response from these people, no matter how good your mailing package. Yet you cannot identify them in advance. So it's cheaper to miss the mark with a self-mailer that costs a few pennies, rather than a full-blown piece costing 30 to 40 cents per package.

Most of the people on your list fall into the first category. As you know, in mail order, response rates of two percent are typical. Even with a dynamite mailing piece and a great offer, more than 90 percent of the people on the list are probably not going to respond.

Category 2: People who want your product and are predisposed to buy it.

There are certain people, again, you can't identify or separate in advance, but who are practically sitting around and *waiting* for your offer. Getting them to buy is a simple matter. *All you* have to do is say, "Here's the product, here's the price, here's the order form." They would, if you could identify them in advance, respond as well to a note scribbled on toilet paper as they would to a costly four-color mailing with all the bells and whistles.

Because they are ready to buy, a self-mailer tells them the basic information just as well as the full-blown package would. In fact, they probably won't bother reading a detailed letter or brochure, because they are already sold.

This group represents a profitable, but extremely small portion of the list—perhaps only 1 percent or less.

Category 3: People who are fence-sitters—another small, but important, group.

These people don't have a preference either way. They have not made up their minds and can be swayed either way. They are prime candidates for being sold through persuasive advertising.

Here, the full-scale mailing package, with its superior persuasive abilities, is much more effective than the self-mailer, which is limited to presenting a much-abbreviated sales pitch. If you could identify the fence-sitters in advance, and separate their names from your list, the full-scale mailing package would probably outpull the self-mailer dramatically.

Of course, if you were somehow able to separate the category 3 prospects (people who need to be sold and will buy if you can persuade them) you might send a separate, more elaborate package to them, as Xerox has done with its Conference Copier.

Marketing Tip

The self-mailer, in effect, allows you to "skim" the list and inexpensively convert a large percentage of the people in the second category—those who are in the mood to buy from you—into paying customers. "Your self-mailer 'skims the cream,' allowing you to reach prospects at low cost and capture those customers who are ready to buy," explains copywriter Richard Armstrong. "Fund raisers use this approach, sending simple, inexpensive packages to people who are predisposed to make a donation to an organization or cause." Richard notes that self-mailers are also widely used by magazine publishers and seminar companies to "skim" large lists of potential subscribers or attendees.

Writing an Attention-Grabbing Outer-Panel Headline

The first thing the reader sees is the headline, or teaser, on the outer panel of your self-mailer.

Unlike a direct mail package, which can be "disguised" to resemble personal mail, a self-mailer immediately identifies itself as advertising material. Therefore, you have no choice but to try to grab the reader's interest with the strongest headline you can.

Here are some headlines from actual self-mailers:

HERE'S A SIMPLE BUT POWERFUL INVESTING TECHNIQUE THAT ANYONE CAN UNDERSTAND

Comment: Some people will believe it; others will be immediately skeptical. But don't you at least want to open the mailer to find out what the story is?

NEED CHEMICAL OR BIOCHEMICAL INFORMATION IN A HURRY? START YOUR SEARCH HERE ...

Comment: If I needed chemical or biochemical information, I would read further.

STOP WATER DAMAGE IN YOUR BASEMENT BEFORE IT'S TOO LATE!

Comment: Fear is always a powerful motivator. Water damage in the basement is something homeowners do worry about. And the phrase "before it's too late" adds a real sense of urgency.

INTRODUCING THE WORLD'S FIRST ANTI-STATIC DISKETTES. And Verbatim Will Pay You To Try Them.

Comment: As a diskette user, I paid attention to this announcement. And the offer of payment for trying the product was a strong incentive to find out more.

The headline on the outside panel is usually what decides whether the reader will open your self-mailer or throw it away. Make sure your headline delivers the most powerful selling proposition possible. The headline should be immediately clear and in no way confusing or vague. And it should give the reader a powerful reason why he or she should look inside.

Marketing Tip

Set the headline of your self-mailer in large, bold type. A headline in large letters catches the eye of people who walk by and see your self-mailer on a table, desk, or the top of the pile in someone's in-basket. Also, put the headline on both the front and back panel. This way the selling proposition is visible whether the reader sees the mailing piece from the front or from the back.

Boosting Response Rates to Your Self-Mailers

Although self-mailers have traditionally been viewed negatively by direct marketing experts, their performance—especially in these days of declining response rates and rising paper costs—has become more competitive with conventional direct mail packages in recent years. The following list has some more tips to help boost your self-mailer's response rates:

➤ **Break copy up into sections.** Use subheads, bullets, borders, boxes, and color tints to segment and highlight various sections of your copy. Experience shows most people only skim self-mailers; few read them through thoroughly. One expert estimates that the maximum amount of reading time given to self-mailers is 90 seconds. The reader should be able to tell, at a glance, what you are selling and the key benefits of your offer.

➤ **Use short sections of copy.** The total length can be long or short, depending on product and offer. But each section of copy should be brief. And each copy block in the section should cover only one sales point or feature. When you want to discuss another sales point, insert a subhead and start a new section.

➤ **Use a bullet format.** Use numbered points, lists, and bullets to make your copy easy to scan. The reader should be able to pick out the selling points that interest him or her by quickly scanning the inside panels of your mailer. Don't bury key points in long-winded paragraphs of text.

➤ **Use visuals to identify the product or service.** If you're selling computer training, show pictures of people sitting at computer terminals. If you're selling a lawn-care service, show photographs of lush, green lawns. The pictures are a visual device that helps the reader instantly identify the nature of your offer and prepares the reader to listen to a sales pitch on the subject.

➤ **Highlight free offers.** If you are offering something free to people who respond, highlight the free offer in a separate block of copy. Use a subhead that says, "Yours FREE" or "Special FREE offer." Show a picture of the item you are giving away.

➤ **Highlight features.** List the features of your product or service in a separate copy block. Don't elaborate on them. A simple listing of the facts in bullet form will suffice. This is especially important in selling books, seminars, or technical equipment. You never know which feature of your product or which chapter in your book will appeal to a particular reader. By including a comprehensive listing, you are certain that you have at least mentioned everything a potential buyer might be looking for.

➤ **Use testimonials from satisfied customers.** These can be grouped together or sprinkled throughout the margins of the self-mailer. I prefer to put all testimonials in one section because I think it makes a greater impact.

➤ **Use a toll-free telephone number.** Highlight the phone number on the reply element and throughout the body of the mailer. You might even consider putting it on the cover; this may prompt calls from "impulse buyers" who are too busy or don't want to bother reading through your mailer.

➤ **Stress the offer.** Unless your mailing is designed merely to build awareness or make an announcement, you should tell readers exactly what you want them to do and what will happen when they do it. Are you offering more information, a free product sample, a free analysis or consultation? Make your offer clear and highlight it, both in the closing paragraphs of your copy and again in the reply card.

➤ **Make bargains apparent.** Highlight sale prices and discounts offered. Provide an incentive for immediate response, such as a cash discount or free gift. This discourages the readers from their natural inclination, which is to put the mailer aside or file it for later consideration—actions which seldom result in a sale for you.

➤ **Highlight the guarantee.** State your guarantee in a separate box highlighted with a certificate-like border or printed over a tint.

➤ **Put a place and date reference on the outer panel.** In a mailing inviting someone to attend a trade show, put the location and date of the show on the outer envelope. If you are advertising a sale, specify the month of the sale. There are two reasons for highlighting the date. First, it tells readers whether they can take advantage of your offer. (If they read that your seminar is on August 15, they can quickly check their calendars to see whether they can make it.) Second, it alerts them to the fact that they have limited time in which to act.

➤ **Consider using a series of self-mailers.** The price of self-mailers is so low that you can afford to mail your prospects a series of two or three mailings for the price of one full-scale, direct mail package. Try it.

➤ **Emphasize the reply element.** Use graphics that draw attention to the reply element. For example, print a heavy dashed line along the border where the reply card is to be torn off or cut out. Show a little picture of scissors along the dashed border. Use a certificate border or other design element to make the reply element look official and important. Give it a title that implies value, such as "FREE TRIAL RESERVATION CARD" or "FREE INFORMATION REQUEST FORM" Or "EXECUTIVE VIP INVITATION RESPONSE FORM."

The point is to make the reply element leap off the page when the reader opens your mailer. Unlike regular direct mail, in which the reply element is separate, in most self-mailers the reply element is attached to the main selling piece. Therefore, you must take extra pains to make it stand out. A reply card that isn't begging to be clipped and mailed is one that won't generate a lot of replies for you.

Try these tips on your next self-mailer and see whether your response rates get a lift as a result.

The Least You Need to Know

➤ Traditional direct mail packages usually outpull self-mailers, but not always. You have to test them.

➤ Self-mailers have a low cost per thousand, making them a viable format for offers with low profit margins or response rates.

➤ Self-mailers are obviously promotional in nature. You can't disguise them as regular mail, so your teaser and headline must be especially powerful to immediately grab the reader's attention.

➤ Make one panel of the self-mailer a tear-off business reply card the reader can detach and mail to request more information on your product or service.

➤ Small self-mailers with limited space for copy, such as postcards, work only when a lot of salesmanship is not required to get an order.

Chapter 10

Catalogs

In This Chapter

➤ Why consumers like catalog shopping

➤ Writing effective catalog copy

➤ Secrets of successful catalog marketers

➤ Capitalizing on catalog space

Catalogs are sales tools designed to generate either leads or direct sales. Catalogs are virtually the only direct response medium, aside from Web sites, that successfully sell multiple products.

Consumer mail-order catalogs for merchandise depend on clear pictures of attractive merchandise with descriptive copy highlighting features and benefits.

Some consumers are avid catalog shoppers. They like the ease, convenience, and privacy of shopping without leaving their home, They also like getting bargains or finding unique merchandise they don't see in stores.

Writing Powerful Catalog Copy

These fundamentals of catalog copywriting can add to the pulling power of your next catalog mailing:

➤ **Use colorful, descriptive language.** Product specification and technical talk don't move buyers to action. Persuasive language does. It's colorful and descriptive, painting a picture in the reader's mind of what the product can do for him or her.

➤ **Use precise language.** Beware of language that is overly colloquial or general. You want your writing to be conversational enough to win the reader over without becoming so vague that it doesn't communicate your meaning.

➤ **Use specific language.** Recently, a Hollywood screenwriter spoke about the secret to her success in writing major feature films. "Specifics sell. When you are abstract, no one pays attention." And so it is with the catalog writer—specifics sell, generalities don't.

➤ **Descriptive heads and breakers.** Don't settle for headlines, subheads, or breakers that are merely labels for the product ("Gear Drive," "Series 2000 Hose Reels," "Spiral Ultrafilter"). Instead, put some sell in your headlines. State a benefit. Promise to solve a problem. Mention the industries that can use the product. Tell its applications. Describe the range of sizes, colors, or models available. Give news about the product, or stress the ease of product evaluation and selection in your catalog.

➤ **Make it easy to order.** If your catalog is one of those monsters jammed with tables of product specsifications, be sure to explain these tables to your readers up front. Tell what's in the tables and how to use them to select the product. Give simple procedures and formulas to aid in product selection. Illustrate with a few examples. Also, make sure your reader knows who to call for assistance or order placement.

➤ **Make it easy to read.** Use short, familiar words. Use short sentences and short paragraphs with space between each. Stick in underlines, bullets, boldface type and breakers for emphasis. A catalog crammed with technical specifications and tiny type is a bore and a strain on the eyes. You can make your business catalog effective and yet fun and easy to read.

In addition to all these tips, make sure you stress the benefits. What the product does for the reader is more important than how it works, how you made it, who invented it, how long you've been making it, or how well it has sold.

Marketing Tip

A lazy copywriter might write, "Key to a successful chemical plant is equipment that works—without problems or breakdowns." The skilled copywriter will write, "Continuous internal lubricating sprays keep our gear drives well-oiled and virtually friction free." Give the particulars. Specifics sell.

Merchandising Your Catalog

Merchandising refers to the selection of merchandise and its organization in the catalog. What products will you feature? Which get the most space?

Although catalogs, unlike ads and solo direct mail packages, sell multiple items, they can't sell everything or anything. Catalogs sell groups of products related by application, style, function, category, or some other theme.

Specifically, here are 10 ways you can organize a catalog:

1. **By product demand.** You can organize your catalog by the sales that each product generates. Put your best sellers up front and give them a full or half-page each. Put slower-moving merchandise at the back of the book with a quarter page or less. Drop dead items altogether.

2. **By application.** Organizing according to application makes it easy for your customer to find the product that solves his or her problem. The disadvantage of this scheme is redundancy: Many products handle multiple applications and must be listed (or cross-referenced) in more than one section.

3. **By function.** A software catalog can be organized by the function each program performs: word processing, financial analysis, database management accounting, inventory, graphics, and communications. Obviously, this scheme won't work in a catalog where all the equipment performs the same task (for example, a catalog of pollution-control equipment or safety valves).

4. **By type of equipment.** This scheme is a natural for companies that carry multiple product lines. For example, Radio Shack's consumer electronics catalogs are organized by product

Marketing Tip

The organizational technique of organizing by product demand takes advantage of a principle first articulated by David Ogilvy (founder of ad agency Ogilvy & Mather): "Back your winners, and abandon your losers." It puts your promotional dollars where they'll do the most good. But be careful. In large or highly technical product catalogs, this organizational scheme may cause some confusion.

Marketing Tip

The technique of organizing your catalog by price is excellent for organizing a catalog of premiums and incentives. After all, an ad manager searching for a premium has a price range in mind, not necessarily a specific product. Make it easy for that person to find the $1 giveaways as well as the $50 executive gifts.

group: stereos on one page, car radios on the next, followed by VCRs, computers, and tape recorders.

5. **By "system hierarchy."** This technique organizes by the level at which each component fits into the overall system. This unit/sub-unit/sub-sub-unit approach is ideal for manufacturers who sell both complete systems and component parts.

6. **By price.** If you sell similar products that vary mainly in quality and price, you can organize your catalog by selling price. If your customers are concerned with savings, start with the cheapest items and work up. If you're selling to an upscale group willing to pay a premium for the deluxe model, start with high-priced versions and work down.

7. **By scarcity.** If your catalog features hard-to-get items, consider putting them up front—even on the cover. This makes your catalog more valuable by offering the buyer products he or she needs, but can't get anywhere else. Don't worry that these hard-to-find items aren't big sellers. When the customer knows your catalog has a stock of rare merchandise (and uses your catalog to order it), that customer will be more inclined to do other business with you, too.

8. **By size.** If you make one product and the basic selection criterion is size, it's natural to organize your catalog by size (dimensions, weight, horsepower, BTUs, or whatever). This is handy for catalogs with boilers, motors, shipping drums, envelopes, light bulbs, air conditioners, and other equipment selected mainly on a size basis.

9. **By model number.** If you've worked out a sensible numbering system for your product line, organize your catalog by model number. If there's a simple meaning to your numbering system, explain it at the start of the catalog. And don't rely solely on the model numbers to describe your products; include headings and descriptive text, as well.

10. **Alphabetically.** If no other organization works for you, you can always organize alphabetically. A large tool catalog can start with adjustable strap clamps and angle plates and end with wing nuts and wrenches. Or a vitamin catalog can start with vitamin A and end with zinc.

Now that you know the various ways you can organize your catalog, the next section will help you with marketing techniques.

Catalog Marketing Techniques That Work

Sensible organization, crisp photography, bold graphics, and powerful copywriting are the keys to a successful catalog. But experienced catalog marketers also use dozens of sales-boosting gimmicks that have little to do with the basics of salesmanship or good copywriting. All we know is that these tricks-of-the-trade work—and that's reason enough to use them. Here are nine that may be helpful to you:

1. **Include a letter.** To add a personal touch to your product catalog, write a "personal letter" to your customers from the president of your firm. The letter can be printed inside the front cover or run off on letterhead and bound into the catalog. You can use this type of letter to introduce the catalog, explain your ordering system, state a company philosophy, stress your dedication to service and quality, or alert the reader to new, discounted, and other special offerings. Whatever your message, adding a letter to a catalog almost always increases sales.

2. **Use bursts.** Often used by cereal makers to alert children to the prize inside the box, the "burst" (a star-shaped graphic with a copy line inside) also can draw a reader to special items within a catalog. Bursts can be used to highlight "price-off" deals, free trials, guarantees, and quantity discounts.

3. **Offer last-minute specials.** Insert into your catalog a separate sheet featuring items added to your product line or discounted at the last minute. Tell the customer these bargains were included just in time for mailing, but too late to print in the catalog. This insert generates additional sales because people like to be "in" on the latest developments.

4. **Put your catalog in a three-ring binder.** Expensive, but people won't throw out a hardback binder as readily as they would an ordinary paperback catalog. Your customer also is more likely to keep your binder on the shelf because it's too bulky for the filing cabinet. This is recommended only for catalogs aimed at purchasing agents and other corporate buyers.

5. **Include product samples.** You get two advantages. First, mailings that have three-dimensional objects inside are more likely to be opened than flat envelopes. Second,

Warning!

Make sure you use bursts and other special graphic techniques (such as underlining, colored or boldface type, fake handwriting) sparingly. Overuse dilutes their effect.

Marketing Tip

If your products can't be ordered by mail, include a "spec sheet." The spec sheet asks the prospect to provide key information on his or her applications (such as, size of plant, hours of operation, type of process, and so on). With this information in hand, you can specify the equipment the prospect needs and tell him or her what it will cost.

133

engineers and other technical buyers often like to play with product samples, keeping them handy on their desks or shelves.

6. **List your customers.** Include a list of a portion of the firms that have bought from you, whether you have 300 or 3,000 names. Seeing such a list in print makes a powerful impression on your customers. They'll think, "How can I go wrong buying from these guys? Everybody in the world does business with them."

7. **Include an order form.** Make it easy to fill out. Leave enough space for customers to write in needed information. Bind it into the catalog so it won't be lost or misplaced.

8. **Include a business reply envelope (BRE).** The BRE is a self-addressed, postage-paid envelope the prospect can use to mail the order form or spec sheet back to you. Practically every consumer catalog has a BRE. Most business catalogs don't. Business-to-business marketers think, "My prospect works in an office; he or she has a supply of envelopes and a postage meter handy. My prospect doesn't care about the cost of postage, and can have the secretary take care of addressing the envelope." This may be true, but a BRE still boosts the response rate in business catalogs. Why? Not because it saves the buyer the cost of postage, but because it flags readers to notice you'd like them to respond to your catalog.

9. **Make it an event.** Your buyers get a lot of catalogs in the mail, so the boredom factor is high. Anything you can do to make your catalog mailing special, to stand out from the crowd, will boost sales and inquiries.

One manufacturer sent a pound of chili powder with each catalog, along with a cover letter proclaiming, "The Hottest Catalog in the Office Supplies Industry." With a little imagination, you'll come up with an approach that fits your catalog and customers.

Catalog Selling Starts on the Cover

Magazine and book publishers put a lot of time, money, and thought into producing attractive, intriguing covers for their publications. They know that if a book or magazine has a dull or uninteresting cover, people won't pick it up and buy it. And so it is with your catalog. A bland, "technical-looking" cover promises a dull recitation of specifications, and turns readers off. A cover with an enticing illustration and a strong selling message arouses curiosity and prods readers to open the catalog.

Here are a few suggestions for spicing up your catalog cover:

1. **Sell the product line.** A catalog is really a "store in a mailbox." The more complete the store, the more likely the customer will return to do all his or her shopping—again and again. A comprehensive product line is a big selling point. Why not stress it on the cover?

2. **Sell solutions.** Sometimes, buyers aren't looking for specific products; they're looking for solutions to problems. You'll win them over if you show how your product solves the problem.

3. **Sell service.** Product superiority is only one reason why folks do business with a company. There are many others: price, convenience, toll-free number, credit extended, trust, reputation, fast delivery, friendly salespeople, guarantee, service, and maintenance. You can generate interest in your catalog by selling these services and intangibles—rather than the products—on the cover. Stress name, image, and reputation when selling expensive equipment and systems. Buyers want to know that you have the resources to support your system for years to come, and that you'll be around at least as long as the product lasts.

Marketing Tip

Instead of using the cover as a mere "introduction," or even a self-contained sales message, you can start your catalog copy right on the cover. This is an effective way to draw the reader inside the book. Naturally, this cover copy should feature your most popular or hard-to-get items.

4. **Put a letter on the cover.** Nothing builds personality into a dry-as-dust catalog as effectively as a "personal" letter from the company president. If getting people to warm up to you is your problem—and it might be with new customers or with customers who have been "burned" by your products in the past—you can address the reader directly with a letter right on the cover. The letter should be written in a warm, friendly, personal style.

5. **Add a wrapper.** Wrappers are used to "shout" a sales message. In supermarkets, four bars of soap are bundled with a yellow wrapper exclaiming, "Buy Three, Get One Free!" The same technique can be applied to catalog covers. If you've got a great new product, a price-off deal, or a major improvement in service, delivery, or reliability—announce it with a bright banner wrapped around the cover.

These techniques add variety to your catalog and help make key sales points, products, and offers stand out.

Ideas to Boost Your Catalog Sales

Catalog marketers pay thousands of dollars to consultants and ad agencies for marketing ideas, but you can get dozens of new ideas, *free* ideas, by studying catalogs produced by other firms. And getting these catalogs is easy. Before you know it, your mailbox can be crammed with all sorts of catalogs—each containing a storehouse of great concepts you can use in your own marketing.

First, get a stack of magazines. Next, request any free catalogs the advertisers offer in their ads. Here, for example, is just a sampling of the kinds of ideas, techniques, and tips you can find in catalogs you could receive this month:

1. **Use product photos that demonstrate the product.** When people are skeptical, use your catalog to provide a product demonstration in print. Take computer paper, for example. With cheap brands, it's hard to tear off the perforated edges and sometimes the printed document rips in the process. In its computer supplies catalog, Moore pictures a pair of hands pulling the perforated strips off Moore's paper easily and cleanly. Kudos to Moore—not many others have thought of a way to demonstrate a piece of paper in a photo.

2. **Add value to the product.** Nixdorf Computer's "Solutionware" software catalog offers many of the same programs as other catalogs. The difference? Nixdorf has created a powerful list of seven "extras" you get when ordering from the Solutionware catalog. This list of goodies appears at the beginning of the book and is repeated on the order form. The reader knows he or she gets more for the money when he or she buys programs through Solutionware, instead of another catalog or a computer store.

3. **Give the buyer free information.** Thomson's 83-page catalog of ball bearings and shafts includes 17 pages on how to select, size, and install the equipment. Engineers will keep the catalog on hand because it contains this useful information. By adding tips on maintenance, repair, troubleshooting, applications, and operation, you can increase demand for—and readership of—your catalog. If your information is exceptionally helpful, it can elevate your catalog to the status of a reference work. Customers will keep it on their shelves for years.

4. **Help the reader shop.** Compatibility is a big problem when selling computers and computer-related equipment and supplies. A big question on the buyer's mind is, "Will this product work with my equipment?" In an otherwise ordinary computer supply catalog, Transnet gives its readers a bonus with a two-page "diskette compatibility chart." The chart lists the major brands and models of microcomputers alphabetically, along with the specific make of floppy disk designed for each machine. Uncertainty and confusion are eliminated. The buyer can place an order with confidence.

5. **Show the *results* of using the product**, not just the product itself. Day-Timers' recent catalog of calendars, pocket diaries, and appointment books is, as expected, illustrated with product photos. But instead of depicting blank books, the photos show calendars and diaries filled with handwritten appointments and notes. This adds realism and believability to the catalog. It also shows how the calendar or diary could help organize the reader's life and schedule.

6. **Turn your catalog into a "shopping system."** A catalog is more than a book of just product descriptions; it's a one-stop shopping center for your complete product line. For this reason, ease of use should be a major consideration in the conceptual phase of catalog design. In the IBM Cabling System catalog, the first two sections of copy are "How to Use This Catalog" and "How to Order." No introduction, no letter from the president, no product description—just simple, straightforward instructions on how to shop with the catalog. Another nice touch is that the price list is printed opposite the order form, so the buyer doesn't have to search through the catalog to find prices for the items being ordered.

Although many prospects throw catalogs away shortly after they get them, yours may get saved for future reference if you implement the ideas above.

Checklist for Effective Catalog Copy

Before you approve your catalog copy and send it to the printer, you want to be sure that it's *right*. Getting it right involves more than the basics of spelling and punctuation. It involves more than avoiding superlatives and generalities about your merchandise.

Here's a handy checklist to help you review your present copy. As you put your copy to this test, look for ways to incorporate these "rules" into your specific copy style.

1. **Is your copy in the right order?** Is there a logical scheme to the presentation of copy points about your merchandise? And have you been faithful to this organizational principle throughout? Is this the best way to organize the items in your catalog? Would another method make more sense?

2. **Is it persuasive?** Does your copy begin with a strong selling message? Have you used copy to indicate your sales message on the catalog cover? Do individual headlines promise solutions to reader problems and draw the readers into the product descriptions? Does the body copy stress user benefits as well as technical features?

3. **Is it complete?** If the catalog is designed to generate direct sales, does it include all the information the reader needs to make a buying decision? Does it make it easy for the customer to specify and order the product? If the catalog is designed to generate leads, does it

Marketing Tip

Most catalogs have strict space limitations on product descriptions. Ask your designer how many characters or words can be written for each product, and stick to that count.

contain enough information to interest qualified prospects? Does it encourage them to take the next step in the buying process? Have you described products fully? Have you included all-important details, such as size, operating efficiency, model numbers, equipment compatibility, materials of construction, accessories, and options?

4. **Is it clear?** Is the copy understandable and easy to read? Are all technical terms defined, all abbreviations spelled out? Is it written at the reader's level of technical understanding?

5. **Is it consistent?** Have you been consistent in your use of logos, trademarks, spellings, abbreviations, punctuation, grammar, capitalization, units of measure, table and chart formats, layouts, copy style, and visuals?

6. **Is it accurate?** Is the copy technically accurate? Has an engineer checked all numbers, specifications, and calculations to make sure they are correct? Have you carefully proofread tables, lists, and other "fine print"? Do the photos show the current models or versions of your product? Have you matched the right photo to each item description?

7. **Is it interesting?** Is your catalog attractive to look at, lively and informative to read? Or is it boring? The typeface you choose for your copy, and the style of layout in which you print it, encourage the viewer's desire to read the copy.

8. **Is it believable?** Is the copy sincere or full of ballyhoo? Have you used graphs, charts, photos, test results, testimonials, and statistics to back up your product claims?

9. **Have you included all necessary "boilerplate" copy?** This includes areas such as: effective and expiration dates of prices, how-to-order information, notification of possible price changes, payment terms and methods, shipping and handling information, returns policy, quantity discounts, credit terms, sales tax, trademark information, copyright line, disclaimers, guarantees, warranties, and limits of vendor liability.

10. **Is it easy to place an order?** Does your copy explain how to order? Is there an order form? Is the order form easy to fill out? And is there enough space to write in the required information? Is a business reply envelope enclosed or attached to the order form?

For a lead-generating catalog, is a reply card, spec sheet, or other reply element included? Have you made clear to the reader what the next step is in the buying process? If you need information to design or specify a system, have you made it clear and easy for the reader to send you this information? If you want the reader to request more literature, have you described the literature and made it easy to send for these brochures?

If you think the words "easy" and "clear" have been overused in these guidelines, you're wrong. Everything you can do to make your message clearer and to keep ordering a simple process will be reflected in your bottom line.

Determining Your Proper Copy "Tone"

"Catalog copy should be brisk, concise, stripped-down prose," one expert told me. "Cram as many facts as you can. Use bullets, sentence fragments, word lists. Don't waste time with fancy sales talk; just pile on the description."

"Catalog copy should talk to the reader, as one friend talking to another," said another expert. "Use conversational copy to build sales arguments that compel the reader to buy the product. The sales pitch—not a pile of product specifications—is what counts."

Should catalog copy be in prose form or bullet form? Should it be clipped and concise or leisurely and conversational? Crammed with facts or written to entertain as well as educate? Though no two experts agree, here are some factors to help you determine the tone and style of your catalog copy:

1. **Space.** This, obviously, is the greatest limitation. If you allocate only a few column-inches per item, you've got to write lean, bare bones, telegraphic copy. Write the basic facts, and nothing more. If you have a full-page per item, you have the luxury of writing a conversational, ad-style sales pitch on each product.

2. **The product.** The copy style varies according to the type of product being sold. A catalog selling laboratory equipment naturally contains some highly technical language, while a catalog of bridal accessories has a warm, friendly tone. The complexity of the product also affects the length of the copy; you can say more about a microprocessor than you can about a stick of chewing gum.

3. **Purpose.** A catalog from which the customer can order directly must have complete product information and technical specifications. Copy has to be clear, comprehensive, and to the point. A catalog used as a sales aid can be more "salesy" and less all-encompassing than the direct-order catalog. A promotional catalog geared to whetting the customer's appetite will contain benefit-oriented headlines and

Warning!

Keep in mind, however, that length alone does not make copy better. Going on and on while saying nothing is not good selling copy. Also remember that a catalog can have as many pages and items as you are willing to pay for. So, if the product can't be adequately described in the space available, you should consider adding more pages.

Warning!

Remember, no matter what the purpose of your catalog, not giving enough merchandise details can be a sales deterrent. A promotional catalog lacking product facts may never stimulate the customer's interest.

subheads, highly sales-oriented copy, and sophisticated graphics to engage the reader's attention.

4. **The buyer.** How sophisticated is the buyer? How much does the buyer already know about the product and its uses? How much more does he or she want to know? A paint catalog aimed at professional painters need only describe the color, composition, and other features of the various paints. A catalog selling paint to the consumer would have to provide more of an education in the basics: types of paints available, pros and cons of each, applications best suited to each kind of paint, plus tips on how to apply paint.

5. **Buyer/seller relationship.** If your buyers are already sold on your firm and have a tradition of doing business with you, your catalog can be a simple, straightforward description of your latest offerings. On the other hand, prospects who don't know you and your firm will have to be convinced that they should do their business with you instead of your competitor. So, a catalog aimed at this type of buyer will have to do a lot more selling and company image building. The type of relationship you wish to have with your customers will also affect the tone you use (warm and friendly, formal and highly professional).

6. **Past experience.** Measure catalog results to your best ability and try to learn from past experience. If cutting copy from a full page of hard-selling prose to a terse quarter-page entry doesn't reduce sales, cut the copy and get more items per page. If increasing each item from a quarter page to a full page boosts sales 500 percent, consider expanding all entries to a full page and increasing the size of the catalog. Remember, every situation is different.

In the final analysis, the best way to set the tone and length of your copy is to know what works with your market and your customer.

Calculating Your Catalog Real Estate

Your catalog is like a piece of real estate—every square inch of space is valuable. And, every square inch of space should be considered selling space—from the front cover to the back cover. The space a product occupies on the printed page must pay its way.

That's why it is important to evaluate the results of your catalog based on some predetermined criteria. Some catalogers like to use traditional *square-inch analysis,* which is common to the industry. In square inch analysis, you divide dollars generated by an item by the size in square inches of the space it takes in the catalog. You can then determine which items are most profitable.

Another method is based on the calculation of a *hurdle rate* to measure the performance of any given product. The goal is to analyze merchandise performance. What sold? What didn't sell? How many pages should the catalog be? How much space should an item have? These are all important questions, which must be answered in order to maximize the earnings potential.

Before we discuss the actual hurdle-rate calculation, let's briefly discuss basic merchandising rules. The "one third, one third, one third" rule as it relates to merchandise in a catalog says that one third of the items in a catalog will be the real winners—the best sellers. One third will perform so-so. One third will be nonsellers.

Insider's Buzzwords

The **hurdle rate** is a method of determining which products are profitable and which should be eliminated from the catalog. **Square-inch analysis** is a method of determining the gross sales of a product in the catalog relative to the space it is given.

If you rank your sales by item, you will probably find this to be true for you, too. It is not brain surgery to realize that some items will sell better than others, and every item is not going to pass the hurdle rate. Obviously, the goal is to know what items to drop, how to adjust the selling space for the marginal items and how to select more top-selling items.

Another point worth mentioning has to do with pricing. Let's start by defining gross margin versus markup. Both mean different things, but the terms are used interchangeably much too often. A 50 percent gross margin represents a 100 percent markup. If our cost for a particular item is $50 and we plan to sell that item for $100, our gross margin is 50 percent and our markup is 100 percent. Many catalogers tend to price based on a formula, such as two times cost, which others feel is the wrong way to set prices.

What about setting prices based on the perceived value of a particular item instead? Remember, the price/value relationship is the perceived value of a product at a given price. When prices are set based on the perceived value of an item, the price is generally set higher, which increases the gross margin and helps improve the bottom line.

A third point has to do with changing out your merchandise from one printing to another. As a rule of thumb, a consumer catalog should change 25 to 30 percent of the merchandise every printing.

Let's assume you print four times annually: spring, summer, fall, and winter holiday. If you print four times a year, you most likely mail 12 times a year. For each printing, you probably are mailing three times—one seasonal drop with two re-mails every season.

For each and every item in the catalog, you can determine a hurdle rate in order to measure the performance of a product. For example, a hurdle rate of 100 percent represents the break-even point. Any item doing less than 100 percent is below break-even. Any item falling above 100 percent is performing better than break-even. Here is the way the calculation is determined.

Let's assume our catalog cost in the mail is $.8222 and our gross margin is 50 percent giving us a break-even point of $1.644 per catalog mailed ($.8222 divided by .50). Please keep in mind that this is a simplified version of the calculation. Customer returns and direct-order processing costs should also be included. Assuming the catalog includes 24 pages, our break-even point is $.0685 per page per catalog mailed.

Assume we mail 525,000 24-page catalogs. We first need to calculate a hurdle rate as follows: $.0685 × 24 pages = $1.644 per catalog. Now, $1.644 × 525,000 = $863,310 in sales required to break-even, and $863,310 ÷ by 24 pages = $35,962 per page needed to break even.

Let's assume we have an item that has 25 percent of a page with $9,500 of gross sales. For an item to occupy 25 percent of a page, it must do $8,991 ($35,962 × .25) in gross sales to do 100 percent of the hurdle rate.

If the item generated $9,500 in gross sales, the item did 1.057 percent (above break-even) of the hurdle rate ($9,500 ÷ $8,991). On the other hand, if the item generated $8,000 in gross sales, it did 88.9 percent (below break-even) of the hurdle rate.

By calculating the hurdle rate, it is easy to separate the winners from the losers at a glance. Obviously, the higher the percentage, the stronger the item. The opposite of this is also true. The products with low hurdle rates will obviously need to be discontinued. By focusing on those items, which fall within the 90 percent hurdle rate zone, you might be able to help improve the results by simply adjusting the amount of selling space, combining an item with another item, or by doing something else. These marginal items are worthy of more attention. You will want to do everything possible to push these products over the hurdle rate next time.

We should also consider the basic merchandising requirements to help make these calculations and numbers work. For example, are you offering an adequate selection of merchandise—in both depth and breadth—to your customers? In general, you should be offering a minimum of 250 to 300 distinct products. If your product selection is too narrow, consumer interest will decline and will lower your response rates.

By calculating a hurdle rate, you will be able to analyze your merchandising results most effectively. This is a constant, on-going, and never-ending process. It's basic. It's necessary. And, it is important to the success of any catalog. I hope your catalog can make the grade, too!

The Least You Need to Know

➤ Catalog buyers want offers they cannot get in stores. They also like the convenience of shopping from home without driving to a mall.

➤ Catalogs can sell many different products, but the products must somehow be logically related.

➤ You can use hurdle rates and square-inch analysis to determine whether items in your catalog are profitable and which are the most profitable.

➤ Don't let personal preferences—especially fondness for a particular product—cloud your judgment. If square-inch or hurdle-rate analysis shows a loser, throw it out.

Chapter 11

Profits from Postcard Decks

In This Chapter

➤ Do postcard decks work?

➤ Best offers to use in card decks

➤ Selecting the right deck

➤ Fundamentals of card design

Years ago, when I worked as the advertising manager for an industrial manufacturer, a product manager asked me to create a full-page advertisement for a new product. "And oh, yes," he added, at the end of our meeting, "I'll also want to run a postcard, too."

I discovered that the magazine in which our ad would run, *Chemical Engineering,* also published a "card deck"—something I'd never heard of before. Frankly, I was unenthusiastic about the deck. Who, I wondered, would want to leaf through a bunch of postcard advertisements, especially when they already received *Chemical Engineering* magazine?

I paid our ad agency to create a brilliant ad. And slapped together the postcard without too much fuss and bother—almost as an afterthought. The ad ran and the postcard ran, and the results shocked me. The full-page ad, which cost over $2,500 to produce and more than $4,000 per insertion, pulled maybe a hundred or so inquiries. But the postcard, which cost less than $300 to produce and approximately $1,000 or so to run, generated more than 500 replies! At this point I began to think, "These postcard decks are worth looking into!" And maybe you're saying the same thing now, also. This is the topic if the chapter, so keep reading to find out how you can use them, too.

What Is a Postcard Deck?

Postcard decks are packs of loose postcards, sealed in a paper, poly (clear plastic) or foil wrapper, and distributed to a mailing list of prospects who, we hope, will be interested in our product, as well as the products and services of the other companies advertised on the rest of the cards. Almost all postcard decks are published by magazine publishers, sent to their subscribers, and contain cards from many different advertisers who pay to be in the deck. Only a few card decks are published by a single advertiser; those that are usually contain cards only for that advertiser, each on a different product.

Although I've seen postcard decks with as few as a dozen cards and as many as a hundred, the average deck probably contains 40 to 60 separate cards. The typical card, which measures $3^1/_2$ by $5^3/_8$ inches, is black and white, although larger folded formats and color cards are available.

Marketing Tip

A few publishers mail decks of postcards bound into booklet form. An example of this is the Executive Mart, published by Hamel Publishing Company, Inc. However, the majority of those published are loose decks.

The front of the card, or *mailing side,* usually contains the advertiser's address, business reply imprint and permit number, so that when the prospect drops it in the mail, the card will be returned directly to them. (You need to get a permit number from the post office; otherwise, they will not process your reply mail.)

The back of the card, or *advertising side,* generally contains a miniature ad. In this tiny space, you must fit a headline, some brief copy, and, if appropriate, a visual. You must also leave a space for the prospect to write in name, address, company, and phone number.

Because the space is so limited, copy must be brief and visuals small. There is no room for complex diagrams or explanations or a detailed listing of features. You have to quickly state your offer, highlight a few key benefits, and prod the reader to respond.

Advertising in Postcard Decks

The first step to advertising in postcard decks is to locate ones that are right for your offer. This process is similar to choosing which magazines to advertise in. The difference is that there are only 600 or so postcard decks that accept outside postcards, while there are more than 6,000 magazines that accept ads.

Also, all postcards in a deck are basically the same size and format, while magazines offer a greater variety of sizes and shapes to choose from. This makes it a little easier to plan postcard advertising. In addition, most postcard decks are mailed only three times a year. This limited mailing schedule, combined with the limited number of decks being published, makes it nearly impossible to rely on postcard decks as your *sole* method of direct marketing.

So, despite the low cost of postcard decks, deck advertising will only be part of your overall effort. You will have to supplement postcard decks with other inquiry and sale-generating activities, such as direct mail and print advertising.

Selecting the Right Postcard Decks

A good place to start is with postcard decks you receive or know about. Take a look at the postcards in these decks. Do they seem to be aimed at the market you are trying to reach? Are their postcards advertising products similar to yours? Also ask your customers which postcard decks they receive.

One alternative to running a postcard in an existing deck is to create your own deck and mail it to your customers and prospects. John Wiley, a book publisher, regularly mails decks featuring business and technical books. The Wiley decks feature only Wiley books and Wiley does not accept outside advertising.

If you have many related products and a large mailing list, creating your own postcard deck may be an option for you. But for most of us, with limited product lines and budgets, it is more likely that we will run postcards in one or more of the existing decks.

Marketing Tip

SRDS (Standard Rate and Data Service; phone 847–375-5000) publishes a directory of postcard decks and their publishers. The listings include the name of the deck, description, price to insert a card, publication schedule, and contact information. SRDS is often available in the reference rooms of larger libraries.

Reviewing Postcard Market Segments

First and foremost, find postcard decks that are mailed to people who are likely to be potential prospects for your product. If you advertise in a magazine, for example, you might also want to run a postcard in that magazine's card deck, if it has one. There's a possibility that if people receiving the deck have read your ad in their magazine, response to your postcard may go up.

Postcards are segmented by markets in one of three different ways:

➤ **Industry.** Many postcard decks are aimed at specific industries, such as chemical processing, pulp and paper, food processing, and pollution control. Most of these are published by companies that also publish trade journals in these fields.

➤ **Affinity.** A second category is postcard decks aimed at people with similar interests, such as investors or personal computer users.

➤ **Geographic.** Perhaps the fastest-growing segment of the postcard deck industry is card packs aimed at businesses within a specific geographic market region, such as Boston, New York, Atlanta, Chicago, Houston, Los Angeles, San Francisco, or Miami. An example is Business-to-Business, Inc., which publishes a card deck mailed three times a year to 75,000 prospects in Manhattan.

Once you've found the card decks that reach your industry—you have to determine which one is the best buy—in other words, which card deck reaches the most prospects for the lowest cost?

Determining Card Deck Advertising Costs

One important measure is cost per thousand, which is how much it costs to reach one thousand prospects with your message. The formula is:

Cost of advertising in the card deck × 1,000 ÷ Number of people card deck is mailed to = Cost per thousand

Let's say a publisher with a deck mailed to 32,000 business executives then charges advertisers $1,200 to run a card in the deck. The cost per thousand is:

$1,200 × 1,000 ÷ 32,000 = $37.50 per thousand

To put it another way, the cost per contact—the amount of money you have to spend to put your postcard in the hands of one prospect—is:

$37.50 cost per thousand ÷ 1,000 = $0.0375 per contact

Thus, using this card deck, you can send a postcard mailing to your prospects for about four cents per person. This is about 10 times less expensive than a regular direct mail package.

The cost per contact, however, tells you only how much you'll have to spend to reach people who receive the card deck. It does not tell you whether they will read your postcard. It also does not tell you whether they will respond to your offer.

Measuring Card Deck Results

The real measure of any card deck is how many leads or sales it produces for you, and at what expense. But this varies widely based on several factors, including whether you are running in the right deck and the quality of the mailing list receiving the deck. As with anything else, there are good card decks and not-so-good decks. Some will perform for you, others won't. Of course, you can't know how well your card will work in a particular deck until you test it.

After running your postcard in a deck, count the number of sales or leads you receive. Then divide the cost of advertising in the deck by the volume or orders or leads generated. This gives you cost per lead (or cost per sale), an accurate yardstick by which to measure performance of the deck.

Cost of advertising in the deck ÷ Number of leads generated = Cost per lead

Cost of advertising in the deck ÷ Number of orders received = Cost per sale

Total sales generated – Cost of advertising = Profit

How many responses will you receive? It depends on whether your product and offer appeal to most of the people receiving the deck or just a fraction of them. And some decks are more responsive than others. You can expect a response of between $1/4$ and 1 percent in returned cards and telephone inquiries—all within a month.

Once you know which card decks generate the most leads or sales per dollar, card-deck success becomes a matter of refining and testing different headlines, visuals, and layouts to come up with the postcard that will pull the most response for you every time you run it.

Items you might consider testing include price, headline, offer (free gift versus no free gift), benefit headline versus free-booklet headline, one-color versus two-color cards, one-color versus four-color, visual versus no visual, or format (number of panels, address block on the front of the card versus on the back of the card).

Marketing Tip

Many card decks allow "split testing," which means the publisher will mail two versions of your card (or two different cards), one to each half of their mailing list. This provides an easy, inexpensive means of testing card A versus card B.

Don't Most People Just Throw Postcard Decks Away?

People read card decks the way you read them: quickly. I picture my prospects flipping through the deck with a wastebasket positioned between their knees.

As quickly as they can, they go through the deck, pitching cards into the trash. After all, they are busy. They have many other things to do. At best, they view reading postcard decks as a necessary evil—something they would avoid altogether except for the fact that they occasionally find an interesting or helpful offer or two buried in with the rest of the cards. One study estimates that the average prospect spends one minute going through the entire deck, using approximately one second per card. Others say that readers spend up to three seconds scanning each card.

The point is that your card is glanced at, not studied in detail. Just as a highway billboard has only five seconds to gain attention and deliver a message before drivers speed by it, a postcard has but a few seconds to catch the reader's eye and say, "Hey, stop a minute. Here's something worth paying attention to." The studies also show that people do not stop and read cards of interest. Rather, they pick out those cards that get their attention and set them aside for later reading.

The most important factor in getting attention as people scan cards is a headline that leaps off the card and grabs the reader. A good visual can also help, especially if it is a picture of something the reader can identify with. Body copy is less important, although some is needed to provide supporting evidence for those readers who like to know a little more about a product before responding. And you need to use a portion of the card as a coupon on which the reader can fill in name, address, and phone.

Since the headline is the most crucial element, let's take a closer look at some successful card deck headlines and how to write one for your offer.

Writing Your Postcard's Headline

Unlike an advertisement, which seeks to build image or awareness over an extended period of time, the postcard headline's main mission is to grab attention so that the reader pauses long enough to decide to remove the card from the deck for immediate response or later consideration.

There are a number of different approaches you can take when writing postcard headlines, the following sections will discuss them.

Mention a Free Offer

The word "free" is pure magic in postcard headlines. I'm sure there are a large number of people who are attracted to postcard decks because of the numerous free offers. (I'm one of them! I love to get things for free.) If you give away a free gift, a free product sample, or a free booklet, stress the free offer (not the product itself) in your headline and body copy. Show a picture of the free sample, gift, or booklet—not the product. Sell your offer, not the product.

Provide a Benefit Headline

Another powerful technique is to state the key benefit of your product in a crisp, to-the-point headline. This benefit can be a low price, cost savings, a wealth-building opportunity, increased efficiency, or the ability to do something you couldn't do without the product.

Advertising writers sometimes write vague or coy headlines. The purpose is to arouse curiosity, then explain the payoff in the body copy. But in postcards you don't have this luxury, because body copy is limited to a few well-chosen sentences. When writing a post-card headline, make your headline as direct, specific, and clear as possible. Try to tell the whole story in the headline. Leave nothing to imagination.

Surprising Secrets

Don't worry about whether your headline is similar in content and style to another card in the deck. People do not sit and comparison-shop between one postcard and another. Rather, they respond to any card in the deck that has a headline and offer that appeals to them. If your main benefit is saving time and money, stress time and money savings in your headline. If you offer a free booklet, say "free booklet" in the headline.

Ask a Question

A proven response-getter in print advertising and direct mail is to ask a provocative question in the headline. You don't see this technique applied much in postcards, but I suspect it would work well. The key is to ask a question that promises a benefit, a reward for reading the postcard, or arouses curiosity on the part of the reader. For example: "Moving your offices?" (asked by Relocation Management Systems); or "Printing crisis? We can help!" (asked by Penn Copy Center).

Use a Command Headline

A classic example of a command headline is Exxon's famous slogan, "Put a Tiger in Your Tank." Command headlines generate action by literally telling the reader what to do. Another example from a recent print ad: "Buy Scott Towels." This type of headline is a logical choice for postcards, because our main job is to tell (or rather persuade) the reader to mail our card back to us.

Use a News Headline

Postcard decks bring people news of new products, new ideas, and new ways to save time and money. As with other forms of direct response, postcards are especially successful when offering products or information that the reader perceives they cannot get elsewhere.

If your product or idea is new, stress the newsy aspect in your headline. You can do this by using such words as *new, discover, announcing, now, it's here, at last,* and *just arrived.* For example: "Announcing a breakthrough" (from Best Power Technology).

Use Mail-Order Headlines

When going after sales rather than leads, many advertisers state the offer directly in the headline. This includes the name of the product, the price, the discount being offered, and, if space allows, a statement summarizing the key product benefit. In selling directly from a postcard, it pays to be direct. Here, subtlety is the enemy of sales. For example: "Save *50%* on ESQUIRE and get this important book—*A Man's Body*—Free!" (from *Esquire* magazine).

Warning!

Avoid headlines that are general, vague, boastful, or involve broad claims or wordplay. Ineffective in ordinary print ads, these say-nothing headlines can dramatically depress response in a postcard deck. Here are a couple actual examples:

"A new breed of flexibility ...." Says nothing and could apply to virtually any product.

"Copier uptime. It's part technology, part people, and all Kodak." This might be appropriate for a corporate brochure or image campaign, but not for a response-getting postcard. Where's the hook?

Writing the Body Copy

Because of their small size, postcard decks are strictly a short-copy medium. Here are some copywriting tips to guide you:

➤ **Keep it short.** You don't have much room on a 3¹/₂-by-5³/₈–inch postcard panel. Copy must be brief and to the point. Maximum length is approximately 100 to 150 words.

➤ **Design your copy.** Do a rough layout showing how your copy should be positioned on the card. Don't just write copy in ordinary paragraph format. Use headlines, subheads, captions, bullets, bursts, arrows, underlining, boldface type, and graphic devices to highlight various components of your copy.

➤ **Get to the promise.** The promise of the headline should be fulfilled in the body copy—immediately. Your first few sentences should immediately explain, elaborate on, and support the promise made in the headline.

➤ **Stress benefits, not features.** Highlight the benefits of what you are selling. For example, if you are selling a machine that folds papers into booklets, don't say, "Stainless steel hopper, 10-inches wide." Say, "Makes up to 600 booklets per hour." Of course, if you are after a direct sale instead of a lead, you have to give a description of exactly what the reader is getting for his or her money, but these features should be secondary to a discussion of the benefits of your product or offer. If you are selling a simple product the reader is already familiar with, such as office supplies, stress the benefits of your offer, rather than the product itself. Talk about your low price, volume discount, free catalog, or fast shipment.

➤ **Include a fill-in blank.** Between a quarter and a third of the advertising side of the card is taken up by a name-and-address block. In this tiny space, prospects fill in their name and address, answer any questions you've asked, and might also check off a box to indicate their area or level of interest. In addition to bringing back an inquiry or order, the

Warning!

Don't use an overly verbose or descriptive style. Write in terse, almost clipped prose. Make sure each sentence gives the reader a new piece of information; you don't have room to repeat yourself. Avoid transitional phrases, warm-up paragraphs, and other stylistic habits that waste words.

Marketing Tip

Postcards are inadequate for explaining complex products and concepts. If the reader needs a basic education in your product before he or she can make a buying decision, postcards may not work well for you. Of course, you can write a booklet or report presenting the background information, then offer it free through a postcard.

name-and-address block can also be used to ask questions for market research purposes or to prequalify prospects. For instance, a card offering free information on computer security might ask the prospects how many computers they have or how many people have access to their system. If you use your card for survey purposes or to screen leads, ask only one or two questions and keep it simple. Don't ask too many questions or you'll discourage readers from responding.

➤ **Include instructions.** Even though it may seem obvious, don't assume the reader knows what to do with your card. Include instructions on what to do next. Copy should tell the reader, "For more information, fill out the space below and mail this card today." A card that doesn't ask for the order just sits flat in the pack. Tell the reader what to do.

Since most readers scan card decks and give each card a brief look before making the decision to toss or read it, you want to catch their eye—and that's where pictures can help. But in such a tiny space, what can you show to possibly capture their interest?

Illustrating Your Postcard

Because you need room for a headline, copy, and a name-and-address block, the space for your visual is extremely limited, usually no more than $2\frac{1}{2}$ inches wide by $1\frac{1}{2}$ inches high. Most postcards are illustrated with either a picture of the product or, if you are offering free information, a picture of the front cover of your free booklet, catalog, or brochure.

Take a look at some postcard decks. The quality of photo reproduction may not match a glossy magazine or annual report, but it's much sharper than a newspaper, so it pays to use good-quality photographs in your card. Diagrams, charts, graphs, schematics, and other complex visuals do not work well in postcard decks. The reason is that the original must be reduced in size to fit the space, rendering fine detail unreadable.

If you are advertising a cassette program or book, and the author is well known to people in the field, you might increase response by showing a photo of the author in addition to the cover of the book or cassette album.

Although some advertisers are successful with postcards that are all copy, I recommend that you include a visual. The picture gives the postcard the graphic appeal needed to catch the reader's eye as he or she rapidly flips through the card deck.

Product photos already taken for slide presentations, print advertisement, or press releases are usually ideal for card-deck advertising. Many advertisers routinely create postcard versions of all of their product ads using the same visual plus an abbreviated version of the ad headline and copy.

The Least You Need to Know

➤ Card decks allow you to direct-market to your prospects at a fraction of the cost of a regular direct mail package.

➤ Your space on a postcard is limited, so you must get to the point quickly.

➤ Sell the offer—a free catalog, free demo disk—not the product.

➤ Make sure there is ample room for the prospect to write in his name and address when responding to you.

➤ Use business reply cards. Do not require the prospect to affix postage.

Chapter 12

Alternative Media

In This Chapter

➤ Deciding to choose alternative media

➤ Knowing your alternative media options

➤ Choosing the package inserts format

➤ Package insert production guidelines

➤ Billboards and transit advertising

"Alternative media" refer to nonmainstream methods of direct marketing. It is of course no surprise that direct marketers rely primarily on the use of outside rented names to grow their house files. Certainly, direct mail is the most proven and the fastest way to generate new buyers.

But there are other cost-effective prospecting methods that can be used to generate new buyers. This chapter will cover some of the different types of alternative media that you might want to consider testing.

Why Alternative Media?

It is so easy to stick with the use of outside rented names and databases for new buyers. Therefore, why should a direct marketer consider alternative methods, which take time to set up and cost money to implement?

To begin with, using alternative media can expand your universe of prospects. Through the use of alternative methods of prospecting, a marketer can identify and attract a wider variety of prospects not always found on an outside rented list. In other words, the use of alternative media can generate new mail-order buyers. The marketer is afforded the opportunity to go beyond the current response list universe to generate new mail-order buyers.

The life-time value of a new buyer generated from an alternative prospecting method can be longer than that of a new buyer generated from a rented list. Obviously, this is not always the case, but the point is that different methods of prospecting do yield differences in the life-time value of the acquired buyer. It is not always the initial conversion rate that should be considered but the value of the name over time—its life-time value.

In addition, alternative methods of prospecting, providing you find the right method, can reduce your cost to acquire a new buyer. Direct marketers are always looking for ways to reduce their cost of acquiring a new buyer.

How much you can afford to spend for a new buyer depends to a large degree on the life-time value of the name being acquired. For example, a cataloger might be able to spend more up front to obtain a new buyer providing there is a reasonable payback in, say, less than 12 months. We tend to rush to judgment with regard to the results from the initial campaign without considering how much a new buyer will return over time.

Alternative Media Options

There are several alternate media that can be effective for some direct marketers. Pricing for alternative media is much more negotiable than standard-list rental pricing. Discounts will be given for volume commitments providing the broker or mailer makes the request. The following sections describe some alternative media sources for you to consider.

Bind-In and Blow-In Programs

Insertspromoting your offer can be placed directly into a catalog. A blow-in is loose and a bind-in is stapled into the catalog. The cost ranges from $30 to $35 per thousand. This distribution has been used in big numbers for years by horticultural marketers (a flier promoting a gardening magazine or a lawn tool is bound into a flower catalog).

Many catalogs are now beginning to offer blow-in space, traditional advertising space, and business reply card (printed three-up to make a page) space in their catalogs to further serve the direct response advertiser. Blow-ins can run as little as half the price of package inserts mailed to the same customers.

Free-Standing Inserts

These are cooperative, full-color, multipage flyers featuring coupons, refunds, sweepstakes, and other promotional offers that are distributed in Sunday newspapers. They reach the mass markets with a low cost of $4 to $8 per thousand.

Package Inserts

In a package insert program, you create a small promotional insert advertising one or more of your products. You then pay other companies to stuff these inserts into the boxes in which they ship their merchandise.

Package insert programs are an ideal way to reach consumers who are known to be responsive to mail-order offers. The insert is delivered to the prospect, for example, in a box containing a shirt the prospect ordered from a catalog. Naturally, the product-shipment types vary dramatically: catalog generated versus space generated, continuity or club oriented, business-to-business versus consumer.

Correspondingly, the responses to the outside insert will also vary. The going rate for package inserts is still an average of $50 per thousand. The number of outside inserts varies from four to eight. Generally, only noncompetitive pieces are included together.

If one goes heavily into a club or *continuity-oriented program,* the rate of duplication needs to be monitored. The response rates also vary significantly depending on a number of other variables: whether the insert is generating a lead or producing an order, the average ticket price of the items being sold, the size of insert, and so on.

A large-ticket item may be satisfied with two responses per thousand, whereas lead-generating devices having a strong affinity between the insert and the products being delivered would require and will produce responses from 2 to 5 percent.

The current universe approaches half a billion and includes distributors like Arizona Mail Order, America Online, and Fingerhut. There are also scores of distributors and specialty companies like Albert Constantine (woodworking), Atlas Pen & Pencil, and Performance Diver.

Package insert programs reach proven mail-order buyers. Costs range from $50 to $65 per thousand (plus the cost of the printed piece).

> **Insider's Buzzwords**
>
> A **continuity-oriented program** is an offer where the consumer is shipped a new item in a series (videotapes, foods, books) for inspection, usually every month. Example: Book of the Month Club. The customer can buy that month's item or return it and owe nothing. He can usually cancel at any time without penalty or further obligation.

Co-Op Mailings

This category, by definition, presents a group of noncompetitive advertisers mailing to a common market in the same envelope. An example is Val-Pack, which reaches 50 million households every year.

Co-ops represent large numbers (up to 40 million) in a single drop, can usually provide demographic selectivity and often provide demographic selections. Although responses are not as high as those generally received from other types of packages, co-ops are priced more competitively, at an average of $15 per thousand.

Other types of co-ops also exist which include mail order and direct response offers, but instead of the package-goods coupons, local coupons are included (for example, dry cleaner, ice cream shop, bank, gas station). These programs are usually sold on a local level by neighborhood franchises. Good examples include SuperCoups (mostly New England), Money Mailer, and of course Val-Pak.

Most co-ops mail in a #10 envelope format, but some mail in a 6-by 9-inch envelope. Circulation exceeds 100 million per quarter. Typically, there are 20 to 30 individual pieces in a co-op mailing package. There are some demographic and geographic selections available to the mailer. With regard to co-ops, it is important to know the list source of the prospect names being mailed. Costs vary anywhere from $10 to $40 per thousand.

Success Story

Although most consumers are hard-pressed to name a mailing list broker or even tell you what a list broker is, many are aware of Val-Pak. According to a study from Elrick & Lavidge, a research firm, Val-Pak has the highest brand awareness among consumers of any direct mail brand.

Statement Stuffers

A statement stuffer or insert program is one in which your promotional offer rides along in the statement or invoice from another company. These inserts are distributed via banks, retail, oil companies, utility companies, cable television companies, and others and carry an implied endorsement from the sender.

Outside inserts are generally limited to one or two because statements get mailed first class (high percentage of deliverability) and additional outside advertising would bump them into the next postal class. The inserts are usually distributed in small envelopes so your insert needs to be no larger than $3^{1}/_{2}$ by $6^{1}/_{2}$ inches to fit. Response tends to be strong. The average price is running $45 per thousand.

Take-Ones

Take-ones are offered to shoppers, usually in consumer information centers in super-markets. These are ads that are placed in the information-center display, and con-sumers are drawn to topics of interest. The costs range from $2.50 to $10 per thousand.

If you use transit advertising (refer to the later section in this chapter, "Transit Advertising: Ads on the Move"), we recommend the use of take-ones to increase in-quiries—attach them directly to the transit ads and point-of-purchase displays. The ad copy should urge the reader to send for a free brochure or other literature using one of the reply cards. On the card, which is usually postage-paid and addressed to the advertiser, the reader can fill in his or her name, address, phone number, and request. "Take-ones" are so-named because they often bear the headline "FREE: TAKE ONE!"—urging transit riders to do just that.

Ride-Alongs

Some companies will allow another company to advertise in the mailing they make to their own customers. This is called a ride-along promotion. The inserts are gener-ally poly-bagged and carried on the outside of the other companies promotional material. Costs range from $40 to $70 per thousand.

In this instance, a company mails a catalog, circular, or announcement to its cus-tomer base and allows outside advertising to ride along. An advertiser can count on this method of distribution because the company doing the mailing has a vested in-terest in getting out their own promotional pieces.

Companies like Columbia House and BMG dominate this category and offer regular mailings in blocks of two to six million to their club members. An advertiser's re-sponse from this category is strong and comparable to package inserts. Outside insert programs typically contain four to six inserts per mailing. Response curves are similar to those of direct mail.

Sampling Program

This method of insertion offers a variety of "goody bags" distributed free to a specific market, like college students, new mothers, and other special interest groups. Samples can be mailed to the consumer's residence or distributed at retail outlets such as su-permarkets.

Inserts accompany product samples and coupons. Packages are usually given out "free" in high traffic situations, such as busy malls or fairs. Pricing ranges from $25 per thousand to $40 per thousand. Shelf life can be difficult to pinpoint.

Getting Started in Package Inserts

If you've never tested package inserts before, the requirements may seem daunting to you. But it's really not rocket science. Following is a list of 10 suggestions for getting involved in the lucrative package insert/co-op field:

1. **Use a broker.** Don't do it yourself. It's tough and unnecessary. "We know all the answers," says Leon Henry, who is perhaps the industry's leading alternative media broker. "We've been there with over a billion inserts for nearly every conceivable company and industry and we (or any reputable broker) will tell you what's good for your product … and what you should avoid."

2. **Test—but test smart.** Some mailers test for "test's sake," which unfortunately means when they are through they don't know what and why they tested. It is axiomatic that you test in the insert market because of its varied nature. But testing smart means testing with a proven insert wherever possible. Test statistically reliable numbers relative to your offer, test with no more than two copy approaches. Test as many programs initially as your budget allows.

3. **Test new programs.** Along with the tried-and-true co-op mailers such as Arizona Mail Order, Columbia House, Viking Office Products, and Fingerhut, you want to test the new ones such as Bedford Fair, PC Mall, and MCI WorldCom. Make some room for the tried and true but don't neglect those that are new today and tomorrow.

4. **Use one insert.** Look at all the smart mailers and you will see that they have been going out with one insert format for years. Why one? Because you want to test the medium and not the message. If you are confident with your message, then each test of the medium (the various package insert programs you go into) will be clear in its results.

5. **Ask questions.** Inquire about the source of the customers, number of year in business, other inserters that have used and continued with the program, the time that it takes for your inserts to be distributed, and so on. The more you ask, the better informed you will be. The better informed, the more likely you will be successful.

6. **Key code inserts by program.** You'd be surprised how many sophisticated mailers forget to key in such a way that when the distribution takes too long, they can't research how and when their inserts were distributed. For example, if the distribution will take three months, it makes sense to key your inserts in such a way that you can tell when the first month is completed and so forth. The small extra expense with the printer can save you headaches and cut your aspirin bill.

7. **Choose the right resources to help you.** Just as you should be using a knowledgeable broker, you should have the right printer, direct mail consultant, and, where necessary, the correct mailing house working for you. Ask for competitive bids from everyone that you use.

162

8. **Ask for proof of receipt and delivery.** Your broker should obtain an insert sample upon receipt and upon completion and keep it on file. Your printer should have receipt of delivery. Your inserts should be boxed professionally and clearly marked by the printer. (The insides of some of the co-op warehouses dwarf the imagination and your insert can get lost.)

9. **Pay the right price.** Because of the variety of insert programs, you want to pick the best for your offer and then decide on the right ones based upon the top price you are willing to pay. After you've received the test results, there's plenty of time to negotiate for price reduction. As with other media, prices change with volume and frequency. After all, the worst your broker can report is that the sponsor won't budget from the published rate card. It pays to ask.

10. **Expect less, get more.** This is a medium that is still being developed. For all the success stories, the package insert field is just like the other forms of direct response. It is a numbers game.

Warning!

Your printer, sad to say, may not be right for the insert market even though the printer is an expert with your catalog. Also, your artist should know that inserts must be machine insertable; that is, the company inserting them must be able to place them on their inserting machine and collate your insert with the others going into the package.

If you watch the cost of printing and the cost of distribution, your response should be sufficient to provide you with a satisfactory cost per inquiry or cost per order. If you expect a miracle, this is not the medium. But for steady production of orders at reasonable and competitive costs, this medium is hard to beat. For ease of entry, low visibility (your competitors are less likely to notice your promotion than if you were rolling out on national television), and low cost, what could be better? Where is the cost of a television commercial, or the heavy postage and four-color envelopes? Not here.

Inserts are inexpensive and, for most products, they reach an extensive audience. Many magazines, catalog houses, clubs, and photo finishers are having tens of millions of inserts distributed yearly. They are making the investment in inserts.

Producing and Shipping Package Inserts

An insert may be used as a means to advertise your message and sell your product or service by mail and/or other alternative print media. The insert can be an order-responsive device or serve as an information request. It travels along with a variety of "host" vehicles such as merchandise packages, co-ops, ride-alongs, catalogs, statements, and samples. By selecting the appropriate type of vehicle, you can target the audience that you feel will be the most receptive to your offer.

It is important that certain specifications and instructions are carefully followed in order to participate in insert advertising. Check with the sponsor's production department.

Size and Format

All inserts should be machine-insertable. While some inserts are placed loose within a package by hand, many are pre-collated into an envelope and then packaged with the merchandise, or pre-collated and stuffed into the co-op or ride-along envelope.

The various sizes and formats are as follows:

➤ Maximum size and weight for package insert programs is $5^1/_2$ by $8^1/_2$ inches, and $^1/_4$ oz (.25 oz).

➤ Maximum size and weight for statements, co-ops, and ride-alongs vary from $3^1/_2$ by 6 inches to $3^3/_4$ by 7 inches, and from $^1/_{10}$ to $^1/_5$ oz.

➤ Most co-ops and ride-alongs can accept the larger package sizing. Consult each program data card for specifics.

➤ Minimum sizes for inserts range from 3 by 5 inches to $3^1/_2$ by $5^1/_4$ inches.

Choosing an Insert Format

Available insert formats include single sheet, half-folds, quarter-folds, tri-folds, and bang-tail envelopes. Accordion and "Z" folds are usually not acceptable.

The typical insert uses 45- to 70-lb. paper-weight stock, either coated or plain, depending upon insert size and format. If the insert or any part of it is used as a self-mailer for order/request response, it must be of an appropriate weight and size to conform with postal machinery and regulation requirements.

Key Coding for Response Tracking

All inserts should be imprinted with a key code (located within the response portion) to track the effectiveness of each program placement. This key may be any combination of letters or numbers that will best serve your monitoring needs.

Most advertisers find it helpful to key in set quantities of 10,000, 25,000, 100,000, or 250,000, depending upon individual and total program selection. Remember that you should produce and ship an additional 1 to 2 percent total inserts for spoilage on hand insertions, and anywhere from 3 to 10 percent on machine insertions. Each program sponsor will advise you on the appropriate percentage required.

Fulfillment

Lead times vary greatly, program by program, as to when your inserts must be received in order to be distributed in accordance with your requested timeframe and the program's mailing schedules.

Some programs are able to begin inserting and distributing at any time, as soon as material is received. Others may require as much time as six weeks in advance of mail date. Consult the shipping information letter that your broker sends you, order by order, for the appropriate date.

Shipping the Inserts

Each carton of inserts must be marked with the following information: the name of the advertiser, a sample of the insert taped to the outside of the box, quantity per box, total quantity, number of boxes, key code, number of boxes per skid or pallet, and month and year of insertion. Boxes should also contain packing slips to verify this information.

In some instances, special packing and shipping instructions may be supplied to you. Usually your printer, fulfillment house, or service bureau is responsible for properly and completely following these directions. Instructions might cover how inserts are to be bundled or banded and placed within the carton, specs on carton weight and sizing, and how cartons must be skidded and palletized. For example, the material should be packed not higher than 42 inches; the skid should be banded or poly-wrapped.

Once you have determined the type of program you would like to use for your insert placement, you can then prepare the best insert to meet those needs. By incorporating these suggested guidelines, you can develop a procedure to smoothly and efficiently process your insert advertising orders.

Big Advertising with Billboards

If you run a hotel, restaurant, gift shop, recreational facility, or other business buried in a remote area bypassed by the major highways, billboards can guide travelers to your door.

To passing motorists, your billboard remains in view for about five seconds—barely enough time to read a single sentence. Therefore, don't fill your billboard with lengthy copy. Just make sure your name and a capsule description of your business ("diner," "children's zoo," "miniature golf") are visible at a glance. And don't forget to include directions ("Take Exit 17, $^1/_2$ mile ahead and turn right").

Standard billboards are 14-feet high by 48- or 25-feet wide. Billboard graphics should be simple, with strong, pure colors and realistic artwork or photography. Legibility is the truest test of a billboard design.

Aside from directing prospects to places off the beaten path, billboards can do little else to tell people about your products or services because of the limited number of words their messages contain. Therefore, for most small businesses in urban and suburban locations, billboards are not an effective promotion. But they can work for direct response advertisers, especially if they have a memorable toll-free number 1-800-RESUMES or Web site address (www.careers.com).

There are hundreds of outdoor advertising companies in the United States. When you have selected the markets for outdoor advertising, you can look up in the Yellow Pages in each city under "Advertising: Outdoor." Or, if you're interested in using a particular board, you can usually find the outdoor advertising company's name posted at the bottom.

Contracts generally run on either a 12, 24, or 36-month period for bulletins, or on a monthly basis for poster panels. You should contact the outdoor advertising company at least 90 days before you would like your ad to appear. While poster production takes from 21 to 45 days, artwork for painted bulletins must be sent to the outdoor company 60 days inadvance.

Costs vary tremendously, according to region of the country, specific billboard location, number of billboards leased, designer, complexity of the design, whether the sign is illuminated, whether the billboard is a bulletin or a poster panel, and whether the billboard is hand-painted or computer-printed.

Average costs for poster panels are $200 to $400 per month, plus about $80 each to produce. But the average cost of a bulletin is typically $1,000 to $3,000 per month, plus about $1,000 each to produce.

You can keep down production costs by agreeing to let the outdoor advertising company rotate the location of your billboard every 60 or 90 days. For the outdoor company, this kind of agreement can take advantage of unrented space. The plus side for the advertiser is that balanced coverage of the market can be achieved with just one billboard.

Marketing Tip

For more information on outdoor advertising, contact the Outdoor Advertising Association of America at www.oaaa.org.

Some companies also give discounts based on volume and length of contract, so that if you rent four or five billboards for a two, three, or even one-year period, 10 to 30 percent may be knocked off the price.

Even without such discounts, cost efficiency can be high. As promotional literature published by the Institute of Outdoor Advertising notes, "Outdoor is seen all day, every day. It cannot be turned off like television, tuned out like radio, or discarded like newspapers and magazines. And the mere size of your ad makes it difficult to ignore."

Transit Advertising: Ads on the Move

Don't look down your nose at writing ads for buses, subways, and commuter trains. If such leading literary lights as F. Scott Fitzgerald and Ogden Nash wrote transit ads, then you can, too.

Actually, for small businesses located in metropolitan areas, transit ads can ensure that your prospects see your message. "Interior" ads—those posters plastered on the insides of buses and trains—are especially effective because they have a captive audience. The ads stay in front of the passengers for as long as they're riding in the vehicle.

The average transit rider spends 22 minutes inside the vehicle on each ride and takes 24 rides a month. So chances are your transit ad will be well-read. But few riders will give up a seat on a crowded bus to walk across the aisle and read an ad. Therefore, keep the copy short so the type can be made large enough to be easily read from the opposite side of the vehicle.

Simplicity is also a virtue in transit advertising, because the rider can't clip and save a transit ad (at least not if there's a transit cop around!). Therefore, your message should be short and sweet. Include the name of your business, a brief description of what it is you're selling, and your address and phone number in large, legible lettering.

The standard interior transit ad unit is 11-inches high by 28-inches wide. But you can't rent an ad just in one vehicle: Transit advertising space is sold on a number of vehicles for a set period of time. You might, for example, pay anywhere from $8,000 to $16,000 a month for a standard unit on 1,200 buses. For the rates in your area, contact the local transit advertising company or sales organization.

Integrating Alternative Media into Your Marketing Mix

As direct marketers look for less expensive ways to develop new customers and generate qualified inquiries, more alternative media will be developed. An experienced broker can help lead you through the maze and find the best alternatives for you.

It costs money to prospect, and direct mail is expensive. Very few direct marketers can prospect much above the incremental break-even point. You won't see a profit from that buyer until the buyer purchases multiple times. Your goal should be to generate new buyers with the most lifetime value at the lowest possible costs. This can only be achieved through testing.

Any business must acquire new buyers if it wants to remain in business. Even if you do not want to grow your business, you need to continue to add new buyers to your house file in order to remain even with the previous year. Your house file has a certain attrition rate. To keep your business from spiraling down, you need to prospect, because only a certain percentage of your existing customers will purchase again.

Customers stop buying for a variety of reasons, most of which are out of your control. So, it is important to prospect. But, it is even more important to do so cost effectively to protect your bottom line.

The Least You Need to Know

➤ Inserts and other alternative media are inexpensive to produce and have a much lower cost per thousand than direct mail.

➤ Alternative media can generate orders from customers whose names are not available on response mailing lists.

➤ The lifetime value of a customer acquired through alternative media can be equal to or better than the lifetime value of a traditionally acquired new customer.

➤ Alternative media should be considered when traditional direct response vehicles see a drop–off in response rate (for example, ads aren't pulling, lists seemed fatigued).

➤ Although billboard and transit advertising are not usually considered to be direct marketing vehicles, they in fact can be. The key response mechanisms include an 800 number, Web site address, and (for transit) a take-one card.

Chapter 13

Direct Response Advertising

In This Chapter

➤ Comparing different ad sizes

➤ Selling more product with space ads

➤ Creating successful space ads

➤ Placing and testing ads

➤ Using the Yellow Pages and business directories

Using print ads to sell mail-order products goes back to the early days of patent medicines. One ad proclaimed, "Send us a dollar and we will get rid of your piles; if not, we will send back your dollar."

Many direct marketers are generating lots of direct response orders with space ads. This chapter shows how you can, too.

Big Versus Small Ads

Today, the full-page ad is the quickest way to mail-order riches. Since full-page ads are so much bigger than small display classified ads, they can potentially generate much more readership and response. This means you can make thousands (or even tens of thousands) of dollars in sales and profits with a single insertion.

Unfortunately, a full-page ad is also fraught with risk. If the ad bombs, you can lose part or even all of the money you invested running the ad. And a full-page ad can cost you $2,000 to $10,000 to run one time in one publication, depending on the magazine or newspaper you select.

Most classified ads, on the other hand, can be run for $50 to $100 per insertion. So if your classified ad fails to pull orders, you have lost only a little money, and can afford to try different ads until one works.

Surprising Secrets

If your product sells for between $10 to $50 or more, you can use a full-page ad to generate direct mail orders. That is, people read the ad and order the product directly from the ad. If your product sells for several hundred dollars or more, you may want to use full-page ads to generate inquiries. If your product is in the range of $50 to $300 or so, you can experiment with both lead-generating and mail-order, full-page ads until you determine which works best for your offer.

Media Buying for Direct Response Advertising

Since the profit from mail-order ads is the ratio of sales generated to the cost of advertising, you have a better chance of making a profit if you can pay less money for an ad. There are several ways to do this:

➤ **P/I (per inquiry) deals.** This is an agreement in which you negotiate with the publication for the following deal: The publication does not charge you to run the ad, but it receives 50 percent of the sales the ad generates. Although you give up more profit if the ad is successful, you minimize your up-front risk. Once a popular form of advertising, P/I is more difficult to do today, because fewer publishers are willing to risk it. But it doesn't hurt to ask.

➤ **Make good.** This means that the publisher reruns the ad for free if there is a mechanical problem with the first insertion (meaning that it doesn't print well or the publication uses the wrong color). Another variation on the make-good is that you and the publisher agree that you will pay the regular rate to run the ad one time. However, if you do not make enough sales to cover the cost of the ad space on the first insertion, the publisher will give you a second insertion free (or at a deep discount). Publishers with new magazines or those having difficulty selling space during a particular month may be agreeable to this deal.

➤ **Remnant space.** Publishers must print a certain number of pages each issue. Sometimes the composition of the magazine (its layout) is such that, for a given month, there are leftover pages with nothing to put on them. This is known as remnant space, and publishers will sometimes sell it at a discount of up to 50 percent off their regular rates. Usually, you can get remnant space only by prearranging such a deal with the publisher: You give them your disk, film, or mechanical, and instruct them to run it for an agreed-upon discount, whenever they have remnant space. The advantage is that you get the ad space at deep discount. The disadvantage is you never know when your ad is going to run.

➤ **Media-buying services.** There are several agencies that specialize in buying mail-order ad space and reselling it to mail-order advertisers. Because these companies buy huge volumes, they get major discounts from the publishers. They pass some of the discount on to you in the form of savings, and keep the rest as their profit.

➤ **Save 15 percent with an in-house agency.** How do ad agencies make their money? Part of it has traditionally come from commissions on the space ads they place for clients. For instance, if an ad costs $10,000 to run, the magazine will give the agency a 15 percent discount, charging it only $8,500. You pay $10,000 to the agency, the agency pays the magazine $8,500, and it keeps $1,500 as its commission. This is a traditional and accepted practice.

➤ **Run your ad in the smaller publications in a particular field.** If you are going to test ads in a particular type of publication, such as supermarket tabloids, the ones with the smaller circulations will be less expensive to test. If your budget is limited, you may want to run in the magazine that charges $5,000 for an ad and has a circulation of 200,000, rather than the magazine that charges $15,000 for a full page ad, but has a circulation of 625,000. If the ad in the smaller circulation magazine is profitable, you can then test it in more expensive magazines with larger circulations. But don't advertise in magazines with too few readers to produce mail-order sales. As a rule of thumb, mail-order ads should be run only in publications with a circulation of 100,000 or more.

Marketing Tip

Years ago, agency discounts were given only to real, bona fide ad agencies. Today, however, many publications give agency discounts to practically anyone. Therefore, if you place the ad yourself, you can often get the publication to give you the agency commission. The result is a savings of 15 percent on the ads you run—a substantial amount of money.

171

To sum up: You will get your best sales results advertising in publications that have large circulations and are used by other direct marketers for advertising.

Getting Your Space Ads to Sell More Product

The following sections describe some techniques that can help improve the odds that the next ad you create will be a winner—one that generates the immediate sales results you desire.

Advertise the Right Product for the Right Audience

The first step is to make sure you are advertising a product that is potentially useful to the people reading your advertisement. This seems to be a simple and obvious rule. Yet, many clients believe that a great ad can sell anything to anyone. They are wrong.

Charles Inlander, of the People's Medical Society, is a master at finding the right product for the right audience. His ad, "Do you recognize the seven early warning signs of high blood pressure?" sold more than 20,000 copies of a $4.95 book on blood pressure when it ran approximately 10 times in *Prevention Magazine* over a three-year period.

Warning!

Who are your prospects? PC users? Runners? Gardeners? Mothers? Does your product fill a need or solve a problem for them? If not, you will have a difficult time. The right product for the audience will sell even if the ad is mediocre. The wrong product, aimed at the wrong group, will not sell even if the ad is dynamite.

"First, you select your topic," said Inlander, explaining the secret of his advertising success, "then you must find the right place to advertise. It's important to pinpoint a magazine whose readers are the right prospects for what you are selling." In other words, the right product for the right audience.

If a publication does not contain ads for offers similar to yours, you should hesitate to advertise there, even if the publication seems to reach the right audience. Here's why: If the publication worked for your type of offer, others with similar offers would already be running there. Their lack of presence indicates that they tried it once and found it wanting. Proceed with caution.

If you advertise in publications in which only a small percentage of the readers are prospects, you will be paying to reach too many people who are not potential buyers—and the ad will not pay off. The more targeted the publication is to your audience, the better your chances for success.

Using an Attention-Getting Headline

Next to the selection of subject matter and the placement of your ad in the proper publication, the headline is the most important element of your ad. People flip through magazines and newspapers quickly. You have only a second or two to get them to stop and notice your ad. The headline plays a major role in doing this, as does the visual.

The main purpose of the headline is to grab the reader's attention and make him or her stop long enough to notice and start reading your ad. You can achieve this in several ways. For example, here's an attention-grabbing headline from an ad published in a newspaper:

IMPORTANT NEWS FOR WOMEN WITH FLAT OR THINNING HAIR

This headline is effective in gaining the attention of the prospect for two reasons: It promises important news, and it identifies the prospect for the service (women with flat or thinning hair). Incidentally, this ad persuaded more than 1,200 readers a month to clip a coupon and send for a free brochure on a hair-conditioning procedure.

To promote a home-study course in writing for children, The Children's Institute of Literature has been using the same successful ad for decades. The headline reads:

WE'RE LOOKING FOR PEOPLE TO WRITE CHILDREN'S BOOKS

This headline works for several reasons. Like the "Thinning Hair" headline, it identifies the prospect for the service: people who want to write children's books. More importantly, it carefully delays any reference to the fact that the ad is selling a home-study course, giving the reader sufficient time to get interested and involved before reading the offer.

In fact, although the headline is completely honest, you get the impression initially that the ad is from a children's book publisher looking for authors, which grabs the attention of the wanna-be authors who are prospects for this course.

A headline does not have to contain just one sentence or phrase set in one uniform type size. Often, you can create a more eye-catching and effective headline using what is essentially a three-part headline.

The first part, or kicker, is an "eyebrow" or short line that goes in the upper left corner of the ad, either straight or at a slant. One good use of the

Marketing Tip

Buy several magazines. Go through them. Clip full-page ads that appeal to you visually or seem to stand out from the others and draw you in. Save these in a file. Emulate their layouts when designing your own ads.

kicker is to select a specific type of reader for the ad ("Attention: COBOL Programmers"). Another effective technique is to let the reader know you are offering something free ("Special Free Offer—See Coupon Below").

Next, comes your main headline, set in larger type, which states your central benefit or makes a powerful promise. Then, in the subhead, you expand on the benefit or reveal the specific nature of the promise. Here are two examples:

$500 A DAY WRITER'S UTOPIA

Here's the breakthrough offer that opens up a whole new world for writers or those who hope to become writers ....

FOR HIGH-SPEED HIGH-PERFORMANCE DATA INTEGRATION, LOOK INTO MAGI MIRROR.

Now you can move data instantly from one program to another right from your PC screen.

If your headline is designed to arouse curiosity or grab attention and does so at the expense of clarity, then be sure to make the nature of your proposition immediately clear in a subhead or within the first sentence. Otherwise, you will lose the interest of the reader whose attention you worked so hard to gain.

Getting to the Point

The lead paragraph should rapidly follow up and expand on the idea expressed in the headline. For instance, if the headline asks a question, the lead should immediately answer it. The promises made to the reader in the headline (for example, "Learn the secret to richer, moister chocolate cake") must be fulfilled in the first few paragraphs of copy. Otherwise, the reader feels disappointed and turns the page.

Here is an example from an ad selling a business opportunity:

QUIT YOUR JOB OR START PART-TIME

Chimney Sweeps Are Urgently Needed Now

My name is Tom Risch. I'm going to show you how to make $200 a day saving people from dangerous chimney fires ....

After writing copy, read through the ad, taking note of the content of all headlines and subheads. Make certain the copy under each heading relates to the topic of the heading. Avoid subheads and heads that sound great but have nothing to do with what's in the copy. Readers are good at spotting this, and it turns them off.

Using a Reader-Friendly Layout

Use a layout that draws the reader into the ad. Some ads just naturally seem friendly or inviting. They draw your eye to the page and make reading a pleasure. This is the type of layout you want to use in your own ads. Avoid layouts that make the ad hard to read or discourage readers from even trying.

Your layout should have a focal point—a central, dominant visual element that draws the reader's eye to the page. This is usually the headline or the visual, but it might also be the coupon, or perhaps the lead paragraph of copy.

Set the body copy in serif type. Serif type has curls and lines at the end of the letter stems, as in this book. It is easier to read than sans serif, which has no such markings at the end of the letter stems. Headlines can be set in either typeface. Do not use reverse type (white on black), and avoid setting type against a colored background, illustration, or photograph. Use black type on a plain white background. It is easiest to read.

Marketing Tip

When there are two or more equally prominent visuals competing for the eye's attention, readers become confused and don't know where to start reading. Always make one element larger and more prominent than the others.

Giving the "Why They Should Buy"—And Proving It

Make sure you write body copy that supports and expands upon the idea presented in the headline and opening paragraphs. What facts should be included in your body copy? Which ones should be left out? Make your decision by listing all the key points, then deciding which are strongest and will best convince the reader to respond to your advertisement.

Start by listing all the features of your products and the *benefits* people get from each feature. For instance, *a feature* of an air conditioner is that its energy efficiency rating is 9.2; the *benefit* is a lower electric bill. Remember the difference between features and benefits from Chapter 5, "Writing Copy That Sells."

After making a complete list of features and benefits, list them in order of importance. Then, begin your body copy with the most important benefit. Incorporate the rest of the benefits on your list until you have sufficient copy. You've written copy that highlights the most important reasons to buy the product, given the space limitations of your ad.

Ads have limited space, so you don't have the freedom to go on at length as you do in a brochure or direct mail package. Editing is an important part of writing good ads. Here's one way to do it. First write the ad copy without regard to length. Get all your sales arguments in. Make the message complete. Then go back, prune, and edit. Trim the copy until it fits.

This can be difficult because it's easy to "fall in love" with your copy and not want to cut any part of it, but you don't want to force the reader to use a magnifying glass to read your ad. Ad body copy should be set in type no smaller than 9 point, and preferably 10 point. Another way of putting this: The type size in the ad should be equal to or larger than the type size in the publication's articles.

Avoiding Generalities

Be specific. "Platitudes and generalities roll off the human understanding like water from a duck," wrote Claude Hopkins in his classic book, *Scientific Advertising* (Harper & Brothers, 1936). "They leave no impression whatever."

The most common mistake we see in advertising today is "lazy copy"—copy written by copywriters who are too lazy to take the time to learn about their audience and understand the features and benefits of their product, the reasons why someone would want to buy it.

Why is so much ad copy vague and general? Two reasons.

First, it takes effort to research and understand information about products and markets. We avoid doing the proper research because it's difficult work, and ads are usually written on tight deadlines. Either there isn't time to gather facts or, more prevalent, the writer takes the easy route and writes only from the material presently in front of him or her.

Second, some ad writers are not research oriented. Some do not believe specifics are important. Many feel tone and emotion are everything, and consumers do not want product facts. Experience shows that, for the most part, those ad writers are wrong.

Good advertising is effective largely because it is specific. There are two benefits to being specific: First, it gives the customer the information he or she needs before making a buying decision; and second, it creates believability. As Hopkins points out, people are more likely to believe a specific, factual claim than a boast, superlative, or generalization.

Does this mean ad copy should be a litany of facts and figures? No. But the copywriter's best weapon is the selective use of facts to support the sales pitch. Here are some examples of well-written, specific, factual copy, taken from real ads:

Surprising Secrets

General advertisers preach, "People don't read body copy; keep it to a minimum." But direct marketers find that the more you tell in an ad, the more you sell. *Direct Marketing* magazine reports of an experiment in which more than 70 retailers tested different ads and measured results. Here's what they found: When advertisers doubled the number of product facts in the ad, sales increased approximately 50 percent.

176

> *One out of every four Americans has high blood pressure. Yet only half these people know it. You may be one of them. If you are over forty, you owe it to yourself to have your blood pressure checked.*

> *The Mobilaire (R) 5000. 59 pounds of Westinghouse air conditioning in a compact unit that cools rooms 12' × 16' or smaller. Carry one home, install it in minutes— it plugs in like a lamp into any adequately wired circuit. Fits any window 19¹/₈" to 42" wide.*

Start with the Prospect, Not the Product

Of course, your ad must contain information about the product. But the information must be *important to the reader*—information that the reader will find interesting or fascinating and will answer his or her questions, satisfy curiosity, or cause the reader to believe the claims you make. Information, in short, that will convince the reader to buy your product.

The reader's own concerns, needs, desires, fears, and problems are all more important to him or her than your product, your company, and your goals. For instance, instead of saying, "We have more than 50 service centers nationwide," translate this statement into a reader benefit: "You'll be assured of prompt, courteous service and fast delivery of replacement parts from one of our 50 service centers located nationwide."

The real "star" of your ad is the reader. Your product is second, and is only of concern in that it relates to a need, desire, or problem the reader has, or a benefit the reader wants. Your company is a distant third—the least important element of your copy. It is only of concern if it reassures those prospects who want to do business with a well-known firm that has a good reputation and is financially stable.

Here are excerpts from three other ads that start with the prospects and their needs and concerns:

> *Every day, law firms struggle with the expense and inconvenience of engraved and preprinted stationery.*

> *Are you sick and tired of your current job? Do you dream of a career that's fun, exciting—and financially rewarding?*

> *Do you enjoy going on vacation, traveling to exotic locations, and seeing the world? If so, the Echols International Tourism Institute has some exciting news for you about career opportunities in today's travel industry.*

177

Promise the Reader a Reward for Reading the Copy

One way to increase readership and response is to promise the reader useful information in your headline, then deliver it in your ad copy. For an ad offering business people a book on how to collect overdue bills, Milt Pierce wrote this headline:

7 WAYS TO COLLECT YOUR UNPAID BILLS.

New from Dow Jones-Irwin ....

A Successful and Proven Way to Get Your Bills Paid Faster.

The information-type ad is highly effective in mail-order advertising. Why? Because so many mail-order buyers are information seekers—much more so than the average consumer.

Using a Friendly, Conversational Style

Write in a clear, simple, conversational, natural style. Copy should not be pompous, remote, aloof, or written in "corporatese." The most effective copy is written in a plain, simple, conversational style—the way a sincere person talks when he or she wants to help or advise you.

Here are some examples, taken from recent print ads, of copy that achieves the natural, easy-flowing tone you want in your ads. Even ads for technical products should sound friendly, inviting, and understandable:

Marketing Tip

A good ad sounds like one person talking to another about a subject of mutual interest. Use informal language. Contractions. Sentence fragments. Conversational language. Even a slang phrase now and then. Colloquial expressions.

You may have read that today the lending climate is friendlier. Don't believe it! The fact is, only larger corporations have ready access to capital. Growing businesses looking for funding are often up against a brick wall.

Chemputers is the only computer users' conference specifically designed for chemical engineers. In just 48 hours, you'll learn things about computers—and chemical engineering—that your colleagues won't get in an entire year of reading journals and going to trade shows.

Your style may be different. That's fine. But we have found that "reader-friendly" ads have several things in common: Simple language, short sentences, and short paragraphs. Copy should address the reader directly; the word "you" should appear frequently.

Don't Forget a Strong Call to Action

Decide what you want the reader to do next. Then ask the reader to do it—and make it easy to reply. There are three easy steps for turning your ad into a response-generating marketing tool. First, decide what type of response you want. What action do you want the reader to take? Do you want your prospect to phone or write you, or clip a coupon and mail it back to you?

Do you want the reader to visit your store or Web site, request a copy of your catalog or sales brochure, set up an appointment to see a salesperson, test-drive your product, or order your product directly from the ad? Decide what you want the reader to do.

Second, tell the reader to do it. The last few paragraphs of your copy should spell out the action you want the reader to take and give him or her reasons to take it. For instance ...

> *Just clip the coupon or call toll-free now and we'll send you this policy FREE without obligation as a special introduction to EMPLOYMENT GUIDE.*

Give the reader a *reason* to respond.

The third step is to give the reader a *mechanism* for responding. Emphasize this mechanism in your ad layout to simplify the process of making contact with you. In print advertising, this is accomplished through the use of a toll-free phone number (usually printed in large type to attract attention to it) or by including a coupon in the ad.

Surprising Secrets

Some magazines also allow you to insert a reply card, which is bound into the magazine and appears opposite your ad. This is an expensive technique, but it can dramatically increase replies.

Making Money with Classified and Small Display Ads

The least expensive way to start in mail order is with small classified ads. Actually, these ads generate a greater return on investment than any other medium, including full-page ads.

You should not ask for an order directly from a classified ad. It won't work. There is not enough copy in a classified ad to make the complete sale. Classified advertising is two-step direct marketing. In step one, you run a small classified ad to generate an inquiry, which is a request for more information about your product.

The way to measure classified ad response for inquiry advertising is to count the inquiries, divide the cost of the ad by the number of inquiries, and thus determine the cost per inquiry. For instance, if you run a classified ad and it costs you $100, and you get 100 inquiries, your cost per inquiry is $1. As a rule of thumb, a successful classified ad will generate inquiries at a cost of between 50 cents and $2 per inquiry.

When people inquire, you send them an inquiry-fulfillment kit, which is a sales package promoting your product. The inquiry-fulfillment kit consists of an outer envelope, sales letter, circular or brochure, order form, and reply envelope.

As a rule of thumb, the inquiry fulfillment kit should convert 10 to 15 percent of the inquiries to orders. Some inquiry-fulfillment kits have achieved conversions rates as high as 20 to 30 percent or even a little higher.

Writing an Effective Classified Ad

Classified ads follow the AIDA principle, meaning they must get Attention, generate Interest, create Desire for the product, and ask for Action.

Sales appeals that work in classified mail-order advertising include promises of obtaining love, money, health, popularity, leisure, security, entertainment, self-confidence, better appearance, prestige, pride of accomplishment, and saving time. Other effective appeals include eliminating worry and fear, satisfying curiosity, success, avoiding work or risk, self-expression, pride of ownership, comfort, creativity, and self-improvement.

Certain words are extremely effective in classified ads. These include: free, new, amazing, now, how to, easy, discover, method, plan, reveals, show, simple, startling, advanced, improved, and you.

One of my most successful mail-order ads, which ran continuously for many years in *Writer's Digest,* reads as follows:

> *MAKE $85,000/YEAR writing ads, brochures, promotional materials for local/national client. Free details: CTC, 22 E. Quackenbush, Dept. WD, Dumont, NJ 07628.*

Marketing Tip

As a rule of thumb, whenever you offer information to generate an inquiry, make it free. The exception might be a very expensive and elaborate catalog, for which you charge $1 to cover your costs.

Phrasing the Offer

The offer that will generate the most response is an offer to supply information, not the product itself. This is done by running a phrase such as "free details," "free information," "free catalog," or a similar phrase, followed by a colon and your address (for example, free details: Box 54, Canuga, TN 44566).

Some mail-order advertisers ask the prospect to pay for the information, either by sending a small amount of money (25 cents, 50 cents, $1, and $2 are typical), or by requiring the prospect to send a self-addressed stamped envelope with the postage already on it. The theory is that asking for postage or a nominal payment brings you a more qualified lead and therefore results in a higher percentage of leads converted to sales. My experience is that it doesn't pay to charge for your information kit, since doing so dramatically cuts down on the number of leads you will receive.

Reducing Word Count (Advertising Costs)

The measure of a successful classified ad is the cost per inquiry generated. Therefore, if you can get your message across in fewer words, you pay less for the ad, and as a result lower your cost per inquiry.

Make your classifieds as short and pithy as possible. Here are some tips for reducing your word count:

➤ **Be concise.** Use the minimum number of words needed to communicate your idea. For example, instead of "Earn $500 a Day in Your Own Home-Based Business," write "Work at Home—$500/Day!"

➤ **Minimize your address.** You pay the publication for every word in your classified, including your address. Therefore, instead of "22 E. Quackenbush Avenue," I write "22 E. Quackenbush." The mail will still get delivered, and I will save one word. This can add up to significant savings for ads run frequently in multiple publications.

➤ **Use phrases and sentence fragments** rather than full sentences.

➤ **Remember your objective.** You are asking for only an inquiry, not an order. You don't need a lot of copy, since all you are asking the reader to do is send for free information.

➤ **Use combination words, hyphenated words, and slash constructions.** For instance, instead of "GROW EARTH WORMS," which is three words, write "GROW EARTHWORMS," which counts as two words, saving you a word.

Dollar for dollar, classifieds generate greater return over breakeven than any other type of ad. The key to maximizing return is to entice the reader to respond in the fewest possible words, since you pay by the word to run the ad.

Placing Your Classified Ads

Place your classified ads in publications that run mail-order classified ad sections. Write to these magazines and newspapers and request a free media kit and sample issue. The media kit includes details on circulation, advertising rates, readership, and a sample issue of the publication.

Look at the classified ad sections in the publications. Are their ads for products similar to yours? This is a good sign. See if these ads repeat from issue to issue. The advertisers would not repeat them unless they were working. If this publication is working for their offers, it can work for yours, too.

Classified ad sections are divided by various headings. Place your ad in the appropriate heading. For example, if you sell information by mail, avoid putting your classified under the heading "Books and Booklets." This will reduce orders. Instead, put the ad under a heading related to the subject matter. If you are selling a book on how to make money cleaning chimneys, place the ad under "Business Opportunities." If you don't see an appropriate heading, call the magazine and ask if it will create one for you.

Marketing Tip

In your classified ads, put a key code in the address. By key coding, you can track which ad each inquiry or order comes from. For instance, in my ad "MAKE $85,000/YEAR WRITING," the key code "WD" in my address refers to *Writer's Digest* magazine. Since the ad runs every month, I don't bother adding a code number to track the month.

Insider's Buzzwords

Lead time is how far in advance you must place your ad insertion order for the ad to run in a particular issue. If a magazine has a 2-month lead time, you must let them know in April that you want your ad to run in June.

Testing Your Ad

We have already discussed the two key measurements of two-step, classified advertising, which are the cost per inquiry and the percentage of inquiries converted to orders. The bottom line is: Did the sales the ad generated exceed the cost of the ad space? If they did, it was profitable. If they didn't, the ad isn't working and a new ad should be tested.

You can test a classified by running it just one time in a publication. The problem is, most magazines and even weekly newspapers have long *lead times*—several weeks or more—for placing classified ads. If you place the ad to run one time only, and the ad pulls well, you then have to wait several weeks or months until you can get it in again.

In a weekly newspaper or magazine, I test a classified ad by running it for one month—four consecutive issues. For a monthly publication, I test it for three months—three consecutive issues. If the first insertion is profitable, I will probably extend the insertion order for several months, so the ad runs continuously.

With a full-page ad, you usually get the greatest number of orders the first time the ad runs in the magazine. Response declines with each additional insertion, and at the point where the ad is not going to be profitable in its next insertion, you pull it and try another ad. The reason is that the first time the ad runs, it skims the cream of the prospects, getting orders from those most likely to buy. Obviously, those who buy from the first insertion of the ad will not buy when it runs again. Therefore, each time the ad runs, it reaches a smaller and smaller audience of potential new buyers.

With a classified ad, however, the total response is much less for each insertion. Therefore, it doesn't materially affect the number of potential first-time customers the ad appeals to. In fact, some people who responded once, got your sales literature, and didn't buy, may respond several times—and get your literature several times—before they eventually break down and buy.

Also, each issue reaches a number of new subscribers via subscriptions and newsstand circulation, so the total audience for a classified remains fairly constant. While response to full-page mail-order ads declines with each insertion, the response to a classified ad can remain steady for many insertions. Indeed, some mail-order operators (and I am one of them) have run the same classified ad monthly in the same magazine for years at a time, with no decline in response.

Response sometimes tends to increase during the first 12 months the ad is run, as people see the ad over and over again, and eventually become curious enough to respond.

Surprising Secrets

According to the Thomas Publishing Company, publishers of *Thomas Register*, a leading industrial-products directory, the surest way to get your directory ad to generate inquiries is to have the biggest ad on the page. The largest ad generates 40 times the response of an ordinary name-and-phone-number listing.

Advertising in the Yellow Pages and Business Directories

There's a *big* difference between directory ads and newspaper and magazine ads, and the difference is this: People reading newspapers and magazines are reading articles for information or entertainment, and they tend to pass over the ads.

Therefore, to be effective, a newspaper or magazine ad must forcefully grab the reader's attention through a novel, interesting presentation—a fascinating photo, a distinctive layout, a compelling headline. But when people turn to a directory, they are prime prospects, *ready to buy and looking for suppliers*. They do not have to be persuaded to buy: They merely have to be persuaded to buy *from you*.

As a result, directory advertising is appropriate for nearly every type of small business, manufacturers, retailers, service businesses, and even wholesalers. And *any* ad is better than no ad—just printing your company name in boldface type will double the response you'd get from a regular listing.

Obviously, it's best to have your ad at the front of your section of the directory, since readers generally start with the A's and end with the Z's. Normally, you won't have much control over this. But if directory advertising is your primary source of new business, you might seriously consider choosing a company name beginning with "A" just to get your ad up front.

Another time-tested gambit is to list everything you sell or do in your directory ad. One New Jersey insurance agent begins his Yellow Pages ad with the direct headline "INSURANCE" and goes on to list the more than 30 different types of items he insures. If he is the only agent to list snowmobiles in his advertisement, then anyone turning to the Yellow Pages with a snowmobile to insure will be hooked by the ad. As a result, his small (2-column-by-2$^1/_2$ inches) display ad generates one or two telephone inquiries on just about *every business day of the year.*

Almost every small business can benefit from an ad in the Yellow Pages. Directory advertising is another story. In some industries, a directory ad is a "must." In others, the standard directories are not often used by customers; advertisers are better off putting their money in trade-magazine advertising or direct mail.

When you have to decide whether it is worth advertising in a given trade or professional directory, consider these four points:

➤ **Completeness.** Does the directory contain enough real information to be useful to buyers? Or is it just one big advertising supplement?

➤ **Ease of use.** Is the directory well organized, indexed, and cross-referenced? Are manufacturers listed by geography, company, *and* product category?

➤ **Reputation.** How long has the directory been around? Is it well-respected and well-used? Check to see if you find it on your customers' desks. Is it considered the leading directory in its industry? Or is it a Johnny-come-lately?

➤ **Circulation.** How many people does it reach? Does this circulation include the majority of your potential customers?

The Least You Need to Know

➤ Mail-order advertising works best in publications that regularly run such types of ads and reach an audience of at least 100,000 subscribers.

➤ You get the most orders the first time you run your full-page ad. Response gradually declines with each insertion. Run the ad until it isn't profitable any more.

➤ Write your ads in an informative, conversational style.

➤ Editorial-style ads—those that sound and look like articles in the publication instead of paid ads—often work well in direct marketing.

➤ Do not overlook low-cost classifieds as a profitable source of inquiries.

Part 3
Electronic Direct Marketing

Increasingly, direct marketing campaigns are conducted using electronic media rather than ink on paper. This part covers both new and old media in electronic marketing.

We discuss direct response radio and TV advertising, including short-form commercials and infomercials. Keep reading to find tips on how to use telemarketing effectively, as well as use the Internet for banner ads, e-mail, Web sites, and e-zines.

Chapter 14

Direct Response TV and Radio

In This Chapter

➤ Infomercials: commercials disguised as shows

➤ TV as a direct response medium

➤ Short–form direct response TV

➤ Creating TV commercials that sell

➤ Selling your product on QVC and Home Shopping Network

➤ Radio as a direct response medium

People not in direct marketing like to make fun of commercials for products like the Pocket Fisherman or the George Foreman Grill, but the fact is that TV and radio can be tremendously effective for selling all types of direct response offers—from exercise videos to financial services.

A number of options exist for direct marketers who want to sell via broadcast media. These include infomercials, short-form TV commercials, QVC, Home Shopping Network, and direct response radio.

Infomercial: The Commercial That Sells Like a Show

The term "infomercial" is short for "information commercial." A half-hour in length, infomercials are commercials produced in the format and style of a TV show. Consumers view them as "programming" rather than commercials, and watch them for information content and entertainment value—and in the process, are sold a product.

Since 1984, hundreds of infomercials have been produced. Hits have produced from 10 to 100 million dollars or more in sales, each. There have been phases where three to six shows are successfully selling a similar product, such as the current ab machine craze.

Marketing Tip

Most products have a life cycle of 9 to 18 months. But a select few don't burn out and are still on the air two to five years after launch. The reasons: quality infomercial, great product, shrewd production, and effective media buying.

Infomercial products must appeal to the masses—because its targeting, by direct mail standards, is very crude. So, how do you select winning products to be direct marketed via the most massive of all mass marketing channels? TV is in 99 percent of all U.S. households—93.1 million of them.

The five key ingredients to infomercial success are:

1. Mass appeal (solves a common problem)
2. Five- or six-to-one markup
3. Highly demonstrable product
4. Capable of "magical transformation" (big benefit or result)
5. Unique

If you've got a product that fits *all* of these categories, you're sitting on a gold mine.

Common Infomercial Blunders to Avoid

One out of 10 movies makes money on its theatrical release. The same hit ratio holds true for most infomercials. Here are some pointers on what not to do in your infomercial scripting and production:

➤ Don't just create an information program and then throw two to three commercials into it. You must sell benefits all the time.

➤ Don't think that a celebrity spokesperson guarantees success. It doesn't. The offer and the copy rule supreme.

➤ Don't over-entertain. Sure, make it glitzy, fun, exciting, and fast-paced—but only if you're selling all the while.

➤ Don't spend lots of money if you can convey the same message with less.

The old adage of "test cheap" still holds true. Spend your money on content—not program packaging such as graphics, sets, music, and professional actors. Spend your money on the scripting, and craft every line. Find only the best testimonials, and create the best offer. And figure it will take from two to four months to create your infomercial.

Key Elements of Infomercial Production

One of your first decisions will be to select a format. Will it be a talk show? Documentary? Lecture format or demonstration show? The lead is critical. You've got seven seconds to grab viewers at the top of the show. It's your headline. Make it hot!

Should you use a celebrity? It will cost you $5,000 to $15,000 for minor talent; $20,000 to $50,000 for a moderate celebrity; $50,000 to $500,000 for a current network, movie, or sports star plus a percent of sales from 1 to 5 percent.

Celebrities are most useful for two reasons. First, their appearance on screen will stop the remote control zappers long enough to possibly capture viewer interest—7 to 10 seconds. Second, celebrities give credibility to the product. Good testimonials can boost response 20 to 50 percent. The celebrities should be real people who are actual product users, and interviewed, not scripted.

Pacing, rhythm, and timing are everything in audiovisual communication. Sell all the time. Mention the product name whenever possible—at least three times a minute. Complete a full sales cycle—attention, interest, demand—before doing your "call for action." Typical sales cycles can be 8, 15, or 27 minutes long—meaning one to three sales cycles per infomercial.

The "call to action" commercials within the infomercial should be a minimum of $2^1/_2$ minutes. The 800 phone number should appear on screen for as long as possible.

Sell with benefit information and close the sale with emotion. Emphasize the "magical transformation" from using your product—dramatic weight loss, better life. Use before and after photos and testimonials.

Test different offers and prices. Common price ranges for direct response TV include $29.95 to $59.95; $49.95 to $89.95; $79.95 to $129.95;

Marketing Tip

Make sure your scriptwriter, director, and producer have documentary and commercial experience. Background in 30-second general advertising image spots or even two-minute direct response spots is not enough to guarantee success.

189

$99.95 to $199.95; $179.95 to $295. Test premiums, bonuses, money-back guarantees, and "call now" motivators.

Test inbound upsells, meaning when the person calls in to buy the advertised product, you try to sell the caller another product or a more expensive, deluxe version. A good upsell can get 15 to 50 percent of callers to buy the more expensive package.

Make sure you ask for the order on your infomercial. Some tips on the offer or ordering opportunity are as follows:

Surprising Secrets

Fifty percent of those who tune into an infomercial will watch the whole show; 25 percent will watch half the show; and 25 percent will watch one quarter to one half of the show. Since 50 percent do not watch the whole show, you've got to keep selling throughout the entire half-hour.

➤ Since you've been talking about benefits throughout the show body, just review them at the close of the show for $1\frac{1}{2}$ to 2 minutes. Keep them concrete and condensed.

➤ Use bullets and graphically list your benefits. This is done on a screen that asks for the order and gives the response information—name of product, credit cards accepted, toll free number to call, and address for mailing checks.

➤ Pace your infomercial appropriately. For instance, infomercials, typically, are interspersed with short straightforward commercial pitches asking for the order. If your show is slow in pace, pick it up during these commercials. Use a voice-over spokesperson. If your show is fast-paced, slow the commercial down. Use an on-camera spokesperson.

➤ If you can persuade your celebrity to do the product offer pitch, do it. A celebrity's direct endorsement can mean 15 to 20 percent increase in response.

➤ State the offer details verbally and very clearly.

➤ Use premiums and bonuses whenever possible. They will lift response 10 to 25 percent.

➤ Repeat the phone number and address a minimum of two times in the closing segment of the show.

➤ Always say "call now."

Getting Your Infomercial on the Air

Buying air time for infomercials is a work apart from buying air time for regular TV commercials. Go to somebody who knows the good cities to test, where and how to negotiate good prices, and how to analyze results.

The average half-hour costs between $800 to $1,200 per half hour, at a cost of 10 to 20 cents per viewing household. And you and your agency will know whether you've got a hit or a miss for just $20,000 to $40,000 worth of testing.

Media time is a perishable commodity. Therefore, unless the market is tight, it's highly negotiable. A few caveats: Don't run in prime time. It's too pricey. And don't run weekday daytime. Fifty percent of response to your infomercial will be male, and they're not home. Try not to run against hometown sports or after somebody else's infomercial. And forget the local cable stations and low-power TV stations. It's not worth the bother.

So where and when do you buy time?

➤ Late nights, or Saturday/Sunday daytimes

➤ Cable networks (about 25 of them)

➤ Broadcast affiliates

➤ Independent stations

➤ Heavy buys (repeating the show many times) in first, fourth, and third quarters—in that order

➤ Light buying (running the show only a few times) April to June (everybody's outside)

A really successful infomercial can run profitably on the air many times—as much as $2 million a year in media costs. Anywhere from 50 to 90 percent of that will be on broadcast stations—about 800 of the nation's 1,100 commercial stations will run infomercials, and seven of the top 10 cable networks air them.

Be prepared to have the cash ready for a *media rollout.* The rule among station sales reps is: Religious programs and infomercials pay cash up front—as much as two weeks in advance.

Within 24 hours of airing, you will have 95 percent of your orders from that telecast. So you know whether to run again or cancel. And within 48 hours, you have credit card receipts deposited in your bank account.

Which brings us to the all-important issue of response. How many orders can you expect per $1,000 spent on air time? Assuming you have an successful product and program, your response will be from .2 to 4 percent or more of total viewers for *one-step orders*; from 4 to 15 percent of total viewers for *lead generators*; and about 4 percent for *900-number programs.*

But response in the infomercial industry is most commonly measured as the ratio of sales generated to air time cost. Two to one is okay, three to one is good; four or five to one is terrific. This means that with a three to one response ratio, for every $100 I spend in media, I generate $300 in sales.

Insider's Buzzwords

A **media rollout** is the expansion of a media schedule to greater frequency and additional markets after a successful test. **One-step orders** are commercials that generate a direct sale, usually requiring the viewer to call an 800 number to order. **Lead generators** are commercials that generate an inquiry, usually a request for more information on a product or offer. **900-number programs** are commercials that get the viewer to call a 900 number, usually to get advice, gossip, or useful information; the viewer is charged by the minute for the call.

Shorter Formats

The most popular commercial for general advertisers is 30 seconds. For them, 60 seconds is a long commercial. But direct marketers do more than just create brand awareness on TV; we actually sell products. And we need more time to do the job.

In direct response TV (DRTV), the long format—the infomercial—is 30 minutes. A short direct response TV commercial is typically two minutes, sometimes one minute.

You will notice that DRTV spots always run at odd hours—late night or daytime—and almost never during prime time. The reason is that the viewer pays less attention to the programmed shows at those times, and therefore is more interested in the commercials. During prime time, focus is on the programming, and commercials are used for bathroom breaks.

According to the Direct Response Television Center, a DRTV producer should be aware of these facts and recommendations:

➤ DRTV spots run on low-interest programs pull well.

➤ Daytime spots are usually more cost-effective than evening spots.

➤ Tests in small-scale markets can be reliable predictors of more expensive campaigns.

➤ Double the number of small-audience spots is better than half the number of large-audience spots.

➤ Use titles to highlight your phone number and emphasize selling points.

➤ Speak the phone number over and over in your commercial.

➤ Have a strong, clear, simple selling proposition.

Copywriter Dean Rieck, writing in *DM News* (March 12, 2001, p. 14) offers these additional DRTV tips:

➤ **Offer a unique product.** Retail is still king because it is faster, easier, and cheaper for most people to buy at a local store. So, if you want people to buy from you on television, you must offer them something special. Example: Louis the Loud Mouth Bass looks like a plaque but starts moving and singing when it senses you are near.

➤ **Dramatize benefits and results.** People believe what they see. Dramatize features and benefits. George Foreman doesn't just tell you that his grill drains off fat; he cooks some burgers and shows you the fat dripping off into a dish.

➤ **Solve a problem.** This is the classic DRTV formula. Can't reach the bolt? The Squeeze Wrench promises to work in tight places where pliers, ratchets, and wrenches won't fit.

➤ **Push your unique selling proposition (USP).** Your USP positions your product and sets it apart from all others. The IGIA is "the world's first and only laser toothbrush."

➤ **Make a powerful promise.** State your primary claim clearly and directly. Example: The Steam Bullet "cleans and disinfects your entire home with just the power of steam."

➤ **Establish high perceived value.** A commercial for Euro Sealer points out first that "an electric sealer costs over $200." Then, it offers you the Euro Sealer for just $19.95.

➤ **Add value with extras.** The Popeil Pasta and Sausage Maker seems like a good deal at $99.95. But the deal appears even better when Ron Popeil throws in, at no extra cost, 12 pasta shaping dies, a pasta measuring cup, automatic pasta cutter, Italian sausage horn, 12 feet of casings, Italian spice seasoning, an instructional video, and a recipe book.

"DRTV is designed to solicit a specific response directly from TV viewers," writes marketing author Jim Daniel. "Tell the viewers exactly what you want them to do. Solicit a response that is direct and measurable."

Marketing Tip

"To be successful, DRTV must demonstrate the product's benefits physically, verbally, and graphically," writes Barbara Kerry, president of Script to Screen, a direct response agency specializing in TV. "The use of experts adds to the product's credibility, and customer testimonials underscore the genuine satisfaction derived from use of the product. Most important, make the customer an offer he or she can't refuse."

Other DRTV Options: HSN and QVC

An alternative to producing your own direct response TV spots is to sell your product on the Home Shopping Network (HSN) or QVC.

The Home Shopping Network reaches over 74 million U.S. households with cable and satellite dishes. Their sales in 1999 were $1.2 billion. Products sold on HSN include electronics, jewelry, beauty, health, fitness, home, crafts, cooking, collectibles, dolls, toys, sports, music, and books. HSN actively seeks new products. They are especially interested in you if you hold a large inventory of merchandise that fits their sales criteria.

The other major DRTV outlet is QVC, which telecasts live 24 hours a day, seven days a week, to more than 70 million U.S. households. They get 110 million phone calls a year resulting in sales of $2.4 billion.

QVC sells a wide range of consumer merchandise including fashion, electronics, home products, kitchen appliances, health, beauty, and consumer electronics. QVC reaches over 80 percent of U.S. cable homes and three million satellite dishes. Last year they shipped over 67 million packages to their customers. Like HSN, QVC is actively looking for quality merchandise at good value to sell on their programs.

Direct Response Radio

Suddenly, radio is "in" again. From tiny transistors to sophisticated Sony Walkmans to huge "boom boxes," radios are everywhere—the streets and the subways, the beach and the park, the bedroom and the bathroom. And where radio goes, advertisers follow.

All fads aside, radio has always made it easy for broadcasters and their sponsors to reach the masses. Today, 99 percent of all households and 95 percent of all automobiles have radios.

Although radio doesn't dominate our lives the way television does, as an advertising medium it has two major advantages over the tube. One is comparatively low cost; the other is selectivity.

Surprising Secrets

More than 7,800 AM and FM stations broadcast music, news, sports, and talk shows daily to some 458 million radios across the country. People *listen* to radio; the average man or woman has his or her radio turned on about 3½ hours a day. And 88 percent of these listeners say they are listening to radio as much as or more than they always have.

Reaching Listeners Through Radio

In order to compete with television, radio stations became specialized in their programming, reaching out to certain select audiences. There are many different types of radio stations: easy listening, religious, Top 40, news, talk, sports, country and western, jazz, hard rock, "middle-of-the-road," Hispanic, black, soft rock, oldies, classical, and disco.

Each type of station reaches a specific segment of the market and this is what the stations sell to their advertisers. As a result, radio advertising is extremely effective for businesses catering to specific groups: teenagers, commuters, housewives, and college students.

For example, research shows that teenagers are the audience for Top 40, heavy metal, rap, and rock and roll stations. The Big Band stations, featuring the music of Benny Goodman, Glenn Miller, Count Basie, and Harry James, attract a more mature crowd; 60 percent of their listeners are between 45 and 64 years old.

A study by Robert E. Balon and Associates reveals that the listener's *mood* is a crucial factor in what station he or she selects. As one would expect, people in their mid 20s to early 30s prefer news, weather, and soft music when they get up to go to work in the early hours of the morning. But coming home after a hard day's labor, they like to hear mostly music shows featuring familiar oldies, with little talk in between.

Buying Radio Time

Naturally, you want your radio spots to reach the right audience at the right time. Here, then, are a few helpful hints on buying radio time. First, make sure you buy time on the right type of station. As we've mentioned, radio stations are narrowly targeted to specific audiences primarily on the basis of age, and sometimes by race, ethnic background, and income, too.

Find out which stations in your area appeal to your particular market. If you own a sporting goods store, for example, you may wish to sponsor a sports show. If your theater is pushing tickets to a highbrow play, the classical music stations would be the place to advertise.

To find out if a local station reaches your market, call the station's advertising sales department and explain what you're selling and who you're selling it to. If the station's listeners don't match your target market, the sales department may recommend another station.

If, however, the station represents a potential advertising vehicle for your product, ask the station to send you a media kit. This package is similar to the kit you'd get from a magazine and contains the following items:

➤ A coverage map that indicates the geographic area the station reaches. Some powerful stations broadcast to people too far away to be potential customers for your business; other stations broadcast signals that are too weak to cover your area adequately.

➤ Market research reports that show how well the station competes with other stations in the area when it comes to attracting listeners.

➤ Descriptions of the DJs and their shows. In some areas, certain DJs can become minor celebrities, and as a result, more people listen closely to their shows.

➤ A list of other businesses in the area that have advertised on the station.

➤ A rate card that tells you the cost of buying airtime. Rates vary with the time of the broadcast (morning, afternoon, early evening, late night) because the size of the audience varies with the time of day.

Radio delivers its largest audience during "drive time" the times when listeners are driving to work (6:00 to 10:00 A.M.) and from work (3:00 to 6:00 P.M.). Naturally, drive time is the most costly time—radio's equivalent to television's "prime time." The least expensive radio spots run from midnight to 5:00 A.M. During this "graveyard" time, few people besides insomniacs and the third shift are tuned in.

Rates vary with time, number of commercials, and type of station. Prices for a 60-second spot to air once a week range from $5 in some rural areas to $400 for drive time in a metropolitan area. Sixty-second spots are by far the most popular, but 30 second and 10 second chunks of time are also available. Radio stations will offer "bonus" spots free to advertisers who buy a number of spots at one time.

Marketing Tip

In addition to spot buying, advertisers can elect to buy sponsorship of certain program segments such as the weather, sports, news, or the traffic report. As a sponsor, your name and product will be plugged by on-air personalities at certain points during the broadcast.

Ask the advertising sales departments of your local radio stations for help in planning your radio advertising. They can set up a schedule and budget, help you plan advertising strategy, recommend an ad agency to produce the commercial, and even help with the writing of the commercial. Best of all, this free service comes with the price of the airtime.

Depending on the nature of your business, the radio sales people may recommend drive time spots, late night commercials, sponsorship of program segments, or a combination of several alternatives. Naturally, as with newspaper and magazine radio advertising, you want to reach the greatest number of *qualified* prospects at the lowest possible cost per thousand.

Writing Effective Radio Commercials

Two major advantages of radio are its short lead time and its minimal production costs. While television spots have to be performed in a studio, recorded on film or videotape, and sent to the station to be aired, a radio commercial can be written, handed to the announcer in script form, and read live on the air all in the same day.

Some companies do hire advertising agencies to produce more elaborate radio spots using professional narrators, actors, singers, musicians, and sound effects. But for most small businesses, a well written "live" commercial—one read by the announcer from a script—can get the word out and eliminate production costs altogether.

Often, the radio station's advertising sales department can help you write the script. In addition, here are some copy tips specifically designed to help you write better radio commercials:

➤ **Make it sound the way people talk.** Radio, after all, involves talking and listening, not reading and writing. By controlling the volume, tone, and inflection of his or her voice, the radio announcer can emphasize certain points, and communicate in ways a printed page cannot. A natural, conversational style in radio helps keep listeners interested; awkward or stiff monologue sounds false and turns them off.

➤ **Repeat the product name and the 800 number.** Ever since Pavlov rang a dinner bell for his hungry dog, we've known that repetition aids the memory. To get listeners to buy your product, repeat the name and ordering information several times.

➤ **Use short words and short sentences.** Two reasons for this. First, although grammarians hate to admit it, people do *talk* this way. They use short sentences. Sentence fragments. And sentences beginning with the conjunctions *and, or,* and *but.* Secondly, short words and sentences are easier to understand and remember. Listeners cannot grasp long, convoluted arguments and complex terms.

➤ **Supply the visual.** The major disadvantage of radio versus newspapers, magazines, and television is that *radio has no pictures.* It is a medium of words and sound. The listener's imagination supplies the visual based on what the ear takes in. So, if it's important that the listener know what your product looks like, you must describe it in the copy. For example, in a radio spot advertising a line of home-baked pies that are packaged in red aluminum foil, end the commercial with a line like: "So, ask for the pie in the bright red wrapper at your favorite supermarket or grocery store today."

➤ **Use sound effects.** A lifeguard's whistle, children laughing, the tinkling of the bell on an ice cream truck—these are the sounds that can add warmth, drama, and believability to radio advertising. Promoting stock car races at the local speedway? Your commercial should include the roar of engines revving up for the big race. Selling mufflers? Let listeners compare the sound of an auto before and after the new muffler is installed.

➤ **Identify with the listener's situation.** In print advertising, you can use hundreds of words plus photos and diagrams to explain the benefits of your product in great detail. In

Warning!

Keep in mind that adding sound effects to your spot means you will have to record your commercial instead of having it read from script live. And that, in turn, adds considerably to the cost of your radio advertising.

radio and television, you have only 10, 30, or at the most 60 seconds of time to hook the listener's interest and explain your selling proposition. Radio and television are better for eliciting an *emotional* rather than a logical response from consumers. One way to make this a positive response is to create a situation that empathizes with the listener's own life, to get the listener to say, "Oh yes, that's me."

➤ **Ask for the order.** Don't forget to give your toll-free phone number or Web address. Some stations will also allow listeners to write to you, the advertiser, in care of the station, and you can mention this, too, just in case listeners forget to jot down your number. In a direct response radio spot, say the 800 number three or four times.

"Don't be afraid to experiment," says Burt Manning, vice-chairman of J. Walter Thompson, one of the world's largest advertising agencies. "Radio's lower production costs are an invitation to do that. And if you make a mistake, you'll know about it fast, and you can fix it." Try a variety of different approaches in your radio scripts—drama, dialogue, humor, warmth, hard sell. Run the spots that work; rewrite the ones that don't.

In one sense, radio is the *easiest* advertising medium to succeed in. Readers will turn the page on a dull or boring ad. TV watchers use commercial breaks to run to the refrigerator. But according to a recent study on radio-audience listening habits, only 4 percent of radio listeners change the station when they don't like the commercial. So practically any commercial you write and broadcast will be heard. The trick is to get people to *listen* and act.

The Least You Need to Know

➤ The average direct response TV commercials runs two minutes. Infomercials run for 30 minutes.

➤ Using a celebrity—even one who is no longer a big star—can increase infomercial response significantly.

➤ The infomercial customer wants to see that she is getting a lot of stuff and a great value for her money. Example: Anthony Robbins's tape set has each tape in its own album, so laid out on a table it looks like you are getting more.

➤ Any direct marketer can submit products to be considered for selling on QVC or Home Shopping Network.

➤ Radio is an effective but underused direct response medium.

Chapter 15

Telemarketing

> **In This Chapter**
>
> ➤ How telemarketing works
>
> ➤ Writing the phone script
>
> ➤ Improving your telemarketing skills
>
> ➤ Combining telemarketing and direct mail

Telemarketing has a bad rap. Many consumers say they hate it. In his book *Dave Barry's Bad Habits* (Henry Holt, 1993), Barry sarcastically comments: "What I like best about the telephone is that it keeps you in touch with people, particularly people who want to sell you magazine subscriptions in the middle of the night. These people have been abducted by large publishing companies and placed in barbed-wire enclosures surrounded by armed men with attack dogs, and unless they sell 350 magazine subscriptions per day, they will not be fed."

Yes, people will tell you they hate telemarketing. But many people say they also dislike direct mail and TV commercials. Yet all of these things work.

Why Telemarketing Works

The telephone is a results-oriented medium. It is not aimed at building image, creating brand awareness, or promoting your reputation. The purpose is to generate an immediate sales lead, qualify a prospect, set up an appointment, or make a sale.

Use of the telephone as a sales tool is growing. According to an article in *Selling* magazine, IBM expects as many as 80 percent of its worldwide sales transactions to be handled by phone. In today's busy world, a telephone call is often the only way to break through the clutter and grab the attention of the businessperson or consumer.

Surprising Secrets

According to an article in the *Newsletter on Newsletters* (February 16, 2001, p. 8), the top 10 telemarketing firms together have the capacity to make 560 calls per second. That translates to over 16 million calls in an eight-hour day, or more than 322 million calls per month—enough to dial every phone in the U.S. several times.

Surprising Secrets

The Telephone Consumer Protection Act (TCPA) of 1991 forbids telemarketers to call consumers who have asked to have their names placed on a "do not call list." If a telemarketer violates such a request, the consumer can sue the telemarketer directly for $500 to $1,500 per violation.

In telemarketing, you pick up the phone, dial a prospect whose name and number you took from some directory or rented telemarketing list, introduce yourself and your company, and try to get him or her interested in learning more about what you are selling. This prospect is a person you don't know: This person hasn't bought from your company and you have never spoken with him or her before.

Using the phone focuses and expedites the selling process. "You get the prospect's undivided attention, if only for three to five minutes, and you usually get a response, even if it's not the one you want," said Bob Woodall, owner of Sales Consultants International, in an interview with *Selling* magazine.

Response rates to telemarketing calls will vary widely, depending on the market, the product or service, and whether you are generating a lead, arranging a meeting, or qualifying a lead. As a rule of thumb, response rates for cold calls to a prospect list can range from 5 to 20 percent. They can be lower but rarely higher. A 5-percent response rate means that for every 20 calls you make, you will get one positive response. That's not bad. After all, how long does it take to make 20 phone calls?

The 5- to 20-percent response rate to telephone sales calls compares favorably with direct mail, which typically generates response rates of $1/2$ to 3 percent. Or with print advertising, where less than a tenth of a percent of the readers of a particular newspaper or magazine will reply to your ad.

A telephone response of less than 5 percent is not necessarily a bad thing. If you sell high-priced products and services, you may be able to achieve your sales goal for the week with just one or two orders. The higher the price, the lower the response rate you need to make a profit. At the same time, you want to constantly refine your approach to see if you can increase response. The better your response rate, the greater your sales.

With a higher response rate, you have to make fewer calls to achieve your sales goal, so you can spend less time selling each day. With a 1-percent response rate, you must make 100 telephone calls to generate one positive response. With a 10-percent response rate, getting that positive response requires only 10 calls.

Creating a Winning Telemarketing Script

A script is the written dialogue for handling the telemarketing call. Telemarketing is most effective when the caller has practiced using word-for-word openings, product presentations, and answers to common objections.

It's important that you get the call off to a good start, and to do this, you must have a pretty good idea of what you want to say and how to say it. You should write an opening script, and practice it many times, until it becomes second nature to you. The goal is to sound like you aren't reading a script.

Later on in the call, you'll be responding intelligently to what the prospect says and how he or she sounds and acts. But at the beginning, you have almost no clues from which to take your lead. That's why, to cold call with confidence, you must be prepared to carry on the first 30 to 60 seconds of your call with little feedback or participation from the prospect.

To be effective, the opening script, when delivered, should tell your prospect the following four points:

1. Who you are—your name and, if appropriate, title

2. The name of your business

3. The reason you are calling

4. The reason why the prospect should be interested in talking with you—or at least hearing what you have to say

Do you really need all this? Yes. If you leave out or try to defer giving away the first three items (your name, the company name, the reason for your call), the prospect is likely to resent your evasiveness and become annoyed.

People want to know who they are talking to, and why. You can't get around this. But you can present the information in a way that arouses interests rather than turns people off. If you leave out the fourth item (why the prospect will want to hear what you have to say), the prospect will quickly lose interest in and motivation for continuing the conversation, and the call is likely to be ended by the prospect in short order.

Fortunately, these four points don't represent an overload of information, and you can get it all in—smoothly, quickly, and without sounding like a salesperson.

There is an endless variety of opening scripts that achieve these objectives with varying degrees of success. But most of them are variations of one of two basic openings:

the benefit-statement opening and the prospect need-qualification opening. Although I have a strong preference for, and almost always use, the latter, let's take a look at both of these proven openers.

The Benefit-Statement Script

In the benefit-statement script, you follow the guidelines of immediately giving the prospect the four key pieces of information—who you are, your company, the reason for your call, and the reason the prospect should be interested. But you do it with a twist.

The twist is this: In the description of your company and the reason for your call, instead of just saying the company name and what its product or service is, you tell the prospect the *benefit* of what you do—not the actual title, product name, service category, or function. For example:

Caller: *Mr. Doakes?*

Prospect: *Yes, how can I help you?*

Caller: *Mr. Doakes, my name is Michael Jones, and I'm a Catalog Production Specialist with Royal Printing. Have you heard of us?*

Prospect: *I don't think so.*

Caller: *We specialize in helping companies like yours produce quality catalogs at a significantly lower production and printing cost than they are now paying. Mr. Doakes, if I could show you how ABC Company can maintain its high standards of quality in your catalogs while cutting printing costs 10 to 20 percent, would you be interested in taking a look?*

Prospect: *Well, how would you do that?*

Note, in this script, that Michael gives his title as a Catalog Production Specialist. The title you use in telephone sales calls should not contain the word "sales" in it. When prospects hear "sales" in your title, they rightly assume you are a salesperson trying to sell them something, and they want to get away from you as rapidly as possible.

After giving his company name, Michael asked, "Have you heard of us?" This inserts a natural break into the conversation that prevents Michael from giving a too-long monologue at the beginning of the call. It gets prospects involved early.

Marketing Tip

Instead of saying you are a financial planner, you say, "I help people become wealthier and retire earlier." Instead of saying you are a color catalog printer, you say "I help companies produce better-looking catalogs while significantly reducing their production lead time and printing costs."

If the prospects haven't heard of you, they appreciate that you're modest enough to realize that and ask them. If they have, they become comfortable talking to a vendor they perceive as well-known. Either way, you win. At the close of his opening script, Michael asks the prospect, "If I could show you a way to achieve [benefit X], would you be interested?" Prospects are more likely to respond positively if you offer a benefit and ask if they want that benefit. Response will often not be as enthusiastic if you merely say, "Are you interested in buying widgets?"

The benefit-statement script is used by numerous telemarketers and can be very effective. The advantage is that it presents your offer in terms of customer benefits, not product or service or seller. The disadvantage is that it can come across as a "sales pitch." And some prospects find it evasive. Their feeling: "If you are a printing broker, just come right out and say it; don't ask me if I want to save money on printing. Of course I do. What kind of idiotic question is that?"

Also, the benefit you stress in your opening may not be the benefit the customer considers most important in evaluating your type of product or service. For instance, if you offer lower costs, and a particular prospect is more interested in higher quality, than you've already disconnected with prospect—you're not talking about what really interests him or her. You're not on the same wavelength. And it's difficult to get back on track, because you've already presented yourself as the low-cost supplier, not the quality supplier. To then say, "Oh, we are also better quality" lacks credibility.

This danger can be avoided by using the prospect need-qualification script. Let's take a look at how it works.

The Prospect Need-Qualification Script

In the benefit-statement opening, you tell the prospect, "Here is what you need, and here is the benefit—the advantage we offer over other suppliers." But, if that benefit doesn't match the customer's concerns, you are in trouble.

In the prospect need-qualification opening, you *ask* prospects, "What benefits are you most interested in when evaluating products or services like mine?" The prospects tell you. And then you present your capabilities as favorable to helping the prospects achieve their goals better than what they're now doing.

Here's how Michael Jones might have used the need-qualification opening with Mr. Doakes:

> Caller: *Is this Mr. Doakes?*
>
> Prospect: *Yes, how can I help you?*
>
> Caller: *My name is Michael Jones, and I'm a Catalog Production Specialist with Royal Printing. Mr. Doakes, are you still the Manager of Communications at ABC?*
>
> Prospect: *Yes, I am.*

> Caller: *And are you the person responsible for buying four-color printing for your company?*
>
> Prospect: *Yes.*
>
> Caller: *May I ask you question?*
>
> Prospect: *Yes.*
>
> Caller: *What would it take for Royal Printing to do color catalog printing for your firm?*
>
> Prospect: *Well, although cost is always important, we're primarily concerned with quality and reliability.*
>
> Caller: *[Begins to talk about Royal Printing in terms of quality and reliability, not emphasizing price.]*

There are some important points to note about this script. First, Michael Jones qualified the prospect. He asked if he has reached Mr. Doakes, if Mr. Doakes is still the Communications Manager, and if he is the person in charge of color catalog printing. Had Mr. Doakes said he was in fact not responsible for buying color printing, Jones would then ask him: "Can you tell me who that would be?" He would then end the call with Doakes and phone the other person, noting, "I got your name from Michael Doakes," turning the conversation from a cold call into a referral.

Second, Michael Jones qualified the need. He learned that ABC still bought color printing and was therefore a prospect for his service. If Mr. Doakes had said, "We do it all in-house and no longer buy color printing outside," Jones would know his chances of making a sale to Doakes were extremely limited.

Third, Michael Jones, having established that ABC buys his type of service and Doakes is the buyer, asks, "What would it take for us to do business together?" Instead of picking one fact about Royal and presenting it to the customer as a benefit, he has asked, "What benefits are you looking for that we might be able to offer you?"

When the prospect answers, Jones knows one of two things: Either Royal can't meet the need, and this is not a good prospect, or Royal can meet the need, because Royal's capabilities are compatible with the customer's requirements. Knowing this, and knowing what those requirements are, Jones can then effectively present Royal's capabilities in a way that maximizes the prospect's interest in the service. The prospect need-qualification opening is so effective and so comfortable precisely because it puts the focus on the prospect, where it belongs.

Try both the need-qualification and the benefit-statement opening scripts, and see which works best for you. Vary the scripts in this chapter to fit your own selling situation. Combine them, or create your own opening.

Surprising Secrets

Ever pick up the phone when it rings, then hear silence? Just when you're ready to hang up, someone finally comes on the line—and it's a sales pitch. The cause is "predictive dialers" used by telemarketers to make calls. These are computer systems with a number of phone lines. The computer keeps dialing numbers. When you answer and say "hello," the call is transferred to an available telemarketing operator. The silence you hear is the lag time between when you answer and when the call is transferred to the telemarketer.

Becoming a Telemarketing Master

What separates a successful telemarketing representative from one whose sole accomplishment is to annoy people at dinner? It's largely a matter of delivery and technique.

Shift Your Delivery to Accommodate Prospect Mood

When delivering your opening script, you can adjust the delivery to fit the reception the prospect is giving you over the phone:

➤ **If the prospect is interested and open to your message,** slow down a bit. Be relaxed, friendly, cordial. Have a real conversation. The prospect is inviting you to do so.

➤ **If the prospect is neutral,** proceed on an even keel. Don't get too informal or comfy. But take your time, remain professional, and move things along at a reasonably brisk pace.

➤ **If the prospect seems bored, disinterested, or hostile,** and your benefit-statement or need-qualification opening doesn't warm the person up, you may want to politely end the call and move to the next prospect on your list. The person is probably not going to respond positively. At least not today.

➤ **If the prospect seems pressed for time,** ask when would be a good time to call back. Make an appointment to call back on that date and time. Make sure the prospect knows it's an appointment. Write it in your appointment calendar. Then follow up and make the call. If the prospect isn't there when you call, keep trying until you do connect.

Improving Your Telemarketing Technique

Telemarketing consultant Mary Anne Weinstein offers these additional tips for tele-marketers making cold calls:

1. Make sure your phone provides a clear sound, is comfortable, sturdy, and easy to use. Touch tone produces a ring 50 percent faster than rotary does.

2. Let each call ring no more than six times. If you get a busy, move on to the next call. Do not replace the receiver after each call. It's a waste of time.

3. Everything rides on your voice. It's more important than your script. Your voice needs to be warm and friendly and properly pitched; not too loud or too soft; not too fast or too slow; not garbled or slurred. It must sound enthusiastic and sincere.

4. Your script needs to tell your listeners who you are, what you are offering, how it will benefit them, and how, when, and what they need to do to buy your product or service. *Don't expect it to be perfect the first time.* You will need to work with it, making modifications as you go. Keep trying. You will get it right.

5. Your list, too, must be tested and qualified. When you have done this you are ready to begin. Pick up the phone and start making more money!

6. Get a good night's sleep before any day you have earmarked as a telemarketing day. Telemarketers take more rejection than most people can stand. "Sleep is na-ture's soft nurse."

7. Take a break after each hour of work, never skip lunch, and don't work for more than four or five hours a day. After four hours, productivity decreases greatly.

To this list I add the tip: Drink water before making telemarketing calls. It avoids dry mouth and helps your voice stay smooth. Also, remember that rejection brings you closer to success. The only telemarketers who don't hear "no" are those who have given up making calls. Every new day presents its own challenge for outstanding achievement and superior performance in our every human endeavor.

Telemarketing and Direct Mail: A Powerful One-Two Punch

Telemarketing can work in tandem with other sales and marketing methods for a syn-ergistic effect. Don't feel forced to choose between telemarketing and other marketing methods. For many businesses, it makes sense to use the telephone in conjunction with other methods. For example …

➤ Calling prospects and customers to invite them to a trade show, seminar, or other event.

➤ Calling customers to renew their contract, lease, policy, or subscription as follow-up to a written notice.

➤ Calling people to remind them to attend a sale, party, meeting, seminar, or other event they have already agreed to come to.

➤ Following up with a phone call to everyone who responded to your ad and requested a brochure or catalog on your products.

➤ Following up with prospects after face-to-face sales presentations.

➤ Calling prospects to set up or confirm an appointment.

➤ Taking a survey and following up with information sent via mail.

➤ Calling prospects after purchase to ensure satisfaction with the product or service and upsell them on additional products.

➤ Letting current customers know about special offers, promotions, discounts, and opportunities.

➤ Updating prospects on new products or new offers.

➤ Periodically reminding customers and prospects about you and your products and services.

Results to direct mailings, for example, can be increased 10 to 25 percent or more when a follow-up call to every prospect is made a week or so after the pieces are mailed.

Telemarketing's Dynamic Duo: Feedback and Flexibility

The telephone is an interactive, two-way marketing tool. Aside from the Internet, the telephone is one of the few marketing vehicles that is interactive and allows instantaneous two-way communication between the seller and the prospect. The interactive nature of the telephone enables you to get instant feedback and adjust efforts accordingly.

Scripts and call guidelines can be changed instantly to increase response and at virtually no cost. The ability to ask questions and get immediate answers enables you to qualify prospects on the spot—and more definitively— better than almost any other selling method.

When you send out a mailing, you don't know why people respond (or do not respond) the way they do. With telephone selling, your prospects frequently tell you what they think of your product, your offer, you, and the phone call. As a result, you can immediately respond to objections that, unanswered, would prevent a sale. You can answer questions, provide additional information, and reason with the person on the other end of the line. In short, you can sell.

Not only does this increase your chances of selling the current prospect, but it gives you a good feel for how your overall sales approach is working. You can call 10 or 20 prospects, analyze the results, and try a different approach on the next 10 to 20 people. And you can repeat this until you find something that works.

The Least You Need to Know

➤ If people ask you not to call them any more, do as they request. To do otherwise is illegal and can result in a financial judgment against you of $500 or more per violation.

➤ Anticipate common objections and script answers to them in advance. Ideally, a telemarketer should not be asked a question to which she does not already have the answer.

➤ Avoid deception. Tell the person who you are, where you are from, and the purpose of your call right away.

➤ Following up a direct mailing with a telemarketing call can lift response 10 to 25 percent or higher.

Chapter 16

The Internet: Direct Marketing for the Digital Age

In This Chapter

➤ Enabling purchasing on your site

➤ Creating the perfect home page

➤ Accepting payments on your site

➤ Increasing sales with links and affiliate programs

➤ Marketing with e-mail and e-zines

If you go to a direct marketing convention today, you can simply peek your head into the seminar rooms and see the concern direct marketers' have for learning to use the Internet profitably. On average, attendance at Internet-focused presentations is three times larger than attendance at sessions focusing on traditional direct marketing.

Direct marketers, as of this writing, have not yet mastered the Internet as a marketing tool or profit center. Right now we are in the testing stage with mixed results and no clear single formula for how to do it right. For instance, Amazon.com sells millions of books on the Web via direct marketing, but they are still missing the key ingredient—profit—by which direct marketers deem a new medium a success or failure.

This chapter explores direct marketing vehicles on the Internet that are already achieving some measure of success.

Integrating E-Commerce into Your Direct Marketing Program

There are three phases in enabling purchasing on your site, and you can start with Phase 1 right away, then gradually evolve your capability as your site expands.

Phase 1: Go beyond merely having product descriptions posted on your Web site to giving actual prices. You also include ordering instructions along with shipping and handling options. You then take orders offline. Web site visitors can call an 800 number posted on your Web pages, just like in your offline catalog. Add an *HTML* (HyperText Markup Language) or pdf (portable document format) order form to your Web site. Encourage people to print the order form, fill it out, and fax or mail it to order—again, just like an order form in a catalog.

Insider's Buzzwords

HTML stands for HyperText Markup Language. It is the computer language that enables graphics to be placed on Web sites and integrated into e-mails.

Phase 2: Replace the pdf or HTML order form with an online order form that is interactive. Visitors no longer have to print the order form and fill it in by hand. They can enter information to fill in fields on the screen and click boxes to indicate their preferences (for example, regular versus priority shipping). When they are finished, they submit the order form with their payment, which is typically credit card information.

On your end, you have to run the credit card number manually to get approval. You may also have to transfer the customer information to a database to keep a record of the transaction. If there is a problem with the credit card, you can send an e-mail to notify the customer and resolve it. You do not have to create such an interactive online order form yourself. You can find several at www.scriptsearch.com. Pick one and download it for use on your own site.

Phase 3: You have a full-fledged online catalog or shopping cart system on your Web site, similar to Amazon.com or other high-traffic commerce sites such as Victoria's Secret. Phase 3 is the online equivalent of a mail order catalog or retail store. You can flip through the pages or walk the aisles, pick the merchandise you want, put it in your cart or on your order form, then check out at a cash register to finalize your purchase.

Unlike Phase 2, a Phase 3 e-commerce site usually checks, authorizes, and charges the credit card automatically, eliminating the need to do this manually. If there is a problem with the credit card, the site automatically notifies the customer and does not accept the order until it is corrected.

Almost all e-commerce Web sites, whether in Phase 1, 2, or 3, offer online shoppers a money-back guarantee of satisfaction. If you do not, online buyers will go elsewhere.

When you implement e-commerce Phase 1, 2, or 3, promote your product sales on your Web site. One way to do this is with banners that pop-up announcing specials and sales.

Building a Web Site

The first step in creating your Web site is to write an outline, or site map. The site map shows the topic of each page and how the pages link. What should the page topics be? In his book *Roger C. Parker's Guide to Web Content and Design* (MIS Press, 1997), my friend Roger Parker says content should consist of two components:

1. Information your prospects need to know in order to buy from you

2. Information you know that will convince prospects to buy from you

Need-to-Know Information

Information your prospects need to know in order to buy from you is the product information a serious potential buyer is likely to ask for. This "need-to-know" stuff includes …

➤ **An overview of your products or services.** This is usually found on your home page or an "About Us" page.

➤ **Pages on individual products and services.** Create one page per product or service.

➤ **Additional product information.** This would include such things as specs, features, options, accessories, models, ratings, upgrades.

➤ **Customers.** Who buys from you?

➤ **Projects.** What are some of the major projects your firm has handled?

➤ **Applications.** What applications is your product used for? What industries do you serve?

➤ **Testimonials.** Are customers satisfied? What do they say about you?

Marketing Tip

Web consultant Amy Africa says special offers should appear in the upper right-hand corner of your home page, because this is the most read area of your site. Africa advises making some noticeable change to your home page frequently—every 8 to 10 days. These changes can include new banners announcing new specials, news items, or graphics. Basic colors and navigation tools should not be changed.

Marketing Tip

Converting a printed color brochure to an HTML file can sometimes be tricky. One company used typography printed over color photos, which was difficult to read when put on a Web page. The Web designer changed the design for the HTML versions, so that the copy was taken off the photo background and printed in black against a white background next to the pictures for greater legibility.

Product information can be of several varieties. A common technique is to post product brochures on the site.

In industrial companies, it is common to photocopy product brochures and circulate copies to different decision makers while evaluating potential vendors. If you serve such a market, consider posting your product data sheets as pdf files which, when printed, look remarkably similar to a printed brochure.

Allow viewers to "drill down" to the level of detail they need. One chemical company has links in its product brochures to MSDs, or "material safety data" sheets, on the safe handling of each chemical it sells. A prospect with a particular safety concern can get his or her question immediately answered by accessing the MSD sheets on-line.

Want-to-Know Information

Your Web site should not only contain everything the prospect wants and needs to know about you—but also everything *you want to tell them*. There are certain facts and information prospects may not look for or ask about, but that you would want to tell them, nonetheless. These are items that establish credibility and expertise.

Marketing Tip

On the Web site for my free-lance copywriting practice, www.bly.com, I post samples of my work—because potential clients want to see promotions I've written for other companies before making the decision to hire me. They can also click on a page showing color images of the covers of the many books I've written on marketing. That's what I want them to see, because it increases their comfort level regarding my expertise in my craft.

Many products are, to a large extent, commodities, with little to differentiate your goods from another vendor's. What determines whether the customer buys from you is whether you can convince the buyer that you are reliable, trustworthy, knowledgeable, and competent. In other words, you know what you're doing, better than your competitors.

Jericho Communications, a New York PR firm, has a large button on its site labeled "Awards." Through that link, you can find all the PR awards Jericho has won. Although you may be more interested in PR results than awards, Jericho knows you'll be impressed.

They also offer a document called "Five Point Equation for Ideas That Work." Even though you may not intend to ask how they come up with PR ideas, they proactively tell you. The method establishes believability—they have a system for producing ideas—and makes you feel you have learned something about creativity when you read it.

Posting content on your billboard site—useful information, such as white papers (reports) or how-to articles—is another, more subtle way of convincing potential customers that you are the qualified source.

After all, if they read and are impressed with your article on how to select a hydraulic pump, they're more likely to buy the pump from you than from another seller.

One technique you might consider is a button on your home page for "Recommended Vendors." It opens to an HTML file or database of resources, in fields allied with yours, that your visitors might find useful. For example: As a copywriter, I provide a list of recommended vendors including graphic designers and HTML programmers. When you post a regularly updated recommended vendors section, visitors come to view your site as a useful resource. Knowing that they can find on your site the other products and services they need to complete their project, increases the likelihood of visitors buying your product as well.

Designing Your Home Page

As you know, a home page is the "title page" of your Web site—the first thing a visitor sees when he or she clicks onto your Web site address. Your home page, at minimum, should contain the following seven elements:

1. **A strong headline.** The headline can welcome visitors to the site ("Welcome to the world of e-speak"), reinforce the company positioning ("your online one-stop printing shop"), or state a benefit ("Find a job fast").

2. **A site introduction.** Two to three paragraphs directly under your headline should explain your site's reason for being, who can benefit, and what those benefits are. The introduction should "orient" the reader to where he or she is on the Internet (your site) and why he or she came (the information or help you offer).

3. **A site menu.** This is a series of buttons the reader can use to access the various sections or pages of the site. These should remain at the sides, top, or bottom of the screen as the user navigates through the site.

4. **What's new.** Internet users are always looking for what's new, so highlight news and new features on your home page, either with a "What's New" button or a banner advertising special offers and new information.

5. **Contact information.** Make it easy for the visitor to find your Internet address, snail mail address, e-mail address, and phone and fax numbers. You never know when or how a potential customer may want to contact you. A buyer with an immediate need may feel the need to speak with a live person on the spot and not wait for an e-mail reply.

6. **Instant e-mail reply.** On the home page and elsewhere display a click-on button that lets visitors instantly send e-mail to you. Be sure someone in your office reads the incoming e-mails at least daily.

7. **Privacy statement.** Show visitors you respect their electronic privacy by posting a privacy statement on your home page. For example, Nike's privacy statement

reads: "Okay, so you're on your computer minding your own business and you get an e-mail telling you about a special offer from Nike for free shoes, or some other golden opportunity. Don't believe it. It's not real. For the record, Nike doesn't send out unsolicited e-mails. From time to time we'll notify consumers who let us know they want to hear from us. Otherwise, any information on the Internet from Nike to the public comes on www.nike.com or www.nikebiz.com.

Web marketers often speak of the "Three C's" of Web sites—commerce, community, and content. *Commerce* is the ability to take orders over the Internet. *Community* means the site provides a forum, chat group, bulletin board, or other mechanism for visitors to share thoughts, opinions, and information about the subject of the site. *Content* is the information available to visitors on the site. Sites that offer all three C's in abundance get more visitors, have those visitors stay longer, and sell them more products.

Taking Product Orders on Your Site

To sell products directly on your Web site, you need a mechanism for taking the orders, as well as the ability to accept payments online. The order mechanism can be a shopping cart or a Web-based order form. When you are just starting out with only a few products, an order form—also called a "guest book," "guest page" or "registration "page"—is the simpler, easier option.

Almost any Web designer can create order pages and shopping carts for you. Programming charges are anywhere from $75 to $150 per hour.

One issue in form design is how much information to ask for. At minimum, you want to get the prospect's contact information: name, company, street address, city, state, zip code, phone, fax, and e-mail address. You can ask additional questions to quality the prospect. For instance, how many employees does the prospect have? Does her she have children? Is the prospect thinking of buying a new car? How soon?

Warning!

People will fill out a form or guest book with one to three simple questions. More than that and response rate drops. So limit your questions to three.

You can think of the guest book on your Web site as the online equivalent of the reply card in a direct mail package. As is the case with reply cards, there is a trade-off in guest books when asking questions: The more questions you ask, the better you qualify the prospect. But ask too many questions, and people will give up. They will stop halfway without completing or submitting the form, and your response rate will decline.

Your guest book should include an "opt-in" box. This is a box followed by text that reads: "Check here if you are willing to receive occasional e-mails about products and offers of interest to" you." When the prospect clicks this box and submits the form, he or she has given you permission to send promotional e-mails. These e-mail marketing messages can be from you or other companies to whom you rent your e-list.

Your Web form should also allow the visitor to give you credit card information if making a purchase. Although some e-commerce sites permit customers to pay with check or C.O.D., the best method is to accept major credit cards at the time of the transaction. It's convenient for the customer and ensures that you get your money.

An article in *The Interactive Multimedia Sourcebook 1997* says that nearly 90 percent of online shoppers pay by credit card. Yet, according to *Business Week* (April 17, 2000, p. 10), only 28 percent of large businesses surveyed say they can process a transaction online.

If you plan on taking orders on your Web site, get "merchant status" with, at minimum, American Express, Visa, and MasterCard. "Merchant status" allows you to accept credit cards for purchase payments both online and offline.

Another payment option is to work through a service bureau that can process the online payments for you. One such company is CyberCash, which promotes itself as "the leading provider of electronic commerce payment services." They can be reached at www.cybercash.com.

Another service bureau, 1ClickCharge, specializes in allowing online purchases for small dollar amounts—typically less than $20. They store the customer's credit card information, so the buyer doesn't have to re-enter the card number and expiration date whenever they visit your site. 1ClickCharge can be reached at www.1clickcharge.com.

Links and Affiliate Programs

Links take you from Web site to Web site. For example, when you use a search engine, you are given a list of Web sites that match your interest. The names of the sites on the list are linked to the home pages of each Web site. You click on the name and go directly to the site.

But what about using strategic links not only to make your site easier to navigate, but to actually increase traffic and add value for your visitors? You will find that many Web sites have a separate button on the home page labeled "Links." When you click on it, you are given a list of sites. The names are highlighted because they are hot links or hyperlinks that, if you click on one, will send you directly to the site. Through a strategic links page, you can give your visitors access to content and resources that are relevant, but that you don't want to (or can't) include on your site.

Another way to improve your Web site with links is to guide visitors to products and services that complement your own but are not in direct competition with you. For example: You sell plants and bulbs through a Web site, and some of your plants require special grades of soil that are not always easy to find in nurseries and gardening stores.

Marketing Tip

Some Web sites link to other sites as a service to their visitors, with no financial arrangements between sites. Often the agreement is reciprocal—if you link to my site, I want, in exchange, to be allowed to link to yours. An increasingly popular arrangement is the "affiliate program." I put a link from my site to your site. If a Web visitor clicks from my site to your site and then makes a purchase, you pay me a percentage—typically 5 to 15 percent—on that sale.

You want to help your customers but do not want to be in the soil or dirt business. What do you do? Add links to the Web sites of companies who sell the soil your customers will need. These links can be on a separate links page. You can also have them appear on the product pages for the plants requiring these soils. Customers will appreciate the convenience. And with the soil concern removed, you will sell more of these particular plants.

Although there is some question as to whether you need permission to put up a link to someone else's site, most people will be glad to have you do it. I have never heard of someone telling another site operator, "Please do not link to my 'site'"—although I suppose it could happen. (If it did, it's easy enough to remove the link.)

Banner Advertising

Banner ads are small ads that pop up on the screen while a visitor is on a Web site. They are, typically, small boxes with a few words in an eye-catching design, created using HTML. To respond, the visitor clicks on the site and is taken to a Web page where he or she can view more information or fill in a guest page or other reply form.

Banner ads tend to generate low response rates. Typically, one half of 1 percent of those who see the ad will click on it to learn more. But their low cost makes them worth a test. Many list brokers who handle e-mail lists also offer banner placement services.

Internet Direct Mail

Internet direct mail, also known as "e-mail marketing," consists of sending an e-mail to a list of prospects. The e-mail can be text or graphics. Text mailings are naturally quicker and easier to produce, and work quite well. If your product lends itself to a visual presentation, you can enhance your e-mail with graphics.

When creating an e-mail marketing campaign, keep these ideas in mind:

➤ At the beginning of the e-mail, put a "From" line and a "Subject" line. The From line identifies you as the sender if you're e-mailing to your house file. If you're e-mailing to a rented list, the From line might identify the list owner as the sender. This is especially effective with opt-in lists where the list owner (for example, a Web site) has a good relationship with its users.

The Subject line should be constructed like a short attention-grabbing, curiosity-arousing outer envelope teaser, compelling recipients to read further—without being so blatantly promotional it turns them off. For example: "Come on back to Idea Forum!"

➤ Some e-marketers think the "From" line is trivial and unimportant; others think it's critical. Internet copywriter Ivan Levison says, "I often use the word 'Team' in the From line. It makes it sound as if there's a group of bright, energetic, enthusiastic people standing behind the product." For instance, if you are sending an e-mail to a rented list of computer people to promote a new software product, your Subject and From lines might read as follows: From: The Adobe PageMill Team/Subject: Adobe PageMill 3.0 limited-time offer!

➤ Despite the fact that the word "free" is a proven powerful response booster in traditional direct marketing, and that the Internet culture has a bias in favor of free offers over paid offers, some e-marketers avoid "free" in the subject line. The reason has to do with the "*spam*-filter" software some Internet users have installed to screen their e-mail. These filters eliminate incoming e-mail, and many identify any message with free in the subject line as promotional.

➤ Lead off the message copy with a killer headline or lead-in sentence. You need to get a terrific benefit right up front. Pretend you're writing envelope teaser copy or are writing a headline for a sales letter.

➤ In the first paragraph, deliver a mini-version of your complete message. State the offer and provide an immediate response mechanism, such as clicking on a link connected to a Web page. This appeals to Internet prospects with short attention spans.

➤ After the first paragraph, present expanded copy that covers the features, benefits, proof, and other information the buyer needs to

Insider's Buzzwords

Spam is unsolicited promotional e-mail messages sent to people who have not given permission for marketing-oriented e-mails to be sent to them.

make a decision. This appeals to the prospect who needs more details than a short paragraph can provide.

➤ The offer and response mechanism should be repeated in the close of the e-mail, just as in a traditional direct mail letter. But they should almost always appear at the very beginning, too. That way, busy Internet users who don't have time to read or who give each e-mail only a second or two get the whole story.

➤ John Wright, of the Internet-marketing services firm MediaSynergy, says that if you put multiple response links within your e-mail message, 95 percent of click-through responses will come from the first two. Therefore, you should probably limit the number of click-through links in your e-mail to three. An exception might be an e-newsletter or "e-zine" broken into five or six short items, where each item is on a different subject and therefore each has its own link.

➤ Use wide margins. You don't want to have weird wraps or breaks. Limit yourself to about 55 to 60 characters per line. If you think a line is going to be too long, just hit the return key to create a new line. Internet copywriter Joe Vitale sets his margins at 20 and 80, keeping sentence length to 60 characters, and ensuring the whole line gets displayed on the screen without odd text breaks.

➤ Take it easy on the all caps. You can use WORDS IN ALL CAPS but do so sparingly. They can be a little hard to read—and in the world of e-mail, all caps give the impression that you're shouting.

➤ In general, short is better. This is not the case in classic mail-order selling where as a general principle, "the more you tell, the more you sell." E-mail is a unique environment. Readers are quickly sorting through a bunch of messages and aren't disposed to stick with you for a long time.

➤ Regardless of length, get the important points across quickly. If you want to give a lot of product information, add it lower down in your e-mail message. You might also consider an attachment, such as a Word document, pdf file, or HTML page. People who need more information can always scroll down or click for it. The key benefits and deal should be communicated in the first screen, or very soon afterward.

➤ The tone should be helpful, friendly, informative, and educational, not promotional or hard-sell. "Information is the gold in cyberspace," says Vitale. Trying to sell readers with a traditional hyped-up sales letter won't work. People online want information and lots of it. You'll have to add solid material to your puffed-up sales letter to make it work online. Refrain from saying your service is "the best" or that you offer "quality." Those are empty, meaningless phrases. Be specific. How are you the best? What exactly do you mean by quality? And who says it besides you? And even though information is the gold, readers don't want to be bored. They seek, like all of us, excitement. Give it to them.

➤ Include an opt-out statement to prevent *flaming* from recipients who feel they have been spammed, and say that your intention is to respect their privacy. It also makes it easy for them to prevent further promotional e-mails from being sent to them. All they have to do is click on Reply and type "unsubscribe" or "remove" in the subject line. For example: "We respect your online time and privacy, and pledge not to abuse this medium. If you prefer not to receive further e-mails from us of this type, please reply to this e-mail and type 'remove' in the subject line."

While e-mail marketing is not the "miracle replacement" for regular direct mail people once thought it could be, Internet direct mail is, nonetheless, extremely effective, generating about twice the response of regular direct mail at about half the cost per thousand.

Insider's Buzzwords

Flaming is an angry response from an irate online user to an unsolicited, unwanted promotional e-mail message they received from you. Flames can range from cursing to threats to tampering with your computer system via hacking.

E-Zines and E-Zine Classified Ads

An e-zine—short for "electronic magazine"—is a newsletter distributed over the Internet. Frequency varies from daily to weekly to monthly. Some are published sporadically only when the sponsor has news. Almost all e-zines are free.

Should you publish an e-zine? It's probably a good idea if you already publish, or would like to publish, a print newsletter, catalog, or other promotion you mail multiple times throughout the year. The e-zine can serve as a supplement to keep your audience informed between issues. You can also mail the print publication less frequently, relying on the e-zine to keep people up to date.

If you are frequently e-mailing your site registrants and customers, an e-zine can serve as an alternate to strictly promotional e-mail. A good program of contact is two e-mails a month, one a promotional e-mail and the other your e-zine.

There are many different e-zine formats, anywhere from simple text (ASCII) to elaborate graphics

Warning!

Be careful about using a pdf or HTML format. Some people consider it a pain to detach files or don't have the Adobe Acrobat Reader needed to open and view pdf files. As for HTML e-zines, they take longer than straight ASCII e-mails to download, and if they take *too* long, it's tempting for the recipient to hit the delete button and move on to the next e-mail.

(HTML) to animation and real audio (rich media). Some e-zines are graphically designed to look like a printed newsletter or bulletin. They are sent either as an attached pdf file or as an HTML e-mail.

Fortunately, fancy design isn't needed or even, necessarily, an advantage in publishing a newsletter, whether it's offline or online. By making your e-zine a simple, straight-text ASCII (American Standard Code for Information Interchange) e-mail, which everyone's computer can read, you can achieve an informational look and eliminate design or html programming costs. You further ensure that all recipients can receive and read your e-zine.

An ideal format for your e-zine is to break it into short sections, each featuring a story on a different issue, problem, or product. Each section should have a headline, the story, and if available, a hyperlink the reader can click on to access the page on your Web site giving additional information on that topic.

What type of response can you expect? According to a survey from *Email Newsletter Advertising*—an e-zine about e-zines—75 percent of e-zines generate click-through rates of 2 to 10 percent. A 2 percent rate would mean that for every 100 people receiving your e-zine, two clicked on at least one of the URLs embedded in the e-zine.

Article length can range from a paragraph to a page or more. Most e-zines keep articles brief, usually just a few short paragraphs. You can separate articles with a dashed line or a row of asterisks if you like.

The articles can be a mix of promotional (for example, "New version 3.0 now available for download") and informational (for example, "Tips for recovering from a hard drive crash"). In both types of articles, keep the tone straightforward and direct; avoid promotional hype and product puffery.

Advertising in Other Marketer's E-Zines

Many e-zines will now accept advertising in their publications. For a fee, you can run a 100-word product ad, similar to a classified ad, in someone else's e-zine. The ad includes a hyperlink to your Web site.

A big advantage of advertising in other e-zines is reach: Some of them reach millions of Internet users. Another is the relatively low cost. Running an ad in an e-zine costs around $40 per thousand versus the $150 to $400 per thousand cost of renting and transmitting to an opt-in e-list.

Today, advertising with and on e-mail newsletters is becoming one of the most popular forms of online marketing. Why? Because it is inexpensive, highly targeted, and produces results. Most e-zines accept only one or two ads per issue, so ad clutter is not a problem. And, the e-zine ads get an implied endorsement from the editors by being positioned inside with the rest of the content.

With e-zines, you get incredibly cost-effective marketing. For example, there are e-zines where you can reach a targeted audience of thousands of readers at 1.5 cents to 3 cents per reader or less, all of whom have opted in to receive the publication that carries your advertisement.

The Least You Need to Know

➤ The Internet has many advantages over paper direct marketing including interactivity, speed, and a low cost per thousand.

➤ For most direct marketers, Internet marketing supplements conventional direct marketing methods, but does not replace them.

➤ If you want to direct market products over the Internet, you need a Web site.

➤ When you want to keep your name before your customers and prospects on a frequent basis at low cost, consider publishing your own e-zine.

Part 4
Direct Marketing Applications

This part presents direct marketing techniques and tips for specific products and services. You will learn how to market merchandise to consumers, and then delve into selling products to businesses via direct marketing. We will also cover how direct marketing can be used to sell professional, trade, technical, consulting, and personal services.

You will find specialized advice for marketers of information products such as newsletters, magazines, directories, books, seminars, videos, audiocassettes, CD-ROMs, and software. Then you will learn how to use direct marketing to generate inquiries, fundraise, and employ other nonprofit direct response applications.

Chapter 17

Direct Marketing to Consumers

> **In This Chapter**
>
> ➤ Understanding the mail-order buyer
>
> ➤ Marketing consumer merchandise
>
> ➤ Choosing your company name
>
> ➤ Consumer offers that work

Although direct marketing, today, is used to sell everything from information products to software to memberships, the discipline has its roots in selling merchandise face-to-face. Infomercials, for instance, owe much of their success to the selling techniques used by old-fashioned traveling salesmen who hawked their wares on street corners or at county fairs.

Getting Started in Consumer Mail-Order Merchandise

A mail-order business is a great business to start, either part-time or full-time. It's exciting because it's always changing and it can be very profitable, if run correctly.

One important thing to remember, though, is that mail-order businesses are easy to start, but take work to maintain. Don't believe the hype you hear about making millions overnight in mail order. It's happened to a few lucky fools, but that's about it.

Meeting Your Mail-Order Customers

Although many people, today, respond to direct marketing in catalogs and on Web sites, there is still a "core mail-order buyer" who, if you can reach that person, will spend a small fortune with you.

Many people buy through catalogs or online because of the shopping convenience, but core mail-order buyers go a step further, actually preferring mail order to retail shopping. They like the whole process, from looking at pictures of the merchandise, to reading colorful descriptions in the copy.

They also like the idea of sending in an order and getting their package in the mail. It is always a surprise when they receive it (the buyer almost always forgets exactly when he or she ordered or the date the merchandise is scheduled to arrive), and opening the box is like unwrapping a gift at Christmas.

Using Low-Cost Marketing Methods to Minimize Your Risk

Too many people jump into a mail-order business with an expensive, flashy full-page ad in a big magazine. That's great if it's successful, but what do you do when your ad pulls only enough orders to cover its cost and you have no marketing budget left over for new ads? Lick your wounds and close down your business. The smart thing to do at the start (and throughout your mail-order career) is to take advantage of all the free and low-cost marketing options at your fingertips.

Send a sample of your product along with a press release to the products reviewers at the magazines your customers read. Also, write a short article about a subject or issue that will interest your potential customers and that has a connection to the product you do sell, and submit it to those same magazines.

For example, if you sell bass-fishing lures, write an article on the best times of day for bass fishing. Offer to talk about the subject on radio or TV talk shows that air programs on this subject. Cable TV, in particular, has plenty of talk shows with specific audiences that are desperately in need of guests. In all of these instances, write a short paragraph with information on how to contact you and a general description of the products you sell. Offer your articles or expertise for free, in return for your contact information and product description either appearing at the end of your article, or being read after the interview.

Expanding Your Marketing with the Profits You Make

You should take at least half of your profits and reinvest it in more advertising. When you make your first batch of sales, don't take your profits and buy a BMW.

A good way to grow your sales is by expanding your advertising. If you can afford only one or two small ads in the beginning, that's fine. If those ads are successful, make sure you take the profits from the sales they generate and reinvest them in four or five of the same ads in different magazines. Then, reinvest the profits from those ads into seven or eight ads, and so on. Don't be concerned about making immediate money. You'll make a larger profit later if you reinvest in your business now.

Before you sink hundreds or thousands of dollars into a large ad or mailing, test the waters. Place a smaller ad with the same message in the magazine for two or three issues, and see if it pulls. Or, if you're renting a mailing list, do a smaller mailing to a small percentage of the list, instead of just rolling out the whole thing.

Testing is important in this business. There are two possibilities that can come out of a test. Either the ad or mailing works, or it doesn't. Now, if it didn't work, it's up to you to figure out *why* it didn't. Either the ad or mailing copy isn't effective, or you're reaching the wrong audience. Review the whole picture, find out what needs to be changed, make the changes, and then retest. When you hit on the right combination, take the big plunge. Until then, don't hesitate to cut your losses if a test bombs.

Mail-order success doesn't come from overnight millions, but from steady trickles. Put another way, mail order is really a "get rich slow" business. If you keep plugging away, keep learning from mistakes, and keep trying new things as you find them, you'll at least be headed for success.

Marketing Tip

You won't hit a home run in this business every time you're up at bat. In fact, just like in baseball, you may strike out more times than not. But, the times that you're lucky to get to first base will make up for your strikeouts. You need to keep a stiff upper lip, admit that you didn't get a hit, and move on.

Consumer Direct Mail Percentage Returns

What percentage of returns should you receive from consumer-direct mail? It depends on how much you are spending and how much you are getting back. If you want to sell a Rolls Royce and you receive only a 1-percent return on your mailings, which is more than enough to pay for the mailer and make a nice profit because the cost of the item is so high. Lower priced items need a higher percentage of response.

A rule of thumb is that your business can usually expect a return of around 10 percent if your mailer is going to your regular customers who expect to receive direct mail from you on a regular basis. No other advertising medium gives you an exact measurement. But when you send out a direct mail piece, you'll know in a few days whether or not your mailer worked. That's why people "test" their mailings.

What's in a Direct Mail Company Name?

Ask 500 people already in business how they decided upon their business name and you will get 500 different answers. Everyone has a story behind how they chose their own business name. Even if the business is named after their own birth name, there's a reason why.

There are several reasons why a good business name is vitally important to your business. The first obvious reason is because it is the initial identification to your customers. No one would want to do business with a company if it didn't have a name yet. This makes you look like an amateur who is very unreliable. Even if you call your company "Kevin's Lawn Service," a company name has been established and you are indeed a company. People will, therefore, feel more comfortable dealing with you.

Marketing Tip

When you open a business, in a sense, you are causing a new birth to begin. This new birth was created from an idea alone by you and your associates. It will have its own bank account, federal identification number, credit accounts, income, and bills. On paper, it is another individual! Just as if you were choosing a name for your own unborn child, you need to spend considerable time in deciding upon your business name.

Secondly, a business name, normally, is an indication as to the product or service you offer. "Mary's Typing Service," "Karate Club for Men," "Jim-Dandy Jack-of-All-Trades," "Laurie and Steve's Laundry," "Misty's Gift Boutique," and "Star 1 Publishers" are all examples of simple business names that immediately tell the customer what product or service you offer.

However, most people will choose the simple approach when naming their business. They use their name, their spouse's name, their children's names, or a combination of these names when naming a business. The national hamburger-restaurant chain "Wendy's" was named after the owner's daughter. However, research has proven that these "cutesy" names are not the best names to use for a business. Many experts claim that it makes the business look too "mom and pop." However, this depends on the business. If you are selling something that demands this mood or theme to appeal to your market, it's best to use this approach.

Personally, I am inclined to name my businesses with catchy names that stick in people's heads after we have initially made contact. Names like, "Sensible Solutions,"

"Direct Defenders," "Moonlighters Ink," "Printer's Friend," "Strictly Class," "Collections and Treasures," and "Starlight on Twilight" are all good examples of catchy names. These types of names relate to your product or service but serve as a type of slogan for your business, as well. This is a big help when marketing.

One marketer owns a business called "Mint and Pepper." He grows and sells his own line of raw seasonings to people in the local area. At a get-together for small businesses, he passed out his business card. The card had a peppermint candy wrapped in plastic glued on the back and the slogan read: "Your business is worth a mint to us." This marketing concept not only got noticed and remembered, but brought in several large orders for the business.

Finally, when coming up with a name for your direct marketing company, try to avoid very long names. Pick a short name, because shorter names can fit into small display ads. Or abbreviate. Amalgamated International Enterprises can be easily presented as AIE, which is easier and shorter to spell.

Marketing Tip

A good name sounds like the company has the expertise to create and support the product being offered. For instance, if you are selling horoscopes by mail, try a name like the American Astrological Institute. This can be shortened to AAI in small display and classified ads.

"Romancing" the Buyer

Earlier I said that the hard-core mail-order buyer likes to be sold. These buyers are particularly receptive to "story copy"—copy that makes the product more alluring by telling an interesting story about it.

Here is a letter, written by copywriter David Yale, that romances a rather ordinary product: jewelry. Notice in the lead that he creates a tension by talking about foreigners, even though this is simply an Australian mail-order firm selling jewelry to Australians:

Dear [First name]:

I'm writing to you because I'm sick and tired of selling our best Australian Opals to foreigners. It's hard work finding these shimmering beauties, and then I have to stand by and watch 90% of them go to Japan, Germany and the USA.

If I'm going to work so hard and live in this dry and dusty place, I want my finest gems to go to Australians.

Why shouldn't Australians like you, [First name], have the chance to wear jewelry with the look of Black Opal? Well, the other night, and it was a hot one here in the outback, I figured out how to do it.

Instead of selling all my finest Opals to foreign middlemen who mount them in tacky settings and sell them back to us Australians for inflated prices—why not work with an <u>Australian</u> jeweler? Why not make the finest Opal jewelry right here, in Australia, for Australians only?

To make a long story short, I found an Australian jeweler who agreed to my terms. I would get him the best Opals on the planet for the best prices in the world. And he would give a limited number of Australian ladies, including you, [First name], the chance to **wear the Black Magic Opal Ring FREE for one month.**

When I went down to Sydney to see the ring he created, I was stunned. The Black Magic Opal Ring is bezel-set in a gorgeous Vogue-style, solid-silver mounting. I know my Opals, and this ring has the look of costly Black Opal that could sell for up to $20,000 a carat.

But the jeweler kept his word, and the Black Magic Opal Ring is affordable—even if you're not rich.

The Opal is cut <u>en cabochon</u>, even though that's more expensive. But a cabochon cut shows off the play of colors better than a less expensive flat cut.

When you look at the shimmering colors, you see the living fire of the ruby, the glorious purple of amethyst, the sea green of emeralds, all glittering together in an incredible mixture of light. And every time you move the ring, the colors flare and change again.

Each Opal has its own color patterns. So the Black Magic Ring we have set aside for [First name] [Last name] is like no other ring in the world!

Your Black Magic Ring comes with a signed, numbered Certificate of Authenticity, and an appraisal by the oldest, most respected Gemologist in Australia. (Take a moment to look at the enclosed sample copy.)

The Opal in your Black Magic Ring has a guaranteed minimum weight of 1 carat, but may weigh as much as 1.5 carats. This top-quality stone is graded 6.000 for color play and 10.000 for cut.

And the inside band of your Black Magic Ring is marked with a special hallmark to show that it's a genuine product of Australia.

When you wear your Black Magic Ring, you'll feel like you're a Queen. (Cleopatra and Queen Victoria adored opals.)

People will stop you in the street and at parties to get a better look. (You know how men love women who wear glamorous jewelry!)

Your friends and family will envy you, and wonder how you could afford it. You can tell them, or you can keep it a secret. That's <u>your</u> choice!

*Although your Black Magic Ring is appraised at $445, you won't pay anything near that. Since I got the jeweler the best Opals on the planet for the best prices on earth, **you can have this stunning ring for just one-third of the appraised price!***

***And you get to wear it FREE for 30 days!** We won't bill your credit card for one month, so you have a chance to try before you buy. We can make this offer because we're sure you'll love your Black Magic Ring so much you wouldn't part with it for anything. If we're wrong, just return it, and you'll owe us nothing.*

But if you want to keep your Black Magic Ring, we'll bill you for 3 monthly installments of just $49.95 each, plus $9.95 for insured delivery and handling.

The jeweler crafted a limited number of Black Magic Opal Rings, so we have to strictly limit this offer to one Ring for each person on our invitation list. If you don't reserve your Ring within 15 days, we'll have to cancel your entitlement, and offer your Ring to the next name on our waiting list.

*Don't let this chance of a lifetime slip by! You may not get another opportunity to own a Ring with the look of Black Opal. Mail your Certificate of Entitlement to the jeweler today. **Or call toll-free: 1-800-xxx-xxxx.***

With kind regards,

Alex Novelli
Mine Superintendent

P.S.   The Black Magic Opal Ring is the first piece in the Great Southern Gems Collection of jewelry made in Australia. As a Black Magic Ring owner, you'll be eligible to preview other items in the Collection FREE!

Warning!

The best piece of direct marketing advice I ever heard comes from copywriter Peter Beteul who says, "Don't get trapped by personal preferences." Whether you like or don't like something—a product, a sales theme, a sales letter, a piece of copy, a design—is irrelevant. The only way to determine whether the approach is "good" is through a test. If it generates a profit, then it's good. If it doesn't, it's bad—no matter how much everyone liked it.

Direct marketing expert Denny Hatch has said that direct marketing doesn't fill needs; it creates wants. In the above letter, the copywriter makes you want the special opals the seller is offering.

Overcoming Buyer Resistance with Endorsed Mailings

One method to overcome resistance is to seek endorsements from reputable organizations. The endorsed mailing approach serves three important purposes:

1. A letter of endorsement gives the product instant credibility so crucial in direct mail marketing.

2. The offer comes from an organization whose members identify and possibly socialize with the person receiving your offer; this changes the essence of the offer.

3. Organizations tend to have members who are older and who, depending on the organization, have high incomes; this brings a significant percentage of mail recipients into the demographic range necessary to achieve optimum results.

Begin with a letter to the president or central office. Explain your program and request an opportunity to make a presentation. Follow up the letter with a phone call and in many cases with a visit. Arm yourself with credentials and important backup information. Organizations are protective of their members and don't want them exploited. Use recommendations from other organizations that have used your services in the past. With credibility and reputation established, you can demonstrate what you have to offer and why it will benefit members of the organization.

The Least You Need to Know

➤ In your travels, be on the lookout for unusual merchandise you've never seen. A product unique to a specific locale and not available in stores beyond the region can often be sold effectively to consumers via direct response on a national basis.

➤ Select a company name that lends perceived credibility to your direct marketing offers.

➤ "Romance" the product, adding an element of interest or intrigue not ordinarily connected with the product. Offer the buyer something he or she cannot get elsewhere.

➤ People who belong to an organization are more likely to respond to your offer if it appears to be endorsed by the organization.

Chapter 18

Business-to-Business Direct Marketing

In This Chapter

➤ Business-to-business versus consumer direct marketing

➤ The business opportunity (biz op) marketplace

➤ Selling to SoHos

➤ Marketing industrial products

➤ Secrets of successful high-tech marketing

➤ Selling to managers and corporate executives

I have a special fondness for marketing to business and industry that the average direct marketer—who concentrates on consumer offers—doesn't. Probably it's my background as a chemical engineer and, later, as a technical writer for Westinghouse.

Because I grew up marketing to industry before expanding into other areas (financial services, publishing, consumer products, e-commerce), I feel well-qualified to guide you in this important—but often ignored—segment of the direct marketing universe. In this chapter, I share with you the best practices I've learned in 20 years of marketing products and services to business and industry.

Getting Down to Business-to-Business

While most of the fundamentals of direct response hold true whether you are selling to a business or consumer audience, there are also some differences between business-to-business direct marketing and consumer direct marketing you should not ignore.

The following sections discuss six factors that you must consider when direct marketing to businesses.

The Business Buyer Wants to Buy

Most consumer advertising offers people products they might enjoy but don't really need. How many subscription promotions, for example, sell publications that the reader truly could not live without? If we subscribe to *Playboy* or *People*, for instance, we do so for pleasure—not because the information offered is essential to our day-to-day activity.

But in business-to-business marketing, the situation is different. The business buyer wants to buy. Indeed, all business enterprises must routinely buy products and services that help them stay profitable, competitive, and successful. The proof of this is the existence of the purchasing agent, whose sole function is to purchase things.

The Business Buyer Is Sophisticated

Business-to-business copy talks to a sophisticated audience. Your typical reader has a high interest in—and understanding of—your product (or at least of the problem it solves).

Most important, the reader usually knows more about the product and its use than *you* do. It would be folly, for example, to believe that a few days spent reading about mainframe computers will educate you to the level of your target prospect—a systems analyst with six or seven years experience. (This realization makes business-to-business writers somewhat more humble than their consumer counterparts.)

The sophistication of the reader requires the business-to-business copywriter to do a tremendous amount of research and digging into the market, the product, and its application. The business audience does not respond well to slogans or oversimplification.

The Business Buyer Will Read a Lot of Copy

The business buyer is an information seeker, constantly on the lookout for information and advice that can help the buyer do the job better, increase profits, or advance his or her career.

"Our prospects are turned off by colorful, advertising-type sales brochures," says the marketing manager of a company selling complex systems software products to large

IBM data centers. "They are hungry for information and respond better to letters and bulletins that explain, in fairly technical terms, what our product is and how it solves a particular data-center problem."

Don't be afraid to write long copy in mailers, ads, and fulfillment brochures. Prospects will read your message—*if* it is interesting, important, and relevant to their needs. And don't hesitate to use free information as an offer in your ads and mailers. The offer of a free booklet, report, or technical guide can still pull well—despite the glut of reading matter clogging the prospect's in-basket.

A Multi-Step Buying Process

In consumer direct response, copywriters' fees are geared toward producing the "package"—an elaborate mailing that does the bulk of the selling job for a mail-order product.

But in business-to-business direct marketing, the concept of *package* or *control* is virtually nonexistent. Why? Because the purchase of most business products is a multistep buying process. A vice president of manufacturing doesn't clip a coupon and order a $35,000 machine by mail. First, he or she asks for a brochure. Then, a sales meeting. Then, a demonstration. Then, a 30-day trial. Then, a proposal or contract.

Thus, it is not a single piece of copy that wins the contract award. Rather, it takes a series of letters, brochures, presentations, ads, and mailers—combined with the efforts of salespeople—to turn a cold lead into a paying customer.

Marketing Tip

A proven strategy for increasing response to business-to-business ads and mailers is to offer free information related to the product—its design, selection criteria, and applications. For instance, if you are advertising mixers to plant engineers, offer a booklet on how to size and select the right mixer for the customer's process.

Multiple Buying Influences

You don't usually consult with a team of experts when you want to buy a fast-food hamburger, a soda, bottle of shampoo, or a pair of shoes, do you? In most consumer selling situations, an individual makes the purchasing decision. But a business purchase is usually a *team* effort, with many players involved.

For this reason, a business purchase is rarely an "impulse" buy. Many people influence the decision—from the purchasing agent and company president, to technical professionals and end users. Each of these audiences has different concerns and criteria by which they judge you. To be successful, your copy must address the needs of all parties involved with the decision. In many cases, this requires separate mailings to many different people within an organization.

Business Products Are More Complex

Most business products—and their applications—are more complex than consumer products. (For example, clients I now serve include a commercial bank, a manufacturer of elevator-control systems, a data-processing training firm, a database-marketing company, a mailing-list broker, a general contractor, and a semiconductor manufacturer.)

Business-to-business copy cannot be superficial. Clarity is essential. You cannot sell by "fooling" the prospect or hiding the identity of your product.

Half the battle is explaining, quickly and simply, what your product is, what it does, and why the reader should be interested in it. "In high-tech direct mail, the key is to educate the "prospect," say Mark Toner, who manages the advertising program for Amano, a manufacturer of computerized time-clock systems. "With a product like ours, most customers don't even know of its existence."

Selling Business Opportunity Offers

A whole industry has been built around selling "business opportunities." These are offers, ranging from a $10 book to a $300 set of videos to a $5,000 "boot camp," that promise to make the buyer rich by pursuing some entrepreneurial venture such as mail order, real estate, or options trading.

Warning!

Every direct marketer offering a trial period with a money-back guarantee naturally gets some customers who return the product for refund. Returns are likely to be higher with a "blind" ad (for example, "Get Rich Without Leaving Your Home") than with an ad that reveals what the business opportunity actually is (for example, "Grow Earth Worms for Fun and Profit"). Generally, to be profitable an ad's return rate should be under 10 percent.

Business-opportunity marketing is a hybrid of business and consumer marketing. It ostensibly discusses a business proposition, but the tone is aggressive, even hard-sell. Copy sells the sizzle rather than the steak. As is typical in this genre (see the sample ad in the following figure), the sales pitch is all "tease," with the nature of the proposition not even revealed.

Some marketers believe all business-opportunity advertising is deceitful or immoral because of its very nature, but I do not agree. All advertising, to some degree, over-promises and paints a rosy picture—and direct marketing, burdened with having to actually sell something, does it more than other media.

If we don't effectively sell our offer in print, we don't close the deal. Therefore, if you are offering a legitimate opportunity or useful information and you don't write a powerful, provocative ad, the buyer is going to send his or her check to someone else, and your book or report won't get read. To me that's doing the customer a real disservice.

Work at Home
Be a Medical Billing Specialist
Earn up to $40,000 a year!

**No previous experience needed...learn at home.
Prepare medical claims for doctors, hospitals, clinics.**

This exciting money-making opportunity is wide open. So if you want to make a good living at home—without commuting, without selling...and working the hours you choose—call the toll-free number below or mail the coupon for free facts about what could be the greatest job opportunity of your life! There are plenty of high-pay office jobs, too!

Experts train you step by step...you can be ready to work in just four months!

The medical profession is in need of skilled medical claims and billing specialists...and you can make almost as much money as you want because there is so much work. You learn medical terminology, procedures and how to prepare medical claims for Medicare, Medicaid and private patients. Experts show you how to do your work to meet the exacting standards of the medical profession.

Compare the money you can make at home as a Medical Claims and Billing Specialist with any other job.

What other job can you start with just four months of training at home and start earning up to $40,000 a year? Plus, you get these extra benefits—no transportation cost or time wasted going to and from your job, no expensive clothes because you can do all your work at home, no child day care costs, work whatever hours you choose...early mornings, late at night, any time, and take "breaks" whenever you want them. And it's not only the money you make that's important—you'll be working in a prestigious job making a valuable contribution to the medical profession.

COMPARE THESE ADVANTAGES WITH ANY OTHER PROFESSION!

- You can work as much as you want
- You can earn $10 to $20 an hour
- Choose your hours...any time of day
- No time wasted traveling to work
- Be your own boss
- Continuing graduate support throughout your career
- Work wherever you want to live
- Prestige of working in the medical profession
- Plenty of high-pay office jobs, too

GET FREE FACTS!
NO COST! NO OBLIGATION!
MAIL COUPON TODAY
OR CALL TOLL-FREE

At-Home Professions
2001 Lowe Street, Dept. PWMA11
Fort Collins, CO 80525

1-800-388-8765 Dept. PWMA11

YES! Rush me free facts on how I can train at home to work as a Medical Claims and Billing Specialist.

Name _____ Age _____

Address _____ Apt. _____

City _____ State _____ Zip _____

Business-opportunity ads are often "blind," meaning the specific nature of the opportunity is not revealed in the ad copy.

(Source: Spare Time Opportunity)

Reaching the SoHo Market

"SoHo" stands for small office/home office. Unlike business opportunity buyers, who are "wanna be" entrepreneurs, SoHo prospects are real entrepreneurs. Many are self-employed professionals. Others are small home-based businesses, or small service businesses or retail operators. Still others are consultants and other self-employed, white-collar professionals.

SoHos are a hybrid market. True, marketing to SoHos is a business-to-business sale, but it doesn't have all the characteristics on our six-point list of what makes business-to-business unique (given at the beginning of this chapter). Most notably, SoHos, working in isolation, can make quick decisions on their own without consulting a committee or getting approval from upper management. Therefore, impulse offers work well with this market.

Success Story

Studebaker-Worthington is a computer-leasing company that offers financing to computer buyers through resellers. To get resellers to recommend Studebaker's leasing services, Studebaker offers the reseller a selection of attractive high-end gifts ranging from VCRs and microwave ovens to stereos and big-screen color TVs.

Also, while buyers in corporations are often restricted from accepting gifts from vendors, which limits the value of the premiums you can offer, SoHos have no such limitations because they are buying for themselves, with their own money. "Big bribes"—extremely nice gifts and premiums—can also work with this market.

Because SoHos are spending their own money and reap all the rewards of the business (unlike a corporate employee who is paid a fixed salary not tied to the company's success), SoHos take more of a personal interest in their businesses. Part of the reason they are entrepreneurs is their passion for their ideas and a fierce sense of independence.

When you can tap into these emotional hot buttons, you can get SoHos to buy. A subscription letter for *Inc.* magazine had the lead, "A special invitation to the hero of American "business." The copy recognizes the SoHo's pride in being an entrepreneur and acknowledges this courage in a flattering manner.

Office products is one category that targets the SoHo market. Computers and Internet services are two others.

Industrial Marketing

"Industrial marketing" refers to the selling of products used in manufacturing operations. These products can range from large capital expenditures (air pollution control equipment) to relatively small items (nuts, bolts, connectors) and everything in between.

The following are 10 time-tested tips for writing industrial copy that sells. Apply them to your next ad, mailer, or catalog, and watch the reply cards come pouring in.

Be Technically Accurate

Industrial marketers sell systems to solve specific problems. Therefore, copy must accurately describe what the product can and cannot do. Being accurate means being truthful. Industrial buyers are among the most sophisticated of audiences. Technical know-how is their forte, and they'll be likely to spot any exaggerations, omissions, or "white lies" you make.

Being accurate also means being specific. Writing that a piece of equipment "can handle your toughest injection molding jobs" is vague and meaningless to a technician; but saying that the machine "can handle pressures of up to 12,000 pounds" is honest, concrete, and useful.

Check the Numbers

Just think of the disaster that would result if a misplaced decimal in a sales letter offered a one-year magazine subscription at $169.50—10 times the actual price of $16.95. You can see why this would stop sales cold.

Well, the same goes for industrial copy. Only, in technical promotions, a misplaced decimal or other math mistake is less obvious to the copywriter, since the material is so highly technical. You and I would suspect an error in a mailer that advertised a $169.50 magazine subscription. But how many direct-response writers could say, at a glance, whether the pore size in a reverse osmosis filter should be 0.005 or 0.00005 or 0.0005 microns? (How many of us even know what a micron is?) Yet, to the chemical engineer, the pore size of the filter may be as crucial as the price of the magazine subscription. Get it wrong, and you've lost a sale.

Warning!

All numbers in industrial and technical promotional literature should be checked and double-checked by the writer, by the agency, and by technical people on the client side. Be extremely cautious and careful, and not just about numbers. A defense contractor I worked for was not allowed to publish a power rating for a product because it was a military secret. The marketing department was careful to make sure this number did not appear in the brochure. But then an engineer in the company told us any reader could figure out the power by looking at the internal components, which were revealed in a large color photo on the front cover. We had to reprint the brochure at great expense.

Be Concise

Engineers and managers are busy people. They don't have the time to read all the papers that cross their desks, so make your message brief and to the point. Take a look at some industrial direct mail. Letters are seldom more than a page long, and you almost never see a four-page letter in industrial selling.

Marketing Tip

The engineer's purchase decision is more logical than emotional. Most books and articles on advertising stress that successful copy appeals to emotions first, reason second. But with the engineering audience, it is often the opposite. The buying decision is what we call a "considered purchase" rather than an impulse buy. That is, the buyer carefully weighs the facts, makes comparisons, and buys based on what product best fulfills the buyer's requirement.

In other words, cram your industrial promotions full of product information and strong sales arguments. But avoid redundancies, long sentences, wordy phrases, and other poor stylistic habits that take up space but add little to meaning or clarity. For example, don't write "water droplets condensed from atmospheric vapor and sufficiently massive to fall to earth's surface" when you're talking about rain.

Simplify

The key to successful industrial copywriting is to explain complex concepts and products clearly and directly. Avoid overly complicated narratives; write in plain, simple English. In the first draft of catalog copy for a line of pollution control equipment, the product manager wrote:

> It is absolutely essential that the interior wall surface of the conduit be maintained in a wet condition, and that means be provided for wetting continually the peripheral interior wall surface during operation of the device, in order to avoid the accumulation of particulate matter about the interior surface area.

Here's how the copywriter simplified this bit of technical gobbledygook to make it more readable:

> The interior wall must be continually wetted to avoid solids buildup.

One way to achieve simplicity in your industrial writing is to avoid the overuse of technical jargon. Never write that a manufacturer's new dental splint "stabilizes mobile dentition" when its function is to keep loose teeth in place.

When you're deciding whether to use a particular technical term, remember Susanne K. Langer's definition of jargon as "language more technical than the ideas it serves to express." Never let your language make things more complex than they already are.

Talk to the Users to Determine Their Needs

Elaborate marketing research is often unnecessary in industrial selling. By talking with a few knowledgeable engineers, the copywriter can quickly grasp what makes a technical product useful to industrial buyers.

Because the products are highly technical, you can't rely on your own feelings and intuition to select the key selling points. The benefits of buying a kitchen appliance or joining a record club are obvious, but how can a layman say what features of a multi-stage distillation system are important to the buyer, and which are trivial?

By speaking with technical and marketing people on the client side, you can find out which product features should be highlighted in the copy and *why* they appeal to the buyer. Then, apply your usual skill in persuasive writing to turn these features into sales-oriented "reasons why they should buy" copy. The kind of copy that generates leads, goodwill, orders—and *money*.

Recently, I was given the assignment of writing a package on a water-filtration system to be sold to two different markets: the marine industry and the chemical industry. In the course of conversation with a few customers in each field, I discovered that marine buyers were concerned solely with quality and price, while chemical engineers considered "technical competence." They wanted to know every detailed specification down to the last pump, pipe, fan, and filter.

Selling the product to the two markets would require two completely different sales letters—but I'd never have known this if I hadn't *asked*.

Understand How the Promotion Fits into the Buying Process

The sale of an industrial product can require many lengthy steps and machinery is seldom marketed by mail order. Sometimes your package can be used to generate the lead. Or it may help qualify prospects. Many industrial marketers use sales letters to distribute catalogs, remind customers of their products, or answer inquiries. Know where your copy fits into the buying process so you can write copy to generate the appropriate response.

Know How Much to Tell

Different buyers seek different levels of technical information. If you're writing for top management, keep it short and simple, and pile on the benefits. If you're pitching to technicians, be sure to include plenty of meaty technical information.

Here's a description of a Dry FGD System (a large piece of industrial equipment) from a promotion aimed at plant engineers:

> *The average SO_2, emission rate as determined in the outlet duct was 0.410 lb/10^6 Btu (176 ng/J). All emission rates were determined with F-factors calculated from flue gas analyses obtained with an Orsat analyzer during the course of each test run.*

This will satisfy the technically curious buyer who wants to know *how* you determined your product specifications, not just what they are. But managers have little time or interest in the nitty-gritty; they want to know how the product can save them money and help improve their operations.

A brochure on this same Dry FGD System aimed at management takes a lighter, more sales-oriented tone:

> *The Dry FCD System is a cost-effective alternative to conventional wet scrubbers for cleaning flue gas in coal-fired boilers. Fly ash and chemical waste are removed as an easily handled dry powder, not a wet sludge. And with dry systems, industrial and utility boilers can operate cleanly and reliably.*

Don't Forget the Features

By all means, stress customer benefits in your copy. But don't forget to include technical features as well. In the industrial marketplace, a pressure rating or the availability of certain materials of construction often mean the difference between a buy or no-buy decision. Although these features may seem boring or meaningless to you, they are important to the technical buyer.

Direct response copywriters often work up a list of product features and the benefits that these features offer the consumer. Then, the benefits are worked into the sales letter. In industrial copywriting, we do the same thing, except we work the *features* into the copy. Features and their benefits are often presented in "cause and effect" statements, such as:

> *Because the system uses L-band frequency and improved MTI (moving target indication), it can detect targets up to 50 times smaller than conventional S-band radars.*

> *No mechanical systems or moving parts are required. Which means that Hydro-Clean consumes less energy and takes less space than conventional pump driven clarifiers.*

Marketing Tip

Use graphs, tables, charts, and diagrams to explain and summarize technical information quickly. Put strong "sell copy" in your headlines, subheads, and body copy; relegate duller "catalog information" to tables, sidebars, charts, and inserts. And don't hesitate to use visuals; photographs add believability, and drawings help readers visualize complex products and processes.

Include Case Histories to Demonstrate Proven Performance

Industrial buyers want to know that your product has proven its performance in real-life applications. Case histories—concise "product success stories"—are a sure-fire way to put the buyer's mind at ease.

In mail order, a simple one-line testimonial from "GK in Portland" or "the Jack Reeds in Jersey City" is all that's needed to demonstrate a product's success. But industrial buyers need to know more, and the typical case history tells what the problem was, how the product solved it, and what the results were in terms of money saved and improved plant performance.

In an ad for the Hitachi chiller-heater, a unit that cools and heats buildings, Gas Energy, Inc. uses a series of tightly written one-paragraph case histories to show readers that the product works. Here's a sample:

> *Miami Hospital (300,000 sq. ft.). Linking a gas turbine generator with one 450-ton Hitachi Cogeneration unit produces all cooling and heating and saves $360,000 yearly vs. purchased electricity and the previous electric centrifugal system.*

The case history approach is one area where industrial and consumer writers agree. After all, every direct response writer knows that the best advertising is a satisfied customer.

Selling Tech Products to Non-Tech Executives

When selling hardware and software to businesses, you often have to appeal to three different buying influences within each company:

1. **Senior management**, including CEOs, CFOs, COOs, vice presidents
2. **End users**, who are often middle managers or administrative staff
3. **Information systems (IS) professionals**, ranging from programmers to systems analysts

The first two audiences consistent primarily of people who are not techies. And these nontechies care about different things, and respond differently, than the traditional IS technology buyer.

Nontechies are results oriented, interested in the ends rather than the means, the bottom line rather than the process. They lack interest in the details, preferring to focus on the "big picture." Most nontechies simply want to resolve problems; engineers, scientists, and programmers enjoy actually working on problems. The result is that nontechies are more interested in benefits, business results, and the reputation and credibility of the vendor.

IS professionals, by comparison, tend to focus on technical issues including platforms, scalability, interoperability with existing systems, reliability, specifications, limitations, and ease of implementation, operation, and maintenance.

But there are some direct marketing methods that work well with both IS and non-IS prospects. For example, when generating leads for expensive enterprise software, quote the price in the terms that seem most palatable—for instance, per user or per site license. Demonstrate, if it exists, the rapid return on investment. A mailing for SurfControl, an application that monitors and controls employee Internet usage in organizations, informs the recipient that surfing the Internet for personal rather than business reasons costs $300 per employee per week. (Copy claims that four out of five hits to the *Playboy* Web site are from Fortune 500 companies!) The letter then positions the license fee of a few dollars per user as a drop in the bucket compared to the savings SurfControl can generate.

Using Premiums

For both lead generation and mail order, premiums are proven response boosters. Premiums that have worked well for technology marketers include white papers, computer books, audio and video cassettes, free software, free support, free training, seminars, and electronic conferences that the user accesses via telephone (for voice) and, optionally, the Web (for visuals).

Another popular premium is to offer a simple calculator that demonstrates the potential return on investment to the prospect if he or she purchases your product. This is typically an Excel application on a disk. The prospect inputs his or her business scenario and instantly discovers whether your product will pay off.

Marketing Tip

For high-end software representing a major corporate investment, the goal is often to get an appointment with the decision maker. The offer then becomes, in essence, not the software, but rather the initial meeting—which is frequently positioned as a needs analysis or assessment—to be followed by recommendations. Of course, the seller's goal is to gain the information needed to provide a quote or proposal the buyer will accept.

Select a premium that is highly desirable and ties in with your product or service. A Web design firm, for instance, offered "four free digital photos of your key staff, postable on your Web site." When the rep visited the prospect, she carried a digital camera, took the photos, and immediately gave the disk to the prospect. Of course, the prospect wanted the photos posted on the company's Web site, something that could be done as part of the "Web site makeover" service the Web consulting firm offered for a fee.

Getting a Response

There are four basic response mechanisms: paper reply forms for mailing (reply cards and reply envelopes), online (e-mail or logging on to a Web site), phone, and fax (using fax-back forms).

Because you never know which reply method a particular prospect prefers, why not offer them all? At a recent marketing conference, one software executive said, "Every software prospect is on the Internet today. It's a waste of time to offer any other response mechanism." A colleague from his company disagreed. "I don't want to log on to the Internet if I'm not already online just to respond to an ad or mailing," he said, insisting that for him, a toll-free number or reply card is more convenient.

While it's generally safe to assume IS professionals are comfortable responding by going to your Web site, don't make that assumption with nontechies. Some can access the Web but are not comfortable with it and prefer not to. Others, amazingly, don't even know how to get onto your site!

The key to success? Talk to businesspeople in their language, not yours. Show that if they give you a dollar, they'll get back two dollars. And test sales appeals, offers, pricing, response mechanisms, copy, graphics, formats, and premiums. Don't assume you know which will work best. Instead, let your prospects tell you. Makes sense, doesn't it?

Writing High-Tech Product Copy

What's the right tone to take when writing about high-tech products? Should you use jargon? How much knowledge can you assume the reader has? When you're writing about high-tech products, keep these tips in mind:

➤ **Make it clear, not too technical.** To stand out from the pack of competitive products, your headline should telegraph what your product does. For example, "Link 8 PCS to your Mainframe—only $2,395" instantly says all the reader wants to know.

➤ **Put the main benefit in the headline or subhead**, especially in high-tech writing. Although technical buyers shop for technical benefits, management types want to see a major benefit of efficiency, productivity, money or time savings. "Develop dBASE Applications Up To Four Times Faster," began a tremendously successful direct mail campaign for a software product. The head not only identifies the function ("Develop dBASE Applications") but also spells out the benefit ("Up To Four Times Faster").

➤ **Make the lead paragraphs identify the reader's problem and present your product as the solution.** Try the two-part approach. The first sentence of a paragraph dramatizes the problem; the second offers the product as the solution. For example, check out the opening of a lead-generating sales letter that pulled an 11 percent response. "Do you have a potable water supply or waste stream that contains organic contaminants? And have you considered activated carbon as the ideal treatment, only to ultimately *reject* deep-bed carbon installations because of the cost? Envira-Plus Filter Precoats may be the answer for you ...." Restating the problem helps you set the stage for your sales pitch, and says you understand the reader's needs, concerns, and fears.

➤ **Stress functions, not just benefits.** Tech buyers look for products to solve specific tasks. They already know the benefits. So the best high-tech copy tells—and shows—exactly what your product can do for them. You don't have to reduce every paragraph to "saves money" or "saves time."

➤ **Use a feature/function table.** Create a box, table, or sidebar showing all the product's features and capabilities at a glance. List features in the left-hand column; their corresponding function in the right. For example, in a spec sheet for a software design tool, a feature is "Automated Balancing." The function performed reads: "Provides automatic proofreading of a project by pointing out errors between diagram levels, dictionary, and text specs." In a typical brochure, the feature/function table might contain 15 to 20 items. Highlight the five or six hottest features in the main text, with hard-sell copy. All the prospect wants to know about the other features is the functions they perform.

➤ **Use a tech-specs box.** Put specifications—hardware, power and temperature needs, software compatibility, operating system—in a separate box or table, typically on the last page. Make specs easy to find. They may not get people excited about products, but prospects want them before they place an order.

➤ **Use subheads and short copy blocks.** Don't try to force tech and business buyers to wade through long, argument-packed copy to get what they need to know. Each subhead should communicate so well, the reader could get the message just by reading subheads. With each new idea, concept, or feature, start a new section. Organize copy so the readers can find what's relevant to them and skip what isn't.

Above all, keep in mind that the technology marketplace is glutted with new products. Yours is likely to get lost in the shuffle unless you can differentiate it clearly from the pack and then prove that your difference delivers real value to the user.

Selling to Middle Managers

The most common mistake in direct marketing to managers is to assume that they are solely motivated by what is best for their company. But the fact is, the business buyer buys for the company's benefit—*and* his or her own.

Of course, the business buyer must acquire products and services that benefit the company. This means the product or service saves the company time or money, makes money, improves productivity, and increases efficiency or solves problems.

Let's say, for example, that you sell a telecommunications network and your primary advantage over the competition is that your system reduces monthly operating expenses by 50 percent. If a prospect is spending $40,000 a month for your competitor's network, you can replace it and provide his or her company with the same level of service for only $20,000 a month. The company benefits because it saves $240,000 a year in communications costs—more than $1 million in a five-year period.

Yet, despite this tremendous benefit, you find that prospects are not buying. They seem interested, and you get a lot of inquiries, but few sales are closed. Why? Because in addition to buying for the company's benefit, the prospect also buys for him- or herself. While the buyer is looking to do right by the company, the buyer has an equal (if not greater) concern for his or her own well-being and selfish interests.

Although the idea of saving $240,000 a year with your telecommunications system is appealing to your prospect, his or her thought process is as follows:

> "Right now I have an AT&T system. Your system sounds good but I don't know you or your company. If I switch and something goes wrong, I will be blamed. I may even get fired. My boss will say, 'You shouldn't have gambled on an unproven product from an unknown vendor—why didn't you stick with good ole reliable AT&T?' He will say this even though he approved my decision. So to be safe, I will stick with my current system—even though it costs my company an extra $240,000 a year. After all, I'd rather see them spend an extra $240,000 a year than me lose my "$60,000-a-year job!"

This play-it-safe mentality is only natural, and it affects buying decisions daily in corporations throughout the country. Data-processing professionals are fond of saying, "Nobody ever got fired for buying IBM." Buying IBM ensures the prospect that no one can criticize his or her decision, even if brand X is the better choice from a business and technical point of view. A corporate-pension fund manager, writing in *Money* magazine, noted that no money manager ever got fired for losing money invested in a blue-chip stock. A different example, but the principle remains the same.

Concern for making the safe acceptable decision is a primary motivation of business buyers, but it is not the only reason why business buyers choose products, services, and suppliers that are not necessarily the best business solution to their company's problem.

Avoiding stress or hardship is a big concern among prospects. For example, a consultant might offer a new system for increasing productivity, but it means more paperwork for the shipping department—and especially for the head of the shipping department. If he or she has anything to say about it, and thinks no one will criticize him or her for it, the head of shipping will, in this case, work to sway the committee against engaging the consultant or using that system, even though the current procedures are not efficient. The department head, already overworked, wants to avoid something he or she perceives as a hassle and a headache, despite its contribution to the greater good of the organization.

Fear of the unknown is also a powerful motivator. A middle manager, for example, might vote against acquiring desktop publishing and putting a terminal on every manager's desk because the manager actually has computer phobia. Even though the manager recognizes the benefit such technology can bring to the department, the manager wants to avoid the pain of learning something that seems to be difficult and frightening. Again, personal benefit outweighs corporate benefit in this situation.

Fear of loss is another powerful motivator. An advertising manager in a company that has handled its advertising in-house for the past decade may resist the president's suggestion that they retain an outside advertising agency to handle the company's rapidly expanding marketing campaign. Even if the ad manager respects the ad agency and believes it will do a good job, he or she may campaign against it, fearing that bringing in outside experts will diminish his or her own status within the company.

In these and many other instances, the business buyer is for him- or herself first; and the company, second. To be successful, your copy must not only promise the benefits the prospect desires for the company; it should also speak to the prospect's personal agenda, as well.

Selling to Corporate Executives

The higher up on the company ladder an executive is, the more difficult he or she is to reach via direct marketing—and the less likely he or she is to respond.

Some techniques that work with the senior executive audience:

➤ Make your direct mail look like professional business correspondence. Mail first class or even certified mail.

➤ Use the "cc" technique. Write to the CEO about an important issue in a particular department or area of operation, and cc the manager in that area. Send the same information to the department manager, tell him or her you already sent it to the CEO, encourage them to discuss it, and cc the CEO.

➤ Make the envelope look important or even semi-official. When mailing to pharmaceutical executives, one mailer made the envelope look like it might be from the FDA.

Keep in mind that managers buy both for themselves and their companies. It's usually not enough that the purchase benefits the business; the manager won't buy unless he sees that the product can also make his life easier (or at least won't make it harder).

The Least You Need to Know

➤ Most business–purchase decisions are made by committees.

➤ Almost every purchase of more than $1,000 must be approved by at least one person besides the person actually placing the order.

➤ When selling to the business–opportunity marketplace, the benefit or result (for example, getting rich, being your own boss) is almost always more important than the method being offered to get there (for example, selling at flea markets, buying foreclosed properties).

➤ SoHos (small office/home office owners) buy lots of office products by mail and respond well to free gift offers.

➤ The larger the purchase price, the longer the sales cycle. Big–ticket items of $50,000 or more may take three to six months or more to get approved for purchase.

➤ Engineers and other technical people respond well to copy written authoritatively and are turned off by lack of solid technical content.

Chapter 19

Selling Services

In This Chapter

➤ Using the telephone to sell your services

➤ Generating referrals

➤ Using direct mail to produce inquiries

➤ Ads that sell services

Once you decide to begin actively marketing and selling your services, how will potential clients learn about the availability of those services?

If you're lucky, perhaps your phone will start ringing right away, without any effort on your part. If that happens—congratulations! You will have all the business you need, and you can skip this chapter.

But for most service providers, self-promotion is an essential activity. Just as Ford must advertise to sell cars, you must advertise and promote yourself and your service business if you expect people to call you with assignments.

Service Selling Is Different

There are a number of differences between selling services versus selling products that make direct marketing of services a unique challenge. Among the key differences:

➤ Products have fixed prices versus most services have variable pricing. And the final price cannot be determined until the seller makes an estimate.

➤ Products have tangible features; services are intangibles.

➤ Product benefits are tangible and can be documented for consistent performance (for example, Crest reduces cavities 80 percent). Service benefits are often intangible and the confirmation of their delivery dependent on the buyer's subjective judgment (for example, one client could hate your interior decorating while another client with the same room loves it).

➤ Products can be delivered via mail or UPS. Services often require the presence of the service provider on site to render the service.

➤ If the buyer is not satisfied with the product, he can return it for his money back—and the marketer can resell it to another customer. But once a service is rendered, it cannot be returned, resold, or reused by another buyer.

Working the Phone Lines

Telemarketing, as it applies to selling services, means picking up the telephone, calling strangers, and asking them if they'd be interested in getting a free estimate or learning more about your services.

Marketing Tip

If you do decide to make cold calls, consider having someone else in your office do it or hire someone to make the calls for you. Reason: Clients only want to hire those service providers who seem busy and successful. If you're so successful and busy, why are you on the phone asking people to hire you? You can test telemarketing for your services using the guidelines presented in Chapter 15, "Telemarketing."

Does this type of cold-call telemarketing work? For many service providers, yes. Cold-call telemarketing campaigns are actively conducted by thousands of firms, most notably home improvement companies (siding, windows, doors, roofing) and financial services firms (gold coins, stockbrokers, mutual funds, and other investments).

Referral Marketing

Referrals are a great way to get new business. One advantage of getting leads through word of mouth is that prospects are already favorably inclined to hire you, because they have been told great things about you by the person who gave them your name.

Whether referrals are frequent and common depends on the type of service business you're in. If referrals are a major source of business in your profession, it's important to learn who does the referring and to contact them and let them know of your service. There are some clients who might refer you but simply never think to do so and never get around to it. These can be sources for referrals, with a little prodding from you.

One referral technique that's especially useful when the client is a large organization is to ask for referrals to other clients within that organization. Typically, most of us are thrilled when we're working for Manager X or Division A of a large Fortune 1000 corporation; this represents lucrative business. But few of us, myself included, ever stop to realize that now that we've got an "in" at the company, other managers and divisions that could buy our service will be much more likely to use us—especially with a referral from Manager X.

To get this referral, say to your client, "Mr. Client, I have a question. Who else in [name of company] do you think could benefit from my service?" When the client gives you one or two names, ask for the complete information, including spelling, title, address, and phone number.

Then say, "Mr. Client, when I get in touch with [name of referred lead], may I mention your name?" When the client answers yes—and the client will—you can then legitimately call other prospects within the corporation and say "[Name of client] told me that you use [type of service you offer] and that I should get in touch with you."

If you are uncomfortable about having this phone conversation, a less aggressive way of asking for referrals is to send a letter. Refer to Part 2, "Direct Response Formats and Media," especially the section "The Sales Letter" in Chapter 7, "The Direct Mail Package."

Testimonials

Testimonials can benefit many self-promotions, including brochures, direct mail, ads, and press releases. A testimonial is a statement from a satisfied client praising you and your services. A typical testimonial might read:

> *"Thanks for the training program on 'People Skills for DP Professionals.' The techniques you taught have already improved relations between users and software developers in our organization and have helped us get through a major bottleneck on one important new system."*
>
> *—May Stoddard, Manager of Training*
> *Big Company, U.S.A.*

Some testimonials are received unsolicited; for example, a client might send you a letter thanking you for a job well done. Naturally, this makes a good testimonial. However, before you use it, get the client's permission—in writing. Otherwise, clients may become angry if they see themselves quoted in your next ad or brochure without consent, and you will have damaged your relationship.

Getting permission is easy. To quote a client, send a standard permission letter similar to the one that follows:

Mr. Sam Smith
Anytown, USA

Dear Sam:

I never did get around to thanking you for your letter of 6/7/01 (copy attached). So, thanks!

I'd like to quote from this letter in the ads, brochures, direct mail packages, and other promotions I use to market my catering services—with your permission, of course. If this is okay with you, would you please sign the bottom of this letter and send it back to me in the enclosed envelope. (The second copy is for your files.)

Many thanks, Sam.

Regards,
Jean Wilson

YOU HAVE MY PERMISSION TO QUOTE FROM THE ATTACHED LETTER IN ADS, BROCHURES, MAIL, AND OTHER PROMOTIONS USED TO MARKET YOUR SER-VICES.

Signature _____   *Date* _____

I always send a self-addressed stamped envelope and two copies of the letter. This way recipients don't have to copy the letter or address and stamp their own envelopes.

"But what if clients don't send me nice letters?" you may ask. That's okay. Most clients won't, because most people don't bother to send notes and thank-you letters nowadays. However, this doesn't prevent you from asking satisfied clients to endorse your services with a testimonial. The following letter solicits favorable comments from clients:

Mr. Andrew Sprecher
Anywhere, USA

Dear Andrew:

I have a favor to ask of you.

I'm in the process of putting together a list of testimonials—a collection of comments about my services, from satisfied clients like yourself.

Would you take a few minutes to give me your opinion of my catering service? No need to dictate a letter—just jot your comments on the back of this letter, sign below, and return it to me in the enclosed envelope. (The second copy is for your files.) I look forward to learning what you like about my service ... but I also welcome any suggestions or criticisms, too.

Many thanks, Andrew.

Regards,
Jean Wilson

YOU HAVE MY PERMISSION TO QUOTE FROM MY COMMENTS AND USE THESE QUOTATIONS IN ADS, BROCHURES, MAIL, AND OTHER PROMOTIONS USED TO MARKET YOUR SERVICES.

Signature _____ *Date* _____

Note that this letter asks for an "opinion" instead of a testimonial and that it urges the recipient to give criticisms as well as positive comments. In this way you are not just asking for a favor; you're getting information that will help you service the client better in the future. You are not the only one who profits; both you and the client do.

Direct Mail: The Powerhouse of Service Marketing

When other service providers ask me "What is the most effective self-promotion for you?" I answer without hesitation: direct mail. You can quickly write an effective sales letter and mail it to prospective clients. It is a relatively inexpensive promotion, and it gives you great control over cost, because you can mail as few or as many letters as you wish.

Direct mail can be as simple as a one-page letter or as complex as a multicomponent package with see-through windows, color brochures, order forms, reply envelopes, computer-personalized letters, and other inserts. It can be produced using only a typewriter or word processor, or you can add color, glossy stock, photographs, drawings, pop-ups, and three-dimensional objects.

In my experience, cheap and simple is best for service providers who mail limited quantities on a limited budget. My standard package consists of a one-page letter (a typed form letter printed on one side) and a reply card mailed in my regular #10 business envelope.

Although I could personalize each letter using my computer, I prefer a form letter because it's faster and easier to produce and mail. If I personalized it, I could mail letters only when I wasn't using my computer to do client work. A form letter can be pulled off the shelf and stuffed in an envelope any time, in seconds.

Also, there's no law that says you have to mail in large quantities. Whenever I learn of potential clients—say, an ad agency with a new account, or a company launching a new product—I can look them up in a business directory, address an envelope to the appropriate person, and drop a form letter in the mail. This is much quicker than writing a personal letter from scratch and allows me to reach many new prospects I might not, otherwise, have time to contact.

Marketing Tip

If you need a lot of leads, you can mail in large quantities. Make sure to "test" any new letter by mailing to 100 prospects. If the letter generates a good response, you can use it in larger quantities—say, 500 or so at a time. If the letter fails to produce any replies, go back to the PC and try again.

The Prospect Letter

Begin with an opening statement that grabs attention. You can promise a benefit, as I do in my headline. Or you might get attention by stating a fascinating fact, quoting a statistic, or asking a provocative question. Next, identify the reader's problem. Then, offer your services as a solution. Do this in the three opening paragraphs of your letter.

Elaborate on your background, showing why you are uniquely qualified to solve the client's problem. Explain why your services are superior, or why you have the best qualifications for the job. In my letter, this section follows the sentence, "Here are my qualifications."

Call for action. Ask the reader to phone or write or mail back a reply form. Offer a reason for the reader to respond, such as free information, a free consultation, a free meeting, a free analysis, or free estimate. Tell readers the specific action you want them to take and spell out the benefits they will receive if they respond *now*.

The Reply Card

Always include a reply card the reader can use to reply and request more information. The typical headline for such a card is "YES, I'd like to know more about how [name of service] can provide [major benefit]." The reply card does not have to be a business reply card; you can put a box in the front upper-right corner that says, "Place stamp here." However, using a business reply card enhances your image a bit and may also lift response slightly.

The reply card should leave ample room for the prospect to fill in name, title, and company name (if mailing to businesses), address, city, state, and phone number. Under the headline, the reader should be able to indicate the desired action by checking a box. Typically, this might read …

❑ *I'm interested. Please call me to arrange a FREE estimate.*

❑ *Please send more information by mail.*

The first offer is the "hard" offer. It is for prospects who have an immediate need, and checking it results in a phone call or visit by the seller. The second offer is called the "soft" offer, because it enables the prospect to find out more without making personal contact with you. Typically, 90 percent of prospects will check the soft offer; only 10 percent will have an immediate need and check the hard offer.

Of the prospects who check either offer, 10 to 25 percent will eventually become clients within a time frame ranging from a month to a year or longer. The rest, for one reason or another, will not become clients. Some were not really interested but were just curious. Some people just like to get brochures in the mail and will respond to any offer. Some had a need but did nothing about it or chose someone else. And your service may not have been right for others.

Marketing Tip

Mail your sales letters in regular #10 business envelopes. Type the recipient's name, title, company, and address directly on the envelope. Do not use labels. A recent article in the *Wall Street Journal* reports that many corporate mailrooms dump mailers sent to titles rather than individual names, so always use the prospect's name.

The advantage of having a tested sales letter—one that will generate a certain percentage response every time you mail it—is that you can quickly produce as many sales leads as you need, whenever you need them. For example, if your letter generates a three percent response, mailing 100 letters will, on average, produce three inquiries.

If your goal is to get 10 sales leads, you will need to mail 300 to 400 letters. As a rule, you'll get the majority of responses to your letter within two to four weeks after you mail it.

Advertising Your Services

Another way to get people to call and ask about your services is to advertise in newspapers, magazines, and directories. While your own experience and judgment may suggest where to run your initial ads, you can't really predict which publication will work best. As with direct mail, you should test your ads—both the content and where you place them. Only by testing do you know which ad and which publications will get the best response.

Although I have run larger ads, I have found that small classified and display ads work best for me. In any case, I recommend that you test small versions of your ad first. If the smaller ad gets good results, you can do a larger version based on the same theme. But if the ad flops, rewrite and try again before spending more money on a bigger version.

Where Should You Advertise?

Obviously, in publications read by your prospective clients. And which are these? It depends on your business, on the services you offer, and the market you want to reach. A useful reference for people who advertise is the Standard Rate and Data Service (SRDS), phone 847-375-5000. SRDS publishes comprehensive directories listing all magazines and newspapers, plus advertising rates for each publication. SRDS directories are available at most local libraries.

However, common sense and experience are at least as useful as SRDS in planning your advertising. In what publications do other service providers in your area advertise? What publications are your clients reading? What publications do *you* read?

You should advertise in publications read by your *prospects,* not by other vendors. If you are a painter, for example, advertise in the town newspaper, not in *Professional House-Painter's Bulletin.*

One good indication that a publication is worth trying is that your competitors are already advertising in it. If no one in your field advertises in a magazine or newspaper, there may be a very good reason for that. Advertise where others do—or, as advertising expert Joe Barnes puts it, "Fish where the fish are biting."

Don't neglect small local publications, such as the newsletters of local business associations or bulletins produced by professional groups and associations. Weekly newspapers, penny savers, and town shoppers are excellent for local service businesses such as real estate agents, insurance agents, financial planners, painters, roofers, and other contractors.

Once, for $2, I placed a 35-word ad in *IABC Employment Letter,* a newsletter published by the local chapter of the International Association of Business Communicators. The first (and only) call I received resulted in an immediate $5,000 assignment to write an annual report.

Once you have been in business for a time, you will begin to receive many solicitations in the mail asking you to advertise in a variety of professional directories. If you decide to try an ad, insist that it be placed in a separate category for your specific type of service. Don't allow your ad to be placed in a category that's too generic; otherwise, no one will find it. For example, if you are an executive recruiter, insist on a category titled "Executive Recruiters." Don't allow the directory to place your ad under the broader category "Management Consultants"; no one thinks of looking under "Management Consultants" for a headhunter.

Some business publications have separate sections for classified and display ads offering business services. People turn to these sections when they are looking for a service, so your best bet is to put your ad in that section under the appropriate category. However, you might also want to test an ad outside of the special section.

Writing Your Ad

In a small ad, you don't have room for a lot of sales talk, so you must stick to the essentials. The ad must communicate in a clear direct fashion: who you are, the services you offer, type of clients you serve, the next step, and how to get in touch with you.

If you are advertising in a magazine where no other service providers in your industry or profession are running ads, you can gain attention simply by stressing your service in the headline. Because there are no other ads for this service, people interested in your type of service will be drawn to the headline.

For instance, if you are the only collection agency advertising in a local business magazine, your ad might read as follows:

COLLECT THOSE OVERDUE BILLS!

We help you get the money owed you to increase your cash flow. To turn old invoices into cash fast, call Watson & Crick Collections, phone XXX-XXXX.

On the other hand, if many other collection agencies advertise in this publication, you would need something special to make yours stand out from the crowd. Some ad writers would elect to use a clever headline. I prefer to target readers by stressing a benefit or specialty. For instance:

BUSINESS-TO-BUSINESS COLLECTION SPECIALISTS

We use proven techniques that get business customers to pay bills while retaining good customer relations. You get cash without losing valued clients. For details call Watson & Crick Collections, phone XXX-XXXX.

Stressing the offer of a free booklet or report can also be a successful tactic:

10 NEW WAYS TO COLLECT OLD BILLS!

Free booklet explains collection secrets that turn your old unpaid invoices into cash-fast! For your copy, call or write Watson & Crick Collections, 100 Main St., Anytown, USA, phone XXX-XXXX.

There are two additional points to keep in mind with small ads. First, although repetition helps create an awareness of your name, most ads gradually lose their impact over time. When the number of responses begins dropping off, you might consider running a new ad. (But save the old one. You may want to rerun it later.)

Marketing Tip

On occasion, you might have to run larger ads in select publications. You can get more response and attention with a larger ad, but the price of the space can be stiff. Although some big ads are successful, the smaller ads are more cost effective in most cases. The exception is in highly targeted business directories or local and regional business publications where small businesspeople can afford even a full-page ad.

Second, competition will hurt your response. When I was one of only a few writers advertising in *Adweek,* response was great. As more and more writers took out ads surrounding mine (many of them lifting sections of my headline and copy and using it in their own ads!), response dropped off.

When the competition gets thick, you must work extra hard to make your ad stand out. On the other hand, no competition may indicate that the publication doesn't work for your type of offer. But you can always test it and see.

Here are some additional tips for making ads generate more response:

➤ The headline should either stress a benefit ("INCREASE PRODUCTIVITY!"), the nature of your service and your specialty ("ROOF REPAIR FOR VICTORIAN HOMES"), or an offer of free information ("NEW FREE BOOKLET TELLS HOW TO REDUCE LONG-DISTANCE PHONE BILLS").

➤ Ask for action. Tell the reader to phone, write, or send a fax for more information.

➤ Offer free information, such as a brochure, catalog, report, pamphlet, or booklet.

➤ Show a small picture of your brochure or booklet.

➤ Describe the contents or special features of your free information ("Includes a 12-month lawn-care maintenance schedule").

➤ Give your literature a title that implies value. "Information kit" is better than "sales brochure." "Resource guide" is better than "catalog."

➤ Include your fax number in your ad, if you have one and are aiming at business audiences.

➤ Put a heavy dashed border or other unusual border treatment around your small ad to make it stand out.

➤ Offer a free consultation, analysis, recommendation, study, cost estimate, computer printout, critique, and so on.

➤ Talk about the value and benefits of this free offer.

➤ Test different small ads. Keep track of how many inquiries each ad pulls. Then, run only those ads that pull best.

➤ Put your name in the ad as well as your company name. Invite the reader to contact you personally.

➤ Use a testimonial from a satisfied client as a headline or in body copy.

➤ Use your photo in the ad to personalize the message.

➤ Consider using a toll-free hotline. Pete Silver, a professional speaker, has a toll-free number, 1-800-MR-SPEAKER.

The Least You Need to Know

➤ Direct marketing's objective should be to move the buyer to the next step in the selling process.

➤ Depending on the service, this next step might be an estimate, quotation, meeting, or an order.

➤ Offering a premium can usually lift response from mediocre to high levels.

➤ Have a hard offer ("call for an appointment") for prospects with an immediate need, and a soft offer ("send for our free tip sheet") for those not ready to buy now.

Chapter 20

Selling "Information Products"

> ### In This Chapter
>
> ➤ Understanding the information buyer
>
> ➤ Competing in the Information Age
>
> ➤ Types of informational products
>
> ➤ Working with online products

"Information products" are printed, recorded, or electronic publications containing data or information sold at a per-unit price. Information products is a broad term referring to everything from pamphlets, special reports, books, audio cassettes, and videos, to CD-ROMs, software, computer-based training, newsletters, fax-advisory services, and online subscriptions. Such products, typically, present in-depth data, information, or discussion of a topic related to a particular area of expertise.

What are the criteria for a marketable information product—especially at a time when we are all suffering from information overload? The answer: Information products provide specific and detailed answers to questions and problems in narrow niche subjects not usually addressed by newspapers, magazines, and general media.

As Richard Saul Wurman observes in his book *Information Anxiety* (Doubleday, 1989), "The information explosion has backfired, leaving us inundated with facts but starved for understanding." Information products cut through the clutter, providing clients with the precise information they want in a minimum of words.

Understanding Information Marketing and the Information Buyer

As has been observed more than once, we live in an "Age of Information." In this world, there exists a species we call "information seekers." These people need specialized data, and they're willing to pay well for it—sometimes hundreds or thousands of dollars for a single product.

What sort of products? Newsletters, magazines, books, special reports, directories, seminars and conferences, audio and video tapes, PC software, online databases, consulting services ... just to name a few. The subjects include management technology, investment, health, travel ... and more.

It can be a fertile, lucrative market. But it's essential to understand this special breed, what motivates them, and how to reach and sell them.

Here are some information-marketing strategies and trends that you probably won't read in textbooks.

Look for Niche Areas

Although there is an oversupply of information, opportunities still exist, even in fiercely competitive areas. There are still niches—places where data may be nonexistent, superficial, or anemic. The trick is to spot these niches, target the right market or market segment, recognize its needs, and fill them.

For example: Travis McFee is a dentist who became fascinated with the process of marketing and building a dental practice. He started a successful newsletter, "The Profitable Dentist," showing other dentists how to duplicate his methods and success and build million-dollar practices.

Research Your Market

Knowing your audience is key. Get customers and prospects talking about their information requirements—and how you can meet them. Identify the forces that drive their decision-making process. As marketing strategist Daniel Piro likes to ask, "What sort of data do they require most intensely? In which market segments is there a high level of uncertainty that information can help reduce?" Assemble the data elements that support these processes; define their relationships, and then package them into a series of information products.

Cultivate the Information-Hungry Core Buyer

Interestingly, the best prospect for information products is often the person who complains that he or she already has "too much to read." This ravenous individual appreciates the value of specialized, high-priced data and buys lots of it. This is why multiple-buyer lists, and the subscriber lists of directly competitive publications, invariably pull so well.

Indeed, your bread-and-butter audience will be composed of just such people. They are the ones who renew year after year, and who eagerly purchase related information products.

Specialized business publications fill a market niche where competitive information sources are nonexistent or weak. By providing only top-quality information, you make price sensitivity less of a problem: People will pay a premium for reliable data whose accuracy they can trust. For example, a newsletter covering trends in consumer marketing, originally targeted toward managers in all kinds of businesses, found its real audience among professional market researchers.

People Pay for Tightly Focused Information

Therefore, successful information marketers often specialize in providing coverage of a sharply defined topic. Beware of the temptation, then, to tinker with a successful information product in order to "widen the universe." The strategy may succeed. But you could achieve an unintended result: losing your product's focus, diluting its unique "positioning," and eroding reader loyalty. At the same time, never write off any *genuine* prospect.

You can preserve your editorial integrity and still pursue the greatest number of subscribers within that orbit. Accomplish this goal by extracting every legitimate benefit from editorial (that is, analyzing the information, what it means to the reader, and how the reader can apply it versus merely reporting information), then write copy that promises something for every potential buyer—including marginal ones.

Transform Editorial Matter into Powerful Promotional Copy

The *editorial* and promotional spheres intersect, but they're not synonymous. By all means, use editorial material as a basis for your promotional copy. But it's essential to select, slant, and dramatize it for maximum selling value. Some things are editorially strong, and some are promotionally strong. The ability to recognize the differences is crucial.

Marketing Tip

Better to be vertical than horizontal. Publications aimed at horizontal markets (such as consumers, and middle-management executives in all industries) often have a tough time, while specialized, vertical business newsletters such as *Bank Mergers & Acquisitions, Fiber Optics News, BOC (Bell Operating Companies Week)* prosper. One reason: The abundance of information, much of it low priced, on consumer and general-management topics.

Remember that a promotion is read in an entirely different context than the information product it is selling. In the case of a promotional piece, the copy is uninvited, an intrusion, so you've got to sell hard and fast. In the case of an information product, they've asked for it, paid for it; there's a built-in commitment and a whole different attitude. Keep in mind how editorial and promotion can help each other, but never forget that they each have a fundamentally distinct nature and purpose.

Insider's Buzzwords

Editorial refers to the literal content of an information product (for example, a newsletter is eight pages). Promotional refers to the benefit of the editorial feature (for example, you can get all the news about this topic in just 25 minutes reading time a month).

To boost credibility and persuasiveness, use proven creative techniques. Today, people are skeptical, critical, and suspicious. Expect increasing resistance to exaggerated copy and unproven assertions. Some solutions: Strong testimonials, media quotes, and other third-party endorsements can help.

To enhance the perceived value of your promotion piece, turn it into an information product. (Some techniques are: sample issue, report or article reprint, simulated editorial format, and information-heavy letter copy.) Remember that specifics add power and punch. Cite recent events or hot issues, and link them adroitly to your editorial promises.

Being negative can yield positive results. To justify the high price of specialized information, however, it's essential to demonstrate a *compelling need* or sense of urgency. That often means emphasizing a problem, threat, danger or fear, and offering information as a solution. Examples: "The Biggest Mistake Executives Make"; "Is Your Tax Return a Time Bomb?"; "The Coming Industry Shakeout—Will Your Company [or: Your Job] Survive?"

Determined Responses

Your response is determined, in part, by an external factor you can't control: the conditions in the field you cover. When times are good, information about business, stock investing, and so on is in demand. When the climate is flat or depressed, it's a much tougher sell.

Obvious? Perhaps. But publishers will sometimes say: "Now, when things are bad in [name your field], there's even *more* need for the information we provide." That may be true, but does the *prospect* see it that way? His or her reaction is more likely to be: "Until things turn around, why should I pay for information? In fact, this is a logical place to trim expenses."

For example: Investment advisories and business newsletters tend to rise and fall with the fortunes of the markets and industries they cover. In October of 1987, publishers clobbered by the stock market crash were forced to re-strategize and reposition.

Selling Information in the Information Age

Is the "information explosion"—the exponential growth of information in general, and the glut of free information on the Internet—a good thing for information marketers? Actually, it's a mixed blessing. People have too much to read and not enough time to read it. More and more information is competing for their attention.

There is a proliferation of low-cost/no-cost information sources eating into the market for your expensive information products. Fortunately, you can still succeed in selling information by mail. It's tougher than it was in yesteryear, I think. So here are some rules and guidelines formulated specifically for information marketers competing in the Information Age.

Narrow the Focus

Although the most profitable product may be one with wide appeal, such as Joe Karbo's book *Lazy Man's Way to Riches* or Bob Kalian's book *A Few Thousand of the Best Free Things in America*, "gold-mine" concepts such as these are difficult to come by. Today we live in an age of specialization. People have narrow, specific areas of interest and eagerly seek the best information in these niche areas. Match your own interests and expertise with the information needs of an identifiable market and you're on your way.

How big must this market be? Jerry Buchanan, publisher of *Towers Club Newsletter*, a how-to newsletter for information marketers and self-publishers, says that "any group large enough that some magazine publisher has seen fit to publish a magazine about them or for them" is large enough for your purposes.

Seize a Subject

The tendency of the typical magazine writer or book author is to wander from subject to subject to satisfy a never-ending curiosity about all things. But the information marketer must behave differently. He or she must latch onto a narrow niche or topic, make it his or her own, and produce a *series* of information products that meet the needs of information seekers buying materials on this subject. Not only does this increase profits by giving you more products to offer your customers, it also helps establish you as a recognized expert and authority in your field.

Marketing Tip

Come up with and plan the back end of related products *before* launching a direct-response campaign. Otherwise, you may lose precious opportunities for repeat sales if you offer only a single product to eager, information-hungry buyers.

Plan the Back End Before You Start Marketing

Many entrepreneurial direct response advertisers dream of duplicating the one-shot success of Joe Karbo who got rich from a single mail-order book. But it rarely happens. This "front end," or first sale, *can* be profitable, if cost-effective marketing techniques are used. But the real profits are in the back end, as discussed in Chapter 2, "Planning Your Direct Marketing Campaign," selling a related line of additional information products to repeat customers.

Test Your Concept with Classified Ads

Most information marketers want to immediately mail thousands of direct mail packages or place full-page ads. That's fine if you can afford to risk $5,000 to $25,000 on an untested idea. However, I prefer to test with small classified ads first, as shown in Chapter 13, "Direct Response Advertising." By doing so, I can determine the product's sales appeal and potential for under $200.

Your ad should seek inquiries, not orders. All requests for information should be immediately fulfilled with a powerful direct mail sales letter, circular, order form, and reply envelope.

What should all this cost? A successful classified ad will bring in inquiries at a cost of 25 cents to 1 dollar per lead. A good sales package will convert 10 percent to 35 percent of these leads to sales. I have run classified ads that pulled up to 17 times their cost in product sales.

The Importance of the Bounce-Back Catalog

A bounce-back catalog is a circular containing descriptions and order information for your complete line of related information products. When a customer orders your lead product, you insert the bounce-back in the package and ship it with the order. Ideally, the customer sees the catalog, scans it, orders more items, and the order "bounces back" to you.

The bounce-back catalog doesn't have to be long or elaborate. For a mail-order business I once owned, I printed a catalog on two sides of a single 8½-by-11–inch sheet in black ink on colored paper.

Additional sales generated by bounce-backs can range in dollar amounts from 10 percent to 100 percent of the front-end sales generated by your original ad or mailing. The only cost is a penny or two to print each catalog sheet. There is no postage cost, because the catalog gets a "free ride" as an insert in your product shipment.

Marketing Tip

When you fulfill a bounce-back order, send out another bounce-back catalog ... and another ... until the customer has bought every item in the catalog.

Create Low-, Medium-, and High-Priced Products

Different buyers have different perceptions of what information is worth and what they will pay. You will get more sales by testing a variety of prices for your lead item and by offering a number of different products reflecting a broad range of prices.

In a former mail-order business, my front-end product was a $12 book. The back-end consisted of a series of $7 and $8 reports, a second book for $20, and a six-tape cassette album for $49.95. Dr. Jeffrey Lant, who sells business development products and services, has products ranging from a $4 report to a $4,800 consulting service.

Recently, I sent an inquiry to a well-known and successful marketer who specializes in selling information on how to make money as a speaker. I didn't buy because the only alternatives were a large cassette album or a one-year newsletter subscription, both of which are fairly expensive, and I wasn't ready to make that kind of commitment to the subject. Most buyers prefer to sample your information with a lower-priced product, such as a book, single cassette, or inexpensive manual in the $10 to $50 range.

Let Your Buyers Tell You What Products to Create

Always put your name, address, and phone number in every information product you produce, and encourage feedback from readers. Many readers become advocates and fans, calling, writing, and establishing a dialogue with you. Welcome this. Not only can you solve their problems and answer their inquiries by telling them which current products to buy, but their questions can suggest new products.

Most of my back-end reports were written to answer specific questions readers asked me repeatedly. Instead of having the same telephone conversation over and over again, I can simply sell them a report containing the answers they seek. It saves time and generates revenue.

Be the Quality Source

Your strongest advertisement is a good product. A clever or deceptive ad can certainly generate brisk sales, and product returns may not be excessive even if your product is poor, but customers will feel cheated and will not favor you with repeat business.

A good product will have people actively seeking you out and will bring in a small but steady stream of phone calls, letters, inquiries, and orders generated by the product itself and not the advertising. You will be shocked at the enormous effort some people expend to locate the source of quality information products that are praised by other buyers.

Building the Buyer's Trust in You

"People buy from people they like and trust" is an established sales truism. This is an advantage for you if you are a well-known information marketer like Boardroom Reports or Rodale Press; a disadvantage if you're a home-based business or solo operator.

How many people receiving your direct mail package have even heard of your publication or editor or you, much less like and trust you? Your direct mail copy must work hard to build the credibility that will get the reader to trust you enough to order and rely on your information. The following descriptions are some techniques copywriters use to establish credibility quickly in their mailings:

➤ Show a picture of your building or establish a physical presence to prove you're more than just a mailbox. Promotions for *Dr. Atkins' Health Revelations* show a photograph of his impressive seven-story clinic in midtown Manhattan and note that tens of thousands of patients have been treated there.

➤ Link the specifics of the editor's (or, if you are a seminar promoter, the speaker's) background to reasons why this particular background enhances his or her value as a researcher and analyst. A promotion for *Forecasts & Strategies* notes that editor Mark Skousen was once with the CIA, which gave him government insider contacts he still uses today to interpret the market for his readers. Likewise, promotions for *Technology Investing* point out that Michael Murphy's proximity to Silicon Valley enhances his ability to research high-tech companies first-hand.

➤ Cite any awards the publication has won or favorable third-party reviews it has garnered. These can include Newsletter and Electronic Publishers Association awards and, for financial newsletters, favorable ratings in *The Hulbert Financial Digest*. (Because some readers may not be familiar with the source of the rating, describe it in impressive terms. Hulbert, for instance, can be described as "The *Consumer Reports*" of the financial newsletter industry.)

➤ Get and use testimonials from subscribers and the media. The best testimonials are specific rather than superlative, and support the key points you are making in your copy.

Stress the editor's credentials and experience. List the books he or she has written (and their publishers) and the periodicals in which the editor's articles have appeared. Also list major conferences and speaking engagements as well as academic or business affiliations. Give the names of the TV and radio shows or stations that have featured the editor as a guest.

If the editor is not a subject matter expert and the publication is not built around him or her, promote the credibility of the publisher (you) instead. Tell how many publications you have and why you have such a great reputation in the market you serve.

One way to get around an editor or publisher credibility problem is to create an Editorial Advisory Board. Have three to five experts agree to serve on this board, and then stress their credentials and achievements in your promotional copy.

Don't forget standard credibility stuff like number of years in business or number of subscribers—especially if you have been in business a long time or have an unusually high number of subscribers. "Our 50th year" impresses some people. Also look for other statistics that can boost your credibility. For example, perhaps you still have your first subscriber who joined 28 years ago when you published your first issue.

Types of Information Products You Can Sell

You can package and sell information in any print or electronic format your buyers can read—from posters and flash cards, to password-protected Web sites and e-mails.

The following sections describe some of the most common types of information products sold through direct marketing.

Magazine Subscriptions

Magazine subscriptions are one of the biggest product categories in direct marketing. Almost every magazine in the world is sold in whole or in part through direct marketing—the only other option being newsstand purchase.

Newsletters

Unlike magazines, which have significant news-stand sales, subscriptions to newsletters are almost wholly sold through direct marketing—some telemarketing and space advertising, but mostly direct mail. The categories of newsletters are …

➤ **Paid consumer.** These are newsletters marketed to consumers. They usually charge between $29 and $79 for a one-year subscription, although consumer newsletters dealing with the stock market and commodities trading may sell for $59 to $149 a year or even higher.

➤ **Paid business.** Business-to-business newsletters give analysis, news, or advice on narrow niche fields. An example is Magna Publishing's *Distance Education Report,* which covers distance learning (online education,

Marketing Tip

Since the use of soft bill-me offers by magazine publishers is so widespread, magazine subscribers have become accustomed to not paying up front. That means you, too, will probably need to use a soft offer which, in turn, means you'll have the problem of getting subscribers to pay up after they receive their first free issue.

Warning!

Many newsletter publishers offer a "bill me" option in which the buyer can order now, and pay later. If your promotion stresses a free premium, many prospects may respond to get the premium only, then cancel and not pay you. Thus, your "pay up" rate—the number of bill-me subscribers who actually pay your invoice and become subscribers—may suffer.

Marketing Tip

When selling directories, stress the urgency and importance of having up-to-date information. Many prospects don't ask "Why buy," when they see your offer; instead they ask "Why buy *now?*" Demonstrate to prospects why they need or should want the most current data available. For instance, bringing a manager up to date on new safety regulations might help him or her achieve compliance at lower cost.

correspondence courses, CD-ROM based programs). Business newsletters are typically more expensive than consumer newsletters, with one-year subscriptions ranging from $59 to $499 and even higher.

➤ **Promotional.** Thousands of companies give away free promotional newsletters as an advertising vehicle. These don't concern us here, although in Chapter 25, "Database Marketing," we'll discuss how to use free newsletters as a database marketing tool.

Directories

Directories are a big business; there is even a directory, *Directories in Print* (Gale, 2000), that tells you where to find them all! Many direct marketers use direct marketing to market both to end users as well as to the library market.

Books

Direct marketing of books has been conducted successfully for decades—by mainstream publishers, direct marketing companies, and mail-order start ups. Books are frequently recommended as a product to sell in "get-rich-quick mail-order promotions," but most people who try to produce and market a book this way fail.

Why? Two reasons. First, the book is not specialized enough or does not appeal to a targeted audience. Second, the average book is too inexpensive to justify the cost of a solo direct mail package. Space advertising is often a better medium for mail-order book selling.

Booklets and Special Reports

If you don't want to make the commitment to producing and marketing a full-blown book, you can scale back and tackle booklet selling instead. Writing, publishing, and selling information booklets is a popular home-based business that has brought many entrepreneurs a nice income. Booklets are generally 4 by 9 inches, so they can be mailed in a standard #10 business envelope.

A booklet is constructed by printing the pages and then saddle-stitching them together (saddle-stitching is binding by stapling through the spine). Booklets typically run anywhere from 8 to 16 pages, although they can be longer. I price booklets at $5 to $12 each. Printing costs can be 25 to 50 cents per unit, depending on volume.

Audio Cassettes

Audio cassettes are a popular medium for disseminating spoken-word business and how-to information. A single audio cassette is easy to produce. Just get a speaking engagement, and tape your talk. Or tape it at home or in a studio. Then make duplicates, put a nice label on it, and sell the tapes. A single audio cassette retails for between $10 and $15. Duplication costs for small quantities are $1 to $2 each, depending on packaging.

Marketing Tip

When you have done a number of tapes on related topics, you can package them in a vinyl album and sell them as an audio cassette program. A six-cassette album can sell for $49 to $79. Albums are a couple of dollars each, and available from any tape duplication service. A "power pack" is a multimedia information product made by combining audio tapes with another medium. Typically, it's a combination of tapes, reports, perhaps a book or CD-ROM, all in a nice package. Power packs can sell for $50 to $150 or more.

Video Tapes

How-to videos on a variety of topics, such as exercise and sex, sell well. *TaeBo,* an exercise video, was one of the best-selling direct-response products of all time. Your video should be edited professionally in a video studio. Add graphics, special effects, charts, and other footage for a varied presentation that's more than just you talking behind a lectern. Have a nice label or package. A single video can sell for $29 to $59 or more.

CD-ROMs

You can put lots of things onto CD-ROMs and sell them—games, directories, reports, books, databases, even software. Price can range from $10 for a CD-ROM with games to $1,000 for a technical or business database.

Software

Software is a popular direct response product. It is most commonly offered online, in ads in computer magazines, and via direct mail. Pricing is not an afterthought but a key ingredient of the marketing mix. How much the software costs is terribly important to buyers—much more so than most marketers seem to believe.

When selling software through mail order, always give the prospect a discount price and identify it as such. Even sophisticated programmers and system analysts like to think they are getting a bargain. If you want $299 for the program, give the list price as $399, and then tell customers they get a $100 discount if they act now.

Seminars

Seminars can be sold via direct response, primarily through course catalogs, the Web (especially good for online registration), newspaper ads, and direct mail. The most popular mailing format for promoting seminar registrations is a four-page self-mailer (see the following figure). Why? Mainly because they are cost-effective. At the low mailing quantities typical of seminar promotion, the standard #10 package (letter, brochure, order card, BRE) is too expensive to allow the seminar promoter to make a decent profit.

What kind of response can you expect? One-fourth to one-half percent is typical, with 1 to 2 percent being the most you could hope for on an outside list. At a response rate of one-half percent, a mailing to 10,000 would bring you 50 registrants.

Seminars are held successfully throughout the year, and every expert publishes a list of preferred months that seems to directly contradict what the other experts say. My own experience is that the best seminar seasons are March through May and September through mid-November. Summer interferes with vacations and winter brings the danger of cancellation due to bad weather.

This self-mailer format is the most common for selling public seminars.

(Source: The Center for Technical Communication)

Online Products

With the growth of the Internet, many prospects like to buy information in electronic form, whether as downloads from a Web site or a subscription newsletter delivered as a pdf file via e-mail.

The rising popularity of the Internet can work to your advantage as an information seller: You can package essentially the same information in multiple media, and sell it many times over. Not only will different people buy information in different formats, but some customers will actually pay for the same information several times over to get it in different formats.

The down side is that the culture of the Internet is one of free information, which clashes with the direct marketer who wants to sell information at a handsome profit.

Some newsletter publishers offer access to a Web site as a supporting service to their print newsletter. When you subscribe, you get a pass code giving access to the advanced information and features on the site. Position the Web site as a value-added service and a way to keep subscribers current between print issues.

Another way to get late-breaking news to subscribers between issues is through e-mail alerts. Position this as a value-added premium. Added benefit to the publisher: You capture the subscriber's e-mail address.

A number of information marketers (as well as many other marketers) now offer their customers a free weekly or monthly electronic newsletter. Get people to sign up for the free e-zine (e-mail marketing campaigns are perfect for this purpose), then upsell them on your paid print or online product.

The Least You Need to Know

➤ In direct marketing of published material, timely news, analysis, or how-to information sells best. Fiction, poetry, and literature cannot usually be sold profitably via direct marketing.

➤ Tell the reader how he or she benefits from buying your information product (for example, a quick-reading newsletter eliminates the need to spend hours searching the Web).

➤ You are probably overestimating how many people will buy your product, but underestimating what they are willing to pay for it. Test the price you think is right versus a higher price and a lower price.

➤ Develop a complete line of information topics centered on a particular topic (for example, computers) or audience (for example, computer resellers). Have a mix of media (videos, books, newsletters, reports, software) and prices.

➤ The person who bought one of your information products is the one most likely to buy your other information products. Constantly market to your buyer list.

Chapter 21

Lead Generation

> ## In This Chapter
>
> ➤ Are leads of any value?
>
> ➤ Leads for the sales force
>
> ➤ Designing your lead–getting programs
>
> ➤ Comparing solo mailings and series mailings
>
> ➤ Offers that increase lead flow
>
> ➤ Keeping track of responses

Are sales leads a waste of time? Not according to a cover story in *The Marketing Report* newsletter (January 29, 2001, p. 1), which reports that between 25 and 45 percent of prospects who respond to marketing campaigns will buy within the coming year.

By generating a steady flow of qualified leads, your direct marketing program can assure a healthy sales curve and prevent the peaks-and-valleys sales cycle companies suffer from when their marketing is erratic or ineffective.

Sales Leads Support the Sales Force

Unless you're Microsoft, and probably not even then, your company does not have an international monopoly. Your company *does* have good competitors. And the competition poses problems for your sales force because …

1. The competition goes after the same potential customers.

2. The competition wants to get your active customers away from your company.

3. If your salespeople could spend all their time soliciting business from just one potential customer, they probably would get that business. But they can't.

4. If your salespeople could spend all their time with just one current customer, they might never lose that customer. But they can't.

Your salespeople must seek business from several prospective companies at the same time that they are working to convince several current customers to remain with your company and increase their purchases. Your salespeople are just too busy to do everything and that's the main reason why they need direct mail.

Direct mail supports your sales force. It is their "calling card" when they cannot be there and it continues their sales efforts and reinforces their messages after they have left the prospect's domain.

Your competitors know their biggest dollars come from their biggest prospects. They logically spend the most time on the biggest prospects. Your salespeople thus need promotional support to go after those companies that can become large customers.

And for those big companies that are now your active customers, your salespeople need promotional support to help prevent the competition from getting your business.

Surprising Secrets

The competition does not spend much sales time on smaller companies that may not be worth several personal sales visits. *Industrial Distributor News* reports that 85 percent of American businesses employ fewer than 100 persons. Those companies are, thus, classified as small businesses, yet they offer tremendous and often-missed sales opportunities at better gross profits. Profits often are better because smaller customers may not buy at bulk sales discounts.

Increasing Sales Force Efficiency

Your company can be smarter than the competition by using direct mail and other lead-generating direct marketing (such as e-mail marketing or banner ads) to support busy salespeople who cannot spend all their time soliciting business from smaller companies.

This direct mail support can …

➤ Familiarize executives at those smaller companies with your products and services.

➤ Warm up those executives for future sales visits.

➤ Produce qualified leads from those companies so the salesperson does not waste his or her time on fruitless visits.

The competition also knows that some potential customers are located far away from a sales office or in areas that are not usually visited. So, the competition does not send its salespeople to call on those prospects. However, your company can be smarter by using direct mail to get the executives at those distant companies to request a visit by your company salesperson. Then, when your salesperson arrives, he or she will be responding to a request for a sales presentation. That beats a cold call.

Direct mail is not intended to replace a good salesperson. You need salespeople to educate prospects, counsel them, explain products, point out the benefits of your company, and produce orders. But demands on your salespeople's time are growing and the personal sales-call rate has been going down because your company salespeople are so busy, and because the executives they call on have many pressures on their time.

This is not a unique problem. It is worldwide. The sales-call rate in the United States, for instance, has slipped from six per day to five per day and is now approaching four per day for many salespeople, while many others are lucky to complete three solid visits in a day. Some international industrial firms count themselves lucky if top salesmen make just two sales visits a day. So, they use direct mail to keep their names in the minds of current customers and potential customers. Their mailings educate prospects about manufacturing care and details, product uses, and benefits.

That's what your new mailings must do for your salespeople.

Reaching the Buying Committee

The next problem you face is that orders are not always produced by a single executive at a prospective company. Often, several executives are involved. But sometimes your salesperson can't see each decision-making executive, or each executive who influences the decision. And just one person in the target company can ruin the salesperson's entire pitch, especially if that person was not at the sales presentation. But, your company direct mail can reach those important people to tell them the details that the salesperson wants them to know.

Sometimes, the target company does not inform your company salesperson about a new requirement for which your products or services would be perfect. Because your salesperson cannot be at the target company every day of the year, he or she may miss a sale when those new products are being planned or produced. But your company direct mail can support your salesperson when he or she is not there, by reinforcing an image of your company so that when your salesperson arrives, his or her job is easier.

Your salesperson's rough job is to face these 10 constant problems:

1. Competition wants your prospective customers.
2. Competition wants your active customers.
3. Salespeople are overly busy.

4. Small target companies may not be worth cold calls.

5. Prospects may be too distant for sales calls.

6. Prospects need familiarization.

7. Prospects need education.

8. Nonqualified leads waste time.

9. Several decision makers are involved.

10. Planning stages are difficult to determine.

Warning!

If you are having trouble determining the relative importance of quality versus quantity in your lead-generation program, err on the side of more quality and less quantity. When salespeople are given bad leads that are not responsive and don't close, they are quick to sour on a lead generation program and won't bother even following up on future leads.

Strategic use of targeted direct mail enables the marketing team to overcome these objections. This gives the sales force highly qualified decision makers from the company's prospecting database and rented lists.

Direct Mail Formats That Work Best for Lead Generation

Direct mail is one of the most effective methods of generating large quantities of high-quality sales leads. Aside from public relations and postcard decks, few promotional methods can even come close to matching direct mail's effectiveness for lead generation.

Direct Mail Letter

A good lead-generating direct mail letter will generate response rates of between 1 and 5 percent—and sometimes higher—when mailed cold to a rented mailing list or directory of prospect names. This response rate is for producing quality leads with a genuine and serious interest in your product or service—or at least in the problem your product or service solves. It can be achieved using copy with a strong sales appeal and an attractive offer that is free and without obligation.

Can response rates be higher? Yes. Some lead-generating mailings have achieved response rates of 10 to 50 percent or more, although this is rare. Response rates are generally two to five times higher when mailing to existing customers versus "cold mailing" to rented prospect lists.

Response rates can also increase when offering expensive free gifts or other "bribes" to prospects in return for their reply. The more costly and desirable the bribe, the more inquiries are produced. But when prospects respond just for the bribe rather than because of a genuine interest in the product or service, conversion of leads to sales becomes poor. With lead generation, you must always balance between quantity and quality of inquiries.

The most effective format for lead-generating direct mail seems to be a one- or two-page letter in an envelope with a business reply card and perhaps one insert, such as a brochure, flier, or article reprint.

Self-Mailers

Self-mailers can also be effective. The most successful self-mailer format for lead generation is the trifold. This is made by taking a piece of paper and folding it twice horizontally so you form three sections (the same way you fold a business letter for insertion into a #10 business envelope). There are infinite variations, but the trifold seem to work best, and they are inexpensive to produce. Try a trifold before spending money on something more elaborate that may not get any better response (and may very well get less).

Postcards

Because of their low cost, a third format—postcards—is growing in popularity. Aside from low cost, their major advantage is that, unlike direct mail packages and trifold mailers, postcards do not require opening or unfolding: The message is completely visible as soon as you pick it up.

The disadvantage of a standard postcard is that there is no reply element. Mailers have found several solutions to this. One company instructs prospects to return the entire postcard as-is in an envelope to receive a free sample copy of their product (the postcard does not have to be filled in since the front panel already contains a label with the recipient's name and address).

Other postcards stress response through tool-free 800 and 888 numbers, 900 numbers, and phone numbers that dial up recorded hotlines with more detailed promotional messages and product information on tape. Sending a fax seems a logical response option, but smaller postcards do not fax well (they do not feed through many machines smoothly).

Marketing Tip

As discussed in Chapter 9, "Direct Mail: Short Formats," another advantage of postcards is they are easy and inexpensive to produce. The postage is also lower than postage on a letter in a first-class envelope.

Marketing Tip

Another innovation is the double postcard, which is two postcards attached via a perforated border. One postcard carries the promotional message; the other is the reply element. While used with considerable success in selling magazine subscriptions, double postcards have not found widespread use in other applications as of yet.

Of all the lead-generating direct mail formats, trifold self-mailers and simple sales letters mailed with reply cards have the longest track record of success, and are, therefore, your safest bets.

Successful Lead-Generating Copy Features

Whether you use a sales letter or a self-mailer, copy for your lead-generating mailing should be simple, clear, conversational, and concise. It should be easy to read and laid out in a fashion that is inviting—short sentences, short paragraphs, subheads and graphics for emphasis, generous margins, and adequate spacing between paragraphs and sections.

The style should be breezy and inviting. Use short words and simple, direct language. Make it sound natural—like one friend talking to another. Each paragraph should convey one simple thought. When you want to begin a new topic, start a new paragraph. Use subheads whenever starting a major new section.

Successful letters are usually simple in style, tone, content, and proposition. Unlike mail-order copy, which is usually lengthy because it has to do a complete selling job, lead-generating copy is designed to accomplish only one part of the selling task: getting a qualified prospect to reply ... in effect, to raise his or her hand and say, "Yes, I'm interested; tell me more."

Surprising Secrets

What if a prospect reading a lead-generating letter is interested but not at the stage where he or she is ready to meet with a consultant to discuss the product? Those who are interested but not ready to act immediately should be given an alternative offer—for example, sending for a free white paper. By offering the white paper as a premium, the consultant increases response. Those who are not ready to buy now can still identify themselves as interested by requesting the white paper. And the premium is an added incentive that probably increases response from those prospects who are potential immediate buyers.

Therefore, the copy must contain just enough information to gain attention, arouse curiosity, and generate interest. Additional information will be communicated in conversation or other sales materials requested by the prospect. The lead-generating mailer only needs to present enough information so that the prospect becomes interested in the product or service. More detail is not required and may even serve to decrease response: After all, if there is nothing left for the prospect to find out, what reason do he or she have to call you?

What is the best length? For a lead-generating sales letter, somewhere between one and two pages. Many marketers feel lead-generating letters should fit on one side of a piece of business letterhead, and I often strive for that degree of brevity myself. But avoid the mistake of cramming too much copy together just for the sake of fitting it on that one side of a sheet of paper. It's better to have a one-and-a-half- or two-page letter with wide margins, readable type, and adequate space than a one-page letter that's a giant block of tiny, tight copy.

Solo Versus Series Mailing

Should you create a single lead-generating piece or a series? It depends on the size of the market, the number of inquiries you can handle, and whether you sell one product or service or a line of products.

A lead-generating mailing can generate inquiries for a single product or a family of products. An old rule of thumb in direct mail selling is, "Sell one thing in one mailing." Following this advice, you would discuss one product or service in a mailing. Discussing multiple products or services risks diluting the impact and confusing the prospect. Therefore, a company with five different services might have one lead-generating mailing on each service.

The rule about selling only one product per mailing can be violated at times, with success. If we focus our copy on the prospects and their problems, not the products, then we don't need to go into the products or services in depth. We can say, "We understand your problem; we offer a full range of products and services to solve this problem; these solutions offer you the following benefits; and call us for more details." So you can focus on a problem or need, then offer more information on either a product or family of products as the solution.

The key to answering the question of whether you need a solo mailing or a series is the size of the market and your capacity to handle inquiries.

Market Size and Handling Capacity

Here's a helpful rule of thumb: If you have an extremely large list of potential customers and a limited capacity to handle leads, you should focus on developing a single lead-generating mailing that gets the maximum response. Then, use it on as many prospects as you can handle in a given time frame.

For example, let's say you have a piece that gets a 5 percent response. Mailing 100 pieces produces 5 leads. If you can't respond to more than 10 inquiries a week, you would mail no more than 200 pieces a week.

Further, let's say the size of the market is 200,000 prospects. Mailing 200 a week, you'd reach only about 10,000 in a year. At that rate, your lead-generating mailing could be used for 20 years before you'd hit every prospect with it!

The key is to reduce mailing costs by increasing the response rate. Therefore, I recommend continually testing different lead generating mailings to increase response. For instance, if you can double response, to 10 percent, you then have to mail only 100 per week, not 200, to get your 10 leads, which cuts your mailing costs in half.

On the other hand, if you can handle a large number of leads, or if the size of the market is extremely limited (or if both conditions exist), then you may need a series of mailings. A one-shot mailing is often not sufficient, because you can quickly expose all prospects to it, at which time you need something fresh to lure them with. Yes, you can mail the same piece to the same group of prospects more than once, but each time you do, response declines, and eventually it declines to the point where the mailing is not making money.

The rule of thumb here is that mailing the same piece to the same audience about four to eight weeks after you mailed it the first time produces about half the response as the initial mailing. Therefore, if you got 5 percent on the first mailing, the second will produce $2\frac{1}{2}$ percent; the third, $1\frac{1}{4}$ percent. So you need a new piece to bring response back up.

Surprising Secrets

Let's say you are a bigger company and can process 200 inquiries a week. Also, your market is specialized, with only 2,000 prospects. If you produce a letter that generates a 3 percent response, the first mailing will generate 60 leads; the second 30 leads. At that point, everyone has seen the mailing twice, and most of those who will respond to it have already done so. I would recommend having a series of three or more mailings to this market. You will build name recognition and generate more leads with a series than repeat mailings of a solo.

Evaluating Your Response

Keep track of the responses. Most respondents will mail back the reply card. Some will fax their reply to you; others will telephone. When you get a phone inquiry, always ask the prospect where he or she heard about you. By tracking inquiries and number of pieces mailed, you can calculate and compare response rates for different pieces and different mailing lists.

In addition to keeping track of the quantity of leads received from each promotion, you also want to measure the quality. This is determined by calculating the conversion rate, which is the percentage of leads that convert to sales. What is typical? As we've said, a good lead-generating self-mailer or letter, mailed to a rented list of names, will generate between 2 and 10 percent response or more (4 to 5 percent is considered excellent, and 2 to 3 percent is quite acceptable).

If the leads are of good quality, you will convert between 10 and 25 percent of them to sales. A conversion rate of less than 10 percent suggests that either the lead-generating letter is misleading, the free offer too much of a bribe and not related to the product or service, or the offer is not right for this market. A conversion rate in excess of one in four leads indicates either that your follow-up is excellent or the leads are of superior quality—or both.

Of course, these figures are intended as a general guideline only. Your response percentages and conversion rates may vary depending on your product, market, list, and offer. As a rule, the higher the product price, the lower the conversion rate, and the longer it takes to close the sale. But the real measure of success is, "How profitable was the mailing?" After all, if your product costs $1 million, one sale can pay for the cost of a lead-generating mailing many times over. If your product costs $1,000, you may need to sell several to make the mailing pay off.

Another rule of thumb is that inquiry response rates are higher for products that are commonly and frequently needed; lower for products that have infrequent or occasional use. Therefore, if you are selling pH meters to industrial scientists, response may be high, because these people buy lots of pH meters. On the other hand, if you are selling brick-lined reactor vessels, response will be lower: Only a few plants use this type of vessel, and those that do may buy a new one perhaps only once every 20 years or so.

Marketing Tip

If your product costs over $1,000, you are probably best off generating leads and following up on those inquiries to convert them to a sale. If your product costs less than $500, you can probably sell it directly from your mailer or ad, and ask for the order instead of an inquiry. If your product sells for between $500 and $1,000, you should probably test lead generation versus direct selling in your marketing.

Other Lead–Generating Methods

We have shown in this chapter how direct mail can be used as a cost-effective lead generator. But many other media and formats are also effective lead generators.

➤ **Postcard decks,** discussed in Chapter 11, "Profits from Postcard Decks," are good low-cost lead generators. They work, however, only if you can find someone who publishes a card deck mailed to your target audience.

➤ **Space ads,** discussed in Chapter 13, "Direct Response Advertising," can bring back inquiries, although not always as cost-effectively as direct mail or card decks. Classified and small display ads are cheaper than full-page ads and, for lead generation, often perform better with a lower cost per lead.

➤ **E-mail marketing,** one of the newest and most effective lead generators, is covered in Chapter 16, "The Internet: Direct Marketing for the Digital Age." Response rates, measured in "click throughs" (percentage of people receiving the e-mail who click on a hyperlink embedded in the e-mail that sends them to a response page on the Web) can range from 4 percent to 10 percent for lead-generating offers.

The Least You Need to Know

➤ A sales letter with a reply card is one of the most effective lead-generating direct response formats.

➤ Other direct-response media and formats effective in lead generation include postcards, trifold a self mailers, e-mail marketing, and print ads.

➤ Lead-generating promotions should have two offers: one for those ready to buy now and another for prospects who may have a need but are not at the stage where they are willing to sit down and talk with a salesperson.

➤ Products over $1,000 are almost always sold via lead generation, not one-step direct marketing.

➤ Salespeople are often skeptical of leads provided by marketing departments, so make sure you produce for them quality leads from qualified buyers, not casual responses from brochure-collectors and tire-kickers.

Chapter 22

Nonprofit Marketing

In This Chapter

➤ Who uses direct marketing to raise money?

➤ Reasons why people donate

➤ Key differences of fundraising versus commercial direct marketing

➤ Fundraising copy that pulls in the money

➤ Political direct marketing

Nonprofit direct marketing is tricky business. Imagine you are raising money for a political candidate's campaign, a community event, your local school or college, a museum, or favorite charity. Marketing a product makes sense to buyers: They pay money, and they get a product they want in return.

But what about nonprofit marketing? When you think about it, asking for donations is downright unnatural. Your fundraising letter must persuade the recipient to take an action that much of humanity thinks peculiar: to give money away. Keep reading to find out more techniques to successful nonprofit marketing.

What Motivates People to Donate?

To bring in checks, your fundraising appeal needs to be built on the psychology of giving. Forget your organization's needs or the worthiness of your cause. Instead, focus on the needs, the desires, and the concerns of the people you're writing. Your job is to motivate them.

The author of a popular book on writing fund-raising letters says there are five "great motivators" that explain response: fear, exclusivity, guilt, greed, and anger. Advertising copywriters typically fall back on a similar short list. But the truth is much more complex.

There are at least a dozen reasons why people might respond to your fund-raising letter. Any one of them might suggest a theme or hook for your letter. It's likely that several of these reasons help motivate each gift.

Why do people send money? The following sections explain some of the reasons.

Marketing Tip

You can raise more money, more profitably, by soliciting past donors than by mailing to people who have never given you money.

You Asked Them To

Public opinion surveys and other research repeatedly confirm this most basic fact of donor motivation. "They asked" is the most frequently cited reason for giving. The research confirms, too, that donors want to be asked.

Focus group research also reveals that donors, typically, underestimate the number of appeals they receive from the charities they support. These facts help explain why responsive donors are repeatedly asked for additional gifts in nearly every successful direct mail fundraising program.

When you write an appeal, keep these realities in mind. Don't allow your reticence about asking for money make you sound apologetic in your letter.

They Can Afford It

The overwhelming majority of individual gifts to nonprofit organizations and institutions are small contributions made from disposable (or discretionary) income. This is the *money left over* in the family checking account—after this month's mortgage, taxes, insurance, credit cards, and grocery bills have been paid. Unless you're appealing for a major gift, a bequest, or a multiyear pledge, your target is this modest pool of available money.

For most families dependent on a year-round stream of wage or salary income, the pool of disposable income is replenished every month or every two weeks. That's, why most charities appeal frequently and for small gifts.

If your appeal is persuasive, your organization may join the ranks of that select group of charities that receive gifts from a donor's household in a given month. If you're less than persuasive, or if competing charities have stronger arguments, or if the family just doesn't have money to spare that month—you won't get a gift.

For example, if you write me a letter seeking a charitable gift, you may succeed in tapping into the $100 or $200 I'll probably have "leftover" for charity during the month your letter arrives. If your appeal is persuasive, I might send you $25 or $50—$100 tops—because I decide to add you to the short list of charities I'll support that month.

They're Proven Donors

Charity is habit forming; giving by mail is a special variety of this benign affliction.

The Direct Marketing Association (DMA), a leading industry trade association, periodically surveys the American public to determine what proportion of the adult population is "mail-responsive" and, thus, susceptible to offers or appeals by mail.

DMA surveys indicate that approximately 50 percent of Americans are mail-responsive. Clearly, the American population is becoming increasingly mail-responsive. Almost gone are the days when people would insist on waiting in line to pay bills in person because they distrusted the mail.

Surveys also reflect the growing importance of direct mail appeals in the fundraising process. Research shows that fundraising letters are the number-one source of new gifts to charity in the United States.

They Support Organizations Like Yours

Your donors aren't yours alone—no matter what you think. Because they have special interests, hobbies, or distinctive beliefs, your donors may support several similar organizations.

A dog owner, for example, may contribute to half a dozen different organizations that have some connection to dogs: a humane society, an "animal rights" group, an organization that trains seeing-eye dogs, or a wildlife protection group.

A person who sees him- or herself as an environmentalist might be found on the membership rolls of five or six ecology-related groups: one dedicated to land conservation, another to protecting the wilderness, a third to saving endangered species or the rain forest, and so on.

Marketing Tip

Think about how well the people on a mailing list match your cause before you rent it. If you are doing a mailing to save the trees, Sierra Club would probably get better results than the Young Republican's Club.

There are patterns in people's lives. Your appeal is most likely to bear fruit if it fits squarely into one of those patterns.

They Want to Make a Difference

Donors want to be convinced that their investment in your enterprise—their charitable gifts—will achieve some worthy aim. That's why so many donors express concern about high fundraising and administrative costs. It's also why in successful appeals for funds, the impact of a gift is often quantified: $35 to buy a school uniform, $40 for a stethoscope, $7 to feed a child for a day. Donors want to feel good about their gifts.

Like everyone else on the planet, your donors are striving to be effective human beings. You help them by demonstrating just how effective they really are.

They Want to See Immediate Results

Urgency is a necessary element in a fundraising letter. Implicitly or explicitly, there is a deadline in every successful appeal: the end of the year, the opening of the school, the deadline for the matching grant, the limited press run on the book available as a premium.

But the strong attraction in circumstances, such as these, is best illustrated by imagining that no such urgent conditions apply. If the money I send you this week *won't* make a difference right away, shouldn't I send money to some other charity that has asked for my support and urgently needs it?

They Want to Be Recognized for Their Good Works

You appeal to donors' egos—or to their desire to heighten their public image—when you offer to recognize their gifts in an open and tangible way.

A listing in your newsletter. A plaque, certificate, lapel pin, house sign, or armband they can display. Screen credit in a video production. A press release. If your fundraising program can provide appropriate and tasteful recognition, you're likely to boost response to your appeals by highlighting the opportunities for recognition in your letter or newsletter.

Even if donors choose not to be listed in print or mentioned in public, they may be gratified to learn you value their contributions enough to make the offer.

They Want the Premium You Are Offering

Another reason people send money is because you give them something tangible in return. Premiums can come in all sizes, shapes, and flavors: bumper strips, gold tie tacks, coffee-table books, membership cards, even a pint of ice cream.

Sometimes premiums (such as name stickers or bookmarks) are enclosed with the appeal, these so-called *front-end* premiums boost response more often than not and are frequently cost-effective, at least in the short run.

In other cases, *back-end* premiums are promised in an appeal "as a token of our deep appreciation" when donors respond by sending gifts of at least a certain amount. Either way, premiums appeal to the innate acquisitiveness that persists in the human race.

Insider's Buzzwords

A **front-end** premium is a small gift enclosed with the fundraising solicitation. A **back-end** premium is a gift the donor receives after she gives money.

They Want to Be Heard

Today, we are bombarded by information about the world's problems through a wide variety of channels. Though we may isolate ourselves inside triple-locked homes, build walls around our suburbs, and post guards at gateposts, we can't escape from knowing about misery, injustice, and wasted human potential. Often, we feel powerless in the face of this grim reality.

Charity offers us a way to respond—by helping to heal the sick or balm troubled souls, to teach new ways to a new generation or feed the hungry. Your appeal will trigger a gift if it brings to life the feelings that move us to act, even knowing that action is never enough.

If you offer hope in a world drowning in troubles, your donors will seize it like the life jacket it really is.

Your Cause Is Endorsed by a Celebrity

There are numerous ways that the identity, personality, or achievements of an individual might be highlighted in a fundraising appeal. For example, that person may be the signer of the letter, the organization's founder or executive director, the honorary chair of a fundraising drive, a patron saint, a political candidate, an honoree at a special event—or simply one of the organization's members or clients.

If the signer's character or accomplishments evoke admiration or even simply a past, personal connection, your donors may be moved to send gifts in response. The opportunity to associate with someone who is well-known or highly esteemed may offer donors a way to affirm their noblest inclinations—or compensate for what they believe to be their shortcomings.

You Help Them Fight Back

There are too few outlets for the anger and frustration we feel on witnessing the injustice and corruption that pervades our society. Both our moral sense and the secular law hold most of us in check, preventing expressions of violence or vocal fury that might allow us to let off steam.

For many, contributing to charity is a socially acceptable way to strike back. Whether a public interest organization committed to fighting corruption in government or a religious charity devoted to revealing divine justice, your organization may help donors channel their most sordid feelings into a demonstration of their best instincts.

Marketing Tip

In a cause where solidarity can be built around a group of donors sympathetic to your objectives, consider using bumper stickers as front or back-end premiums. They're fun, people like them, and the cost is less than $1 a piece.

They Want to Be Part of Your Inner Circle

Your most fundamental task as a fundraiser is to build relationships with your donors. That's why so many organizations use membership programs, giving clubs, and monthly gift societies.

The process of solicitation itself can help build healthy relationships. For some shut-ins, for example, or for elderly people left with distant family and few friends, the letters you send may be eagerly anticipated. Most of us are social animals, forever seeking companionship.

You Give Them a Forum for Their Opinions

The act of sending a gift to some nonprofit organizations might, itself, constitute a way to speak out. Consider, for example, the ACLU, or the Campus Crusade for Christ, or Ross Perot's United We Stand; support for such a group makes an obvious statement about a donor's views.

But almost any charity can offer donors an opportunity to state an opinion by including in an appeal an "involvement device" such as a membership survey, a petition, or a greeting card that might later be sent to a friend or family member.

Even though most donors may ignore the chance to offer suggestions, they may regard the invitation to do so as a strong sign of your respect and concern for them.

You Give Them Access to Inside Information

Even if your organization or agency isn't an institution of higher education or a research foundation, you still hold knowledge many donors crave. Nonprofit organizations are often on the front lines of everyday, hands-on research, gathering important data day after day from real-world clients, visitors, or program participants. Their staff members are likely to be specialists, often experts in their fields.

Every nonprofit organization possesses information that is not widely known to the public and that donors may perceive as valuable. A loyal supporter may be vitally interested in the health and well being of your executive director (who was ill lately), the progress of that project you launched last year (after a spectacular start), or what your field staff learned last month (three months after the hurricane).

Disseminating inside information, which is intrinsically valuable and, thus, constitutes a gift from you, also helps build strong fundraising relationships by involving your donors in the intimate details of your organization.

What Makes Fundraising Different?

Although fundraising has much in common with other direct marketing, it also has key differences. And to some extent, it also is harder, more difficult to master. The following sections explain some reasons why.

You Have No Commercial Product

In regular marketing, you have a product or service you want to sell that will benefit your prospects. You simply take what you have, extract the benefits, outline the features, then go to work writing sizzling copy. Generally, your product or service appeals to the greed, comfort, or self-interest of your prospects.

However, with fundraising, you have no such product or service (at least, not in the same sense as commercial enterprises). Instead, you have a cause. A heart-felt need. Instead of appealing to a person's greed, you ask them for money, appealing to their heart, their faith and dignity and sometimes compassion for others.

"The spirit behind all ethical development work has to do with what Eric Hoffer, the late philosopher-longshoreman, once called 'things which are not,'" wrote Don Fey in *The Complete Book of Fund-Raising Writing* (The Morris-Lee

Marketing Tip

Do not be dismayed that there is no appeal to the prospect's greed or fear in your fundraising appeal. As Michael Masterson of the American Writer's and Artist's Institute points out in his copywriting course, appealing to a person's benevolence can, in itself, be an effective motivator to action. Wanting to help others is a core human desire that can be exploited in direct marketing for profitable effect.

Publishing Group, 1995). "Fundraisers are futurists selling ideas, opportunities, prestige, and even immortality of a sort."

Think about it. It's much easier to receive money from a person in exchange for a product or service. But try asking—with nothing to exchange but a dream—and you will see why fundraising is not for the timid.

You Offer No Solutions for Individual Prospects

In business-to-business marketing, you generally offer a product or service that will solve some type of problem faced by your prospect. But in fundraising, the focus shifts to people other than the your prospect. Oh, you involved the prospect, but you goal is to persuade him or her to help you solve another person's problem. Ideally, the other person is someone with whom your prospect can relate to or someone (or something) your prospect cares about. Instead of offering solutions to your prospects for their own good, you recruit them to become a solution for others.

You Have a Single Cause—Not a Full "Product Line"

As with other direct marketers, nonprofit groups need "repeat business"—contributions from previous donors—to survive. But, while commercial marketers can return to past customers with new products each time, nonprofit groups must often return to the same people with the same, single cause. Which is harder? You be the judge.

In fundraising, when a campaign is launched, the initial focus is on generating a list of donors. A couple of months later, you try to convince them to make another donation—for the same cause. Before the year is up, you go back to them—the same people—for yet another donation. Near the end of the campaign, you go back to the same donors and ask for another donation as a cause for celebration.

But that isn't all. The next year, you call on those donors to become partners by contributing on a monthly basis. And that's all for the same cause.

So, you can see that fundraising is not the same as selling products or services where you have more to offer prospects. True, the fundraiser must be creative in providing a "new" reason for giving, but the giving, primarily, is for the same cause.

You Target Multiple Audiences

In consumer direct marketing, you write to specific target markets (for example, people who garden for a hobby, parents, pet owners). But in fundraising, you must take a single cause and make it appealing to a wide range of prospects. That includes individuals as well as giant corporations.

Sometimes funding will be sought of both consumers and corporate sponsors, members and strangers. Depending on the cause, the fundraiser doesn't have the luxury of focusing on one audience. He or she must be versatile and creative, able to reach anyone on any level—as the need arises.

Your Approach Is Somewhat Restricted

If you were selling computers by mail or television, you could change your tone and not hurt sales. You could be serious or silly, or downright outrageous, and still sell the product. You could do the same thing selling steak knives or barbells. But try that with fundraising and you'll be scarred for life. That is, unless your cause or group is about popular entertainment.

I know that celebrities and comedians are often used for various fundraising events. Who can forget Bob Hope and his overseas travels to encourage soldiers in war? But again, depending on the nature of the event (or cause), it is best to maintain a consistent tone of sincerity in your communications. That's especially true in direct mail where prospects cannot see you face-to-face.

Writing Powerful Fundraising Copy

When a fundraising giant was asked about the secret to his success, he gave a simple response. "I'm a beggar," he said. "I know when to beg ... where to beg and how to beg ... for money. Begging is all I do." The same may be said of successful copywriters who use words and phrases to raise money for worthy causes. They know the essential elements for generating response. They know what does and what doesn't work. They know how to beg in print.

Although some rules are made to be broken, as the saying goes, there are some you will break at your own peril. If you'd like to try your hand at "begging in print" and raising money for a good cause, then keep the rules in the following sections in mind.

Begin with a Worthy Cause

You can sell a good product with a weak direct mail package, but you'll be hard-pressed to sell a weak product with even a good package. Bottom line: Fundraising, as with general marketing, must begin with a good cause.

To convince a prospect to pull out his or her checkbook and write you a check, you must first convince the prospect of the worthiness of your cause. It must be something the prospect cares about. Whether its saving birds, rescuing homeless teenagers, building a memorial, or supporting a political candidate, your cause must resonate with your prospective donor.

Lead with Emotions

Good copy should be emotion driven. That's true whether you're writing a letter, a feature article, or a brochure. You have to reach out and touch the heart of your prospect.

In a way, fundraising copy is heart-to-heart communication. It is helping another person to feel what you feel about a particular need. It's all about emotions. "An emotional appeal will outpull an intellectual appeal," wrote Herschell Gordon Lewis in *How to Write Powerful Fund Raising Letters* (Bonus Books, 1989). "Logic has its place in debate—but we aren't debating with prospective donors, we're asking them for money."

Marketing Tip

Donors want to know how their money will be spent. So, tell them. For instance, you could say: "$50 will feed a family of five each month ..." or "Your monthly gift of $25 will provide food for 10 children in this orphanage ...."

Follow with Facts

Once you have hooked a prospect with an emotional appeal, you must hold him or her with some solid facts about your cause. Give details. Show what you did in the past and what you hope to do in the future—with their help. For example: "Last year we rescued 125 teenagers from the streets of New York. The year before, we saved 79. So you can see we are making a difference. And it's all possible because of people like you."

Use Plenty of "You" References

It's been said that next to "free," the word "you" is the strongest word in all forms of marketing. It can transform an otherwise formal document into a personal letter that reaches the heart. "Use 'I' and 'you' but mostly 'you,'" said Mal Warwick in *How to Write Successful Fundraising Letters* (Strathmoor Press, 1999). "'You' should be the word you use most frequently in your fundraising letters. Your appeal is a letter from one individual to another individual."

Marketing Tip

Be direct in asking for money. Don't leave it to words like "support" and assume prospects will know what you mean. Say up front that you need financial help. If you are asking in a letter, do so at the beginning, in the middle, and at the end.

Explain the Urgency

People need a reason to respond. For that reason, you must explain why their help is needed *now!* Do you have a deadline? Share it. Then explain what may happen if they don't respond. Will more children die of starvation? Will a "rotten candidate" end up in office? Will more people continue to drive drunk? Whichever point you choose, be sure to drive it home.

Offer a Gift as a Token of Appreciation

Prospective donors are human and desire approval. They want to feel appreciated. Therefore, offer a plaque or certificate bearing their name. Create a monument in their honor. Encourage them to see they are valued and are joining a special, exclusive group of people.

Appeal to Their Need for Prestige

Send them a book, or a photo of the person (or people) they're helping. For example: Programs where you donate to support a child and in return get regular letters from the child telling how your money is helping him or her.

Give Options for Giving

Instead of asking for a single amount, give the prospect a few options. In your letter or on your response card, provide something like: $100 ___ $50 ___ $25 ___ Other $___.

Get More from Your P.S.

Use the P.S. to repeat your offer or your need for help. Restate your request and remind the prospect of the urgency of the moment. Then close with a nice "Thank You."

Ask for the Next Donation

When asked what made him a great pool player, the legendary Minnesota Fats said a good pool player makes the shot, but a great pool player also lines the balls up for the next shot. In the same way, fundraisers who maximize their profits are sure to ask recent donors for their next contribution.

I am a regular contributor to Covenant House. After giving $100, I got this thank-you letter. The request for donation was extremely soft sell, but it was there. A donation envelope was enclosed with this letter:

> Dear Robert,
>
> I just wanted to drop you this quick note to let you know that we received your recent $100 donation and we are all so very, very grateful for your support!

I sometimes think saying simple things like "thank you" has become a lost art in our culture, but I wanted to let you know that our kids are forever and truly thankful for every single act of kindness that comes their way.

I suppose a lot of their sincere gratitude stems from the painful reality that they just haven't been given a lot in their young lives, and any act of kindness is a blessing to them. I also think a lot of their heartfelt thanks stems from the fact that these kids within our shelter are simply great kids, the types of young men and women you'd be proud to call one of your own kids (in some ways, they already are!). So, on their behalf, I want to tell you how thankful they are, and I am, for all you have given us.

We are forever grateful for your friendship, and your prayers. I am praying for you. Please stay in touch ….

Gratefully,

Sister Mary Rose McGeady

Of course, this isn't just a "thank you" … the message is also "and please favor us with another donation again soon." The point was made subtly by Covenant House by enclosing a reply envelope.

Marketing Political Candidates

Most winning political campaigns are based on a formula. According to this formula, there are four attributes each candidate has in varying amounts. A successful campaign will convince voters that one candidate is the right choice because he or she has these attributes, which are: past performance, future promise, credibility, and ideology.

Past Performance

What has the candidate done for voters in the past, either in government service, business, or other capacities? One way to demonstrate good past performance is by citing specific track record; for example, the candidate voted against tax hikes for property owners three times.

Another method is to infer that generally good conditions in the candidate's voting district are largely a result of his or her being in office. For instance, President Clinton enjoyed a high performance rating due to the good economy, and voters are not asking for proof he directly created those conditions.

Future Promise

Past performance is "What have you done for me?" Future promise is "What will you do for me if I elect you?" Sometimes this future promise is a platform of intended actions. In other campaigns, it can hinge mainly on how the candidate says he or she will act regarding a key issue (attacking fraud, for example).

Credibility

Credibility is "Who is this person? Should I trust him or her? Should I believe he or she will do what he or she says?" Creating credibility can be done many ways.

For example: Dwight Eisenhower stressed experience as a successful general in World War II to create a rugged war-hero image contrasting with Adlai Stevenson's intellectual-liberal label. Ross Perot and Steve Forbes make the analogy they are successful at running businesses, therefore can do the same with the government.

Factors that tie the candidate to his or her constituency also work well in building credibility and connections with voters. If you are running for office in Florida, for example, and your children and grandchildren live in the state, saying so builds your image as a Florida family man or woman.

Ideology

Ideology is "What is your belief system?" Are you conservative or liberal? Democrat or Republican? Believe in big or minimal government? The important point is that your candidate need not possess each attribute in equal measure to win. Think of these four attributes as four legs of a stool (this analogy comes from copywriter Michael Masterson). A stool with four legs can stand even if one leg is missing, or if two legs are weak. Likewise a politician can be weak on past performance (for example, someone entering politics for the first time) and still win if his or her credibility and current platform are strong.

The Least You Need to Know

➤ Fundraising copy must give the reader a reason to donate, which unlike commercial direct marketing, usually does not involve receiving a product in return.

➤ Often, fundraising appeals to benevolence—getting people to give because it's a basic human desire to help others.

➤ The person who has just given is the one most likely to give again.

➤ Nonprofit direct mail requires a high degree of copywriting skill to get the reader to give money.

➤ Do not overlook the possibility of offering a premium as an outright bribe for a donation. Many people who like the cause and are on the edge may be pulled over the fence with the offer of an attractive desirable gift.

Part 5

Measuring and Monitoring Your Results

Direct marketers pride themselves in measuring, to the penny, the results of their direct marketing campaigns. This part shows you how to measure response and analyze the results, so you can cut your losses and multiply your profits.

Testing is perhaps the most important element of direct marketing, and you will find solid, sensible advice on how to conduct statistically valid direct response tests. You also learn what variables are worth testing and which are probably not.

Find out how to track and analyze results, including the most common metrics such as percentage response, conversions, cost per order, and break-even. And finally, discover how to turn your list of mail-order customers into a profitable database you can sell more and different products to, again and again.

Chapter 23

Testing Your Way to Direct Marketing Success

In This Chapter

➤ Learning through testing

➤ Tracking responses with key codes

➤ Determining quantities to test

➤ Using statistically valid testing

➤ Figuring out what to test

➤ What to do when the piece is not a success

In direct marketing, testing is the process of putting a letter or package in the mail—or an ad in a magazine, or a TV commercial on the air—counting the replies, and coming to some conclusion based on the results.

In traditional direct marketing tests, two or more variations of a single variable are tested against one another simultaneously. For instance, you might test letter A against letter B to see which pulls more orders. Or, you might take letter A and mail it to two different lists, to see which list produces the better response. But testing doesn't have to be an A versus B proposition, even though that's the way it's traditionally viewed.

Even if you mail only one package or one letter or use only one list at a time, you can still learn something from the mailing—as long as you keep track of the results. Learning is the real purpose of direct mail testing. By counting replies and monitoring results, we learn what works for us in direct mail—and what doesn't.

Although discussions of testing can get elaborate and complex, this chapter has been deliberately kept simple, so you can immediately apply the information to your on-going direct mail activities. If you already have a sophisticated testing program in place, you probably won't get much new help here. But you are probably like many marketers, in that you do minimal testing—or at least not as much as you could. If that's the case, I hope this chapter gives you the motivation to begin testing and tracking all your mailings from now on … and provides some helpful yet easy-to-follow hints and techniques for conducting simple tests on low budgets and in limited quantities.

Why Not Learn While You Test?

"Every time you do a mailing you should test something," writes James E. A. Lumley in his book, *Sell It by Mail* (John Wiley & Sons, 1986). "If you don't, you've wasted an opportunity to learn something about the prospects who respond to your offer." I agree with Lumley and urge you to measure leads and sales on every mailing you do.

Some say, "You can only test one thing versus another, such as package A versus package B." I disagree. If you mail 5,000 letters and get two responses, you have learned something about how that particular audience of 5,000 people responded to the particular product and offer you featured in that particular mailing.

For instance, you can quickly and inexpensively discover whether a new product or service has appeal to a given market by doing a small test ad or mailing. Using direct mail to test the waters in a new market can actually be much less expensive than hiring a market research firm or creating a new ad campaign.

Many direct marketing experts also say, "There is no sense testing a mailing list unless it is large enough to allow for a full-scale mailing if the test mailing should be successful." In other words, don't test 10,000 names unless there are another 90,000 people on the list you can mail to after you learn the test results. Again, I disagree. Even if your list is only 10,000 or even 5,000 names, why not split it in two sections and test something—an offer, a product, a price? Why settle for just selling when you can also learn in the process?

Tracking Results with Key Codes

To test, you must be able to track response. That is, when you receive a reply, you must be able to identify that reply as coming from a specific mailing or ad, or from a reader whose name was on a specific mailing list or publication. There are several ways to do this.

The simplest is to put a key number or code on the reply element. The code can be a series of numbers and letters in fine print tucked away in the corner of the reply card. Or, it can be worked into the address. For example, you might use the return address, "USA Engineering Associates, Dept. DM-2, Yorktown, PA." The code "Dept. DM-2" tells us this reply card came from package 2 as opposed to package 1.

The same thing can be done for telephone response using either an extension ("call Ext. 123") or a person's name ("ask for Jennifer Smith"). If the person asks specifically for extension 123 or Jennifer Smith, the operator knows the call is in response to a specific mailing package.

If you are affixing labels to your reply card or order form, the mailing list owner can use his or her computer to put a key code directly on the label. The charge for this service is nominal—usually about one dollar per thousand names. "Let your mailing house key the order cards or reply envelopes while labeling," advises letter shop expert Lee Epstein. "This will save you many on-press keying and inventory control headaches."

For the Internet, you can track response by setting up a unique Web site address for each promotion. For instance, www.products.com/a, www.products.com/b, and so on. If the response mechanism is e-mail, you can have the recipients e-mail to a unique address for each promotion. For instance, salea@products.com, saleb@product.com, and so on.

Marketing Tip

This coding technique is also used in print ads. Try calling the toll-free numbers used in print ads; ask for the specific extension listed in the ad. Often, you are not switched and the operator who answers handles your call. This is because there is no such extension; the number is solely a tracking device. If the ad is keyed to a fake name ("Ask for Cindy"), the employee who takes orders on the phone is assigned to be Cindy.

Using Employees to Help Track Response

All the keying and coding in the world is useless if you don't train your people to keep track of response. Obviously, it's very important to track all responses if you're going to have accurate test results. In particular, you must keep track of six types of responses:

1. People who respond by mailing or faxing the reply card or order form you have provided

2. People who write on their own letterhead or send a company purchase order or a personal check without your order form

3. People who phone in and ask for the person or extension you have specified

4. People who call and don't specify the extension or person

5. People who don't reply to you directly but are motivated by the mailing to contact their local sales representative or distributor

6. People who go to your Web site.

Keeping track of responses 2, 4, and 5 is admittedly a difficult task. You will always get some leads and sales for which you can't pinpoint the source. But be diligent about tracking those responses you *can* identify. The more accurate your counts, the more meaningful the conclusions you draw from your tests.

Statistically Valid Responses

If you become a student and practitioner of direct marketing, you will read a great deal about tables and formulas for calculating whether a response is *statistically valid*.

Insider's Buzzword

A **statistically valid** response means that, based on the results from your test mailing, you can pretty accurately predict that an identical mailing to other portions of the same mailing list will give you similar results.

Generally, you need to mail several thousand pieces to get a statistically valid response (more specifics on this in the following section). So, does this mean the results of a smaller test should be ignored because they are not statistically valid? The experts will tell you: yes. I say: no. In my opinion, all results tell you *something*. Just be sure to let common sense be your guide.

Recently, I wrote a sales letter for a local print shop. The client called me the other day and said, "I am very excited, I tested your letter and got a 10 percent response!"

I replied: "I'm delighted. But I didn't know the list had even been delivered yet. Tell me … how did you arrive at this test result?"

"Oh," said the client. "That's easy. I mailed 10 letters to people whose names I had on file and got one call back!"

Obviously, you see the danger of this thinking. With a mailing of only 10 pieces, you cannot get a statistically valid result in terms of percentage response. For example, if that one person who responded had been too busy to read his or her mail that day, our rate would have plummeted from 10 percent to zero!

Success Story

Even a small test is meaningful if the information it reveals is good enough for your purposes. For instance, a good friend of mine runs a management-consulting firm. They mail low volumes to local corporations; 1,000 is a big mailing for them. I asked him how he tested. "We do a letter and mail out 500 copies to a portion of our house list, which has about 10,000 names on it. Or we may use a rented list," he replied. "If we get back 25 replies, we call that 5 percent and assume it's a good mailing (5 percent is good for us). I know that in some circles that isn't exactly scientific. But it satisfies our needs, and based on a result like that, we might mail out another 500 to 2,000 copies of that letter—depending on how many new business leads we needed to generate."

How Many Test Pieces Must You Mail?

Okay. Let's say you want to be more sophisticated. How many test pieces do you have to mail? Actually, test results are based on the number of responses—not pieces mailed. So the real question is, "How many *replies* do we have to get back in order for the test to be considered statistically valid?"

Different authorities quote different numbers. James Lumley says 20 responses. Ed Burnett, writing in *The Handbook of Circulation Management,* says between 30 and 40 responses. Milt Pierce, who teaches the direct, response copywriting workshop at New York University, says you need 100 replies to get a statistically meaningful result.

In my experience, the most accurate measure of how many replies you must receive (and therefore, of how many pieces you must mail) to get a statistically valid response is shown in the following table, reprinted from *The Basics of Testing,* written by Ed McLean (and now out of print).

Determining Test-Cell Size: The Number of Returns Required for a Statistically Valid Test

Confidence Level	Deviation or Decline Percent*			
	50%	25%	12.5%	6.25%
75%	1.8	7.3	29.2	116.8
85%	3.5	14.0	56.0	
90%	6.6	26.2	104.8	
95%	11.0	42.8		
99%	21.7	86.9		

The estimated return and your break-even point or the decline percent you wish to protect yourself against.

Take a look at the chart. Go along the top line until you reach the deviation or decline percent column labeled 25 percent. This means that the result from a large-scale mailing should deviate no more than 25 percent from the test result.

So, if the test pulls 1 percent, the "roll-out"—expanded mailing after a successful test—should pull between 0.75 percent and 1.25 percent. Warning: The response rate almost always declines after the test. It rarely goes up.

Now, look at the rows. They show the confidence level, which indicates how certain you can be of your test results. Naturally, the higher the confidence level you seek, the more pieces you must mail to get that level of statistical certainty.

Let's say we are seeking an 85 percent confidence level. Go down the 25 percent deviation column until you reach the 85 percent confidence level. You'll find the number 14, which is the number of responses you must set up your test sample to get. To find the correct sample size, divide the number of returns (14 in this example) by the percent return you expect.

Let's say your mailings, typically, generate a 1.5 percent response. You divide 14 by 0.015 and get 933. So each test cell should be 933, or 1,000 to make it even. So, if you are testing two lists, A and B, you mail 1,000 pieces to list A and 1,000 to list B. Your test cell size is 1,000 each.

On the other hand, if you anticipate a 1 percent response, then you need to mail 1,400 pieces per mailing list in your test (14 is 1 percent of 1,400). To be on the safe side, I'd make it an even 2,000. Therefore, when people ask me, "How many pieces do I need to mail to get a statistically valid test result?" my recommendation is 2,000 names per list, based on the above analysis.

Is this accurate? The formula I just showed you was introduced to me not by Ed McLean (who is now a good friend and valued colleague) but by a large mailing list brokerage that has been involved in thousands of mailings. "We have been using this formula for more than 30 years, and we find over and over that you can get a statistically valid test result mailing 2,000 names, not 5,000," says the president of the firm. I have since used it numerous times with clients doing smaller mailings, and have found it to be valid.

Often, we arrange tests with more than two cells so we can test several factors at once. For instance, let's say we want to test two lists—A and B—and two mailings: a #10 package versus a self-mailer. Here's how our test cells might be arranged:

List:	A	B
#10 package	2,000 pieces	2,000 pieces
Self-mailer	2,000 pieces	2,000 pieces

Therefore, we have four test "cells" of 2,000 each for a total test mailing of 8,000 pieces. At the end of the test, we will know whether list A or B pulled best, and whether a self-mailer worked better than a #10 package. We might also find that the variables are dependent: List A might be the best list with the self mailer, while list B pulls better with the #10 package. (Unlikely, but possible—which is why you must always test.)

Rolling Out After a Successful Test

Can the results of a small test mailing remain statistically valid regardless of how many additional names we mail to? The answer is no. The rule of thumb for roll-outs is that the total quantity you mail to should be no more than *10 times* the number of names you tested.

Therefore, if you got a 5 percent response in a test of 5,000 names, you can mail to as many as 50,000 additional names on the list with the confidence that test results are repeatable in the roll-out. No matter how sorely you may be tempted, never do a roll-out to more than 10 times the test quantity. Results may not hold valid in these large numbers.

Let's say you have a list of 80,000 names. If you tested 2,000, you can roll out to up to 20,000 names and expect the decline percentage not to exceed the percentage you selected when using the "Determining Test Cell Size" table we reviewed earlier to conduct your test. Should results prove profitable on the 20,000 names, you can then safely mail to the remainder of the list.

What Should You Test?

You can test almost everything, but everything is not worth testing. Given a limited budget and time, you should test only those variables that are likely to have a significant effect on your response rate. Well, what are the most significant factors you can test?

Number one is the mailing list. As discussed in Chapter 4, "Mailing Lists," there may be half a dozen mailing lists that might be right for your offer—maybe more. You cannot assume you know which one is best, based on your personal prejudices. The only way to know for certain which list will pull best with your package is through a test mailing.

The second most important factor to test is the price. This applies mainly to mail-order selling. For instance, let's say you've published a 1,000-page report on the telecommunications industry. How much will people pay for it? $195? $495? $1,200? You simply do not know until you test. And frequently, you will be amazed at how many people place orders at prices you thought were sky-high.

The third most important factor to test is the offer. For example, should you try for mail orders or leads? Should you offer a premium—a free gift? Will you get better response offering a gift item, such as a clock radio, or free information, such as a booklet or special report? You won't know which works best unless you test.

Make your mailing list broker your partner in testing. For instance, when you want to test a small portion of the list, ask your broker to supply you with what is called an *nth name selection*.

Insider's Buzzword

An **nth name selection** is a random selection of every nth name. For instance, if you wanted to test 5,000 names in a 50,000–name list, you would select every 10th name.

How does this work? Let's say the list has 70,000 names, and you are going to test-mail to 7,000. In this example, 70,000 divided by 7,000 equals an "n" of 10. That means the computer will select (for your test mailing) every tenth name as it randomly goes through the list. A random nth name selection ensures that you get an average, unbiased sample that represents a typical cross section of the list.

This is much better than ordering the entire list and then picking the test names by hand. The danger of doing it that way is that you subconsciously select the names that will give you the best results (because you want your mailing to be a success). Test results are artificially elevated because of this favorable selection, and roll-outs don't bring the results you would have expected.

Ten Essential Rules of Tested Direct Marketing

Here are the 10 best practices you should follow when creating and testing direct marketing promotions:

1. Make every promotion a test.

2. Establish goals for each test. Determine the information you want to get out of the test—the degree of reliability needed in your data—and how much money you can afford to spend on the test.

3. Test significant factors that make a substantial difference in direct marketing results. These include the list, the offer, and the price.

4. Also test to find out things you need to know or want to know. There may be issues specific to your industry, product, or market that have never been tested in direct mail before. If there is no reliable data from other sources, you have to be the pioneer in your field.

5. Use direct mail tests to settle questions, debates, and disagreements concerning strategy, format, lists, design, and copy. Instead of arguing theory, put ideas to the test.

6. Test even if you are using a small list with minimal or no roll-out. Try to split the list for an A versus B test of a mailing package or a direct mail element, such as letter length or offer.

7. Be consistent in your testing. For example, if you are testing a single factor, such as an envelope teaser, all other factors in the two test packages must be identical—including the mailing list from which the names are taken and the date on which the packages are mailed.

8. Don't assume you know what will work. Test to find out. More often than not, the results will shock you. Direct mail tests are great for shaking up so-called marketing and advertising "experts" who think they know it all.

9. Even if you don't have enough money or names for a statistically valid test, test anyway. Some information is better than no information. Just be aware of the fact that the test is not statistically valid—and act upon the results accordingly.

10. To learn more from a direct mail test, make a list of questions you want answered. Call up some of the people who did not respond, and ask them your questions. In addition to learning a great deal about why your mailing failed to motivate these people, you may be able to turn nonresponders into responders and generate a lot of additional inquiries or orders.

Marketing Tip

Clients often ask me, "Does it pay to follow up my mailings with a phone call to those who did not respond?" This answer is: It may be worth a test. You might find that telemarketing does indeed, for your offer and audience, turn enough nonresponders into responders to make the effort worthwhile. According to Dwight Reichard, telemarketing director of Federated Investors, Inc. (Pittsburgh, Pa.), direct mail followed by telemarketing generates 2 to 10 times more response than direct mail with no telephone follow-up.

When the Verdict Goes Against You

Every direct marketer has had the unsettling experience of waiting for test results, only to have them come back negative—meaning the campaign didn't generate the sales you had hoped. What then?

For one thing, ask yourself if your objectives were realistic to begin with. Most novices have expectations way out of line with reality. Professionals are often happy to do 130 to 150 percent of break-even (see Chapter 24, "Tracking and Analyzing Response," for more information), meaning for every dollar spent, they get back $1.30 to $1.50 in revenues.

Marketing Tip

When something fails, it makes sense for everyone on your team to have a postmortem meeting in which to discuss what may have gone wrong and toss around ideas for either reviving the project or taking it in a different direction.

As you'll recall from reading Chapter 2, "Planning Your Direct Marketing Campaign," in direct marketing most of the profits are made on the back end. So set realistic expectations for the front end. Don't be shocked when your new ad or mailing doesn't beat the control. Most don't. Even most professional direct marketing copywriters say that their copy beats the control only between 25 to 50 percent of the time.

For new product launches, the hit rate is even lower. Probably only between 10 to 20 percent of new product launches in direct marketing are successful. The odds are against you because not only does the promotion have to be strong, but the product must be, too.

Can a promotion that has failed be saved? Maybe. Some direct marketers look to see how they can "tweak" a promotion—make changes here and there to make it better. But if your test pulled only 25 percent of break-even and you double response, you're still losing 50 cents for every dollar you spend.

A marginal performer can be nudged into profitable territory through creative tweaking. You might add testimonials, offer another premium, strengthen the guarantee, or test a payment plan. But a promotion that bombs is either dead or can only be saved by major surgery. The change that can make the most difference, aside from offer, price, and list, is sales theme—the selling proposition communicated in the headline, lead paragraphs, and first page or two of copy. You may be able to save a dud with major revisions and rethinking in those areas.

The Least You Need to Know

➤ You need to mail 1,000 to 2,000 names per test cell in direct mail to get statistically valid results.

➤ Based on a successful test, you can roll out with confidence to a mailing between 5 and 10 times the quantity of the test cell.

➤ By arranging test cells in a matrix, you can test multiple variables, such as prices, lists, mailing formats, and offers.

➤ For a new product, keep testing simple. On a launch (new product test), you might test one mailing package on several lists, and nothing else.

➤ The variables likely to yield the most dramatic differences in response in a test include list, offer, pricing, and sales appeal.

Chapter 24

Tracking and Analyzing Response

In This Chapter

➤ Keeping track of your responses

➤ Analyzing and interpreting results

➤ Calculating lifetime customer value

➤ Boosting your response rates

Scientist Lord Kelvin once said, "When you can measure something and express it in numbers, you know something about it."

This chapter is about direct marketing "metrics"—the numbers we care about, the jargon we use to describe them, how to collect the data and calculate the results, and what they mean.

Counting Returns

The first step in being able to measure direct marketing results is to count the responses that come in. This is not always as easy as it sounds.

For instance, if you enclose a reply card in an envelope and the prospect completes and return it, how do you know which of your mailings it came from? The solution, as we've discussed, is to key code the mailing label, then affix it to the reply card. The label shows through a window on the envelope, and comes back to you when the reply card is returned.

But a significant number of responses are not made using the key-coded reply element you provide. Some people send an e-mail or make a telephone call. Others write or fax. What then? There are some responses whose source will never be known to you. But whenever possible, try to track each response to its source.

People who answer the phones should be trained to ask, "Where did you hear about us?" If it was from a mailing, ask them to read the key code on the label. (Consumer catalog marketers do this all the time.) If the prospect says he or she saw an ad, ask the person which magazine he or she saw it in. Once your inbound telephone staff gets in the habit of asking prospects what prompted them to call, your data collection will improve.

Response Metrics

A "metric" means a measurement or number. Response metrics are the criteria by which direct marketers measure cost, response, and profit. The major direct-response metrics are as follows:

➤ **Cost per thousand.** This is what it costs to reach 1,000 prospects with your advertising message. Say your ad in *Hub Cap Collector* Magazine costs $1,000, and the magazine reaches 50,000 subscribers. Your cost per thousand is $20. Space advertising usually has a much lower cost per thousand than regular direct mail or Internet direct mail sent to rented lists, but the response rate to print advertising is lower than the response rate for direct mail or e-mail.

➤ **Percentage response.** This measures how many people who received your direct mail package replied. If you mail 100 letters and get back 3 reply cards, 1 phone call, and 1 fax, for a total of 5 inquiries, your response rate is 5 out of 100, or 5 percent.

➤ **"Click throughs."** In Internet direct marketing, response is measured in click-throughs. This is the number of people who received your e-mail or saw your banner and clicked on it to link to your Web site or response page. If your banner ad is seen by two million people, and you get 10,000 hits (visits) to your Web site, then your click-through rate is half a percent.

➤ **Cost per inquiry.** This is how much it costs you to get a sales lead. If you receive 50 inquiries for every 1,000 pieces mailed, you are generating a

Marketing Tip

For more cost-per-thousand conversions: A direct mail package to generate inquiries works out to 28 cents postage per package; printing is 25 cents per piece, and letter shop costs are 5 cents per piece. Mailing list rental is $120 per thousand, which works out to 12 cents per label. The total is 70 cents a piece, or $700 per thousand—a typical cost per thousand for direct mail.

5 percent response. If the cost per thousand for your mailing is $700, your cost per inquiry is $14 each.

➤ **Conversion rate.** In traditional direct marketing, conversion refers to the percentage of leads that convert to sales. Say, with follow-up, you can get orders from one out of every 10 leads. That's a 10 percent conversion rate.

➤ **Cost per order.** If you spend $700 per thousand, get 50 leads per thousand pieces mailed, and have five of those leads place an order, then the cost per order is $700 divided by five orders, or $140 per order.

➤ **Break-even.** This is the response rate at which the revenue from the orders equals the cost of the mailing. If each order received is for $1,000 and the 5 orders we get from every 1,000 pieces we mail, that means the mailing generates $5,000 in revenue. Because the mailing costs $700 per thousand, we divide $5,000 in revenues by the $700 cost and get a return of more than 7:1 over break-even. The mailing is generating revenue of more than seven times cost. You often hear direct marketers talk in terms of percentage break-even. If a direct marketer says a mailing pulled 150 percent of break-even, that means they generated $1.50 in revenue for every dollar spent in the mail. If our $700 per thousand mailing pulled 150 percent of break-even, it would have made $1,050 per thousand in revenues. Therefore, to achieve break-even on this mailing, we needed less than one order per thousand, but we got five.

➤ **Dollar return.** This is simply another way of speaking about break-even. A direct marketer will say, "We are getting $1.75 per name." That means that for every dollar they spend on direct mail, they get $1.75 in orders.

Marketing Tip

Sometimes direct marketers use different definitions of "conversion rate." I have heard some Internet direct marketers refer to the conversion rate as a measure of the orders produced by an e-mail or banner ad. For instance, a promotional e-mail generates a 6 percent click-through rate. One hundred are transmitted, and six recipients click through to the Web site. One third of those six people place an order while on the Web site. That means you have two orders, and the Internet marketer would say you have 2 percent conversion. Unlike a conventional direct marketer, the Internet marketer measures percentage of recipients who order, not percentage of leads who order.

➤ **Doubling day.** This is the day on which you receive half of all the responses you are going to get from a particular promotion. You can determine doubling day by keeping track of your responses by the day. Experience will soon reveal when you can expect to have half of your responses for direct mail, display ads, classified ads, e-mail, and other types of promotions. When you know how long it takes to reach doubling day, you can make an accurate early prediction of your total response to a campaign.

The calculations I just listed are all based on the initial order you get from the customer in response to a promotion. But many customers return to order from you again and again. The next section will talk about the value of lifetime customers.

Lifetime Customer Value

The total amount of money a direct marketing customer spends with you during the time he or she remains a customer is called lifetime customer value. For instance, let's say the average order is $500. The average customer orders three times a year and remains a customer for three years. The average lifetime customer value is, therefore, $500 × 3 × 3 = $4,500.

Or take the customer who buys a product or service for an annual fee, such as an insurance policy, Web hosting, or a newsletter subscription. According to an article in *Hotline* (March 5, 2001, p. 1), the newsletter of the Newsletter & Electronic Publishers Association, the formula for calculating lifetime customer value (LCV) is …

LCV = [1 ÷ (1 − Renewal rate)] × annual fee

Say you sell term life insurance policies for a $300 annual premium and your policy renewal rate is 80 percent. The lifetime value of your policyholder would be 1 divided by 0.2 (1 − 0.80) times $300, or $1,500. Knowing lifetime customer value is a competitive advantage, because it gives you a more accurate picture of what you can afford to spend to acquire a customer.

In our insurance policy, say Insurance Agent Joe Jones knows only that the premium is $300, and hasn't calculated lifetime value. He is willing to spend $100 in marketing to sell a policy, because he figures that leaves him $200 in profit. If he spent $250 in marketing to sell a policy, he'd make only $50 on the sale—and he thinks it isn't worth it.

But Insurance Agent Sally Smith has calculated the lifetime customer value at $1,500. She knows that even if she spends $300 in marketing to acquire a customer, that will leave her a profit of $1,200 over the lifetime of that customer. Armed with this knowledge, she spends $300 to acquire a customer, outspending Jones three to one, and she gets more business. He can't figure out what is going on, but consoles himself that she must be operating at a loss—not realizing that she's making a handsome profit the whole time.

Response Boosters

When you use the previous response rate calculations, and your numbers are not where you want them to be, try the following response boosters for improving bottom-line results. Each of these topics has been explained in earlier chapters in the book, but refer particularly to Chapter 5, "Writing Copy That Sells," for more information.

➤ **Test more mailing lists.** The most common direct mail mistake is not spending enough time and effort up front selecting—and then testing—the right lists. Remember: In direct marketing, a mailing list is not just a way of reaching your market. It *is* the market.

➤ **Test more packages, offers, and creative approaches.** In direct mail, you should not *assume* you know what will work. You should test to find out. Big consumer mailers test all the time. Publishers Clearinghouse tests just about everything—even (I hear) the slant of the indicia on the outer envelope. Smaller direct marketers, on the other hand, often don't track response accurately or rigorously test one mailing piece or list against another. As a result, they repeat their failures and have no idea of what works in direct mail—and what doesn't. A mistake.

➤ **Try a sales letter.** The sales letter—not the outer envelope, the brochure, or even the reply form—is the most important part of your direct mail package. A package with a letter will nearly always out pull a postcard, a self-mailer, or a brochure or ad reprint mailed without a letter.

➤ **Stress the features that make your product unique.** Perhaps the oldest and most widely embraced rule for writing direct mail copy is, "Stress benefits, not features." But in certain situations, that doesn't always hold true, and features must be given equal (if not top) billing over benefits.

➤ **Emphasize your offer.** As discussed in Chapter 3, "Make Your Buyers an Offer They Can't Refuse," an *offer* is what the reader gets when he or she responds to your mailing. To be successful, a direct mail package should sell the offer, not the product itself. Make sure you have a well-thought-out offer in every mailing. If you think the offer and the way you describe it are unimportant, you are wrong.

Marketing Tip

The best mailing list available to you *is* your house list—a list of customers and prospects who previously bought from you or responded to your ads, public-relations campaign, or other mailings. Typically, your house list will pull double the response of an outside list. When renting outside lists, get your ad agency or list broker involved in the early stages.

➤ **Say "free."** Don't forget to use the "magic" words of direct marketing. What *are* the magic words? Say *free* brochure. Not brochure. Say *free* consultation. Not initial consultation. Say *free* gift. Not gift.

➤ **Guarantee the customer's satisfaction.** This is important when you are offering anything free. If prospects aren't obligated to use your firm's wastewater treatment services after you analyze their water sample for free, say so. People want to be reassured that there are no strings attached.

➤ **Promise that no salesperson will call.** If true, this is a fantastic phrase that can increase response by 10 percent or more. Most people, including genuine prospects, hate being called by salespeople over the phone. Warning: Don't say "no salesperson will call" if you *do* plan to follow up by phone. People won't buy from liars.

➤ **Tell the buyer to open the envelope.** One of those should follow any teaser copy on the outer envelope. You need a phrase that directs the reader to the inside.

➤ **Make your offer for a limited time only.** People who put your mailing aside for later reading or file it will probably never respond. The trick is to generate a response *now*. One way to do it is with a time-limited offer, either generic ("This offer is for a limited time only"), or specific ("This offer expires 9/20/87"). Try it!

Surprising Secrets

If the English teacher in you objects that "free gift" is redundant, let me tell you a story. A mail-order firm tested two packages. The *only* difference was that package A offered a gift while package B offered a free gift. The result? You guessed it. The free gift order in package B significantly out pulled package A. What's more, many people who received package A wrote in and asked whether the gift was free!

➤ **Introduce your product with phrases like , "announcing/at last."** People like to think they are getting in on the ground floor of a new thing. Making your mailing an announcement increases its attention-getting powers.

➤ **Let prospects know whenever you are selling a product that is new.** "New" is sheer magic in consumer mailings. But it's a double-edged sword in industrial mailings. On the one hand, business and technical buyers want something new. On the other hand, they demand products with proven performance. The solution? Explain that your product is new or available to them for the first time, but proven elsewhere— either in another country, another application, or another industry. For example, when we introduced a diagnostic-display system, we advertised it as "new" to U.S. hospitals but explained it had been used successfully for five years in leading hospitals throughout Europe.

By putting these response boosters to work, you may be able to convert a weak promotion from the red to the black, and transform a marginal winner into a real profit powerhouse.

The Least You Need to Know

➤ If you do not measure the profitability of your direct marketing, you are flying blind and throwing money down the drain.

➤ By tracking responses to the sources that generated them, direct marketers know how every marketing dollar is performing and can stop spending those that aren't.

➤ Response is the name of the game, and is the only meaningful measurement. Forget subjective and aesthetic judgment; they count for naught.

➤ If a promotion is working, tweak and improve it, then split test the old version versus the improved version. If the new version works better, you've just increased your profits with very little expense and effort.

Chapter 25

Database Marketing

In This Chapter

➤ Understanding database marketing

➤ Measuring with database marketing

➤ Staying ahead of the competition

➤ Building your marketing database

➤ Data modeling

➤ Renting your house file

In the past, management was likely to place advertising (space, broadcast, outdoor) and automatically assume there was a cause and effect relationship between advertising expenditure and increased sales. Now, top management is more bottom-line oriented. They want to know that if they spend X, that they will receive Y return on their investment. The key here is not sales but "profitable sales."

With database marketing, you can focus your marketing on the prospects and customers who have the highest likelihood of responding to your offer. In this chapter, you will find out what database marketing is and what it can do for you. The goals should be higher response rates and lucrative repeat sales to your best customers.

What Is Database Marketing?

Database marketing means having an ongoing marketing program aimed at current customers whose names and contact information are stored in your customer database. Marketing to your customer database can routinely yield response rates 5 to 10 times higher than marketing to rented customer lists.

The three basic database marketing techniques are as follows:

➤ **Regular customer contact mailings.** Postcards, company newsletters, and e-zines (see Chapter 16, "The Internet: Direct Marketing for the Digital Age") are all popular vehicles for keeping in contact with customers on a regular basis. Not only does this remind customers of your existence and your product and services, but it also alerts them to new products and offers.

➤ **Goodwill communications.** Marketers find it pays to send an occasional customer mailing that is not a direct solicitation, but rather a communication to build goodwill.

➤ **Special offers.** Database marketing allows you to treat your customers as special. Not only does this build goodwill, but it also increases sales. Special offers can be one-shot deals such as discounts or free gifts. Or you can do ongoing programs, such as the frequent-flier points used by airlines to encourage air travel.

Marketing Tip

How often should you market to your customers? As often as is profitable. Increase the frequency until the next offer doesn't pay. Then you know you've reached the maximum frequency at which customers want to hear from you and will still respond. The frequency of customer contact varies with every marketer, but marketing expert Dr. Jeffrey Lant has a guideline he calls "The Rule of Seven." It says a good starting point for estimating frequency of customer contact is seven times within an 18-month period. That works out to a little over four times a year, or quarterly.

Database Marketing Is Measurable

Database marketing is the computerized use of information in a way that allows you to identify, target, and segment your best prospects and customers and analyze their performance over time.

Through the use of sophisticated statistical models, database marketing enables you to classify every prospect and customer based on previous historic data and trends. This gives you the ability to predict, accurately and confidently, the potential for each individual's future business. Consequently, marketing programs may be customized to target an individual based on his or her probable return on investment.

This means that an individual with the highest probability for a profitable response can be targeted more often and differently than the individual with a low score, vastly increasing the overall profitability of your mailings while simultaneously reducing your costs.

How do you perform this statistical analysis? Your IT department may have a database administrator on staff who can handle the job. Or you can outsource to a consultant, freelancer, or service firm. Many mailing list brokers offer database services.

Gain Competitive Advantage and Control

Database marketing gives you a sustainable advantage to help you stay ahead of your competition. Today's marketers have witnessed an explosion of products all vying for the same target audience. Yet, the costs of all forms of advertising have steadily increased. Once again, database marketers have the edge:

➤ By knowing which individuals have the greatest probability of responding, and armed with in-depth knowledge about the demographics of their prospective buyer, database marketers have an overwhelming competitive advantage.

➤ By concentrating your efforts on the most responsive segments, you can deliver personalized messages to your prospective buyer and overpower competitors who use traditional mass-marketing methods.

Database marketing lets you precisely control the number of times and messages reaching your prospective buyer. Through a marketing database, you can keep track of how many times an individual has been contacted, and which product offerings he or she received. You can also suppress your competitor's names (purge them from lists so they are not sent your mailing) so that they will not know your marketing strategy until it's too late to react.

Building Profitable Private Prospecting Databases

There are two types of databases you may want to build. A customer database is a file of your customers. A prospecting database is a file of your best prospects.

A prospecting database contains names and addresses of as many people as you can identify who would be potential customers for your products and services. The prospecting database is created by identifying appropriate lists, merging these lists, eliminating duplicate names, and organizing the remaining names in a relational database management system.

Such systems, typically, have query capability that allows you to get quick reports on response data and analysis, for example, "How many existing customers bought product X at our special September discount price?"

The advantage of a private prospecting database is that it contains a complete record of the actions taken by a firm's customers and prospects over time. Here are some tips for building and using private prospecting databases to improve direct marketing results:

➤ **Base list selection on "nonresponse" history.** When you rent mailing lists for one-time usage, you have records only of those names who respond. When you own a private prospecting database, you maintain a complete record of the actions—and nonactions—taken by everyone on the database. So, not only can you target those most likely to respond, but you can save money by not mailing to those who are *least* likely to respond.

➤ **Test a list before incorporating it into your permanent database.** A large number of the names used in private databases are taken from mailing lists. But before you incorporate names from a list into your private prospecting database, test those names in a mailing outside your database. Only those lists that test well should be added to your database, assuming they meet your other criteria.

➤ **Use database analysis to enhance mail plans.** A software marketer, for example, mailed mostly to IS managers, thinking this was the primary audience. Database analysis confirmed that IS managers were the largest portion of the customer base, accounting for 43 percent of all sales. Other senior executives, such as CFO and CEO, were mailed to only infrequently. But even though the company didn't target financial executives, further analysis of the database showed that CFOs were the second largest portion of the customer base, accounting for 21 percent of sales. The software marketer was able to virtually double its prospect universe by adding many more qualified CFOs to its prospecting database, and increase its sales by mailing to these CFOs more frequently.

➤ **Use demographic overlays to add information to your private database.** A database or list company can take your private database, run it against large public databases, match

Marketing Tip

Analyze your database results by job title, industry, size of company, state or region, and other demographics. Identify large audiences that buy your product but aren't a priority in your current marketing plan, and mail them more frequently.

names between your database and the public data sources, extract additional information from the public databases on each customer, and add it to your private database. You gain instant added intelligence on your buyers to enhance your database marketing efforts. Overlays are discussed in more detail in the next section.

➤ **Make logical connections between records.** Data found in one record can be propagated onto related records, enhancing database information. For instance, let's say you market business software to companies running Windows NT. But most of the records in your private prospecting database don't indicate computing platform. A few do. You find that Joe Jones at XYZ Company is running Windows NT. Chances are, then, that his company has standardized NT as the platform of choice for the whole organization. You can cross-propagate this information, adding it to all records of people working at XYZ Company. Now these names will show up when you run the NT selection on your database.

Success Story

One direct marketer was getting much lower response from Fortune 1000 companies than other companies to which it mailed its safety products catalog. The feeling was that the promotional-looking catalog was screened in the mailroom (and by secretaries in larger organizations). The solution: The database was split into Fortune 1000 and non–Fortune 1000 firms. The regular firms received the standard catalog via third-class bulk rate mail, as before. But for the Fortune 1000 firms, the catalogs were placed in a plain envelope and mailed first class. Response rate among this group increased, becoming equivalent to the rest of the prospects.

Usually we search and manipulate the database to implement an idea we've already thought of, such as a special offer to customers who recently dropped their maintenance contracts or ordered $100 or more worth of goods within the last three months. This is fine, but you should also spend time analyzing and looking at your database without a specific campaign or plan in mind. Often the data will suggest new marketing ideas.

Demographic Overlays

The proliferation of data sources and today's high-speed computer processing, now, enable a rapid, cost-effective technique for adding more and better customer information to your customer lists: demographic overlays.

Using this method, a database or list company can take your house file, run it against large databases, match names between your list and the data sources, extract additional information from the data sources on each customer, and add it to your customer records. You gain instant added intelligence on your buyers to enhance your marketing efforts and those of the direct marketers who rent your list.

A good example of a successful list enhancement is Insight Direct. Insight is a Tempe, Arizona-based direct marketer of computers and peripherals. Mail-order sales are generated primarily via mail-order catalogs.

An analysis of orders received shows Insight has 934,000 mail-order buyers—business and consumer—with an average order of $675. The list can be segmented by hotline buyers (45,000 quarterly) who have made a purchase within the last three months. Multibuyers (350,000)—customers who have made repeat orders—are also available as a selection.

As with many mail-order lists, Insight selections were limited to information gleaned from orders received. To enhance the list, Insight asked its list manager, Edith Roman Associates, to overlay additional demographic information on its mail-order computer buyers.

Insider's Buzzwords

SESI, which stands for socio-economic status indicator, is a measure of neighborhood quality. Using census block group data, statistical analyses of 25 variables—including income, education, occupation, home ownership, and location—yields an SESI code ranging from 0 to 99. The higher the score, the higher the neighborhood quality.

By running the Insight list against other data sources, demographic information on these buyers from the other sources was added to the Insight file. SIC (Standard Industrial Classification) codes and number of employees were added to business buyer records. Gender, household income, age, and presence and age of children were added to consumer records. Other information added to consumer records includes: whether the customer has a credit card; types of donations made in response to fundraising solicitations; other types of mail-order products purchased from other firms; and *SESI* code.

Insight—and other direct marketers who enhance their customer lists with demographic data overlays—enjoy a number of advantages:

➤ **More knowledge.** Thanks to computer databases and technology, it's not necessary to do a costly survey to gain customer intelligence. Much of the information you need can be inexpensively acquired from other data sources and integrated into your existing computer files.

➤ **Greater selectivity.** Customer records are tagged so all files with a particular demographic enhancement can be selected as a group. This adds many more selection criteria to your customer file.

➤ **Higher direct mail response rates.** By selecting only those portions of your list likely to respond to their offer, marketers who rent your list can significantly increase their direct mail response rates. They also reduce mailing costs by not sending their mailing pieces to nonprospects for a given product or offer.

➤ **Increased list rental income.** When marketers get favorable results on a test of your list, they'll then mail to additional names. A list with a good test and continuation record (ratio of mailers who test versus those who come back to rent more names) makes the list easier to market to brokers and mailers. Also, you can charge $5 per thousand or more for each selection criteria used, increasing your list rental income on those orders for which the mailer selects specific list segments.

➤ **Better direct marketing results.** Overlays enhance your house files not just for list renters, but also for your own marketing purposes. This means customers with the highest probability of responding to a particular offer can be targeted for that offer, with more intensive or frequent mailings than customers whose demographics do not indicate a predisposition toward the offer. This can vastly increase the overall profitability of your mailings while simultaneously reducing your marketing costs.

Many marketers would like to know more about their customers, but feel a survey is impractical, impossible, too costly, or unlikely to yield the results they need. Fortunately, the information you want about your customers is likely to already be available in other computer files. By simply running your customer list against these files, you can quickly and affordably enhance your list with this data. The result: low-cost customer intelligence that enables you—and those who rent your list—to get better direct mail results while reducing marketing expenditures.

Modeling Your Marketing Database

Sound familiar? Response rates are dropping, lists are suffering from fatigue, old selects just aren't working like they used to, and the universe of available names that you can mail profitably is slipping. Many mailers are turning to new ways to combat this decline using sophisticated statistical analysis and modeling.

By modeling a database or list, you can transition unprofitable lists into profitable ones, and profitable lists into stellar performers. Many different modeling techniques

Surprising Secrets

In many ways, the statistician's role is similar to that of a physician diagnosing a patient. The physician must evaluate the situation, and subsequently, prescribe the most effective remedy. The statistician must evaluate business objectives, as well as the information available, and prescribe a correct methodology for achieving these objectives. An incorrect technique, much like an incorrect prescription, can lead to ineffective or even disastrous results.

are available. Some are better than others for specific business objectives. Some are completely inappropriate. You also need to know the lingo so that you can speak with the statistician in his or her own language.

Analysis begins with a definition of the business challenges or objectives. In direct marketing, that's usually (but not always) increased response. The statistician then determines, based upon the objectives, which analytical methods are most appropriate for the job.

Creating a good model starts with an exploratory data analysis (EDA). The EDA helps the statistician understand the "personality" of the data to be modeled.

Comparing the customers generated by your mailing against the lists mailed, for instance, tells you who responded. Matching records mailed and the responses to demographics and transactional/promotional information, and examining the interplay between variables that give you the greatest lift in response, further enhances understanding of who's responding to what.

To gain knowledge about your customers' demographic profile, and what variables are important in predicting response, a good statistician uses some combination of the following EDA techniques in developing a model for you.

Uni-Variate Analysis

Uni-variate analysis measures the effect of single variables (such as age, income, employee size, SIC) on our target variable—response. For example, as income increases, does response increase or decrease?

Other key factors to evaluate include whether the predictor variable contains enough data to be statistically valid, contains valid information or garbage values, or needs to be transformed into a more "modeler friendly" format. Your statistician may do a frequency distribution and other descriptive measures to see if patterns in the data emerge.

Bi-Variate Analysis

Bi-variate analysis is similar to uni-variate analysis, except that you are doing cross tabulations of two variables (for example, SIC by number of employees) to see if more complex patterns emerge. This type of analysis may reveal relationships not detectable through uni-variate analysis.

For example, uni-variate analysis may reveal that SIC is not predictive of response, and number of employees at a site is not predictive of response either. However, viewing SIC and number of employees simultaneously with respect to response may indeed reveal a relationship. It may turn out that SIC 80 (health care professionals) with less than five employees in their offices are extremely predictive of response. However, health care professionals by themselves (without the presence of less than five employees) are not predictive of response.

Factor Analysis

Sometimes referred to as "dimensionality reduction analysis," factor analysis helps to group similar variables such as home value and income to identify if they are statistically redundant. Redundant variables can be eliminated from the analysis, or grouped together into composite measures. An exaggerated example of redundant variables are age and date of birth. Factor analysis helps to identify the true number of independent pieces of information by eliminating redundancies in the data, which in turn helps to simplify the analysis process and make your model more intuitive.

Suppose that, within your marketing database, you have information on product purchases for over 100 products. You are having a model developed to predict responsiveness to a particular catalog promotion, and you know that product purchase history is likely to be a significant attribute in predicting responsiveness. In theory, each product purchased could be used as a predictor variable. But this would yield 100 possible predictors, far too many to include in a single model.

Also, many of the 100 products may have an affinity to one another and thus be somewhat redundant in predicting response. Factor analysis may help by grouping the products into a smaller number of more manageable categories, thus reducing the number of predictor variables and ultimately leveraging more information than if these product variables were considered separately.

Cluster Analysis

Factor analysis is commonly, though by no means exclusively, used as a precursor to cluster analysis. Cluster analysis evaluates a large, heterogeneous population of businesses or consumers and breaks it down into smaller segments with "like" characteristics. The primary benefit of cluster analysis is that it makes it easier to target these more homogenous, well-defined universes.

Suppose you profile your customer base in its entirety and learn that the average number of employees at your customers' locations is 75. It may be that not one of your customers has 75 or even close to 75 employees. Perhaps roughly one half of your customer base consists of smaller businesses with 25 employees on average, and one half of your customer base consists of larger businesses with 125 employees on average. Targeting your customer base as a whole would lead you to believe that companies with 75 employees (the overall average across your customer base) are your ideal target, when in fact, they are not a core market.

Cluster analysis extracts these sub-markets within your database, making it easier to target—both from a modeling perspective as well as a creative marketing perspective—these dynamic groups of customers. Each submarket may have different performance (response) patterns. Let's say your database pulled a 1 percent response to a particular promotion. But the 25-employee segment pulled a 1.5 percent response, while the 125-employee segment pulled a 0.5 percent response.

In actuality, cluster analysis would use several variables (not just number of employees) in determining the various market segments resident within a database. The greater the number of variables to evaluate, the more clusters you are likely to find.

Discriminant Analysis

Often referred to as "cross validation analysis," discriminant analysis is a test to see if the groups being used are valid discriminators. For instance, a university uses a formula for its entering freshmen to determine in which level of a foreign language they are to be placed. If the freshmen completed one to two years of high school Spanish, they are classified as level A. If they completed two to three years, they are classified as level B.

Next, the university administers a test to the incoming students already classified into levels and finds that the scores are very similar. The determination is made that the number of years of a foreign language taken in high school is not a sufficient discriminator to determine a freshmen's knowledge. The idea here is that if the groups perform the same, there is no reason to keep them apart.

Discriminant analysis is often used to cross-validate cluster groupings identified within a database, or assign new customers into such clusters identified within the database.

CHAID Analysis

Short for "Chi-Square Interaction Detector," CHAID is a technique used to segment a population with respect to its relationship to a target variable, such as response. Responders are compared with nonresponders for various attributes to determine whether a statistically valid difference exists.

CHAID can be viewed as a "tree" with branches. The trunk is usually a variable within the database found to have the greatest impact on the target variable. The branches are different variables and combinations of variables that produce an even greater impact on response. As you move up the branches, the impact on response intensifies. For example, within the database, the trunk is made up of individuals with incomes exceeding $100,000. This group responds 1 out of every 100 times mailed. Further up the tree, the first branch consists of a group of individuals with incomes exceeding $100,000 who are between age 35 to 45. This group responds 5 out of every 100 times mailed.

Still further, is a second branch comprised of a group of individuals with incomes exceeding $100,000, ages 35 to 45, and are females who respond 10 out of every 100 times mailed. Climbing of the tree stops when the desired lift in relation to the potential universe is maximized.

Choosing the Right Methodology

Now that you've done your exploratory data analysis, it's time to pick a modeling methodology. It is theoretically possible to get to a model that predicts a fantastic result but does not provide you with sufficient quantity to justify a mailing. This is why you must get involved in the modeling process.

You must examine the interplay between variables that gives you the greatest lift for the quantity you must mail to have a profitable business. If you can't scale up your mailings, it won't matter that you've gotten the best response anyone ever had on the list.

Marketing Tip

There are a few software programs on the market that claim to do all the different types of regression modeling automatically. The problem with this is that the model can be effective only if you understand the data, its relationships to each other, and the type of methodology to use for the information to be discovered. For example, using linear regression to answer a yes- or no-type question will probably result in poor results. Yet these programs could and do sometimes show the best results using the wrong methodology. So be careful, and remember most importantly to clearly communicate your business objectives or challenges. Only then can your statistician prescribe the appropriate medicine for your marketing challenges.

There are three basic multi-variate modeling techniques commonly used in direct marketing:

➤ **Linear regression**, known as "least squares estimation," seeks to find the smallest variance between points. Linear regression can be used on anything that can be averaged (such as dollars, lifetime value, average order size).

➤ **Logistic regression** uses a technique known as "maximum likelihood estimation," which seeks to find a model that gives you the greatest proportion of successes. Use logistical regression in situations whose outcomes are characterized as a yes or no, response or nonresponse, or better, same, or worse.

➤ **Neural net** is a technique that is good at finding patterns in the data that are nonlinear. Its strength is that it can test for all the combinations of variables, not easily detectable through traditional statistical methods, to find positive and negative patterns that determine response.

The Least You Need to Know

➤ Direct marketing to your customer file will yield 5 to 10 times the response as direct marketing to a rented list of prospects.

➤ Database modeling can allow you to target specific offers to customer segments likely to be most responsive to those offers.

➤ You should market to your customer file as frequently as is profitable.

➤ You can use modeling to identify segments *least* likely to respond to your mailings and save money by mailing to them infrequently or not at all.

Glossary

account executive   A member of an advertising agency staff who directs and services a client's advertising. Acts as principal contact between agency and advertiser.

attendee list   A mailing list consisting of people who have attended a specific event, such as a trade show or seminar.

average order   The size of the average order placed by mail-order buyers on a given response list.

bill-me   An offer where the buyer is shipped the product prior to payment and then is sent a bill later.

blind mailing   A direct mail piece designed to look like personal mail.

bookalog   A direct mail piece designed to look like a paperback book.

border   The outer edge of a coupon or ad.

break-even   The point at which the response generated by a direct marketing piece pays for the cost of the promotion.

buck slip   A small insert in a direct mail package.

bullet   A short line of copy, usually set off with a solid circle. Bullet items usually appear in groups.

business reply card (BRC)   A reply card that can be mailed back to the sender at no cost to the recipient (the postage is paid by the advertiser for each reply card returned).

business reply envelope (BRE)   A reply envelope that can be mailed back to the sender at no cost to the recipient (the postage is paid by the advertiser for each reply envelope returned).

campaign   A series of coordinated advertisements or mailings using a definite theme or appeal planned to accomplish a specific task. May last from a few weeks to several years.

Cheshire   A type of mailing label that can be affixed to a direct mail piece via a machine.

compiled list   A mailing list in which the names have been compiled from various sources, such as the Yellow Pages.

controlled circulation   A publication that is given away free but only to qualified prospects who fill out and sign a card indicating their qualifications.

data card   A sheet describing a mailing list.

data overlay   The process of taking a house file or other database and running it against another file or database, for purposes of adding new data to the house file or database. For instance, you can run your customer list against a file of known credit-card holders and add to each record on your house list the customer's credit-card information.

database   A collection of computer files that can be sorted, segmented, and selected according to multiple criteria.

double postcard   Two postcards printed as a single piece with a perforation separating them. One of the postcards is designed as a business reply card that can be detached and returned.

doubling day   The day on which you have received half of the total responses you are going to get to a particular mailing.

envelope teaser   Copy on the outer envelope designed to entice the recipient into reading the message inside.

fascination   A bullet that teases and arouses curiosity by hinting at, but not directly revealing, its subject (for example, "bills that are okay to pay late").

freemium   A premium (see **premium** later in this glossary) included in the mailing itself rather than delivered when the product is ordered.

hotline names   Buyers on a mailing list who have made a purchase recently, usually within the last 12 months.

house list   A company's own files of customers and prospects.

house organ   A publication prepared periodically by a business organization and issued to its employees or to clients and prospects.

hurdle rate   A calculation to determine which items in a catalog are most profitable.

institutional advertising   Advertising devoted to creating good will for the advertiser rather than for the immediate sale of specific products.

keeper   A premium the customer can keep even if he or she returns the product.

keying   Inserting in the address, reply card, or coupon a different code for each medium used, so that inquiries can be traced and media effectiveness compared.

kicker   A premium the customer must return with the product if requesting a refund of payment.

lift note   A second, smaller letter inserted into a direct mail package to accompany the main letter.

magalog   A direct mail piece designed to look like a magazine. Pages are approximately the same size as a magazine.

mailing list   A list of names you can rent for purposes of sending a direct mail piece.

membership list   A mailing list consisting of the members of a particular club, association, society, or group.

merchandising   Arrangement of merchandise in a store or catalog designed to maximize product sales.

merge/purge   The process of running multiple lists against each other in the computer to remove duplicate names and produce a single unduplicated list for mailing purposes.

Monarch envelope   A $3\frac{7}{8} \times 7\frac{1}{2}$ inch envelope.

multi-buyer   A customer who has purchased from a given direct marketing company more than once.

nixie   A bad name on a mailing list, undeliverable because the person has moved or the company is out of business.

opt-in list   A mailing list of Internet buyers with e-mail addresses in which the buyers have said they are willing to receive promotional e-mails.

paid circulation   A magazine that charges a subscription fee.

per inquiry (PI)   Advertising arrangement in which the advertiser pays for space or air time based on the number of responses the ad generates, instead of the published rate.

poly bag mailing   A direct mail piece mailed in a transparent plastic wrapper.

premium   An offer of merchandise, either free or at a reduced price, as an incentive to buy a product.

premium sheet   An insert in a direct mail package, usually $8\frac{1}{2}$ by 11 inches, printed on one or both sides, highlighting the premiums.

press release   A written account or notice of a newsworthy subject sent to newspapers and other publications for editorial use.

rate card   A card that shows the standard advertising rates for a publication, or radio or TV station.

recency, frequency, monetary (RFM)   Criteria for rating direct-response buyers by how recently they made their last purchase, how often they buy, and the amount of money they typically spend.

response list   A mailing list of people who have responded to direct marketing offers.

rollout   Expanding an advertising or direct mail campaign to more publications and lists after completion of a successful test (see **test** later in this glossary).

sampling   The distribution of free samples of a product to encourage its use or to introduce it for future sale.

sectional center facility (SCF)   The geographic region represented by the first three numbers on a zip code.

select   The criteria by which names on a mailing list may be selected, including gender, zip code, state, buying habits, job title, size of company, and so on.

self-mailer   A folder, booklet, or other direct mail piece that provides space for addressing, postage, and sealing, and therefore requires no envelope for mailing.

signature   A printed sheet folded and trimmed as part of a book which may yield from 4 to 64 pages.

slim jim   A brochure designed to fit in a #10 envelope, usually made by folding two or three times a letter-size or legal-size sheet.

slogan   A sentence or phrase that, through repeated usage, becomes identified with the advertiser's product or service.

snap pack   A direct mail package with multiple plys (pages) that must be torn open using a perforation at the outer edge.

square-inch analysis   A calculation of the gross sales each item in a catalog has produced in relationship to the size of its picture and description.

subliminal advertising   A TV commercial technique that flashes a visual message on the screen for a split second so that the viewer is not consciously aware of having seen it.

tabloid   A magalog (see **magalog** earlier in this glossary) with oversized pages bigger than 8½ by 11 inches.

tag line   A slogan that always appears immediately after the advertiser's logo in printed and online materials.

tear sheets   Pages upon which an advertisement appears, and which are torn or cut out of publications and sent to the client as proof of insertion.

teaser campaign   A series of advertisements, usually in a small space, designed to arouse curiosity and create interest before and leading up to the date when an important announcement is made. In direct mail, postcards are often used for teaser campaigns.

test   The try-out of an advertising or direct mail campaign on a smaller basis before proceeding on a large-scale basis.

trade advertising   Advertisements of consumer items directed to "the trade," which are wholesalers and retailers in the distribution channel.

trade name   A name identifying a business. Also, a brand name of a product or service.

trademark   Any mark or design affixed to a product that identifies and distinguishes it from others.

traffic department   The department in an advertising agency which schedules work through the various departments and follows up to see that jobs are completed on time.

unique selling proposition (USP)   A selling point used to distinguish your product from all others in its category.

zone plan   A method of concentrating advertising in a limited geographic area instead of covering the entire country at once. Used for new products, limited appropriations, sampling, and so on.

Resources

Books

Benson, Richard. *Secrets of Successful Direct Mail.* Chicago: NTC Business Books, 1992. A how-to direct mail book by one of the all-time greats.

Bly, Robert. *The Copywriter's Handbook: A Step-by-Step Guide to Writing Copy That Sells.* New. York: Henry Holt & Co., 1990. How to write effective copy.

———*Selling Your Services.* New York: Henry Holt & Co., 1994. Selling skills for service providers.

———*The Perfect Sales Piece.* New York: John Wiley & Sons, 1993. A guide to creating effective brochures, catalogs, and other sales literature.

Bly, Robert, Steve Roberts, and Michelle Feit. *Internet Direct Mail: The Complete Guide to Successful E-mail Marketing Campaigns.* Chicago: NTC Business Books, 2000. How to write, design, transmit, and track responses to e-mail marketing messages.

Boone, Louis E., and David L. Kurtz. *Contemporary Marketing.* Chicago: Dryden Press, 1989. A solid textbook designed for introductory college courses on marketing.

Bruno, Michael, ed. *Pocket Pal: A Graphic Arts Production Handbook.* New York: International Paper Company, 1986. A guide to pre-press and printing.

Caples, John. *Tested Advertising Methods.* Englewood Cliffs, N.J.: Prentice Hall, 1974. Secrets of writing effective space ads.

Clark, Sheree. *Creative Direct Mail Design*. Rockport, MA: Rockport Publishers, 1998. How to illustrate and design direct mail pieces.

Floyd, Elaine. *Marketing with Newsletters*. St. Louis: Newsletter Resources, 1994. How to create effective promotional newsletters.

Goss, Frederick. *Success in Newsletter Publishing: A Practical Guide*. Newsletter Publishers Association, 1993. How to market subscription newsletters.

Harris, Godfrey, with J. Harris. *Generate Word-of-Mouth Advertising: 101 Easy and Inexpensive Ways to Promote Your Business*. Los Angeles: The Americas Group, 1995. Interesting, innovative, low-cost promotions for yourself and your clients.

Hiebing, Roman, and Scott Cooper. *How to Write a Successful Marketing Plan*. Chicago: NTC, 1999. Focuses on creating the marketing plan.

Kauffman, Maury. *Computer-Based Fax Processing: The Complete Guide to Designing and Building Fax Applications*. New York: Telecom Books, 1994.

Lant, Jeffrey. *No More Cold Calls*. Cambridge, MA: JLA Publications, 1994. How to generate leads for your service business.

Levy, Sidney J., George R. Frerichs, and Howard L. Gordon. *The Dartnell Marketing Manager's Handbook*. Chicago: Dartnell, 1994. A collection of marketing articles.

Lewis, Herschell Gordon. *The Complete Advertising and Marketing Handbook*. Bonus Books, 1998.

Muldoon, Katie. *How to Profit Through Catalog Marketing*. Chicago: NTC Business Books, 1996. Recommended for anyone writing catalog copy.

Novick, Harold J. *Selling Through Independent Rep*. New York: Amacom, 1994. How to hire, motivate, and compensate sales reps.

Ogilvy, David. *Ogilvy on Advertising*. New York: Crown, 1989. Required for every copywriter writing print ads.

Reeves, Rosser. *Reality in Advertising*. New York: Alfred A. Knopf, 1985. An excellent book on how to increase advertising effectiveness.

Romano, Frank. *Pocket Guide to Digital Prepress*. Albany, N.Y.: Delmar Publishers, 1996. A comprehensive yet readable guide to digital prepress.

Sackheim, Maxwell. *My First 60 Years in Advertising.* Englewood Cliffs, N.J.: Prentice Hall, 1970. A combination memoir and how-to book by the copywriter who invented the Book of the Month Club.

Stone, Bob. *Successful Direct Marketing Methods, 6th Edition.* Chicago: NTC Business Books, 1996. A comprehensive book on the basics of direct marketing.

Sugarman, Joseph. *Advertising Secrets of the Written Word; Marketing Secrets of a Mail Order Maverick; Television Secrets for Marketing Success.* Las Vegas: DelStar Books, 1998. A three-volume set on how to succeed in mail order, written by a successful entrepreneur.

Warwick, Mal. *How to Write Successful Fundraising Letters.* Berkeley, CA: Strathmoor Press, 1996. An insightful guide on why people donate—and how to get them to do so—by the "dean" of fundraising direct mail.

Wheildon, Colin. *Type & Layout.* Berkeley, CA: Strathmoor Press, 1995. The best guide ever written on designing print materials that are clear and readable.

Wunderman, Lester. *Being Direct.* New York: Random House, 1996. Great information on direct-response advertising and direct mail, with insights into Internet, electronic, database, and other emerging marketing technologies.

Wysocki, Patricia. *The Ultimate Guide to Newsletter Publishing.* Washington, DC: Newsletter Publishers Association, 1999. How to market newsletters and other information products both in print and online.

Zwicker, Milton W. *Successful Client Newsletters.* Chicago: American Bar Association, 1998. How to create promotional newsletters. Written for law practices, but can be used by anyone.

Periodicals

Advertising Age
740 N. Rush Street
Chicago, IL 60611
312-649-5200

Adweek Magazine
49 E. 21st Street
New York, NY 10010
212-529-5500

Exhibitor Magazine
206 S. Broadway, Suite 745
Rochester, MN 55904
507-289-6556

Industrial Marketing Practitioner
1661 Valley Forge Road, #245
Lansdale, PA 19446
215-362-7200

American Demographics
PO Box 68
Ithaca, NY 14851-0068
607-273-6343

The Art of Self Promotion
PO Box 23
Hoboken, NJ 07030
201-653-0783

Business Marketing Magazine
740 North Rush Street
Chicago, IL 60611
312-649-5260

Catalog Age
911 Hope Street
Six River Bend Center
Stamford, CT 06907
203-358-9900

Commerce Business Daily
Nepac, Inc.
55 Maple Ave., Suite 304
Rockville Centre, NY 11570
(800) 932-7761

Direct Marketing Magazine
Hoke Communications
224 Seventh Street
Garden City, NY 11530
516-746-6700

DM News
Mill Hollow
19 W. 21st Street
New York, NY 10010
212-741-2095

Memo to Mailers
National Customer Support Center
U.S. Postal Service
6060 Primacy Parkway, Suite 201
Memphis, TN 38188
www.usps.com

Newsletter on Newsletters
89 Valley Street
East Providence, RI 02914
491-431-2381

Public Relations Journal
33 Irving Place
New York, NY 10003

Sales and Marketing Management
633 Third Avenue
New York, NY 10017
212-986-4800

Target Marketing Magazine
North American Publishing Co.
401 N. Broad Street
Philadelphia, PA 19108
215-238-5300

Telemarketing Magazine
One Technology Plaza
Norwalk, CT 06854
1-800-243-6002

Web Sites

American Association of Advertising
Agencies
www.commercepark.com

Advertising Media Center
www.amic.com

Advertising Professionals Online
www.webcom.com

American Marketing Association
www.ama.org

Bob Bly
www.bly.com

Carl Galletti
www.copycoach.com

Company Sleuth
www.companysleuth.com

Creative Freelancers
www.freelancers.com

Direct Marketing Association
www.the-dma.org

Direct Marketing Club of New York
www.dmcny.org

Direct Response
www.direct-response.com

Dun & Bradstreet
www.dnbmdd.com

Edith Roman Associates
www.edithroman.com

FIND/SVP
www.findsvp.com

Freelance Online
www.FreelanceOnline.com

Graphic Arts Information Network
www.gain.com

IBM
www.ibm.com/patents

Jeffrey Lant Associates
www.worldprofit.com

Mark Johnson
www.healthcopywriter.com

MarketResearch.com
www.marketresearch.com

Newspaper Advertising Association
www.naa.org

Profit Boosters Copy
www.profitboosterscopy.com

Public Relations Society of America
www.prsa.org

Radio Advertising Bureau
www.rab.com

Rene Gnam Consultation Corporation
www.renegnam.com

Shell Alpert
www.shellalpert.com

Steve Wexler
www.wexdirect.com

U.S. Post Office
www.usps.com

Writers for Hire
www.mindspring.com/~lhill

Direct Marketing Association Code of Ethics (Selected Excerpts)

Honesty and Clarity of Offer

Article #1: All offers should be clear, honest, and complete so that the consumer may know the exact nature of what is being offered, the price, the terms of payment (including all extra charges), and the commitment involved in the placing of an order. Before publication of an offer, marketers should be prepared to substantiate any claims or offers made. Advertisements or specific claims that are untrue, misleading, deceptive, or fraudulent should not be used.

Accuracy and Consistency

Article #2: Simple and consistent statements or representations of all the essential points of the offer should appear in the promotional material. The overall impression of an offer should not be contradicted by individual statements, representations, or disclaimers.

Clarity of Representations

Article #3: Representations which, by their size, placement, duration, or other characteristics, are unlikely to be noticed or are difficult to understand should not be used if they are material to the offer.

Actual Conditions

Article #4: All descriptions, promises, and claims of limitation should be in accordance with actual conditions, situations, and circumstances existing at the time of the promotion.

Disparagement

Article #5: Disparagement of any person or group on grounds addressed by federal or state laws that prohibit discrimination is unacceptable.

Decency

Article #6: Solicitations should not be sent to consumers who have indicated to the marketer that they consider those solicitations to be vulgar, immoral, profane, pornographic, or offensive in any way and who do not want to receive them.

Photographs and Artwork

Article #7: Photographs, illustrations, artwork, and the situations they describe should be accurate portrayals and current reproductions of the products, services, or other subjects they represent.

Disclosure of Sponsor and Intent

Article #8: All marketing contacts should disclose the name of the sponsor and each purpose of the contact. No one should make offers or solicitations in the guise of one purpose when the intent is a different purpose.

Accessibility

Article #9: Every offer and shipment should clearly identify the marketer's name and postal address or telephone number, or both, at which the consumer may obtain service. If an offer is made online, an e-mail address should also be identified.

Solicitation in the Guise of an Invoice or Governmental Notification

Article #10: Offers that are likely to be mistaken for bills, invoices, or notices from public utilities or governmental agencies should not be used.

Postage, Shipping, or Handling Charges

Article #11: Postage, shipping, or handling charges, if any, should bear a reasonable relationship to actual costs incurred.

Use of the Word "Free" and Other Similar Representations

Article #16: A product or service that is offered without cost or obligation to the recipient may be unqualifiedly described as "free."

If a product or service is offered as "free," all qualifications and conditions should be clearly and conspicuously disclosed, in close conjunction with the use of the term "free" or other similar phrase. When the term "free" or other similar representations are made (for example, two-for-one, half-price, or one-cent offers), the product or service required to be purchased should not have been increased in price or decreased in quality or quantity.

Price Comparisons

Article #17: Price comparisons including those between a marketer's current price and a former, future, or suggested price, or between a marketer's price and the price of a competitor's comparable product should be fair and accurate.

In each case of comparison to a former, manufacturer's suggested, or competitor's comparable product price, recent substantial sales should have been made at that price in the same trade area.

For comparisons with a future price, there should be a reasonable expectation that the new price will be charged in the foreseeable future.

Guarantees

Article #18: If a product or service is offered with a guarantee or a warranty, either the terms and conditions should be set forth in full in the promotion, or the promotion should state how the consumer may obtain a copy. The guarantee should clearly state the name and address of the guarantor and the duration of the guarantee.

Any requests for repair, replacement, or refund under the terms of a guarantee or warranty should be honored promptly. In an unqualified offer of refund, repair, or replacement, the customer's preference should prevail.

Use of Test or Survey Data

Article #19: All test or survey data referred to in advertising should be valid and reliable as to source and methodology, and should support the specific claim for which it is cited. Advertising claims should not distort test or survey results or take them out of context.

Testimonials and Endorsements

Article #20: Testimonials and endorsements should be used only if they are:

 a. Authorized by the person quoted;

 b. Genuine and related to the experience of the person giving them both at the time made and at the time of the promotion; and

 c. Not taken out of context so as to distort the endorser's opinion or experience with the product.

Index

A

actions (generating responses), product advertising, 179
active versus inactive lists, 53
addresses
  databases, 325-327
  mailing lists, 49
advertising agencies, in-house, 171
advertisements, 5-6, 146
  audiences, 172
  banners, Web sites, 216
  business directories, 183-184
  buying tips, 170-172
  campaigns, 11-12, 26
  classifieds, 179-180
    AIDA (Attention, Interest, Desire and Action) principle, 180
    costs, 169-170
    phrasing the offer, 180
    placing the ads, 181-182
    reducing word count, 181
    testing ads, 182-183
    testing information marketing concepts, 268
  e-zines, 219-221
  graphic design guidelines, 77-78
  mail teasers, 88-89
  package inserts, 159
  postcard decks, 146-150
    costs for advertising, 148
    headlines, 150-152
    illustrating, 154
    measuring results, 149
    segmented markets, 147-148
    selecting, 147
    writing the body copies, 152-154
  print costs and sizes, 169-170
  products
    attention-getting headlines, 173-174
    avoiding generalities, 176
    business directories, 183-184
    classified ads, 179-183

features and benefits, 175-176
generating responses, 179
layouts, 175
lead paragraphs, 174
prospects, 177
rewards for reading the copy, 178
writing styles, 178
yellow pages, 183-184
programs
  billboards, 165-166
  campaigns, 11-12, 26
  package insert, 160-163
  ride-alongs, 161
  sampling, 161
  statement stuffers, 160
  take-ones, 161
  transit, 167
radio, 194
  audiences, 194-195
  buying radio time, 195-196
  writing effective commercials, 196-198
selling services, 257-258
  writing ads, 259-260
space
  direct marketing tools, 16
  lead-generating direct marketing, 286
testimonials, 253-255
writing, 70-73, 152-154, 178, 181-182, 196-198, 259-260
yellow pages, 183-184
advertising, differences from direct marketing, 9-12
affiliate programs, Web sites, 215-216
agencies, in-house, 171
AIDA (Attention, Interest, Desire and Action) principle, 180
air time, infomercials, 190-191
alternative media and prospecting
  bind-in programs, 158
  blow-in programs, 158
  cost, 167-168
  direct marketers, 17, 167-168
  free-standing inserts, 159
  life-time value, 157-158

methods, 157-158
options, 158
Amazon, internet direct marketing, 9
analysis
  databases, modeling lists, 329-330
  EDA
    bi-variate analysis, 330-331
    CHAID (Chi-Square Interaction Detector) analysis, 332-333
    cluster analysis, 331-332
    discriminant analysis, 332
    factor analysis, 331
    uni-variate analysis, 330
  mailing list databases, 326
  statistical, database marketing, 324-325
  tests, 308-309
arguments, sales, 27-28
attendee lists, 48
attention-getting headlines, 65, 173-174
audiences. *See also* buyers; customers
  advertising, 172
  business-to-business direct marketing, 234
  fundraisers, 294
  radio, 194-195
  selling products, 24-26, 243-245
  targets, 24-26

B

back end planning, information marketing, 267-268
back-end premiums, 291
back-end products, 22-23
banner advertising, Web sites, 216
bar code zone, direct mail packages, 79-82
base lists, databases, 326
Basics of Testing, 307
benefit-statement scripts, 202-203

benefits
direct marketing, 68
indutrial marketing, 242
postcard deck headlines, 151
products, 27-28, 175-176
selling tech products, 245
Betuel, Peter, direct marketing, 9
Bezos, Jeff, internet direct marketing, 9
bi-variate analysis, 330-331
bill-me, payment options, 39-40
billboards, advertisement programs, 165-166
bind-in programs, alternative media, 158
blind mailings, promotional mail, 89-91
blow-in programs, alternative media, 158
body copy
postcard decks, 152-154
sales letters, 94
focus, 96-97
graphics, 97-98
information, 97
offers, 95-96
personalizing, 96-97
reader's needs, 94-95
strong leads, 95
bonuses, 42
book catalogs, format and packaging, 105
bounce-back catalogs, 21, 268
branding, direct marketing, 10
break-even, response metrics, 317
BREs (business reply envelopes), 37, 99-100
brochures, 98, 253-255
brokers, lists, 50-54
budgets, project planning and management, 29-30
business directories, mail-order ads, 183-184
business reply envelopes. *See* BREs
business reply mail, response options, 37
Business Week, 121
business-to-business direct marketing, 5, 234
audience, 234
buying influences, 235
deferred offers, 36
information, 234-235

multi-step buying process, 235
negative offers, 34-35
products, 236
purchasing products and services, 234
buyer versus prospect lists, 53
buyers. *See also* audiences; customers
information marketing, 264-265, 271-271
payment options, 38-40
response options, 36-38
resistance, overcoming with endorsed mailings, 232
buying influences, business-to-business direct marketing, 235

C

C.O.D. (cash on delivery), payment options, 39
calculations
costs, examples. 75-76
hurdle rate, 140-142
calls (sales), response boosters, 320
campaigns, 26
consistency, 11-12
timing, 29-30
candidates (political), nonprofit marketing, 298-299
cards, reply, 4-7, 256-257
cash
order bonuses, 42
payment options, 38
cash on delivery. *See* C.O.D.
cassettes (audio), information marketing, 273
catalog copy
checklist, 137-139
tone and style tips, 139-140
catalogs
bounce-back, information marketing, 268
Catalog Success, 8
copywriting fundamentals and techniques, 129-134
cost, 140-142
covers, 134-135
direct mail packages, 131-132
direct marketing tools, 16
hurdle rate, 140-142
mailing fundamentals, 129-130

marketing strategies and techniques, 132-137
merchandising, 131-132
organization skills, 131-132
product descriptions, checklists, 137-139
real estate, 140-142
sales, 135-137
square-inch analysis, 140-142
categories, mailing lists, 47
celebrities
infomercials, 189
nonprofit marketing, 291
cells, test analysis, 309
CHAID (Chi-Square Interaction Detector) analysis, 332-333
charity, nonprofit marketing, 289-293
checks, payment options, 38
Cheshire, mailing lists, 56
circulation (magazines), mail-order ads, 171
classified ads, 179-180
AIDA (Attention, Interest, Desire and Action) principle, 180
costs, 169-170
e-zines, 219-221
phrasing the offer, 180
placing the ads, 181-182
reducing word count, 181
testing ads, 182-183
testing information marketing concepts, 268
click-throughs, response metrics, 316
cluster analysis, 331-332
co-op mailings, 160
commands, postcard deck headlines, 151
commercials
DRTV, 192-193
infomercials, 188
blunders to avoid, 188-189
buying air time, 190-191
key elements for production, 189-190
radio, 4-7, 194-195
buying radio time, 195-196
writing effective commercials, 196-198
television, 4-7
common market advertisers, co-op mailings, 160

communications, database marketing, 324
companies
    names, mail-order businesses, 228-229
    selling to corporate executives, 248
    selling to middle managers, 246-248
competition
    advantages of database marketing, 325
    lead-generating direct marketing, 277-278
        direct mail formats, 280-282
        evaluating responses, 284-285
        increasing sales force efficiency, 278-279
        market size and handling capacity, 283-284
        other methods, 285-286
        reaching the buying committee, 279-280
        solo mailings versus series, 283
        successful copy features, 282-283
compiled lists, 48
computer personalization, personalized direct mail, 82-83
computers, SoHo markets, 237-238
consumer advertising, 6
consumer marketing, 6
contact information, Web site home page, 213
continuity-oriented programs
    mail orders, 159
    self-mailers, 120
conversational writing styles, product advertising, 178
conversion rates, 317
copies, direct marketing, 11
copy content, direct mail, 63-64
copy features, lead-generating direct marketing, 282-283
copy platforms
    direct mail, 64-65
    writing, 109-111
copywriters
    business-to-business direct marketing, researching products, 234
    direct mail, 62-63

four P's, 111-112
    writers, 70-71
copywriting
    catalogs, 132-134
    techniques, 108
core complex
    customer profiles, 109-111
    direct marketing and research, 108-109
corporate executives, selling, 248
cost per inquiry, response metrics, 316
cost per order, response metrics, 317
cost per thousand
    prices, 51
    response metrics, 316
costs. *See also* prices
    advertisements, 169-172
        e-zines, 220-221
        selling services, 258
    calculations, 75-76
    celebrities, infomercials, 189
    classified ads, reducing word count, 181
    infomercials, 190-191
    Insight Direct, demographic overlays, 328-329
    Internet programming charges, 214-215
    postcard deck advertising, 148
    products, infomercials, 189
    radio commercials, 195-196
    response metrics, 316-318
    savings, 19 tips, 79-82
coupons, response, 4-7
covers, catalogs, 134-135
creativity, 9
credit cards
    holder lists, 48
    orders, 44-46
    payment options, 39
criteria selections, 53
customer satisfaction guaranteed, response boosters, 320
customers, 15. *See also* audiences; buyers
    databases, 325-327
    lifetime customer value, 318
    payment options, 38
        bill-me, 39-40
        C.O.D., 39
        cash, 38
        checks, 38

credit cards, 39
    money orders, 38
    purchase orders, 40
percentage returns, 227
profiles, 109-111
response options, 36-38
self-mailers, 119-120
starting mail-order businesses, 226
cutting printing costs, 19 tips, 79-82

D

data
    lifetime customer value, 318
    measuring response results, 315-316
    response metrics, 316-318
data analysis (EDA), 329-330
    bi-variate analysis, 330-331
    CHAID (Chi-Square Interaction Detector) analysis, 332-333
    cluster analysis, 331-332
    demographic overlays, 328-329
    discriminant analysis, 332
    factor analysis, 331
    uni-variate analysis, 330
database marketing, 4
    advantages, 325
    communications, 324
    demographic overlays, 328-329
    EDA (exploratory data analysis), 329-330
        bi-variate analysis, 330-331
        CHAID (Chi-Square Interaction Detector) analysis, 332-333
        cluster analysis, 331-332
        discriminant analysis, 332
        factor analysis, 331
        uni-variate analysis, 330
    mailing lists, 324
    modeling databases or lists, 329-330
        bi-variate analysis, 330-331
        CHAID (Chi-Square Interaction Detector) analysis, 332-333
        cluster analysis, 331-332

discriminant analysis, 332
    factor analysis, 331
    uni-variate analysis, 330
multi-variate modeling tech-
    niques, 333
special offers, 324
statistical analysis, 324-325
techniques, 324
types of databases, 325-327
databases
    analysis of mailing lists, 326
    customer, 325-327
    demographic overlays, 326
    nonresponse histories, 326
    prospecting, 325-327
    record connections, 327
    testing mailing lists, 326
dates (expiration), 42
deadlines, 42
decks, postcards, 16
deferred offers, 36
delivery, telemarketing, 205-206
demography, 328-329
    private databases, 326
    target markets, 25
descriptions, lists, 51
designers, typography, 77-78
designing a home page,
    213-214
designs, direct marketing, 11
digest, letters, 101-102
dimensional mailers, formats,
    119
dimensionality reduction analy-
    sis, 331
direct mail, 6-7.
    advertisements, guidelines,
        77-78
    blind mailings, 89-91
    bookalogs, 105
    closing deals, tips, 99
    copy content, 63-64
    copy platform, 64-65
    copywriters, 62-63
    cost, 75-76
    direct marketing tools, 16
    evolution, 7, 9
    families, 62-63
    formats
        lead-generating direct
            marketing, 280
        letters, 280-281
        postcards, 281-282
        self-mailers, 281
    human appeal, 63-64
    large volumes, 122

lists, 52
long-copy formats, 102
magalog, 101-102, 104
mail preparations, 99
packages, 109-111
    bar code zone, 79-82
    catalogs, 131-132
    printing preparations,
        79-82
    tips, 125-127
selling services, 255-256
    prospect letters, 256
    reply cards, 256-257
testimonials, 253-255
using with telemarketing,
    206-207
direct marketing
    alternative media, 167-168
    Betuel, Peter, 9
    brochures, 98
    business-to-business,
        234-236
    core complex, 108-109
    corporate executives, 248
    customers, 15
    database marketing, 4
    definition, 4, 6-7
    differences from other adver-
        tising, 9-12
    DRTV, 192-194
    e-zines, 219-221
    elusive targets, 120-121
    features and benefits, 68
    graphic design guidelines,
        77-78
    guidelines, 77-78
    history, 9
    illustration considerations,
        78-79
    industrial marketing,
        238-243
    infomercials, 188-191
    information marketing,
        264-276
    Internet
        banner advertising, 216
        Bezos, Jeff, 9
        building a Web site,
            211-213
        designing a home page,
            213-214
        direct mail, 216-219
        links and affiliate pro-
            grams, 215-216
        steps to enable purchas-
            ing on Web site,
            210-211
        taking orders, 214-215

jargon, 4, 6-7
lead-generating, 277-286
lifetime customer value, 318
lift notes, 98
list brokers and managers,
    50
market research, 108-109
market practicality, 70
measuring response results,
    315-316
media kit, 54-55
middle managers, 246-248
multi-variate modeling tech-
    niques, 333
nonprofit marketing,
    287-299
offers, 32-36, 42-43
payment options, 38-40,
    44-46
photography, 78-79
planning offers, 28-29
powerful headlines, 67
profits, 75-76
project planning and man-
    agement, 29-30
radio, 194-198
response options, 36-38,
    316-321
sales letters, 91-98
sales markets, 69
sales tax, 43-44
self-mailers, 120-121,
    125-127
selling business opportunity
    offers, 236
selling products, 20-28
selling services, 251-260
SoHo markets, 237-238
tech products, 243-246
test analysis, 308-309
testing, 303-313
tools, 16-17
Wunderman, Lester, 8
Direct Marketing Association.
    See DMA
Direct Marketing Association
    Code of Ethics, 344
direct response advertising,
    media buying tips, 170-172
direct response marketing. *See*
    direct marketing
direct response TV. *See* DRTV
directories
    advertisements, selling serv-
        ices, 257-258
    business advertisements,
        183-184
discount offers, 28-29, 41

discriminant analysis, 332
distribution companies, package inserts, 159
DMA (Direct Marketing Association), 289
dollar returns, response metrics, 317
donations, nonprofit marketing, 287-293
donor lists, 48
double postcards, 117-118
doubling days, response metrics, 318
DRTV (direct response TV), 192-193
   commercial formats, 192-193
   HSN and QVC, 194
   tips, 192-193
duplicate names, mailing lists, 57

E

e-commerce. *See* Web sites
e-mail
   direct mail, 216-219
   instant replies, Web site home page, 213
   marketing, 216-219, 286
   response options, 37
e-zines, 219-221
EDA (exploratory data analysis), 329-330
   bi-variate analysis, 330-331
   CHAID (Chi-Square Interaction Detector) analysis, 332-333
   cluster analysis, 331-332
   discriminant analysis, 332
   factor analysis, 331
   uni-variate analysis, 330
editorials, information marketing, 265-266
efficiency, increasing sales force (lead-generating direct marketing), 278-279
electronic magazines. *See* e-zines
electronic mail. *See* e-mail
elusive targets, 120-121
employees, tracking test results, 305-306
endorsed mailings, overcoming buyer resistance, 232

engineers, sales markets, 69
enthusiasts, sales strategies, 68
entrepreneurship, 10
envelopes
   business reply envelopes, 99
   outer, 88
      blind, 89-91
      teasers, 88-89
   response boosters, 320
equipment, sales markets, 69
evaluations
   mailing lists and list recommendations, 51-54
   responses, lead-generating direct marketing, 284-285
evolution, direct marketing, 7-9
exclusives, list brokers, 58
executives (corporate), selling, 248
Exhibitor Magazine, 341
exploratory data analysis. *See* EDA

F

factor analysis, 331
facts supporting selling, 27-28
families, direct mail, 62-63
faux reports, issuelog and magalog, 104-105
fax machines
   response options, 37
   tech products, 244-245
feature/function tables, selling tech products, 246
features, 68
   industrial marketing, 242
   lead-generating direct marketing, 282-283
   products, advertising, 175-176
feedback
   information marketing, 269
   telemarketing, 207-208
FIND/SVP, Web sites, 343
flaming, 219
flexibility, telemarketing, 207-208
focus, sales letters, 96-97
folded self-mailers, formats, 118
formats
   bookalog, 105
   dimensional mailers, 119

direct mail
   lead-generating direct marketing, 280
   letters, 280-281
   long-copy, 102
   postcards, 281-282
   self-mailers, 281
   double postcards, 117-118
   e-zines, 219-221
   folded self-mailers, 118
   four U's, 112
   long-copy mailing, 101-102, 106-108, 112
   magalogs, 101-102, 107
   postcards, 116-117
   posterboards, 118
   self-mailers, 115-116, 121-122
   short-copy mailing, 116
   snap packs, 118
   urgent mailers, 119
formulas, calculating cost, 75-76
four U's, formats, 112
four-panel postcards, self-mailers, 115-116
Franklin, Ben, *Catalog Success* publisher, 7
free offers, 28-29
   gifts, response boosters, 320
   Kalian, Bob, 15
   postcard deck headlines, 150
free tests, list brokers, 58
friendly writing styles, product advertising, 178
front-end premiums, 291
front-end products, selling, 22-23
functions, selling tech products, 246
fundraisers, nonprofit marketing, 287-298

G

gadgets, products, 21-22
general advertising, 6. *See also* image advertising
generalities, product advertising, 176
geography, target markets, 25
gimmicks, products, 21-22
goals, marketing objectives, 23-24
graphic design guidelines, 77-78

graphics
  direct marketing, 11
  sales letters, 97-98
guarantees
  customer satisfaction, 320
  list brokers, 58
  satisfaction or your money
    back, 43
guidelines, 77-78

H

handling capacity, lead-generating direct marketing, 283-284
hard offers, 34
hardware, selling tech products, 243-244
  premiums, 244
  responses, 244-245
  writing product copies, 245-246
headlines
  attention-getting, 173-174
  postcard decks, 150
    benefits, 151
    commands, 151
    free offers, 150
    mail-orders, 152
    news, 152
    questions, 151
  selling tech products, 245
  Web site home pages, 213
  writing, 67
high-tech advertising, 6
history, direct marketing, 7, 9
history (nonresponse), databases, 326
home page designing, 213-214
Home Shopping Network. *See* HSN
hotlines, 52
house lists, 47
HSN (Home Shopping Network), 194
HTML (HyperText Markup Language), 210
human appeal, direct mail, 63-64
hurdle rates, catalogs, 140-142
HyperText Markup Language. *See* HTML

I

Ideal Prospect Profiles, 25
illustrations, postcard decks, 154
image advertising, 6. *See also* general advertising
in-house agencies, 171
in-house lists, 47
inactive versus active lists, 53
incentive offers, 42
income earning mailing lists, 57
indicia, preprinted postal permits, 79-82
industrial marketing, 6-7, 238
  accuracy, 238-239
  checking the numbers, 239
  concise mailings, 239-240
  features and benefits, 242
  information, 241-242
  marketing research, 240-241
  sales letters, 241
  simplify writing, 240
  testimonials, 242-243
infomercials, 188
  900 number programs, 192
  blunders to avoid, 188-189
  buying air time, 190-191
  costs, 190-191
  key elements for production, 189-190
  lead generators, 192
  media rollout, 191
information
  business-to-business direct marketing, 234-235
  contacts, Web site home page, 213
  density, long-copy mailing, 111-112
  industrial marketing, 241-242
  sales letters, 97
information marketing, 264-267
  bounce-back catalogs, 268
  building buyer's trust, 270-271
  editorial and promotional spheres, 265-266
  feedback, 269
  focused topics, 265
  narrowing the focus, 267
  niches, 264
  online products, 275-276
  planning the back end, 267-268

product prices and quality, 269
products, 263
prospective buyers, 264-265
researching the market, 264
responses, 266
selling information products, 271-274
subject areas, 267
testing concepts with classified ads, 268
infomercials, one-step orders, 192
inquiry costs, response metrics, 316
Insight Direct, demographic overlays, 328-329
Internet. *See also* online; Web sites
  banner advertising, 216
  building a Web site, 211-213
  designing a home page, 213-214
  direct mail, 216-219
  direct marketing tools, 17
  e-zines, 219-221
  links and affiliate programs, 215-216
  mailing lists, 54-55
  response metrics, click-throughs, 316
  SoHo markets, 237-238
  steps to enable purchasing on Web site, 210-211
  taking orders, 214-215
introductions
  response booster phrases, 320
  Web site home page, 213
issuelog, faux reports, 104-105

J

jargon, 4-7
Johnson box, sales letters, 92
junk mail, 7. *See also* direct mail

K

Kalian, Bob, free things book, 15
key codes
  package inserts, 164
  tracking test results, 304-305

L

labels, personalized direct mail, 82-83

laws, sales tax, 43-44

layouts, advertising products, 175

lead paragraphs, 174

lead times, 182-183

lead-generating direct marketing
  competition, 277-278
    increasing sales force efficiency, 278-279
    reaching the buying committee, 279-280
  direct mail formats, 280
    letters, 280-281
    postcards, 281-282
    self-mailers, 281
  evaluating response, 284-285
  infomercials, 192
  market size and handling capacity, 283-284
  other methods, 285-286
  premiums, tech products, 244
  solo mailings versus series, 283
  successful copy features, 282-283
  two-step direct marketing, 33-34

leaders, loss, 41

leads (strong), sales letters, 95

length tips, sales letters, 93

letters
  digest, 101-102
  lead-generating marketing, 280-281
  magalogs, 101-102, 106-107
  minilogs, 106-107
  prospect, selling services, 256
  sales, 91
    body copy, 94-98
    industrial marketing, 241
    Johnson box, 92
    length tips, 93
    outer envelope, 88
    personalized versus non-personalized, 91-92
    response boosters, 319
    salutations, 92-93
    signatures, 94
  Yale, David, romancing the buyer, 229-232

lifetime value, 157-158, 318

lift notes, 98

limited time offers, response boosters, 320

linear regression, multi-variate modeling techniques, 333

links, Web sites, 215-216

list brokers
  direct marketing, 50
  mailing lists, 50-56
  marketing tips, 58-60

list managers and owners, 50

lists
  active versus inactive, 53
  buyer versus prospect, 53
  descriptions, 51
  direct mail-generated, 52
  mailing
    tests, 310
  modeling, 329-330
    bi-variate analysis, 330-331
    CHAID (Chi-Square Interaction Detector) analysis, 332-333
    cluster analysis, 331-332
    discriminant analysis, 332
    factor analysis, 331
    uni-variate analysis, 330
  questions, mailing lists, 54-55
  sizes, 51
  usage reports, 53

location, target markets, 25

logistic regression, multi-variate modeling techniques, 334

long-copy mailing, 101-102
  formats, 108, 112
  writing, 111-112

long-form mailing, 106-107

loss leaders, 41

low-response offers, self-mailers, 120

M

magalogs, 101-104
  faux reports, 104
  formats, 107
  letters, 101-102, 106-107
  magazine catalog, 102, 104
  minilogs, 105
  tabloids, 104

magazines. *See also* e-zines; periodicals
  advertisements, selling services, 257-258
  Business Week, 121
  circulations limits, mail-order ads, 171
  classified ads, lead times, 182-183

mail. *See also* direct mail
  advertisements, teasers, 88-89
  business reply mail, 37
  direct, 6
    direct marketing tools, 16
    e-mail marketing, 216-219
    selling services, 255-257
  e-mail, 37
  junk, 7
  preparations, 99

mail orders. *See also* orders
  advertising, 172
    attention-getting headlines, 173-174
    avoiding generalities, 176
    business directories, 183-184
    classified ads, 179-183
    generating responses, 179
    in-house agencies, 171
    layouts, 175
    lead paragraphs, 174
    media buying services, 171
    P/I (per inquiry) deals, 170
    product features and benefits, 175-176
    prospects, 177
    remnant space, 171
    rewards for reading the copy, 178
    writing styles, 178
    yellow pages, 183-184
  buying tips, 170-172
  continuity-oriented programs, 159
  credit cards, 44-46
  one-step direct marketing, 33-34
  package inserts, 159
  payment options, 38-40
  postal regulations, 84
  postcard deck headlines, 152
  premiums, tech products, 244

response options, 36-38
sales tax, 43-44
self-mailers, 121-122
selling, hard and soft offers, 34
mail-order business
    company names, 228-229
    overcoming buyer resistance with endorsed mailings, 232
    romancing the buyer, 229-232
    starting, 225-227
mail-order selling, 7
    Franklin, Ben, 7
    Sear, Dick, 8
mailing labels, 56
mailing lists, 56
    available sources, 49
    categories, 47-49
    Cheshire, 56
    cost, 56
    database analysis, 326
    database marketing, 324
    demographic overlays, Insight Direct, 328-329
    duplicate names, 57
    examples, 47-49
    income earning, marketing lists, 57
    Internet lists, 54-55
    large volumes, 122
    list brokers and owners, 50-56
    list questions, 54-55
    list recommendations, 51-54
    marketing tips, 58-60
    merge/purge operations, 57
    modeling a database, 329-330
    payment options, 47-49
    placing orders, 56
    response boosters, 319
    self-mailers, 122
    subscriber lists, 54-55
    telemarketing, 54-55
    tests, 304, 310, 326
mailings
    amount of tests distributed, 307
    blind envelopes, 89-91
    brochures, 98
    endorsed, overcoming buyer resistance, 232
    lift notes, 98
    solo versus series, lead-generating direct marketing, 283

managers
    list, 50
    middle, selling, 246-248
    projects, 29-30
marketing, 7
    business-to-business, 5, 234
        audience, 234
        buying influences, 235
        information, 234-235
        multi-step buying process, 235
        products, 236
        purchasing products and services, 234
    catalogs, 132-137
    consumer, 6
    corporate executives, 248
    database, 4, 324-325
    direct reponse, 4
    e-mail, 216-219, 286
    e-zines, 219-221
    industrial, 6-7, 238
        accuracy, 238-239
        checking the numbers, 239
        concise mailings, 239-240
        features and benefits, 242
        information, 241-242
        marketing research, 240-241
        sales letters, 241
        simplify writing, 240
        testimonials, 242-243
    information, 264, 267
        bounce-back catalogs, 268
        building buyer's trust, 270-271
        editorial and promotional spheres, 265-266
        feedback, 269
        focused topics, 265
        narrowing the focus, 267
        niches, 264
        online products, 275-276
        planning the back end, 267-268
        product prices, 269
        product quality, 269
        prospective buyers, 264-265
        researching the market, 264
        responses, 266
        selling information products, 271-274

subject areas, 267
testing concepts with classified ads, 268
Internet, building a Web site, 211-213
lead-generating, 277-278
    direct mail formats, 280-282
    evaluating response, 284-285
    increasing sales force efficiency, 278-279
    market size and handling capacity, 283-284
    other methods, 285-286
    reaching the buying committee, 279-280
    solo mailings versus series, 283
    successful copy features, 282-283
list brokers, 58-60
lists, income earning mailing lists, 57
methods for starting mail-order businesses, 226
middle managers, 246-248
nonprofit, 287-293
    fundraisers, 293-298
    political candidates, 298-299
objectives, 23-24
postcard decks, 149-150
    costs for advertising, 148
    headlines, 150-152
    illustrating, 154
    measuring results, 149
    segmented markets, 147-148
    writing the body copies, 152-154
radio commercials, 194-195
    buying radio time, 195-196
    writing effective commercials, 196-198
referrals, 252-253
selling business opportunity offers, 236
SoHo markets, 237-238
tech products, 243-244
    premiums, 244
    responses, 244-245
    writing product copies, 245-246

telemarketing, 199-200
  delivery and techniques,
    205-206
  feedback and flexibility,
    207-208
  scripts, 201-205
  using with direct mail,
    206-207
marketing (direct). *See direct
marketing*
markets
  research, 108-109
  sales, engineers and scien-
    tists, 69
  size, lead-generating direct
    marketing, 283-284
  target, selling products,
    24-26
materials, 4-7
measuring results
  postcard deck advertising,
    149
  responses, 315-316
media
  buying services, 171
  direct marketing tools, 17
  direct response advertising
    tips, 171-172
  infomercials, 191
media kits, 54-55
membership lists, 48
merchandising catalogs,
  131-132
merge/purge operations, 57
merged database lists, 48
methodology, multi-variate
  modeling techniques, 333
metropolitan areas, transit
  advertisement programs, 167
middle managers, 246-248
minilogs
  digest, 105
  letters, 106-107
modeling databases or lists,
  329-330
  bi-variate analysis, 330-331
  CHAID (Chi-Square
    Interaction Detector)
    analysis, 332-333
  cluster analysis, 331-332
  discriminant analysis, 332
  factor analysis, 331
  multi-variate modeling tech-
    niques, 333
  uni-variate analysis, 330
money orders, payment
  options, 38

mood, telemarketers delivery
  techniques, 205
motivation
  nonprofit marketing,
    287-293
  sequence steps, 65
    asking for orders, 67
    getting attention, 65
    identifying problems,
      65-66
    product postioning, 66
    proving a case, 66-67
    step 5, 67
multi-step buying process,
  business-to-business direct
  marketing, 235
multi-variate modeling techniques, 333

N

names
  companies, mail-order busi-
    nesses, 228-229
  databases, 325-327
  mailing lists, 49
National Change of Address. *See*
  NCOA
NCOA (National Change of
  Address), 59
need-to-know information,
  building a Web site, 211-212
negative offers, 34-35
negative selling, advertisement
  concepts, 72-73
negative test results, 312-313
net-net deal, list brokers, 58
Neural Net, multi-variate modeling techniques, 334
new products, response boosters, 320
news, postcard deck headlines,
  152
newspapers
  advertisements, selling serv-
    ices, 257-258
  classified ads, lead times,
    182-183
niches, information marketing,
  264
nonpersonalized sales letters,
  91-92
nonprofit marketing, 287-293
  fundraisers, 293-298
  political candidates, 298-299
notes, lift, 98
nth name selections, 310

O

objectives
  marketing, 23-24
  project planning and man-
    agement, 29-30
offers, 34
  components, 32-33
  deferred offers, 36
  free, postcard deck head-
    lines, 150
  hard offers, 34
  incentives, 42
  infomercials, 189
  limited time, response boost-
    ers, 320
  negative offers, 34-35
  nonprofit marketing,
    290-291
  payment options, 38-40
  phrasing, classified ads, 180
  planning, 28-29
  response boosters, 319
  response options, 36-38
  sales letters, 95-96
  sales tax, 43-44
  satifaction guarantees, 43
  selling business opportuni-
    ties, 236
  soft offers, 34
  special, database marketing,
    324
  strengthening, 41
  tests, 310, 319
office products, SoHo markets,
  237-238
one-step orders, infomercials,
  192
one-step direct marketing,
  33-34
online. *See also* Internet; Web
  sites
  ordering, 214-215
  products, information mar-
    keting, 275-276
  tech products, 244-245
opt-in lists, 48
orders. *See also* mail orders
  average size, 51
  credit cards, 44-46
  infomercials, 190
  Internet, steps to enable pur-
    chasing on Web site,
    210-211
  mail-order selling, 7
  mailing lists, 56

motivating sequence steps, 67

payment options, 38-40

response options, 36-38

Web sites, 214-215

originality, products, 22

outer envelopes

blind mailings, 89-91

sales letter, 88

teaser, 88-89

outpull, 11

overlays, demographic, 326-329

owners, lists, 50

P

P/I (per inquiry) deals, 170

package inserts

advertisements, 159-163

formats, 164

fulfillment, 165

key coding, 164

mail orders, 159

producing and shipping, 163-164

programs, 159, 163-164

shipping instructions, 165

sizes and formats, 164

tracking programs, 164

packages

direct mail, 109-111

testing, response boosters, 319

paper reply forms, tech products, 244-245

paragraphs, lead, 174

payment options, 38

pdf (portable document format), 210

percentage response, response metrics, 316

percentage returns, consumers, 227

personal checks, payment options, 38

personalized direct mail, 10

tips, 82-83

personalized sales letters, 91-92, 96-97

phone, tech products, 244-245

phone numbers (toll-free), response options, 36-37

phones, telemarketing, 199-200

delivery and techniques, 205-206

scripts, 201-205

photography, 78-79

phrasing offers, classified ads, 180

placing classified ads, 181-182

planning

back ends of information marketing, 267-268

offers, 28-29

projects, 29-30

point-of-purchase displays, take-ones, 161

political candidates, nonprofit marketing, 298-299

populations, target markets, 25

portable document format. *See* pdf

postal regulations, 84

postcard decks, 146, 149-150

advertising, 146-147

costs for advertising, 148

direct marketing tools, 16

headlines, 150-152

illustrating, 154

lead-generating direct marketing, 286

measuring results, 149

segmented markets, 147-148

selecting, 147

writing the body copies, 152-154

postcards

formats, 116-117

lead-generating marketing, 281-282

posterboards, formats, 118

powerful headlines, 67

premiums, 41

back-end and front-end, 291

nonprofit marketing, 290-291

preprinted postal permits, indicia, 79-82

press releases, testimonials, 253-255

prices. *See also* costs

cost per thousand, 51

indomercials, 189

products, 21, 269

tests, 310

variable, list brokers, 59

principles, AIDA (Attention, Interest, Desire and Action), 180

print advertisements

costs, 169-170

printing preparations, 79-82

sizes, 169-170

privacy statements, Web site home page, 213

private databases, 325-327

problem identification, motivating sequence steps, 65-66

products

advertising

attention-getting headlines, 173-174

audiences, 172

avoiding generalities, 176

features and benefits, 175-176

generating responses, 179

layouts, 175

lead paragraphs, 174

prospects, 177

rewards for reading the copy, 178

writing styles, 178

benefits, 27-28

business-to-business direct marketing, 234-236

descriptions, catalog checklists, 137-139

fundraisers, 293-294

industrial marketing, 238-243

information marketing, 263-274

lines, selling, 20

motivating sequence steps, 66

new, response boosters, 320

office, SoHo markets, 237-238

ordering, Web sites, 214-215

selling, 20

back-end products, 22-23

campaigns, 26

front-end products, 22-23

gadgets, 21-22

HSN and QVC, 194

marketing objectives, 23-24

originality, 22

prices, 21

refillable, 22

sales appeal or theme, 26-27

store availability, 21

story-rich, 21

supporting facts and sales arguments, 27-28

target markets, 24-26

tech, 243-246

uniqueness, response boosters, 319

profits
    expanding mail-order busi-
        nesses, 226-227
    response metrics, 316-318
project planning and manage-
    ment, 29-30
promotions
    blind mailings, 89-91
    information marketing,
        265-266
prospect need-qualification
    scripts, 203-205
prospect versus buyer lists, 53
prospecting databases, 325-327
prospects
    letters, direct mail selling
        services, 256
    products, advertising, 177
    self-mailers, 119-120
proving a case, motivating
    sequence steps, 66-67
psychography, target markets,
    25
publications
    advertisements, selling serv-
        ices, 258
    mail-order ads, 171
publishers, 170-171
pull, 11
purchase orders, payment
    options, 40

Q

quality of products, informa-
    tion marketing, 269
questions, postcard deck head-
    lines, 151
quick-response bonus, 42
QVC, 194

R

radio, 194
    audiences, 194-195
    buying radio time, 195-196
    commercials, 4-7, 197
    direct marketing tools, 17
    writing effective commer-
        cials, 196-198
reader's language, writing,
    71-72
reader's needs, sales letters,
    94-95
real estate catalogs, 140-142

research (copywriters), business-
    to-business direct marketing,
    234
recency, frequency, monetary.
    See RFM
recommendation lists, 51-54
record connections, private
    databases, 327
references
    books, 339-341
    periodicals, 341-342
    Web sites, 343
referral marketing, 252-253
refillable products, 22
remnant space, 171
reply cards, 4-7, 244-245,
    256-257
reports
    databases, 325-327
    list usage, 53
representatives, telemarketing,
    205-206
research
    industrial marketing,
        240-241
    information marketing, 264
resources
    books, 339-341
    periodicals, 341-342
    Web sites, 343
response boosters, 319-321
    envelopes, 320
    free gifts (free quotes), 320
    guaranteed customer satis-
        faction, 320
    introduction phrases, 320
    limited time offers, 320
    mailing lists, 319
    new products, 320
    offers, 319
    product uniqueness, 319
    sales calls, 320
    sales letters, 319
    testing, 319
response coupons, 4-7
response lists, 48
response metrics, 316-318
    break-even, 317
    click-throughs, 316
    conversion rates, 317
    cost per inquiry, 316
    cost per order, 317
    cost per thousand, 316
    dollar returns, 317
    doubling days, 318
    percentage response, 316

response options
    business reply mail, 37
    e-mail, 37
    fax machines, 37
    offers, 36
    toll-free phone numbers,
        36-37
    Web sites, 38
responses
    banner advertising, 216
    evaluating lead-generating
        direct marketing, 284-285
    improving techniques, 41
    information marketing, 266
    Internet direct mail, 216-219
    measuring results, 315-316
    product advertising, 179
    tech products, 244-245
    telemarketing, 199-200
    writing advertisements, sell-
        ing services, 260
results, negative tests, 312-313
rewards, product advertising,
    178
RFM (recency, frequency, mone-
    tary), target markets, 26
ride-alongs, advertisement pro-
    grams, 161
risks, starting mail-order busi-
    nesses, 226
roll-outs, testing, 308-309
romancing the buyer, mail-
    order businesses, 229-232
rules for testing, 311-312

S

sales
    appeal, 26-27
    arguments, 27-28
    calls, response boosters, 320
    forces, increasing efficiency,
        278-279
    markets, 69-70
    performances, catalog tips,
        135-137
    representatives, closing deal
        tips, 99
    strategies, 68
    telemarketing
        delivery and techniques,
            205-206
        feedback and flexibility,
            207-208

scripts, 201-205
  using with direct mail,
    206-207
  tools, telephones, 199-200
sales letters, 91
  body copy
    focus, 96-97
    graphics, 97-98
    information, 97
    offers, 95-96
    personalizing, 96-97
    reader's needs, 94-95
    strong leads, 95
    tips, 94
  industrial marketing, 241
  Johnson box, 92
  length tips, 93
  long copies, 62-63
  outer envelope, 88
  personalized versus nonper-
    sonalized, 91-92
  response boosters, 319
  salutations, 92-93
  short copies, 62-63
  signatures, 94
sales tax, state laws, 43-44
salespersons, potential problems, 279-280
salutations, sales letters, 92-93
sampling programs, advertisement programs, 161
satisfaction guarantees, 43
scientists, sales markets, 69
scripts
  benefit-statement script,
    202-203
  prospect need-qualification
    script, 203-205
  telemarketing, 201-202
Sears, Dick, mail-ordering, 8
selection criteria, 53
self-mailers
  attention-grabbing head-
    lines, 124-125
  categories, 122-123
  continuity, 120
  cost, 119
  customers, 119-120
  direct marketing, 120-121,
    125-127
  double postcards, 117-118
  formats, 115-116, 119-122
  four-panel postcards,
    115-116
  lead-generating marketing,
    281

low-response offers, 120
  mail order, 121-122
  mailing lists, 122
  prospects, 119-120
  secrets, 122-123
  short message, 120
  tips, 125-127
  writing, 124-125
selling
  business opportunity offers,
    236
  campaigns, 26
  direct marketing, 10-11
  industrial marketing, 238
    accuracy, 238-239
    checking the numbers,
      239
    concise mailings, 239-240
    features and benefits, 242
    information, 241-242
    marketing research,
      240-241
    sales letters, 241
    simplify writing, 240
    testimonials, 242-243
  information products,
    271-274
  mail-order, 7
  marketing objectives, 23-24
  products, 20
    back-end, 22-23
    front-end, 22-23
    gadgets, 21-22
    HSN and QVC, 194
    originality, 22
    prices, 21
    store availability, 21
    story-rich, 21
  sales appeal or theme, 26-27
  services, 251-252
    advertising, 257-260
    direct mail, 255-257
    referral marketing,
      252-253
    telemarketing, 252
    testimonials, 253-255
  supporting facts and sales
    arguments, 27-28
  target markets, 24-26
  tech products, 243-246
seminars, lists, 48
series mailings, lead-generating
  direct marketing, 283
services, 41
  business-to-business direct
    marketing, 234
  media buying, 171

selling, 251-252
  advertising, 257-260
  direct mail, 255-257
  referral marketing,
    252-253
  telemarketing, 252
  testimonials, 253-255
SESI (socio-economic status
  indicator), 328
shipping , 165
shopping carts, ordering online,
  214-215
short messages, self-mailers, 120
short-copy mailing, formats,
  116
signatures, sales letters, 94
site menus, Web site home
  page, 213
sizes, lists, 51
snap packs, formats, 118
socio-economic status indicator.
  See SESI
soft offers, 34
software, selling tech products,
  243-246
SoHo markets (small
  office/home office), 237-238
solicitations, families, 62-63
solo mailings, lead-generating
  direct marketing, 283
sound effects, radio commercials, 197
sources, mailing lists, 49
space ads
  direct marketing tools, 16
  lead-generating direct mar-
    keting, 286
spam, 217
special offers, database marketing, 324
SRDS (Standard Rate and Data
  Service), 258
Standard Rate and Data Service.
  See SRDS
statement stuffers, advertisement programs, 160
statistical analysis, database
  marketing, 324-325
statistically valid responses,
  306-307
stores, product availability, 21
story-rich products, 21
strategies, features and benefits,
  68
subject areas, information marketing, 267
subscription lists, 48, 54-55,
  271
sweepstakes, 41

T

tabloids, magalog, 104
take-ones, advertisement programs, 161
tapes (video), information marketing, 273
target markets, 24-26
    demography, geography, psychography, 25
    RFM (recency, frequency, monetary), 26
TCPA (Telephone Consumer Protection Act, 200
teasers, 88-89
tech products, 243-244
    premiums, 244
    responses, 244-245
    writing product copies, 245-246
technical promotions
    checking the numbers, 239
    concise mailings, 239-240
    features and benefits, 242
    information, 241-242
    marketing research, 240-241
    sales letters, 241
    simplify writing, 240
    testimonials, 242-243
techniques
    copywriting, 108
    telemarketing, 205-206
telemarketing, 199-200, 252
    delivery and techniques, 205-206
    direct marketing tools, 17
    feedback and flexibility, 207-208
    mailing lists, 54-55
    scripts, 201-202
        benefit-statement script, 202-203
        prospect need-qualification script, 203-205
    using with direct mail, 206-207
Telephone Consumer Protection Act. *See* TCPA
telephones, telemarketing, 252
television
    commercials, 4-7
    direct marketing tools, 17
    DRTV, 192-194
    infomercials, 188-191

testimonials, 211, 253-255
    building buyer's trust, information marketing, 270-271
    industrial marketing, 242-243
testing
    analysis, 308-309
    classified ads, 182-183
    concepts in classified ads, information marketing, 268
    direct marketing, 303-304
        amount of tests distributed, 307
        mailing lists, 304
        statistically valid results, 306-307
        tracking results, 304-306
    essential rules, 311-312
    mailing lists, 310, 326
    negative results, 312-313
    offers, 310
    price, 310
    response boosters, 319
    roll-outs, 308-309
    variables to test, 310
themes, selling, 26-27
timing, campaigns, 29-30
tips
    advertisement buying, 170-172
    DRTV, 192-193
toll-free phone numbers, response options, 36-37
tone, catalog copy, 139-140
tools, 16-17
tracking
    programs, package inserts, 164
    results, 304-306
transits, advertisement programs, 167
trust, information marketing, 270-271
two-step direct marketing, 33-34

U-V

uni-variate analysis, 330
up-sell bonus, 42
updating, frequency, 53
urgent mailers, formats, 119

variable pricing, list brokers, 59
variables to test, 310

W-X

want-to-know information, building a Web site, 212-213
word counts (reducing), classified ads, 181
writers, 70-71
Writers for Hire, Web sites, 343
writing, 67, 70-71
    advertisements, 71-72, 259-260
    attention-grabbing headlines, 124-125
    body copies, postcard decks, 152-154
    catalog copywriting, 129-130
    classified ads, 180-181
    copy platforms, 109-111
    enthusiasts, 68
    four P's, 111-112
    fundraising copy, 295-298
    long-copy mailing, 111-112
    powerful headlines, 67
    product copies, tech products, 245-246
    radio commercials, 196-198
    reader's language, 71-72
    self-mailers, 124-125
    simplifying industrial marketing, 240
    styles, 72-73, 178
    telemarketing scripts, 201-205
    testimonials, 253-255
    tips, 70
Wunderman, Lester, 8

Y-Z

Yale, David, letter romancing the buyer, 229-232
yellow pages, mail-order ads, 183-184